To Ruby, Izaac, Isabel and Miranda

Praise for the second edition of The Theory and Practice of Change Management

'This is a wonderful book on organizational change and development, ideally suited to graduate courses in change management. The book is especially well researched and well written and offers a rare blend of scholarly insight and application. Students are in for a treat with the book's clever mixture of text, exercises, and cases. The first edition of the book was strong. This second edition is even stronger with the addition of seven new chapters. Taken as a whole, the book provides students with a deep understanding of organizational change management and its nuances.' – **John Harris, Associate Professor of Management, University of Wisconsin–Green Bay, USA**

'This book is a primer in change management. It is excellent and timely as changes are on the top of most managerial agendas. The book provides a thorough theoretical platform, useful examples, valuable exercises and practical guidelines for how to conduct change management in practice. A must read for a broad audience concerned about transforming organizations to survive and to grow further.' – **Flemming Poulfelt, Professor of Management & Strategy, Copenhagen Business School, Denmark**

'This is a major development upon the first edition, and a "must have" volume on anyone's bookshelf of introductory texts to change management in the UK.' – **Dr Richard J. Badham, Professor of Management, Macquarie Graduate School of Management, Sydney, Australia**

'From the systemic to the individual, this book provides a holistic account and examination of change across a wide range of analytical levels. Effectively blending empirical and theoretical material, the book represents a significant contribution to our understanding of change management. Essential reading for students and practitioners alike.' – **David C. Wilson, Professor of Strategy, Chair European Group for Organization Studies and Head of MSM Group, Warwick Business School, University of Warwick, UK**

'The change management literature is full of consultancy-like anecdotal texts. Hayes strikes the very rare balance between practice and theory and equips students and practitioners alike to design and successfully implement situation-specific and effective interventions. The exercises throughout the book help personal reflection and increase the implementability of the theories and methods. Our Executive MBAs have truly enjoyed the first edition. I'm sure they will be even more satisfied with the second edition with its increased emphasis on creating helping relationships.' – **Hanne Harmsen, Dean, ASB Aarhus School of Business, Denmark**

The Theory and Practice of Change Management

Second edition

John Hayes

First edition 2002
Reprinted five times
Second edition 2007

Published by
PALGRAVE MACMILLAN
Houndmills, Basingstoke, Hampshire RG21 6XS and
175 Fifth Avenue, New York, N.Y. 10010
Companies and representatives throughout the world

PALGRAVE MACMILLAN is the global academic imprint of the Palgrave
Macmillan division of St. Martin's Press, LLC and of Palgrave Macmillan Ltd.
Macmillan® is a registered trademark in the United States, United Kingdom
and other countries. Palgrave is a registered trademark in the European
Union and other countries.

ISBN 13: 978-1-4039-9298-7
ISBN-10: 1-4039-9298-3

This book is printed on paper suitable for recycling and made from fully
managed and sustained forest sources.

A catalogue record for this book is available from the British Library.

A catalog record for this book is available from the Library of Congress.

10   9   8   7   6   5   4   3   2   1
16   15   14   13   12   11   10   09   08   07

Printed and bound in China

Contents

Part III   Managing the people issues   147

List of figures

List of tables

List of case studies

Preface

The Theory and Practice of Change Management is designed to help you:

- develop your investigative and diagnostic skills so that you will be more effective in assessing what is going on in organisations
- extend your ability to manage issues arising from internally planned and externally imposed organisational changes
- improve your awareness of how people can facilitate or resist change and extend your ability to manage the human resource in the context of change.

The book is distinctive in at least four respects:

- *Core concepts* Part I reviews some of the main theoretical perspectives on organisational change. This provides a robust conceptual framework for a more detailed consideration of the practice of change management that is presented in Parts II–VII.
- *Exercises to raise your awareness of your own implicit theories* At several points throughout the book you will be presented with exercises designed to help you articulate and critically examine your own implicit theories of change and change management. You will then be invited to compare your own theories with those presented in the literature and, where appropriate, revise your own theories.
- *Exercises to apply theory to practice* In order to help you consider how you might apply theory to improve your practice of change management you will also be presented with a series of exercises that involve relating theory to your own experience. This will help you reflect on the practical utility of the ideas presented in each chapter.
- *Consulting skills* The final two chapters give explicit attention to the high-level *skills* that will enable you, in your role as change agent, to develop effective working relationships with clients and facilitate change.

This book was originally written for practising managers and for MBA students and others who have considerable experience of working in organisations. In this second edition the many exercises that are designed to help experienced managers apply theory to their own practice of management have been supplemented with a range of examples and case studies that will be of interest to all readers, but will be of particular value to undergraduates and others who may not have much direct experience of managing change in organisations:

- *Case studies*   Illustrative Case studies are used throughout the book to illustrate many of the points that are discussed. Sometimes these examples are short and embedded in the text but sometimes they are longer and presented in tinted boxes – for example, the Site Security and Secure Escorts case (Case study 7.1), the BBC cases (Case study 15.2 and 15.3) and the multinational auto components manufacturing company case (Case study 25.1).
- *Case studies to help you apply theory to practice*   Case studies that provide a framework for diagnosing problems and/or formulating interventions are designed to help you apply theory to a variety of problematic situations unrelated to your own experience of change. All of the case studies can be completed on an individual basis but they can also be used to facilitate learning in groups. The case studies are all based on actual events, although in some instances the name of the organisation has been changed.

The case studies are used in different ways. Sometimes they are presented at the end of a chapter to test your understanding of theory. For example, at the end of Chapter 1 you are invited to use a typology of change presented in the chapter to identify the kind of change confronting the BBC, UK Coal, Leicester Royal Infirmary, McDonald's restaurants and GNER (Case study 1.1–1.5). In some chapters the case studies are presented at the beginning or early in the chapter to encourage you to think about how you might manage a situation before you are introduced to theory that will help you diagnose the problem and formulate a course of action. Examples include cases such as The Active Sports Equipment Company and AT&T in Chapter 6 (case study 6.1 and 6.2), and Asda in Chapter 15 (Case study 15.1). Sometimes a case study is broken down into a series of related mini-cases to help you discover ways in which theory can improve your practice of change management. An example in Chapter 9 (Case study 9.1–9.3) involves the merger of two hospitals. The first part of this case invites you to identify all those who might be affected by and/or could affect the outcome of the change. The second part, presented later in the chapter, involves mapping stakeholders in accordance with how much power and influence they have and their attitude towards the change. The final part, presented near the end of the chapter, involves developing strategies for managing relationships with each group of stakeholders.

Sometimes cases relate to a part of the book rather than specific chapters. At the beginning of Chapter 17 Case studies 17.1–17.4 invite you to imagine that you are a consultant who has been asked to design an intervention that will address the issues raised. Case study 17.1 is set in southwest India and involves improving the effectiveness of primary health care centres. Case study 17.2 involves designing an intervention to increase the motivation and flexibility of the workforce of a Danish dairy company operating in the UK. Case study 17.3 involves designing an intervention to improve the treatment offered by the trauma orthopaedic care department of a large UK NHS hospital. Case study 17.4 involves reducing absenteeism in the elderly care sector of the Silkeborg Council in Denmark.

The case studies relate to public and private sector organisations, operating in a variety of areas such as healthcare, local government, broadcasting, energy, dairy, fast-food, leisure, manufacturing and security. The case studies also relate to situations in the UK, Denmark and India and to multinational companies (MNCs) that operate in several countries. Although not presented as a case study, enterprise-level training in Australia is discussed in some detail in Chapter 12.

Changes to the content of the second edition

The content of the book is organised into seven parts and twenty-five chapters. This structure reflects some of the theoretical and practical issues that have been important in my experience consulting with a wide variety of clients on a range of change-related issues.

New chapters

The second edition includes seven new chapters. In Part III, the original Chapter on Power, 'Leadership and Stakeholder Management has been split into two new chapters:

- *Chapter 9* (Power, Politics and Stakeholder Management) reviews different types of stakeholder theory and elaborates an instrumental approach (based on the work of Jawahere and McLaughlin) that draws on resource-dependence theory, prospect theory and lifecycle models. This conceptual framework will help you identify which stakeholders are likely to be most important at different stages in a change project and provide you with a basis for deciding how to manage relationships with these and other groups of stakeholder.
- *Chapter 10* (The Role of Leadership in Change Management) extends the original discussion to consider the role of collective leadership in the management of change.
- *Chapters 18–21* are completely new, and provide a detailed discussion of four widely used types of intervention: action research, appreciative inquiry, high-performance management and business process reengineering.

Part VII, on developing and maintaining helping relationships, is also completely new and contains two chapters:

- *Chapter 24* explores the helping skills required by effective change agents. Attention is focused on intervention styles – high-level approaches to facilitating change. The Intervention Style Inventory provides you with the opportunity to assess your own style of intervening.
- *Chapter 25* presents a six-stage model of helping and facilitating that is designed to provide you with a cognitive map that will help you understand your relationship with those you are trying to help and to give you a sense of direction when thinking about ways of facilitating change.

Changes to other chapters

- *Chapter 1* has been extended to include a more detailed discussion of the punctuated equilibrium and the continuous models of change. The implications of these models for the practice of change management are elaborated, with particular reference to the locus for change, the purpose and sequence of steps in the change process and the role of the change agent.
- *Chapter 4* has been extended to include a discussion of the role of knowledge transfer within and between organisations and the impediments to inter- as well as intra-organisational learning.
- *Chapter 6* has been extended to include a more detailed discussion of what organisations can do to improve their ability to sense the need for change.
- *Chapter 8* has been elaborated with the inclusion of a new exercise that involves using force-field analysis for diagnosing and planning action.
- *Chapter 11* has been extended to include a review of communication strategies and the factors that can promote organisational silence, the widespread withholding of information, opinions and concerns.
- *Chapter 12* has been extended to include a review of the relationship between organisational change and enterprise-level training. This review is based on developments in Australia over a period of ten years from 1994 to 2003. Australia was chosen because from the early 1980s companies operating in Australia have been exposed to increasing levels of international and domestic competition.
- *Chapter 15*, on shaping implementation strategies, has been almost completely rewritten around Beer's seminal work on strategies for managing change.

In addition, there have been minor additions to most other chapters in the book.

A *tutor's guide* is available at www.palgrave.com/business/Hayes2 for those who use this book. It includes a set of PowerPoint slides and a full debrief for many of the case studies, including the Asda case in Chapter 15 and the four cases presented at the beginning of Chapter 17.

JOHN HAYES

Acknowledgements

The author and publishers wish to acknowledge the following for permission to use copyright material: John Wiley & Sons, Inc., for Figures 1.3 and 6.1, from D.A. Nadler, R. Shaw and A.E. Walton, *Discontinuous Change* (1995), p. 11 and p. 24, and for Figures 3.2 and 3.3 and Table 3.2 from E.E. Lawler, D.A. Nadler and C. Cammann, *Organizational Assessment* (1980), p. 274, p. 282 and pp. 292–3 respectively, and also for Exercise 7.1, based on N.M. Tichy and H.A. Hornstein, Chapter 7 in E.E. Lawler, D.A. Nadler and C. Cammann, *Organizational Assessment* (1980), Pearson Education Ltd for Figure 7.2 from P. Strebel, 'Breakpoint: How to Stay in the Game', *Mastering Management*, Part 17 (1996); Sage Publications for Figure 7.3 from M.R. Weisbord, *Organizational Diagnosis* (1978); Elsevier Science, Inc., for Figure 7.6 from W.W. Burke and G.H. Litwin, 'A Causal Model of Organizational Performance and Change', *Journal of Management* (1992), 18 (3), p. 528; Academy of Management for Figure 11.1 adapted from E.W. Morrison and F.J. Milliken, 'Organizational Silence: A Barrier to Change and Development in a Pluralistic World', *Academy of Management Review* (2000), 25 (4) p. 709; Da Capo Press, a member of Perseus Books for Figure 14.1 from W. Bridges, *Managing Transitions: Making the Most of Change* (1991), p. 70; South-Western, a division of Thomson Learning, for Figure 17.2 adapted from T. G. Cummings and C. G. Worley, *Organizational Development and Change* (2001), p. 146; and Elsevier for Table 14.1 adapted from T. Holmes and R. Rahe, 'The Social Readjustment Rating Scale', *Journal of Psychosomatic Research* (1967), 11, p. 215.

Every effort has been made to trace copyright holders, but if any have inadvertently been missed the publishers will be pleased to make the necessary arrangements at the first opportunity.

List of abbreviations and acronyms

A&E	Accident and emergency
AI	Appreciative inquiry
AR	Action research
BPR	Business process reengineering
CEO	Chief executive officer
ERP	Enterprise resource planning
HR	Human resources
HRM	Human resources management
IT	Information technology
JIT	Just-in-time
MBO	Management by objectives
MNC	Multinational corporation
NHS	National Health Service
OD	Organisation development
OR	Operations research
PDSA	Plan, Do, Study, Act
PEST	Political, Economic, Social, Technological
POS	Point-of-sale
QC	Quality circle
R&D	Research and development
SARS	Severe acute respiratory syndrome
SBU	Strategic business unit
SME	Small- and medium-sized enterprise
SWOT	Strengths, Weaknesses, Opportunities, Threats
TQM	Total quality management

Core concepts

Part I reviews some of the main theoretical perspectives on the management of change and provides a robust conceptual foundation for a more detailed consideration of the practice of change management in Parts II–VII.

Chapter 1   The nature of change

This chapter considers the nature of change and the challenges it poses for managers. After reading this chapter you will be invited to assess your understanding of some of the issues discussed by identifying the nature of change involved in Case studies 1.1–1.5. You will also be invited to reflect on the nature of the changes confronting the organisation you work for, or another organisation that you know well.

Chapter 2   Organisational effectiveness and the role of change management

Change management is about modifying or transforming organisations in order to maintain or improve their effectiveness. This chapter considers:

● alternative definitions of organisational effectiveness
● the degree to which managers can intervene to affect the way organisations respond to change – change agency.

Before reading the chapter you will be asked to list the indicators of effectiveness that you believe are used to assess the effectiveness of your organisation *and* your department/unit within the organisation. Partway through the chapter you will be asked to consider whether these indicators/criteria of effectiveness need to be revised. (The measurement of organisational performance will also be considered in Chapter 23.)

   At the end of the chapter you will also be asked to reflect on the beliefs about change agency in your organisation, and how they affect the way change is managed.

Chapter 3   Systems models and alignment

This chapter makes a distinction between component and total system models of organisational functioning and goes on to consider organisations from an open systems perspective. Particular attention is given to the organisation's alignment with the wider environment and the alignment of the organisation's internal elements.

After reading this chapter you will be invited to:

- Think about your department in terms of a process that transforms inputs into outputs
- Analyse the quality of 'fit' between your department and:
  - (a) those departments (or other constituencies) that supply your department with inputs
  - (b) those departments or other customers who receive the outputs produced by your department.

Chapter 4   Organisational learning and organisational effectiveness

This chapter provides a brief overview of strategic change management (where the focus is on finding the best 'fit' between the organisation and the wider environment) and the contribution that individual and organisational learning can make to ensuring that the organisation survives and grows.

After reading this chapter you will be invited to assess the quality of organisational (collective) learning within your department or the organisation as a whole. A series of questions will provide a framework for this assessment.

Chapter 5   Process models of change

This chapter explores some of the issues and choices involved in developing an approach to managing organisational change.

Before reading this chapter you will be presented with an exercise that involves managing a change. The exercise is presented at the start of this chapter in order to help you think about and articulate your implicit model of how change should be managed before you are exposed to some of the most widely cited process models of change.

The nature of change

*T*he Shorter Oxford Dictionary (1973) offers several definitions of change, ranging from the 'substitution or succession of one thing in place of another' to the 'alteration in the state or quality of anything'. Changes can be large or small, evolutionary or revolutionary, sought after or resisted. This chapter examines the nature of change, reviews theories relating to patterns of change, considers some of the factors that facilitate or limit change and explores some of the implications of different types of change for change management practice.

The chapter ends with two exercises. The first invites you to analyse the nature of the change involved in four case studies. The second invites you to reflect on the nature of the changes confronting the organisation you work for, or another organisation that you know well, and classifying these changes using the conceptual frameworks presented in this chapter.

Until recent times, almost all received models of change were *incremental* and *cumulative*. This theoretical consensus had implications for change management practice. The aim of planned change efforts tended to be continuous improvement (what the Japanese refer to as *kaizen*) and most attention was focused on changing sub-systems or parts of the organisation in turn, rather than attempting to change the whole organisation at once. Since the 1980s, however, many traditional assumptions about the incremental nature of change have been revised.

The rate of change is not constant

Starting in the late 1970s Tushman and his colleagues at Columbia University studied hundreds of companies in several industries over time. They found evidence to support what many already knew. The rate of change, as an industry evolves, is not constant. It follows a sigmoidal (s-shaped) curve with a slow beginning (lag phase) associated with experimentation and slow market penetration, a middle period of rapid growth (log phase) as the product gains acceptance and as dominant designs emerge, and finally a tapering off as more advanced or completely different products attract consumers' attention (Figure 1.1). The pattern then starts all over again (see Tushman and Romanelli, 1985; Tushman, Newman and Romanelli, 1986).

Similar variations in the rate of change were identified much earlier by Ryan and Gross (1943) when they studied how 259 farmers in Iowa

Figure 1.1   Pattern of industry evolution

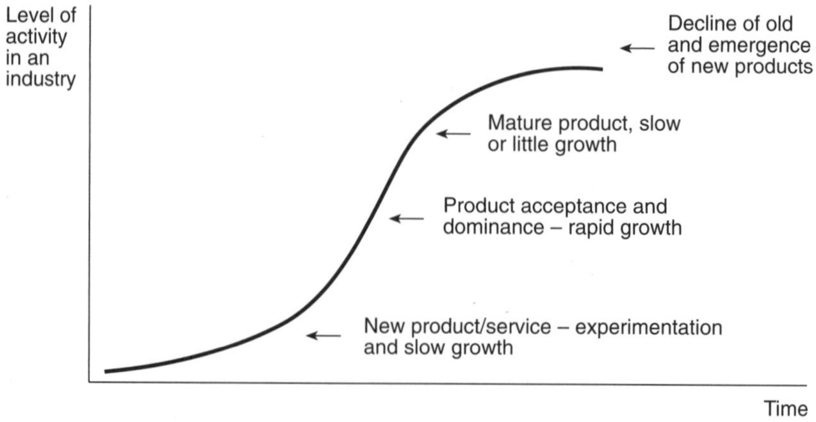

responded to the introduction of a new superior hybrid seed corn. The new seed was available in 1928 but it was 1932 before the first farmers began planting. In 1934 sixteen farmers adopted the new seed, followed by slightly higher numbers in the following two years. But it was nine years after the seeds were first available before there was widespread acceptance. The breakthrough came in 1937. The first users were innovators who 'infected' the early adopters, a group who carefully monitored the success of the initial trials before deciding what to do. This group was followed by a mass of movers, the early and the late majority. The last group to adopt the seeds were the laggards, and it was 1942 before all but two of the 259 farmers were planting the new seeds.

Gladwell (2000), in his book *The Tipping Point*, cites some more dramatic examples, including the sudden and dramatic decline in crime in New York in 1990 and the take-off of fax machines in the US (when, only three years after they were first introduced, over a million machines had been sold) to support his assertion that many social changes do not occur gradually. They spread like viral epidemics and change, when it happens, is sudden. The 'tipping point' is the name he gives to the dramatic moment in an epidemic when everything changes at once.

The proposition that some changes happen quickly, over relatively short periods of time, whereas others gradually evolve, suggests that the tempo of change might provide a useful basis for thinking about the nature of change and the implications of different types of change for change management practice.

The punctuated equilibrium paradigm

Gould (1978) challenges the notion of gradual, continuous change. He is a natural historian with an interest in Darwin's theory of evolution.

Traditionalists assert that evolution involves a slow stream of small changes (mutations) that are continuously being shaped over time by environmental selection. While Gould accepts the principle of natural selection, he rejects the proposition that change is gradual and continuous. He asserts that the evidence points to 'a world punctuated with periods of mass extinction and rapid origination among long stretches of relative tranquillity' (1978: 15). Some of his essays focus on the two greatest 'punctuations'. After 4 billion years of almost no change there was the Cambrian explosion of life (about 600 million years ago) and, after another longish period of very slow change, the Permian extinction that wiped out half the families of marine invertebrates (225 million years ago).

Gersick (1991) has studied models of change in six domains (individual change, group development, organisation development, history of science, biological evolution and physical science) and found support for the *punctuated equilibrium paradigm* in every domain. The paradigm has the following components: 'relatively long periods of stability (equilibrium), punctuated by compact periods of qualitative, metamorphic change (revolution)' (p. 12).

Gersick goes on to assert that in all the models she studied across the six domains:

> the relationship of these two modes is explained through the construct of a highly durable underlying order or deep structure. This deep structure is what persists and limits change during equilibrium periods and is what disassembles, reconfigures, and enforces wholesale transformation during revolutionary periods. (p. 12)

The essence of the punctuated equilibrium paradigm is that systems (organisations) evolve through the alternation of periods of equilibrium, in which persistent *deep structures* permit only limited incremental change, and periods of revolution, in which these deep structures are fundamentally altered. This is in stark contrast to the traditional gradualist paradigm which suggests that (a) an organisation (or an organisational sub-system) can accommodate any change at any time so long as it is a relatively small change, and (b) that a stream of incremental changes can, over a period of time, fundamentally transform the organisation's deep structure.

Deep structure

Gersick refers to deep structure as the fundamental choices an organisation makes which determine the basic activity patterns that maintain its existence. She argues (1991: 16) that deep structures are highly stable because the trail of choices made by a system (organisation) rules out many options and rules in those that are mutually contingent ('early steps in the decision tree are the most fateful'). She also argues that the activity patterns of a system's deep structure reinforce the system as a whole through mutual feedback loops.

Tushman and Romanelli (1985) identify five key domains of organisational activity that might be viewed as representing an organisation's deep structure. These are organisational culture, strategy, structure, power distribution and control systems. Romanelli and Tushman (1994: 1144) go on to assert that it takes a revolution to alter a system of interrelated organisational parts when it is maintained by mutual dependencies among the parts, and when competitive, regulatory and technological systems outside the organisation reinforce the legitimacy of the managerial choices that produced the parts.

Greenwood and Hinings (1996) offer a slightly different perspective based on neo-institutional theory, but the core argument is the same: there is a force for inertia that limits the possibility for incremental change, and that this resistance to change will be strongest when the network of mutual dependencies is tightly coupled. Greenwood and Hinings' argument is that a major source of resistance to change stems from the 'normative embeddedness of an organisation within its institutional context'. Organisations must accommodate institutional expectations in order to survive. They illustrate this point with reference to the way that institutional context has influenced the structure and governance of accounting firms. They were (and most still are) organised as professional partnerships, not because that form of governance facilitated efficient and effective task performance, but because it was defined as the appropriate way of organising the conduct of accounting work.

The parameters offered by such an archetypal template provide the context for convergent change. Greenwood and Hinings suggest, for example, that an accounting firm operating as a professional partnership could, as it grows, introduce some form of representative democracy in place of the traditional broadly based democratic governance. This kind of incremental change could be achieved because it is perceived to be consistent with prevailing core ideas and values. However, a move towards a more a bureaucratic form of authority and governance might encounter strong resistance because it is perceived to be inconsistent with the prevailing template. Such a radical change would involve the organisation moving from one template-in-use to another.

These templates work in the same way as Gersick's deep structures. However, the degree of embeddedness and the strength of these templates may vary between sectors, and this will affect the power of the template to limit the possibility for incremental cumulative change in any particular organisation. In the case of the accounting profession the partnership organisational form, with its commitment to independence, autonomy and responsible conduct, is supported by a strong network of reciprocal exchanges between professional associations, universities, state agencies and accounting firms. The outcome is a situation where individual accounting firms are tightly coupled to the prevailing archetypal template. Greenwood and Hinings argue that radical change in tightly coupled fields will be unusual, but if it does occur it will be revolutionary. However, in loosely coupled fields radical change will be more common and will tend to be evolutionary and could unfold over a relatively long period of time.

Equilibrium periods

Gersick introduces the analogy of the playing field and the rules of the game to describe an organisation's deep structure, and the game in play to describe activity during an equilibrium period. How a game of football is played may change over the course of a match, but there is a consistency that is determined by the nature of the playing field and the rules of the game. The coach and the players can intervene and make changes that will affect team performance, but they cannot intervene to change the nature of the playing field or the rules of the game (the deep structure). In terms of organisational change, during periods of equilibrium, change agents can intervene and make incremental adjustments in response to internal or external perturbations, but these interventions will not fundamentally affect the organisation's deep structure.

An important question is: 'Why do organisations find it hard to change?' According to the punctuated equilibrium paradigm, organisations are resistant to change in equilibrium periods because of forces of inertia that work to maintain the status quo. Gersick argues that so long as the deep structure is intact it generates a strong inertia to prevent the system from generating alternatives outside its own boundaries. Furthermore, these forces for inertia can pull any deviations that do occur back into line.

Gersick identifies three sources of inertia: cognitive frameworks, motivation and obligations. Organisational members often develop shared cognitive frameworks and mental models that influence the way they interpret reality and learn. Shared mental models can restrict attention to thinking 'within the frame'. With regard to change, attention may be restricted to searching for ways of doing things better. In periods of equilibrium assumptions about the organisation's theory of business (Drucker, 1994) often go unchallenged and organisational members fail to give sufficient attention to the possibility of doing things differently, or even to doing different things.

Motivational barriers to change are often related to the fear of loss, especially with regard to the sunk costs incurred during periods of equilibrium. Gersick (1991: 18) refers to the fear of losing control over one's situation if the equilibrium ends, and argues that this contributes heavily to the human motivation to avoid significant system change.

Obligations can also limit change. Tushman and Romanelli (1985: 177) note that even if a system can overcome its own cognitive and motivational barriers against realising a need for change, the networks of interdependent resource relationships and value commitments generated by its structure will often prevent it being able to achieve the required change. This view, at least in part, adds support to Greenwood and Hining's (1996) proposition that the normative embeddedness of an organisation can limit change.

Episodes of discontinuous change occur when inertia (the inability of organisations to change as rapidly as their environment) triggers some form of revolutionary transformation.

Revolutionary periods

Gersick asserts that the definitive element of the punctuated equilibrium paradigm is that organisations do not shift from one 'kind of game' to another through incremental steps. This, according to Romanelli and Tushman (1994), is because resistance to change prevents small changes in organisational units from taking hold and substantially influencing activities in related sub-units. Consequently small changes do not accumulate incrementally to transform the organisation.

Weick and Quinn (1999) note that punctuated equilibrium theorists posit that episodes of revolutionary change occur during periods of divergence, when there is a growing misalignment between an organisation's deep structure and perceived environmental demands. They report that the metaphor of the firm implied by conceptions of episodic change is an organisation that comprises a set of interdependencies that converge and tighten (become more closely aligned) as short-run adaptations are pursued in order to achieve higher levels of efficiency. This focus on internal alignment deflects attention away from the need to maintain external alignment and, consequently, the organisation is slow to adapt to environmental change. Inertia, as discussed above, maintains the state that Lewin (1947) described as 'stable quasi-stationary equilibrium' until misalignment reaches the point where major changes are precipitated. The only way forward is for the organisation to transform itself. Gersick argues that the transformation of deep structures can only occur through a process of wholesale upheaval:

> According to this logic, the deep structures must first be dismantled, leaving the system temporarily disorganised, in order for any fundamental change to be accomplished. Next, a subset of the system's old pieces, along with some new pieces, can be put back together into a new configuration, which operates according to a new set of rules. (1991: 19)

This process of revolutionary change and organisational transformation provides the basis for a new state of equilibrium. However, because of forces of resistance that inhibit continuous adaptation, this new equilibrium gives rise to another period of relative stability that is followed by a further period of revolutionary change. This process continues to unfold as a process of punctuated equilibrium.

Those who subscribe to the punctuated equilibrium paradigm argue that revolutionary episodes may affect a single organisation or a whole sector. Marks & Spencer is an organisation that was faced with the need to reinvent itself when, even after a long period of incremental change, it found itself misaligned with its environment and performing less well than other leading retailers. An example of a whole sector that was faced with the need to change its deep structure is the electricity supply sector in the UK. When the Conservative government decided to privatise the industry, this created a new playing field and a new set of rules for all the utility companies in the sector.

Support for the punctuated equilibrium paradigm

Numerous case histories offer support for the paradigm. Pettigrew (1987) reports a study of change in ICI over the period 1969–86. He found that radical periods of change were interspersed with periods of incremental adjustment and that changes in core beliefs preceded changes in structure and business strategy. Tushman, Newman and Romanelli (1986) examined the development of AT&T, General Radio, Citibank and Prime Computers, and observed periods during which organisational systems, structures and strategies converged to be more aligned with the organisations' basic mission. They also observed that these equilibrium periods were punctuated by very brief periods of intense and pervasive change that led to the formulation of new missions and then the initiation of new equilibrium periods.

The first direct test of the paradigm was Romanelli and Tushman's (1994) empirical study of the life histories of twenty-five minicomputer producers founded in the US between 1967 and 1969. They defined 'organisational transformation' as a discontinuous event involving the domains of an organisation that are important to its survival and central to its organisational activities. Five domains were identified but, because of measurement problems, data was only collected for changes in three of these: structure, strategy and power distributions. The key findings of the study were that:

1 A large majority of organisational transformations were accomplished via rapid and discontinuous change.
2 Small changes in strategies, structure and power distribution did not accumulate to produce fundamental transformations.
3 Triggers for transformations were major environmental changes and chief executive officer (CEO) succession.

The gradualist paradigm

The gradualist paradigm posits that fundamental change (organisational transformation) can occur through a process of continuous adjustment, and does not require some major discontinuous jolt to the system in order to trigger a short episode of revolutionary change. Change is *evolving* and *cumulative*.

Brown and Eisenhardt (1997) argue that many firms compete by changing continuously. They cite companies such as Intel, Wal-mart, 3M, Hewlett-Packard and Gillette as examples and suggest that for them the ability to change rapidly and continuously is not just a core competence but is at the heart of their cultures. They refer to Burgelman (1991) and Chakravarthy (1997), who suggest that continuous change is often played out through product innovation as companies change and sometimes transform through a process of continually altering their products. Hewlett-Packard is identified as a classic case. The company changed from an instruments company to a computer firm through rapid, continuous product innovation, rather than through a sudden punctuated change.

Continuous change, when it occurs, involves the continuous updating of work processes and social practices. Weick and Quinn (1999) argue that this leads to new patterns of organising in the absence of *a priori* intentions on the part of some change agent. It is 'emergent' in the sense that there is no deliberate orchestration of change. It is continuous and is the outcome of the everyday process of management. They cite Orlikowski (1996), who suggests that continuous change involves individuals and groups accommodating to and experimenting with everyday contingencies, breakdowns, exceptions, opportunities and unintended consequences and repeating, sharing and amplifying them to produce perceptible and striking changes.

Weick and Quinn (1999) observe that the distinctive quality of continuous change is the idea that small continuous adjustments, created simultaneously across units, can cumulate and create substantial change. They identify three related processes associated with continuous change: improvisation, translation and learning. Improvising facilitates the modification of work practices through mutual adjustments in which the time gap between planning and implementing narrows towards the point where composition (planning) converges with execution (implementation). Translation refers to the continuous adoption and editing of ideas as they travel through the organisation. Learning involves the continuous revision of shared mental models that facilitates a change in the organisation's response repertoire. They suggest that:

> organisations produce continuous change by means of repeated acts of improvisation involving simultaneous composition and execution, repeated acts of translation that convert ideas into useful artefacts that fit purposes at hand, or repeated acts of learning that enlarge, strengthen, or shrink the repertoire of responses. (1999: 372)

Brown and Eisenhardt (1997) studied product innovation in six firms in the computer industry at a time of rapid product development associated with the Pentium processor, multimedia, internet development and the convergence of telephony with consumer electronics. Three of their case studies related to firms with a record of successful product innovation and business performance and three related to firms with a relatively poor record of developing multi-product portfolios. They identified three characteristics of the firms that were able to manage change as a continuous process of adjustment: semi-structures that facilitated *improvisation*, links in time that facilitated *learning* and *sequenced steps* for managing transitions.

While the punctuated equilibrium paradigm stresses the interdependence of organisational sub-units and a web of interdependent relationships with buyers, suppliers, and others that legally and normatively constrain organisations to established activities and relationships (Romanelli and Tushman, 1994), the gradualist paradigm emphasises the relative independence of organisational sub-units. This loose coupling facilitates change within sub-units. Over time, as unit managers repeatedly alter their goals and relationships to accommodate changes in local environments, the organisation as a whole can be transformed. As noted above, Greenwood and Hinings (1996) support the view that tightly coupled relationships are resistant to change but when change does occur it tends to be revolutionary, whereas in loosely coupled fields radical change can be evolutionary. Weick and Quinn (1999), however, suggest that when interdependencies are loose, continuous adjustments can be confined within sub-units and remain as pockets of innovation.

Continuous adjustment, therefore, may not always lead to fundamental change.

Burke (2002) speculates that more that 95 per cent of organisational changes are, in some way, evolutionary, but he questions Orlikowski's assumption that this can lead to sufficient modification to achieve fundamental change. He asserts it is very difficult to overcome inertia and equilibrium without a discontinuous 'jolt' to the system:

> Organisation change does occur with continuous attention and effort, but it is unlikely that fundamental change in the deep structure of the organisation would happen. (2002: 69)

The nature of change confronting most organisations

Dunphy (1996) argues that planned change is triggered by the failure of people to create a continuously adaptive organisation, the kind of organisation that is referred to in Chapter 4 as an 'effective learning organisation'. Weick and Quinn (1999) suggest that this holds true whether the focus is episodic or continuous change, and they propose that the ideal organisation in both cases would resemble the successful self-organising and highly adaptive firms that Brown and Eisenhardt found in the computer industry. However, while some organisations may achieve this ideal and become so effective at double-loop collective learning (see Chapter 4) that they are never misaligned with their environment, most do not. The majority of organisations, if they survive long enough, experience episodes of discontinuous revolutionary as well as continuous incremental change.

There are three main categories of organisations that may not experience periods of discontinuous change:

1   The kind of self-organising and continuously changing learning organisations identified by Brown and Eisenhardt.
2   Companies operating in niche markets or in slow-moving sectors where they have not yet encountered the kind of environmental change that requires them to transform their deep structures.
3   Organisations that are able to continue functioning without transforming themselves because they have sufficient 'fat' to absorb the inefficiencies associated with misalignment.

With these exceptions, most organisations experience change as a pattern of punctuated equilibrium. This pattern involves relatively long periods of equilibrium, during which an organisation may engage only in incremental change, punctuated with short episodes of discontinuity during which an organisation's survival may depend on its ability to transform itself.

Incremental change

According to the punctuated equilibrium paradigm, incremental change is associated with those periods when the industry is in equilibrium and the focus for change is 'doing things better' through a process of continuous tinkering, adaptation and modification. Nadler and Tushman (1995) make the point that incremental changes are not necessarily small changes. They can be large in terms of both the resources needed and the impact on people. A key feature of this type of change is that it builds on what has already been accomplished and has the flavour of continuous improvement. According to the gradualist paradigm incremental change can be cumulative and, over time, can lead to an organisation transforming its deep structures and reinventing itself. However, according to the punctuated equilibrium paradigm incremental change is incapable of fundamentally transforming the deep structures of an organisation.

Transformational change

According to the punctuated equilibrium paradigm, transformational change occurs during periods of disequilibrium. Weick and Quinn (1999) and Gersick (1991) refer to this kind of change as revolutionary, but most writers – for example Tichy and Devanna (1986), Kotter (1999) and Burke and Litwin (1992) – use the term transformational change. It involves a break with the past, a step function change rather than an extrapolation of past patterns of change and development. It is based on new relationships and dynamics within the industry that may undermine core competencies, and question the very purpose of the enterprise. This kind of change involves doing things differently rather than doing things better. It might even mean doing different things. The reprographics industry provides a good example of a sector that was faced with a major discontinuity. Companies found that their core competence in optical reproduction was undermined when digital scanning technology was developed and made available to their customers.

The studies undertaken by Tushman and colleagues (summarised in Nadler and Tushman, 1995) suggest that most companies not only go through periods of continuous incremental and discontinuous transformational change, but that:

- this pattern of change repeats itself with some degree of regularity
- patterns vary across sectors (e.g. periods of discontinuity may follow a thirty-year cycle in cement, but a five-year cycle in mini computers)
- in almost all industries the rate of change is increasing and the time between periods of discontinuity is decreasing (Figure 1.2).

This last point is important because it predicts that all managers will be confronted with an ever-greater need to manage both incremental and transformational change.

Not all organisations are able to successfully negotiate episodes of discontinuity, and those that fail to adapt may drop-out or be acquired by others. Forester and Kaplan (2001) provide chilling evidence of the consequences of failing to adapt. They refer to changes in the *Forbes* top 100 companies between 1917 and 1987. Out of the original 100 companies only eighteen were still in the list in 1987 and sixty-one no longer existed.

Figure 1.2   Punctuated equilibrium: a recurring pattern of continuous and transformational change

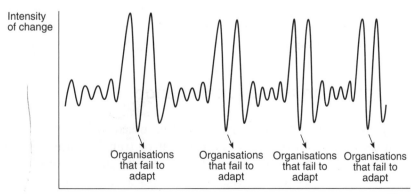

The possibility of anticipating change

Sometimes it is relatively easy to anticipate the need for change. For example, companies operating in the European Union (EU) can, if they pay appropriate attention, anticipate the impact of new regulations that are currently being discussed in Brussels. Companies competing in markets where margins are being squeezed can anticipate the need to secure greater efficiencies or generate new income streams. There are, however, occasions when organisations are confronted with changes that are very difficult to anticipate – for example, the effects of the 9/11 terrorist attacks or the SARS epidemic.

Some organisations are much better at anticipating the need for change than others. They are *proactive*. They search out potential threats and opportunities. They prepare for destabilising events that might occur or anticipate changes that they could initiate to gain competitive advantage. Other organisations are much more *reactive* and act only when there is a clear and pressing need to respond.

Whether the need is for incremental continuous or transformational change, the earlier the need is recognised the greater the number of options managers will have when deciding how to manage it. Whenever managers are forced to react to an urgent and pressing need to change they are relatively constrained in what they can do. For example:

1 *There is less time for planning*   Careful planning takes time, something that is more likely to be available to those who are proactive and anticipate the need for change.
2 *There is unlikely to be sufficient time to involve many people*   Involving people and encouraging participation in the change process can aid diagnosis, reduce resistance and increase commitment, but this also takes time.
3 *There will be little time to experiment*   Early movers not only have time to experiment, they may also have the time to try again if the first experiment fails. When there is a pressing need for change it is more difficult to search for creative solutions.
4 *Late movers may have little opportunity to influence shifts in markets and technologies*   Early movers may have the opportunity to gain a competitive advantage by not only developing but also protecting new products or technologies (for example, through patents).

A typology of organisational change

Combining two of the dimensions of change discussed so far – the extent to which change involves incremental adjustment or transformational change and the extent to which the organisation's response to change is proactive or reactive – provides a useful typology of organisational change (see Figure 1.3).

Figure 1.3   Types of organisational change

	Incremental	Transformational
Proactive	Tuning	Re-orientation
Reactive	Adaptation	Re-creation

Source: Adapted from Nadler, D.A., Shaw, R. and Walton, A.E., *Discontinuous Change* (1995): 24. Reprinted with permission of John Wiley & Sons, Inc.

Nadler *et al.* (1995) identify four types of change:

1 *Tuning* is change that occurs when there is *no immediate requirement to change*. It involves seeking better ways of achieving and/or defending the strategic vision. For example, improving policies, methods, procedures; introducing new technologies; redesigning processes to reduce cost, time-to-market, etc. or developing people with required competencies. Most organisations engage in a form of fine tuning much of the time. This approach to change tends to be initiated internally in order to make minor adjustments to maintain alignment between the internal elements of the organisation and between the organisation's strategy and the external environment.

2 *Adaptation* is an incremental and adaptive response to a pressing *external demand for change*. It might involve responding to a successful new marketing strategy adopted by a competitor or to a change in the availability of a key resource. Essentially, it involves, within broad terms, doing more of the same but doing it better in order to remain competitive. An example of adaptive change might be what happens when one company (for example, Nestlé) is forced to respond to a competitive move by another (for example, Mars may have either increased the size or reduced the price of some of its confectionary products). This kind of change is not about doing things in fundamentally different ways or about doing fundamentally different things.

While tuning and adaptation can involve minor or major changes, they are types of change that occur within the same frame, they are bounded by the existing paradigm. Re-orientation and re-creation, on the other hand, are types of change that, to use Gersick's analogy, target the playing field and the rules of the game rather than the way a particular game is played. They involve transforming the organisation and bending or breaking the frame to do things differently or to do different things:

3 *Re-orientation* involves a *re-definition of the enterprise*. It is initiated in
   anticipation of future opportunities or problems. The aim is to ensure
   that the organisation will be aligned and effective in the future. It may
   be necessary to modify the frame but, because the need for change has
   been anticipated, this could involve a gradual process of continuous
   frame- bending. Nestlé offered a good example of re-orientation in the
   mid- 1980s. At a time when it was doing well it embarked on a major
   change programme to ensure it would remain aligned to its environment
   over the medium term. It initiated a 'top-down review' to decide which
   businesses it should be in. (Should it, for example be in the pet foods
   business, should it continue to manufacture baked beans at a time when
   margins on that product were diminishing or, as a major consumer of tin
   cans, should it supply its own or buy them in on a just-in-time (JIT)
   basis?) It also embarked on a major project to reengineer the supply
   chain across the business and a 'bottom-up' analysis of the added value
   contributed by each main activity. British Gas provides another example.
   After it had been privatised as a monopoly suppler of gas the company
   was referred to the Monopolies and Mergers Commission (MMC). It
   was obvious to the top team that when the Commission delivered its
   report the company would be forced to change and might even be
   broken up. In order to prepare for this, a team of ten very senior
   managers was created to explore and test possible scenarios and help the
   organisation develop the capability to respond to the inevitable (but at
   that time unspecified) changes it would have to face.

   In those cases where the need for change is not obvious to all and may
   not be seen as pressing by many, senior management (as in the British Gas
   example) may need to work hard in order to create a sense of urgency and
   gain widespread acceptance of the need to prepare for change.

4 *Re-creation* is a reactive change that involves *transforming the organisation* through the fast and simultaneous change of all its basic elements.
   Nadler and Tushman (1995) state that it inevitably involves organisational frame-breaking and the destruction of some elements of the
   system. It can be a very disorienting process. An often-cited example of
   this kind of change is that introduced by Lee Iacocca when he moved to
   become the new CEO at Chrysler. He embarked on a process of revolutionary change that involved replacing most of the top team, withdraw-
   ing the company from the large-car market and divesting many foreign
   operations.

The most common type of change is incremental (either fine tuning or
adaptation) but it is not unusual for a single organisation to be involved
in more than one type of change at the same time. Confronted with ever-
diminishing opportunities to grow the mining business, UK Coal reap-
praised its assets and considered how it might revise its theory of
business. The way forward was to explore the possibility of redefining the

company as a land and property management *and* mining company. This re-orientation involved many changes, including bringing in new people with competencies in the area of land and property management. However, while this transformational change was being implemented at the highest level, the company was also pursuing incremental continuous improvement programmes to increase the efficiency of individual deep mines.

Implications of different types of change for change management practice

Different types of change can affect the focus for change efforts, the sequence of steps in the change process and the locus for change.

The focus for change efforts

With incremental change, the aim is to improve alignment between existing organisational components in order to do things better and improve the efficiency of the organisation. With transformational change, the aim is to seek a new configuration of organisational components in order to re-align the organisation with its changing environment. As noted above, this often leads to doing things differently or doing different things.

The sequence of activities required to achieve a desired outcome

Inertia is often one of the major barriers to change. As an organisation moves through a period of equilibrium interdependencies tighten, ideologies that prescribe the best way of operating become more widely accepted and the fear of losing benefits associated with the status quo strengthens resistance to change. The first step in the change process, therefore, involves equilibrium breaking, a step that Lewin (1947) referred to as 'unfreezing'. This unfreezing creates the conditions that facilitate transitioning, moving the organisation to a new state. The need to unfreeze is not limited to transformational change. Even when the change is a relatively small incremental change there may still be resistance from 'local' organisational members and other stakeholders. Thus with most incremental and all transformational change unfreezing is an essential first step in the change process. However, in a minority of cases, where constantly adapting organisations (of the type identified by Brown and Eisenhardt, 1997) are operating in high-velocity environments, the issue may not be overcoming inertia and unfreezing the organisation but re-directing the continuous process of change that is already under way. Weick and Quinn (1999) suggest that the appropriate change sequence required to redirect this kind of continuous change starts with *'freezing'* in order to take stock and highlight what is happening, then moving on to *'rebalancing'*, a process that involves reinterpreting history and re-sequencing patterns so that they unfold with fewer blockages, followed by *'unfreezing'* to resume improvisation, translation and learning 'in ways that are more mindful of sequences, more resilient to anomalies, and more flexible in their execution'.

The locus for change

Nadler and Tushman (1995) argue that an important factor that determines how change will be managed is the intensity (level of trauma and dislocation) of the change. With reference to the typology of change presented above, transformational change is more intense than incremental change. Gersick (1991) observes that since organisations are no longer directed by their old deep structures, and do not yet have future directions, organisational members (including senior managers) experience uncertainty, often accompanied by powerful emotions. Reactive change is also more intense than proactive change. Nadler and Tushman (1995) contend that during reactive change everybody is aware that failure may threaten survival. Furthermore, organisational members may find that their efforts are constrained by time pressures, and often by a shortage of resources. They go on to argue that the change with the lowest intensity is tuning, followed by adaptation. There is a jump in intensity associated with re-orientation but the highest level of intensity is associated with re-creation.

The main thrust of Nadler and Tushman's argument is that when the intensity of change is low it can usually be managed through project management and other forms of implementation associated with normal management processes and systems of accountability. As the intensity of change increases, so does the burden of change management until it reaches a point where it cannot easily be managed through normal management processes. When the intensity of change reaches this level senior management often create special structures and roles to aid the process and they may even appoint an internal or external change agent to facilitate the change. Nadler and Tushman (1995: 32) refer to this approach to change management as *transition management*:

> [It] involves mechanisms specially created for the purpose of managing a specific change . . . the senior team plays a supporting role, and the organisation continues to be run as it was before. If the change is intense enough, it may appear on the senior team's agenda as one of a number of important items to be reviewed and managed over time. (1995: 32)

However, as the intensity of changes increases still further change management is no longer just one of the items on the senior team's agenda, it *is* the senior team's agenda and the CEO assumes responsibility for directing the change rather than delegating it to others.

New patterns of change

Gersick's (1991) multi-level and multi-domain exploration of punctuated equilibrium suggests that this pattern of change is not new. What is new is how people are experiencing it. When the pace of change was slower, a good number of people could spend their entire working life in organisations that were never significantly misaligned with their environment. Consequently their experience of organisational change might have been confined to incremental fine tuning and adaptation. However, with the increasing pace of change many more organisations have experienced periods of *strategic drift* (Johnson and Scholes, 1999) and misalignment with their environment to the point where the only way forward requires some form of radical transformation.

Nadler and Tushman (1995) report research findings indicating that the periods between episodes of revolutionary change are becoming shorter and shorter. Therefore, while the underlying pattern of change may not be changing, an acceleration in the *pace of change* is affecting the way many organisations and organisational members are experiencing change.

The impact of change on organisational members

It is over thirty-five years since Toffler, an eminent futurologist, published his book *Future Shock* in which he discussed three aspects of change and speculated about how they would affect people. Toffler (1970) argues that, in many respects, 'future shock' is similar to culture shock, but with one very important difference – there is no going back. If people find it difficult to adapt to a new culture there is often the alternative of returning to the familiar culture they left behind. For example, if emigrants fail to settle in a new country (national culture) it may be possible for them to return home. However, when confronted with future shock this option is unlikely to be as available.

'Future shock' is the product of three related trends:

1 *Transience* Toffler notes that impermanence and transience are increasingly becoming important features of modern life because of a major expansion in the scale and scope of change and the accelerating pace of change.

The accelerating pace of change affects people's relationship with things, places, people, organisations and ideas. As acceleration occurs, these relationships become foreshortened, telescoped in time. People respond to this increase in the pace of change in different ways. Those who internalise the principle of acceleration make an unconscious compensation for the compression of time – they modify their durational expectancies. But some find this more difficult than others.

2 *Novelty* is the second major trend identified by Toffler. He argues that having to live at an accelerating pace is one thing when life situations are more or less familiar, but having to do so when faced by unfamiliar, strange or unprecedented situations is distinctly another, and this is the reality for increasing numbers of people. Today the balance between the familiar and the unfamiliar is changing. In Toffler's words, the novelty ratio is rising.

3 *Diversity* is Toffler's third major trend. The Orwellian view that people will become mindless consumer-creatures, surrounded by standardised goods, educated in standardised schools, fed a diet of standardised mass culture and forced to adopt standardised styles of life could not be further from the truth, according to Toffler. The reality is that most of us are faced with a paralysing surfeit of choice that, especially at work, complicates decision making.

Toffler summarises the consequence of these trends:

> When diversity converges with transience and novelty we rocket society toward an historical crisis of adaptation. We create an environment so ephemeral, unfamiliar and complex as to threaten millions with adaptive breakdown. This breakdown is future shock. (1970: 285)

The changes that confront individuals and groups as a consequence of organisational adjustments are often incremental. People may be required to develop additional competencies or modify their ways of working. Such changes may be regarded as incremental in that they build on what is already there. However, sometimes a change can destroy, rather than modify, the relationship that exists between individuals and the organisation. The change may undermine the assumptions that people make about themselves and how they relate with the world around them. Just as an organisation may have to redefine its theory of business, individual organisational members may find that, as a result of an organisational change, they have to redefine their theory of being. This may not always be easy and, as noted above, Toffler points to the possibility of adaptive breakdown. Many reports document the increasing levels of stress experienced by workers. Much attention has also been focused on those who believe that the 'psychological contract' between themselves and their organisation has been violated.

All of these developments affect performance, commitment and the physical and psychological wellbeing of individual employees, and they also create problems for managers, supervisors and co-workers. They have to manage people who are upset by change at a time when the same changes are increasing their own workloads.

With increasing frequency, especially in times of discontinuous transformational change, organisational members have to cope with multiple and concurrent changes. At such times, having to cope with other peoples' emotional response to change is an added burden that sometimes is difficult to manage. This issue will be given more consideration in Chapter 14.

Conclusion

The management of change poses many challenges for managers. Burnes (2005) observes that:

> Managing and changing organisations appears to be getting more rather than less difficult, and more rather than less important. Given the rapidly changing environment in which organisations operate, there is little doubt that the ability to manage change successfully needs to be a core competence for organisations. (2005: 85)

Many, and some argue the majority, of change projects fail to achieve there intended outcomes. This book addresses this problem and explores how theory can help to improve the practice of change management.

This chapter ends with a series of case studies of organisations adapting to changing circumstances. You are invited to reflect on the content of this chapter and consider how it applies to these cases.

Exercise 1.1   Types of change

Read the following five case studies (Case studies 1.1–1.5) and use Nadler, Shaw and Walton's typology of change presented below (1995: 24) to identify the type of change described in each case.

	Incremental	Transformational
Proactive	**Tuning**	**Re-orientation**
Reactive	**Adaptation**	**Re-creation**

Types of organisational change

1 The BBC

2 UK Coal

3 Leicester Royal Infirmary

4 McDonald's restaurants

5 GNER

Case study 1.1   The BBC

After a long period of stability, during which the BBC had developed a reputation for honest reporting and programmes of outstanding quality, the Corporation had become complacent. Staff believed that the Corporation was financially secure and that the BBC was the best programme maker and broadcaster in the world. But then the world began to change and the Corporation was slow to respond.

The situation when John Birt came to the BBC

John Birt came to the BBC, as Deputy Director General, in 1987 and was appointed Director General in December 1992. In his autobiography The *Harder Path*, he reports that he was surprised to learn that there was little hard information about the Corporation's basic business. He described the culture within the BBC as a kind of imperialism, where every regional commander in every part of the Corporation acquired a full fleet of facilities, irrespective of need. The result was a vast excess of facilities: 'We could have covered Wimbledon, the World Cup and a world war, and still have had unused resources to spare.' He also found that staff utilisation was low and that in some areas there was between 25 and 50 per cent more staff than necessary. Part of the problem was that facilities, overheads and support services were funded by the centre and not charged to particular programmes. One result of this was that nobody had the slightest idea how much it cost to make a programme.

Until the mid-1980s the Corporation was able to survive in spite of its inefficiencies because, for a period of sixty years, its income from the licence fee had grown, on average, 4 per cent per annum. But, because of a new political climate, this changed in 1985.

Political pressures for change

In 1979, Margaret Thatcher and a Conservative government came to power with an agenda for change that included plans to privatise much of the public sector. Thatcher viewed the BBC as a bloated bureaucracy that was over-manned, inefficient and, therefore, ripe for reform.

In 1985 the government froze the licence fee (paid to the BBC by everybody in the UK who owns a radio or television) in order to force the Corporation to become more efficient. Even though over the next decade the licence fee remained constant or was reduced in value, costs continued to rise. Thatcher's intention of delivering a 'rude shock' to the BBC did not have the intended immediate impact because Birt's predecessor had begun his term of office with a huge cash surplus which he spent on funding the growing gap between licence fee income and costs. When this surplus was used up the Corporation started borrowing until, in 1992, it faced a deficit of £100 million. Birt recognised that this situation could not continue and that major changes were required.

Technological developments and new market pressures

The problem was further complicated by a wave of technological developments that threatened to undermine the BBC's traditional ways of working. The biggest challenge came from the development of digital technologies that opened up the possibility of many more channels, better technical quality, video-on-demand and interactivity. There was also increased competition from new players, for example, Murdoch's launch of BSkyB.

Birt's strategy for change

Birt felt that he had no option other than to introduce radical reforms as quickly as possible in order to ensure the Corporation's survival.

Case study 1.2   UK Coal

The state-owned coal industry in the UK was privatised in 1994–5. At that time UK Coal operated about twenty deep mines and the same number of surface (open cast) mines. By 2004 turnover was down by half and the number of mines had fallen by more than 50 per cent.

The main reason for the closure of many of UK Coal's deep mines was the exhaustion of economically viable reserves. New mines were not developed to replace those that had been closed because the continuing downward trend in world coal prices had undermined the business case for new investment.

The exhaustion of economically viable reserves was not the only problem. Others included environmental opposition to the burning of coal with a high sulphur content. Imported coal was more attractive to major customers (the power generators) on this count, as well as on price. Another factor was the very considerable capital investment required to develop a new deep mine.

The change strategy

The reduction in the number of deep and surface mines encouraged UK Coal to begin looking for ways of improving the company's operating efficiency. One way of achieving this was to reduce the overhead cost of its central corporate headquarters by making each mine more autonomous and delegating to each unit a wider range of activities than used to be the case. Alongside this re-structuring, UK Coal introduced a continuous improvement programme across all the remaining deep mines in order to make them more efficient and ensure their long-term survival.

Confronted with ever-diminishing opportunities to grow the mining business, UK Coal also began to reappraise its assets and consider how it might revise its theory of business. It decided to explore the possibility of redefining the company as a land and property management *and* mining company. This re-orientation involved many changes, including bringing new senior managers into the organisation with competencies in the area of land and property management.

However, while this change was being implemented at the highest level, the company continued to pursue continuous improvement programmes to increase the efficiency of individual deep mines.

Case study 1.3   Leicester Royal Infirmary

The hospital is one of the largest teaching hospitals in England with 1,100 beds and 4,200 staff. By the late 1980s it had developed a reputation for being well run and it was near the top of the National Health Service (NHS) efficiency league tables. However, even though the hospital was at the forefront of change (for example, it was one of the first hospitals to introduce general managers in the mid-1980s, it was an early adopter of clinical directorates in 1986 and it gained NHS Trust status in 1993), there were growing pressures for further change.

The new pressures for change

The city of Leicester had three acute hospitals located close to each other and integrated by a common medical school. When the opportunity of gaining more independence presented itself the original proposal was that all three hospitals would become a single NHS Trust. The Department of Health rejected this proposal and in the end three separate Trusts were established. This created the possibility for competition between the three hospitals. For example, the District Health Authority (DHA, the body that purchased services from providers – hospitals – on behalf of the community) adopted a policy of service rationalisation which raised the prospect of the Leicester Royal losing contracts to one of the other hospitals.

The NHS internal market, introduced in 1991, led to another competitive pressure from the primary care sector as community-based doctors (those who were General Practitioner (GP) Fundholders with delegated budgets to purchase certain elective services) began 'shopping around' the three hospitals to obtain the most cost-effective and best quality provision. Purchasers also began to put considerable pressure on the hospitals to reduce patient waiting times.

In addition, the introduction of national targets to improve efficiency placed new demands on all hospitals to make year-on-year savings.

The change strategy

The Leicester Royal was much better placed than most hospitals to face these challenges and the leadership team proactively sought additional funding from the government to embark on a major change programme (see McNulty and Ferlie, 2002).

Because of the Leicester Royal Infirmary's earlier success in eliminating inefficiencies there were few easy targets for further cost-cutting. McNulty and Ferlie (2002) quote one member of the Trust Board as saying 'I believe that there is no way we could improve the effectiveness and efficiency of this hospital simply by trying to do better that which we already do'.

Leicester Royal Infirmary, like hospitals generally, was organised according to functional principles. However, early experiments that involved introducing process-based principles of organising led to some dramatic improvements in parts of the organisation. In neurology, for example, the introduction of a single visit clinic reduced the time from visit to diagnosis from twelve weeks to one day, and in hearing services the time to fit a hearing aid was reduced from fourteen months to six weeks.

These early successes encouraged the hospital to embark on an ambitious organisation-wide programme of business process reengineering. It was introduced in 1994 as a 'top-down' programme to redesign two of the hospital's core processes – patient visits and diagnostic tests. The aim was to transform the organisation from one that was characterised by fragmented functional thinking that directed attention and activity towards narrow departmental priorities to one where everybody worked together across functional boundaries to achieve wider organisational goals.

Case study 1.4   McDonald's restaurants

McDonald's is the world's largest quick-service restaurant chain. In 2004 the company operated 1,250 outlets in the UK, of which 35 per cent were franchised. McDonald's experienced rapid growth in the UK market from the early 1970s until the late 1990s. However, from the late 1990s it began to experience a slow-down in growth leading, in 2000, to a fall in both total sales and market share.

Over the last forty-five years its core business had been selling burgers, fries and soft drinks. Over this period McDonald's introduced only occasional and relatively minor changes to its menu. Some commentators have suggested that because of its track record of sustained success McDonald's was slow to recognise and respond to changes in its external environment.

Several factors appear to have contributed to the change in the company's fortunes:

- Greater competition from new entrants into the market, including new chains of coffee shops and sandwich bars
- A desire on the part of consumers for a wider choice of food
- A greater awareness of the importance of leading a healthy lifestyle and eating healthy foods
- New evidence on the causes of obesity
- Media interest that has publicised possible links between certain kinds of 'fast- food' and obesity.

An additional threat that has received media attention, and that could affect the company in the future, is the possibility that the UK government might introduce restrictions on advertising to children. There have also been rumours that it might consider imposing new taxes on those foods that are deemed to be 'unhealthy'.

McDonald's response to the new situation

In 2004 the company broadened its food offering and focused more attention on healthy eating with the launch of 'Salads Plus'. This was the biggest change to the McDonald's menu since it started business in the UK in 1974. The 'Good Food Fast' menu strategy involved the simultaneous introduction of eight new items to the McDonald's menu: caesar salad, bacon ranch salad, mixed salad, quorn sandwiches, chicken-filled sandwiches, yogurt and berry pot, fresh apples and muffins.

This major change to the company's product line involved a series of related changes:

- The introduction of new cooking equipment in all 1,250 outlets
- Training 70,000 staff to cook and serve the new products
- Training restaurant managers how to order and store new raw ingredients, and how to manage the introduction of the new menu in a way that enhanced profitability
- Preparing managers at all levels, who had a wealth of experience of how to manage in a steady-state environment, to lead the introduction of these changes.

Case study 1.5   GNER

GNER is a train-operating company and a part of Sea Containers Ltd; a highly entrepreneurial Bermuda-registered company with regional operating offices in London, Genoa, New York City, Rio de Janeiro, Singapore and Sydney. GNER started business in 1996 when it won a seven- (later extended to nine-) year franchise to operate the East Coast high-speed intercity routes from London to all major cities on the eastern side of the UK. From 2005 the franchise for the following ten years was to be awarded on the basis of open competition. For GNER it was a 'win or die' situation. The only way it could retain its business was to submit the winning bid. If it was unsuccessful all the company's assets would be transferred to a new operator.

The company's response was to establish a new development team, headed by a director of development, charged with preparing the company's bid for the East Coast franchise. The bid was successful and GNER won the franchise until 2015. The company decided to build on this experience and grow its business through bidding for other railway franchises as and when opportunities presented themselves. Its first venture was to join forces with the MTR Corporation, which runs the highly successful mass-transit railway in Hong Kong, to bid for the Integrated Kent Franchise that includes the commuter rail services between southeast England and London and the new high- speed line from London to the channel tunnel. This first bid for new business was unsuccessful but, at the time of going to press, GNER (again in partnership with MTR) has been short-listed for the new South Western franchise.

The change strategy

GNER's change strategy is to develop the existing East Coast railway and generate additional revenue through the provision of enhanced services. Plans include rebuilding all the electric fleet carriages, introducing an innovative on-board wireless internet service on all trains and increasing the number of daily intercity services to London from fifty-three to eighty. Alongside this development of the intercity East Coast business the company plans to grow by acquiring more franchises in the UK. It is anticipated that these will include different types of railway (intercity, regional and commuter) each with different risk patterns, and a portfolio of franchises with different expiry dates that will help to provide the company with greater stability.

Exercise 1.2   The nature of the changes that confront your organisation (or some other organisation that you are familiar with)

You may find it useful to reflect on the nature of the changes that have confronted the total organisation or the part of the organisation that you know best over the last year:

● Overall, would you describe the main type of change as incremental or discontinuous?

In terms of the organisation's typical response to change, think back and consider how the organisation has responded to change over the last few years. How does this compare with the organisation's current way of responding to change?

● Is the organisation's typical response to change reactive or proactive?

Make a note of your answers on a separate sheet or in the space provided below.

Notes on the nature of change confronting your organisation

Summary

This chapter has considered the nature of change, giving particular attention to issues of continuity and time pressure. The effects of change on individuals and organisations have also been examined and a typology specifying four types of change has been presented.

References

Birt, J. (2002) *The Harder Path*, London: TimeWarner.

Brown, S.L. and Eisenhardt, K.M. (1997) 'The Art of Continuous Change: Linking Complexity Theory and Time-Paced Evolution in Relentlessly Shifting Organizations', *Administrative Science Quarterly*, 42, pp. 1–34.

Burgelman, R.A. (1991) 'Intraorganizational Ecology of Strategy Making and Organizational Adaptation: Theory and Field Research', *Organisational Science,* 22, pp. 239–62.

Burke, W.W. (2002) *Organizational Change: Theory and Practice*, Thousand Oaks, CA: Sage.

Burke, W.W. and Litwin, G.H. (1992) 'A Causal Model of Organizational Performance and Change', *Journal of Maangement,* 18 (3), pp. 523–45.

Burnes, B. (2005) 'Complexity Theories and Organizational Change', *International Journal of Management Reviews.* 7 (2), pp. 73–90.

Chakravarthy, B. (1997) 'A New Strategy Framework for Coping with Turbulence', *Sloan Management Review,* Winter, pp. 69–82.

Drucker, P.F. (1994) 'The Theory of the Business', *Harvard Business Review,* 72 (5), pp. 95–104.

Dunphy, D. (1996) 'Organisational Change in Corporate Settings', *Human Relations*, 49 (5), pp. 541–52.

Forester, R.N. and Kaplan, S. (2001) *Creative Destruction: Why Companies that are Built to Last Under-Perform in the Market – and How to Successfully Transform Them*, New York: Currency.

Gersick, C.J.G. (1991) 'Revolutionary Change Theories: A Multilevel Exploration of the Punctuated Equilibrium Paradigm', *Academy of Management Review,* 16 (1), pp. 10–36.

Gladwell, M. (2000) *The Tipping Point: How Little Things Can Make a Big Difference*, London: Little, Brown & Co.

Gould, S.J. (1978) *Ever Since Darwin: Reflections in Natural History,* London: Burnett Books.

Greenwood, R. and Hinings, C.R. (1996) 'Understanding Radical Organizational Change: Bringing Together the Old and the New Institutionalism', *Academy of Management Review*, 21, 1022–54.

Johnson, G. and Scholes, K. (1999) *Exploring Corporate Strategy*, London: Prentice Hall Europe.

Kotter, J.P. (1999) *On What Leaders Really Do*, Boston, MA: Harvard Business School Press.

Lewin, K. (1947) 'Frontiers in Group Dynamics', in D. Cartwright (ed.) (1952) *Field Theory in Social Service*, London: Social Science Paperback.

McNulty, T. and Ferlie, E. (2002) *Reengineering Health Care: The Complexities of Organisational Transformation,* Oxford: Oxford University Press.

Nadler, D., Shaw, R. and Walton, A.E. (1995) *Discontinuous Change*, San Francisco: Jossey-Bass.

Nadler, D.A. and Tushman, M.L. (1995) 'Types of Organizational Change: From Incremental Improvement to Discontinuous Transformation', in D.A. Nadler, R.B. Shaw and A.E. Walton, *Discontinuous Change: Leading Organizational Transformation*, San Francisco: Jossey-Bass, pp.15–34.

Orlikowski, W.J. (1996) 'Improvising Organisational Transformation Over Time: A Situated Change Perspective', *Information Systems Research*, 7 (1), pp. 63–92.

Pettigrew, A.M. (1987) 'Context and Action in the Transformation of the Firm', *Journal of Management Studies,* 24 (6), 649–69.

Romanelli, E. and Tushman, M.L. (1994) 'Organizational Transformation as Punctuated Equilibrium: An Empirical Test', *Academy of Management Journal*, 37 (5), 1141–66.

Ryan, B. and Gross, N. (1943) 'The Diffusion of Hybrid Seed Corn in Two Iowa Communities', *Rural Sociology*, 8, 15–24.

The Shorter Oxford Dictionary (1973) Oxford: Oxford University Press.

Tichy, N.M. and Devanna, M.A. (1986) *The Transformational Leader*, Chichester: Wiley.

Toffler, A. (1970) *Future Shock*, New York: Random House.

Tushman, M.L., Newman, W. and Romanelli, E. (1986) 'Convergence and Upheaval: Managing the Unsteady Pace of Organization Evolution', *California Management Review*, 29 (1), pp. 29–44.

Tushman, M.L. and Romanelli, E. (1985) 'Organizational Evolution: A Metamorphosis Model of Convergence and Reorientation', in B. Staw and L. Cummings (eds), *Research in Organization Behavior*, 7, Greenwich, CT: JAI Press, pp. 171–222.

Weick, K.E. and Quinn, R.E. (1999) 'Organizational Development and Change', *Annual Review of Psychology*, 50, pp. 361–86.

Organisational effectiveness and the role of change management

Change management is about modifying or transforming organisations in order to maintain or improve their effectiveness. Managers are responsible for ensuring that the organisation (or the part of the organisation they manage) performs effectively. To do this, they need to know what constitutes effective performance and have some means of assessing whether or not the organisation as a whole, or their particular sub-system, is performing effectively. They also need to know, if performance is unsatisfactory, what elements of the organisation can be changed in order to improve performance and what steps they can take to secure these changes.

This chapter:

- considers some of the factors that need to be taken into account when assessing organisational effectiveness
- reviews arguments relating to the manager's ability to affect the way an organisation responds to changed circumstances
- examines some of the factors, such as the availability of conceptual models, management tools and beliefs about change agency, that can affect the manager's ability to successfully manage change.

Assessing organisational effectiveness

Before reading on, make a note, in the space provided opposite, of the indicators that you believe could be used to assess whether or not your organisation – and your department or unit within the organisation – are effective.

When you have completed this chapter you might like to review these indicators, and consider whether any of them need to be revised.

```
                    Indicators of effectiveness

    Organisation                Department/unit




```

Definitions of organisational effectiveness

Organisation effectiveness has been defined in many different ways. This section examines a range of criteria that you might need to consider when assessing the effectiveness of an organisation or a unit within an organisation.

Purpose

Many commercial organisations use profit as one of the main indicators of effectiveness, but this indicator may not apply to all organisations. While financial viability may be necessary for the survival of organisations such as religious orders, universities, hospitals or charities, profit might not be viewed as a critical indicator of their effectiveness. The effectiveness of hospitals in the British NHS, for example, might be judged on indicators such as bed utilisation, waiting lists and morbidity rates rather than 'profit'. Indicators of effectiveness need to be relevant to the *purpose* of the organisation or unit within an organisation.

Stakeholder perspective

Different stakeholders often use different indicators to assess an organisation's effectiveness. Profit might be more important to shareholders than to workers or customers. Suppliers, customers, employees and people in the wider community affected by the products and services (and pollution) produced by an organisation will all have their own views on what should be taken into account when assessing whether or not it is effective.

Level of assessment

Effectiveness can be assessed at different *levels* (such as the organisation, sub-unit, or individual employee), and in terms of the *linkages* between the different elements of the organisation (such as Kotter's processes and cause and effect relationships: see Chapter 3).

Alignment

Assessments of effectiveness need to be *aligned* up, down and across the organisation. The indicators used to assess the effectiveness of sub-units need to be aligned vertically to the indicators used to assess the effectiveness of individuals who are members of each unit (via the appraisal process) and to the overall effectiveness of the organisation. The indicators used for different units also need to be aligned 'horizontally' across the organisation. Figure 2.1 depicts a simplified model of the functional structure of an organisation and presents examples of indicators of effectiveness for each function and objectives that each function might pursue in order to achieve an effective performance.

Managers working in sub-units of the organisation represented in Figure 2.1 might lose sight of the overall goal of the organisation and focus their attention on the achievement of more immediate goals related to functional performance. For example, marketing and sales, in the face of strong price competition, might seek to secure increased sales (related to their goal of maximising revenue from sales) by offering customers fast delivery and customised products. While this strategy might help marketing and sales achieve its own performance targets, it might undermine the effectiveness of

Figure 2.1   Examples of functional mis-alignment

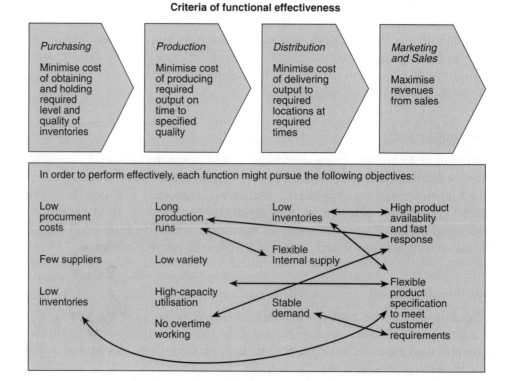

the manufacturing and distribution functions (and consequently the effectiveness of the overall organisation). In order to customise products and offer an immediate and flexible response to satisfy customers' JIT delivery requirements, the manufacturing function might have to introduce short product runs, make greater use of overtime working and hold higher stocks of work in progress. The distribution function might have to hold higher inventories of finished goods and, because of unpredictable demand, make more deliveries that involve part loads. The cost of meeting these new manufacturing and distribution requirements might be greater than the net benefits achieved from the increased sales revenue and might threaten the organisation's overall effectiveness. A few examples of sources of possible mis-alignment are indicated by the double-headed arrows shown in Figure 2.1. As will be seen from this example, it is not uncommon for organisation sub-units (and individual employees) to be rewarded for behaving in ways that have little to do with overall organisational effectiveness.

Time perspective

It has already been noted that in some cases profitability can be a useful indicator of organisational effectiveness. However, just because organisation *A* is currently more profitable than organisation *B* does not mean that *A* is the most effective organisation. Organisation *B* may be incurring higher costs and lower profits today in order to invest in new plant, product development and staff training in the belief that this will help secure survival and growth over the longer term. The implication of this is that some reference to *time perspective* needs to be included in any definition of effectiveness.

Bench mark

Another common feature of definitions of effectiveness is that they are presented in terms of some output:input ratio such as the number of units produced per man-hour. It is assumed that any increase in output with constant or decreasing inputs represents greater effectiveness, and vice versa. When making this kind of assessment reference needs to be made to a standard or *bench mark*. For example, all producers within a given product category or industrial sector may have experienced efficiency gains because of the introduction of a new and widely available manufacturing system. In this context, the assessment of whether one particular producer has maintained or improved its effectiveness might need to involve a comparison of this producer's performance relative to the performance of others. A company may have improved its output:input ratio (and therefore improved its efficiency) but may have achieved smaller improvements than other comparable producers. In these circumstances the company may be deemed to be more efficient than it used to be, but less effective than comparable other companies.

Constraints and enabling factors

Account also needs to be taken of any *constraints* that inhibit performance (or *enabling* factors that boost performance) relative to comparable other organisations. The new manufacturing system referred to above might produce levels of toxic emissions greater than the levels permitted by environmental regulations. These regulations may apply only to a minority of producers located in a particular region or country. In these circumstances, while a producer faced with the strict environmental regulations might not have improved output:input ratios as much as some of its competitors, it might have achieved considerable success in modifying its production processes in a way that enables it to adopt the new manufacturing technology and improve efficiency enough to produce sufficient profit to survive. A failure to respond in this way might have resulted in the company going out of business. In terms of its ability to minimise the effect of the constraint imposed by the environmental legislation, it might be deemed to be an effective organisation.

Summarising the discussion so far, a full definition of organisation effectiveness needs to take account of:

- purpose and desired outcomes
- the stakeholder perspective from which the assessment is made
- level of assessment
- alignment with the various indicators used at different levels and across different functions
- specified time frame (short-, medium- or long-term)
- bench mark standard
- any special constraints or enabling factors that affect performance.

At this point it might be useful to distinguish between *effectiveness* and *efficiency*. Carnall (2003) defines efficiency as achieving stated goals within given resource constraints. His definition of effectiveness includes the efficient use of resources to achieve immediate goals but also embraces the need to adapt to changing circumstances in order to remain efficient over the longer term.

Effectiveness and conceptualisations of organisations

This discussion of what constitutes organisational effectiveness can be elaborated further. Goodman and Pennings (1980) argue that our preferred definitions of organisational effectiveness are closely linked to the way we conceptualise organisations:

- The *goals perspective* presents organisations as rationally constructed entities that are formed, and their existence legitimised, in the quest for certain identifiable goals. The meaning of effectiveness is derived from the accomplishment of these goals.

- The *systems perspective* focuses on the functional complementarity of parts of the organisation and the nature of the organisation's relationship with the environment. The organisation is viewed as an open system that imports inputs from the environment, transforming them into outputs which are then exported. The fundamental task of the organisation is to survive and this is seen to depend on the maintenance of functional complementarity within the organisation and between the organisation and the wider environment. According to Goodman and Pennings, the systems perspective views functional complementarity as being more important than the achievement of some particular goal.

- The *organisation development (OD) perspective* is concerned with the processes of organisational learning that promote organisational renewal and long-term survival. Porras and Robertson (1992) define organisational development as a set of behavioural science-based theories, values, strategies and techniques aimed at the planned change of the organisational work setting for the purpose of enhancing individual development and improving organisational performance through the alteration of organisational members' on-the-job behaviour. Beer (1980) defines organisational development as a system-wide process of data collection, diagnosis, action planning, intervention and evaluation aimed at (a) enhancing congruence between organisational structure, process, strategy, people and culture; (b) developing new and creative organisational solutions; and (c) developing the organisation's self-renewing capacity.

The OD perspective emphasises a set of values that concerns the nature of man and the way he or she is employed in an organisational context. Marguilies and Raia (1972) summarise these values as:

1   Providing opportunities for people to function as human beings rather than as resources in the productive process.
2   Providing opportunities for each organisational member, as well as for the organisation itself, to develop its full potential.
3   Seeking to increase the effectiveness of the organisation in terms of all its goals.
4   Attempting to create an environment in which it is possible to find exciting and challenging work.
5   Providing opportunities for people in the organisation to influence the way they relate to work, the organisation and the environment.
6   Treating each human being as a person with a complex set of needs, all of which are important in his or her work and life.

While this perspective has a strong foundation rooted in systems theory and recognises the importance of alignment, it is normative in so far as it emphasises the importance of individual development. This is reflected in (a) indicators of effectiveness that embrace the quality of working life, and (b) determinants of effectiveness that focus on the contribution that organisational members can make to the process of improving organisational effectiveness.

- The *political arena perspective* presents organisations as a collection of internal and external constituencies, each pursuing their own objectives. Organisational effectiveness is defined in terms of the attributes valued by the most powerful constituencies. A constituency's power is determined, at least in part, by the importance of its contribution to the input–transformation–output process. Suppliers or customers are powerful if they are vital to the survival of the organisation. Groups of employees, such as members of a particular trades union, or specific departments, are powerful only so long as the organisation needs to rely on them to survive. The more central is the contribution of a constituency to the survival and prosperity of the organisation, the greater its power – so long as there are no rival constituencies that can offer an alternative/substitute contribution (see the discussion of Jawahare and McLaughlin's stakeholder theory in Chapter 9). This political perspective views the organisation as the product of a *negotiated order* that is managed by the dominant coalition of constituencies, and reflects aspects of both the goals and systems conceptualisations of organisations.

  There are common threads in all these different conceptualisations of organisations that point to the essential elements of any definition of effectiveness. Organisations are interdependent open systems that comprise a range of constituencies, each with their own interests and goals. The constituencies (stakeholders) that dominate the political process define the purpose of the organisation and the key indicators of organisational effectiveness. Whether or not an organisation performs effectively (at least over the medium term – see Chapter 3) will be determined by the extent to which the various elements of the input–transformation–output system are aligned. Over the longer term, organisational effectiveness entails developing and maintaining the processes necessary to adapt as necessary in order to survive and prosper.

- The *Balanced Scorecard* In the early 1990s Robert Kaplan and David Norton embarked on a collaborative research project to explore new ways of measuring performance that addresses many of the issues discussed above. A guiding hypothesis was that managers and employees focus their efforts on those aspects of performance that can be measured and give relatively little attention to, or even neglect, those aspects of organisational functioning that cannot be measured. One of their early observations was that in the majority of organisations the primary measurement system was financial accounting 'which treated investments in employee capabilities, databases, information systems, customer relationships, quality, responsive processes, and innovative products and services as expenses in the period in which they were incurred' (Kaplan and Norton, 2004). At a time when knowledge-based assets are becoming more important in almost every business these financial reporting systems fail to measure, or provide a basis for managing, the value created by the organisation's *intangible assets*. Their early research led Kaplan and Norton to develop the concept of the Balanced Scorecard. Financial measures, which provide a useful summary of the results of actions previously taken, are supplemented by measures of three other aspects of organisational functioning that Kaplan and Norton believe are important drivers of future financial performance. The 'scorecard' approach enables managers to attend to short- and long-term objectives and lagging and leading indicators through a process that reviews performance from a number of different perspectives (financial, customer, internal business process and learning and growth). In Chapter 23, the ways in which the Balanced Scorecard can be used as a change management tool are discussed.

The assessment of effectiveness in your organisation

Review the notes you made at the beginning of this chapter on how you might assess the effectiveness of your organisation and/or your unit in the organisation. In the light of the content of this chapter, do you think that you need to revise the criteria/indictors you would use? If so, make a note of the revised indicators below.

Revised indicators of effectiveness	
Organisation	**Department/unit**

Change agency and organisational effectiveness

'Change agency' refers to the ability of a manager or other agent of change to affect the way an organisation responds to change.

One approach to the study of change and change management portrays the manager (and other organisational members) as pawns affected by change rather than as agents who can affect change. This approach, which emphasises the forces of economics, environment and context, is referred to by Wilson (1992) as 'determinism'. 'Voluntarism' is an approach to the study of change and change management which emphasises how the actions of managers and other change agents can affect outcomes.

The *deterministic view* is that the ability of the manager to influence change is limited because the main determining forces lie outside the organisation and the realms of strategic choice for managers. Wilson (1992: 42) notes that advocates of this approach view organisations as interdependent elements of a much greater open system and they regard the characteristics of the wider organisation–environment linkages as the key determinant of strategic change. Thus, for example, no matter how good the CEO of an organisation might be, when faced with a dramatic downturn in the trade cycle or very unfavourable exchange rates, he or she may be able to do little to improve the immediate fortunes of the organisation. Greenwood and Hinings (1996) echo this view when they discuss how, in some circumstances, an organisation's institutional context can limit the possibilities for change, especially when the organisation is embedded in a wider system that has tightly coupled relationships. Mellahi and Wilkinson (2004) note that one of the points that classical industrial organisation and organisational ecology scholars can agree on is the deterministic role of the environment in constraining management action.

The *voluntarist view* rejects the assumption that managers are powerless and argues that managers are the principal decision makers who determine the fate of the organisation. The strategic choice framework provides an example of how the voluntarist approach can work. It challenges the view that there is an 'ideal type' of organisation and a 'one best way' of managing. It recognises functional equivalents and the possibility of equifinality whereby organisational outcomes can be achieved in a variety of different ways. One of the key factors that determines the effectiveness of an organisation is the quality of the strategic choices made by members of the dominant coalition. This approach emphasises the role of human agency and asserts that managers can intervene to affect change in ways that will either promote or undermine organisational effectiveness.

Pettigrew and Whipp (1991) report the outcome of a study of firms in four sectors (automobile manufacture, book publishing, merchant banking and life assurance) and conclude that there are observable differences between the ways that higher-performing firms manage change compared to lesser-performing firms. Five factors appear to characterise the way that higher-performing firms, in all sectors, manage change. One of these, environmental assessment, will be considered in some detail in Chapter 4.

From the perspective of change agency the deterministic view offers an over-fatalistic perspective. While, in some situations, there may be external forces that exercise a very powerful effect on organisational performance, there will almost always be scope for managers to intervene in ways that will promote the organisation's interests. Burnes (2004) argues that, despite the constraints they face, managers have a far wider scope for shaping decisions than most organisation theories acknowledge. He asserts that 'the scope for choice and the development of political influence is likely to be more pronounced where change, particularly major change, is on the managerial agenda' (2004: 198).

Problems can arise, however, when managers and others do not believe in their own ability to act as agents of change. As a consequence they may fail to behave proactively. Their response, and therefore the response of the organisation, may be to react passively in response to external forces for change.

Voluntarism and change agency

Two assumptions underpinning the approach to managing change adopted in this book are that (a) managers can make a difference and (b) they can be trained to manage change more effectively. Effective change managers require (and can be helped to acquire)

- conceptual models and action tools/interventions
- change management skills
- confidence in their own ability to make a difference.

Conceptual models

Change managers require a range of concepts and theories. Essentially, they fall into two categories: process models of change which are concerned with the *how* of change management, and diagnostic models of change that focus on identifying *what* it is that needs to be changed.

Change managers need concepts and theories that will help them:

- identify the *kind of change* that confronts them (for example, incremental or discontinuous)
- understand the *process* of changing
- help them identify *what needs to be attended to* (through a process of diagnosis and goal setting) if they are to achieve desired outcomes.

Types of change were discussed in Chapter 1 and process models are considered in Chapter 5. Diagnosis involves the application of the many theories that exist about the behaviour of individuals and groups in organisations, about organisational processes such as power and influence, leadership, communication, decision making and conflict, and about the structure and culture of organisations. These individual, group and organisational performance models can be used to help managers identify *what needs to be changed* in order to protect or improve organisational effectiveness. Organisational-level diagnostic models are considered in Chapter 7.

Action tools/interventions

In addition to the conceptual tools that can help change managers understand the change process and diagnose what needs to be changed, they also need to be familiar with a range of different *types of intervention* that they can use to secure a desired change. These will be considered in Chapters 17–22.

Change managers also need to have some basis for *deciding which interventions to use* in specific circumstances, taking account of contingencies such as the pace of change, the power of stakeholders to resist, etc. Models that can be used for this purpose are considered in Chapter 22.

Change agency skills

While conceptual understanding is necessary, it is not sufficient to guarantee that change agents will be able to secure the desired changes. When managers are acting as change agents they need to be able to communicate, offer leadership, work with teams, confront, negotiate, motivate and manage relationships with others effectively. Change agency requires these and many other skills that managers use in everyday life. Sometimes change agents are less effective than they might be because they fail to recognise the importance of some of these skills, or fail to apply them when required. Some of these skills are discussed later (Chapter 10 on leadership, Chapter 11 on communicating, Chapter 13 on motivating others to change and Chapter 14 on helping others to manage their personal transitions). A more detailed discussion of some of the interpersonal skills associated with helping others to change can be found in Chapters 24 and 25.

Beliefs about change agency

Some managers may have the conceptual knowledge and necessary skills to equip them to intervene and make a difference, but they may fail to act because they have insufficient faith in their own ability to affect outcomes.

Often ineffective change managers are ineffective because they fail to act in ways that enable them to exercise the control necessary to achieve desired outcomes. Rollo May (1969) argues that in many walks of life people are hypnotised by their own feelings of powerlessness and use this as an excuse for doing nothing. He describes the central core of modern man's neuroses as the undermining of his experience of himself as responsible, and the sapping of his will and ability to make decisions. According to May:

> the lack of will is much more than merely an ethical problem: the modern individual so often has the conviction that even if he did exert his 'will' – or whatever illusion passes for it – his actions wouldn't do any good anyway.

This inner feeling of impotence is a critical problem for some managers, and can undermine their ability to act as agents of change.

Two psychologists (Rotter and Phares), after observing that some of their clients seemed to attribute outcomes to luck rather than to factors over which they had some control, embarked on a programme of research which led them to develop the concept of the *locus of control* (Rotter, 1971). The locus of control reflects the degree to which people believe that their own behaviour determines what happens to them. Those who attribute outcomes to their own efforts are referred to as 'internals' and those who attribute outcomes to external factors such as luck, fate, other people, the state of the economy or other factors over which they have no control, are referred to as 'externals'. In the context of change management, those who are over-committed to a deterministic view of change may be inclined to believe that the locus of control is external to themselves and to the organisation and, therefore, may develop the view that there is little that they can do to influence events. Those who think this way are less likely to attempt to adopt a proactive approach to the management of change than those who have a more internal view about the locus of control.

Locus of control is related to Seligman's (1975) theory of *learned helplessness*. This theory argues that a person's expectation about his or her ability to control outcomes is learned. It suggests that managers may begin to question their ability to manage change if, when confronted with a new problem or opportunity, old and well-tried ways of managing fail to deliver desired outcomes. Furthermore, if their early attempts to experiment with alternative ways of managing are equally unsuccessful this questioning of their own ability may develop into an expectation that they are helpless and the associated belief that there is little that they can do to secure desired outcomes. Seligman argues that this expectation will produce motivational and cognitive deficits:

- Motivational deficits involve a *failure to take any voluntary actions designed to control events* following a previous experience with uncontrollable events. If managers believe that they cannot exercise any control over outcomes, they will not be motivated to even try.
- Cognitive deficits involve a *failure to learn* that it is possible to control what happens. If managers believe that they cannot affect outcomes in a particular set of changing circumstances, this belief may stop them recognising opportunities to exercise control, even if there is evidence that their own behaviour has actually had an important impact on outcomes.

The theory suggests that the incentive for managers and others to initiate activity directed towards managing change will depend upon the (learned) expectation that their action can produce some improvement in the problematic situation. If they do not have any confidence in their own ability to manage the change and achieve any improvements, they will not try to exercise influence.

Both individuals and organisations can develop the expectation that there is little they can do to secure desirable outcomes when confronted by change. However, individuals and organisations can also learn that they can affect their own destiny, and can learn how to exercise this influence.

The role of learning in change management will be considered in more detail in Chapter 4.

Beliefs about change agency in your organisation

Do people in your organisation behave as though they believe that they can make an important difference to the way the organisation will develop in the future? What are the consequences for successful change management?

Notes

Summary

This chapter has defined change management as the process of modifying or transforming organisations in order to maintain or improve their effectiveness.

The first section of the chapter considered the attributes of organisational effectiveness and the factors that need to be taken into account when assessing the effectiveness of an organisation or unit within an organisation.

The second section of the chapter considered the ability of the manager (and other agents of change) to affect the way an organisation responds to change. After briefly reviewing the deterministic and voluntaristic schools of thought, it was argued that managers can intervene and make an important difference.

The final section focused attention on the attributes of effective change managers. It was noted that they need to be familiar with relevant conceptual and action tools, possess a range of change agency skills and believe in their own ability to affect the change process.

References

Beer, M. (1980) *Organisational Change and Development: A Systems View*, Santa Monica, CA: Goodyear.

Burnes, B. (2004) *Managing Change: A Strategic Approach to Organisational Dynamics*, Harlow: Pearson.

Carnall, C.A. (2003) *Managing Chang in Organisations*, 3rd edn, Harlow: Prentice Hall.

Goodman, P.S. and Pennings, J.M. (1980) 'Critical Issues in Assessing Organizational Effectiveness', in E. Lawler, D. Nadler and C. Cammann, *Organizational Assessment*, New York: Wiley, pp. 185–215.

Greenwood, R. and Hinings, C.R. (1996) 'Understanding Radical Organizational Change: Bringing Together the Old and the New Institutionalism', *Academy of Management Review*, 21, 1022–54.

Jawahare, M. and McLaughlin, G.L. (2001) 'Toward a Descriptive Stakeholder Theory: An Organizational Life Cycle Approach', *Academy of Management Review*, 26 (3), pp. 397–414.

Kaplan, R.S. and Norton, D.P. (2004) *Strategy Maps: Converting Intangible Assets into Tangible Outcomes*, Boston, MA: Harvard Business School Press.

Marguilies, N. and Raia, A.P. (1972) *Organisational Development: Values, Process and Technology*, New York: McGraw Hill.

May, R. (1969) *Love and Will*, New York: W.W. Norton.

Mellahi, K. and Wilkinson, A. (2004) 'Organisational Failure: A Critique of Recent Research and a Proposed Integrative Framework', *International Journal of Management Reviews*, 5–6 (1), pp. 21–41.

Pettigrew, A. and Whipp, R. (1991) *Managing for Competitive Success*, Oxford: Blackwell.

Porras, J. and Robertson, P.J. (1992) 'Organizational Development Theory, Practice and Research', in M.D. Dunette and L. M. Hough (eds), *Handbook of Organizational Psychology*, 2nd edn, Palo Alto, CA: Consulting Psychologists Press, pp. 718–822.

Rotter, J.R. (1971) 'External Control and Internal Control', *Psychology Today*, June, 37.

Seligman, M.E.P. (1975) *Learned Helplessness*, San Francisco: W.H. Freeman.

Wilson, D. (1992) *A Strategy for Change*, London: Routledge.

3

Systems models and alignment

This chapter considers the attributes of holistic models of organisational functioning, summarises the main features of open systems models of organisations and discusses the utility of the concept of alignment or 'fit'.

It was noted in Chapter 2 that there are many theories and models (of motivation, decision making, group functioning, organisation structure, etc.) that change agents can use to help them understand the functioning of the various components of an organisation. It was also noted that they can use this understanding to help them identify what needs to be changed. Nadler and Tushman (1980) acknowledge the utility of such 'component models' but caution against combining, in some additive manner, the specific assessments they provide in order to produce an overview of organisational functioning and effectiveness. They argue that there is a need for frameworks and models that provide an understanding of the way in which the *total system* of organisational behaviour functions, and they advocate a more holistic approach.

Open-systems theory

Open-systems theory provides such a framework, and views organisations as a system of inter-related components that transact with a larger environment. From the perspective of open systems, some of the main characteristics of organisations are that they are:

1 *Embedded within a larger system*   Organisations are dependent on the larger system (environment) for the resources, information and feedback that they require in order to survive.

2 *Able to avoid entropy*   Through the exchange of matter, energy and information with the larger environment organisations can forestall entropy, the predisposition to decay. They can even increase their vitality over time. People are partially closed systems in that while they can import food, water and air to breathe, there are parts of their body that cannot be renewed or replaced. Groups and organisations, on the other hand, have the potential for indefinite life. In their simplest form, as illustrated by

Figure 3.1   The organisation as an open system

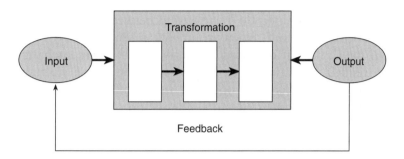

Figure 3.1, organisations can be portrayed as open systems in a dynamic relationship with their environment, receiving various inputs that they transform in some way and export as outputs. In order to survive, organisations need to maintain favourable input–output transactions with the environment.

3 *Regulated by feedback*   Systems rely on information about their outputs to regulate their inputs and transformation processes. Feedback loops also exit between the various internal components of the system. Consequently changes in any one component can affect changes in other components.

4 *Subject to equifinality*   The same outcomes can be produced by configuring the system in different ways.

5 *Cyclical in their mode of functioning*   Events are patterned and tend to occur in repetitive cycles of input, throughput and output. For example, the revenue generated from selling outputs is used to fund inputs (purchase more raw materials, pay bank charges, wages, etc.) that are used to produce more outputs.

6 *Equilibrium seeking*   Open systems tend to gravitate to a state where all the component parts of the system are in equilibrium and where a steady state exists. Whenever changes occur that upset this balance, different components of the system move to restore the balance. (Note the links with Lewin's field-theory, discussed in Chapter 5.)

7 *Bounded*   Open systems are defined by boundaries. External boundaries differentiate the organisation from the larger environment and regulate the flow of information, energy and matter between the system and its environment. Internal boundaries differentiate the various components of the system from each other and regulate the inputs and outputs of sub-systems.

The notion that organisations are systems of inter-related elements embedded in, and strongly influenced by, a larger system is not new. Burns and Stalker (1961) and Lawrence and Lorsch (1967) produced interesting research findings that suggested a link between the internal characteristics of an organisation and the external environment.

Contingency theories

Burns and Stalker examined the relationship between the internal structure of twenty British firms and the environments in which they operated. They found that the firms that operated in relatively stable and unchanging environments tended to have more highly structured and formal internal arrangements than firms that operated in unstable environments. They described firms that operated in stable environments as 'mechanistic' because they were characterised by many rules and procedures and were dominated by hierarchy of authority. The firms that operated in less stable environments were described as 'organic' because they tended to have a free-flowing, decentralised and adaptive internal organisation. Table 3.1 summarises the main features of mechanistic and organic organisations.

The contingency approach advanced by Burns and Stalker received further support from a later study undertaken by Lawrence and Lorsch. They examined three departments (manufacturing, research and sales) in ten US companies and found that departmental structures varied with environmental uncertainty. The results of their research indicated that production departments tended to have the highest degree of structure, followed by marketing and then research. Their results also indicated that the more complex and uncertain the external environment the greater the internal differentiation between departments. This happened as departments developed their own attitudes, goals, work orientation and internal structures and processes to accommodate the requirements of their specialised sub-environments. Lawrence and Lorsch's findings also suggested that this internal differentiation tended to lead to problems of internal coordination between departments and, consequently, to a greater need for internal integrating mechanisms.

There are some who question the utility of contingency theory and argue that it fails to provide a convincing explanation for the way in which organisations operate (see Burnes, 2004: 79–80). Congruency theorists, however, interpret the results of these and other studies as offering support for a broader proposition that the alignment or 'fit' between an organisation and the environment, and also between the various internal elements of the organisation, is a critical determinant of organisation effectiveness.

Table 3.1   Mechanistic and organic organisation forms

Mechanistic	Organic
1 Specialised tasks, narrow in scope.	1 Common tasks and interdependencies
2 Tasks rigidly defined	2 Tasks adjusted and redefined as required
3 Strict hierarchy of authority	3 Less adherence to formal authority and rules
4 Centralised knowledge and control	4 Decentralised knowledge and control
5 Hierarchical communication	5 Network communication, diffused channels

Alignment as a determinant of organisation effectiveness

Open systems theory predicts that changes to any one of the internal or external elements of an organisation's system will cause changes to other elements. This implies that in order to understand the performance of an organisation one must view it as a system of *interconnected choices* (Siggelkow, 2001).

Kotter (1980) elaborated this proposition when he developed his integrative model of organisational dynamics. His model comprises seven major elements. Figure 3.2 shows these as a set of five key organisational processes plus six structural elements.

Figure 3.2   Kotter's integrative model of organisational dynamics

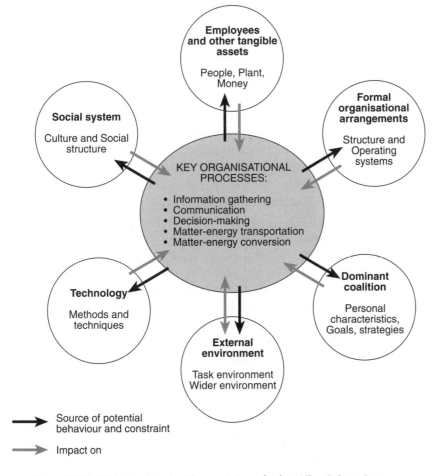

Source: Kotter (1980: 282). Reprinted with permission of John Wiley & Sons, Inc.

The key organisational processes are classified under two main headings, informational processes such as information gathering, communication and decision making, and processes that are concerned with the conversion or transportation of matter/energy. Specific processes can be labelled according to their purpose and might include the market research process, the product development process, the manufacturing process or the leadership process.

The six structural elements in Kotter's model are:

- *external environment*, including the immediate task-related environment and the wider environment (which includes public attitudes, the political system, etc.)
- *employees and other tangible* assets, such as buildings, plant, inventories and cash
- *formal organisational arrangements* – structure, job design and operating systems
- *social system* including the organisation's culture and social structure
- *technology* (or technologies) associated with the organisation's core products
- dominant coalition – the objectives and strategies of those who control policy making.

In the *short run*, organisation effectiveness can be defined in terms of the nature of the cause–effect relationships that link all the elements of the system together. For example, if demand for a major product produced by organisations operating in a particular industrial sector begins to slump, the dominant coalition in some organisations will recognise this and take corrective action much faster than the dominant coalition in other organisations. An organisation's response will be influenced by the effectiveness of its information gathering and decision making processes and by how quickly these processes can affect other elements in the organisation to adjust matter/energy conversion and transportation processes in ways that will maintain their efficiency. Adjustments might involve cutting production, finding new customers or reducing prices in order to minimise any build up of stocks of finished goods. Any delays in reacting to changes will result in a wasteful use of resources. In the short run, therefore, effective organisations are those that have key processes that are characterised by levels of decision making effectiveness and matter–energy efficiency that help to ensure that resources are used effectively.

Kotter argues that over the *medium term* (which he defines as a few months to a few years) the effective organisation is one that is capable of maintaining its short-run effectiveness. He suggests that organisations do this by maintaining the key process elements in an efficient and effective state because it is this that enables them to ensure that the other (six) structural elements are aligned to each other. Sustained mis-alignment (sometimes referred to as 'poor fit') leads to levels of waste that will eventually threaten the survival of the organisation. He suggests that what constitutes a mis-aligned relationship between any two or more structural elements is often 'intuitively obvious'. He cites several examples to illustrate the point:

- If the goals and strategies championed by the organisation's dominant coalition are based on inaccurate assumptions about the task environment, the dominant coalition and the task environment are obviously mis-aligned
- If the size of the work force or the organisation's other tangible assets are not sufficient to take advantage of the economies of scale inherent in the organisation's technologies, the two elements are obviously mis-aligned
- If the level of specialisation called for in the formal organisational arrangements are inconsistent with the skills of the work force, then again the two elements are mis-aligned.

The most common sources of non-alignment are changes in the external environment and growth. Kotter argues that organisational systems correct mis-alignments by taking the path of least resistance; they move towards the solution that requires the minimum use of energy. This usually involves realigning around the element or elements of the organisation that are most difficult and expensive to change (or emerge as the driving force over the longer term, see below). However, if the organisation can afford the waste associated with mis-alignment, minor examples of poor fit could go uncorrected for a considerable period of time. This argument suggests that, over the medium term, the focus of change management needs to be ensuring that the elements of the organisation are appropriately aligned.

Over the *longer term* (six–sixty years) Kotter predicts that it is the adaptability of the six structural elements that will be the underlying determinant of effectiveness. He notes that over time one or more of the structural elements (for example, the external environment, technology, the employees, or the dominant coalition) typically begins to exert more influence on the key organisational processes than the other elements. This element (or elements) emerges as the driving force that shapes the development of the company. Kotter argues that because of the nature of the interdependence among all of the elements (and the equilibrium seeking disposition of systems), if one or two elements emerge as the driving force the natural tendency is for the others to follow. They adapt to the driving force in order to maintain alignment. However, this process may not always be as rapid or smooth as required to maintain a sufficient level of alignment, with inevitable consequences for effectiveness. Sustained mis-alignment will threaten the survival of the company.

Building on the proposition that the organisation's ability to adapt to change over the long term is a function of the state of its structural elements, Kotter provides examples of structural states that do, and do not, facilitate system adaptation. These are presented in Table 3.2.

Table 3.2   Examples of element states that do and do not facilitate system adaptation

	States that are highly constraining and *hard to align* with, thus inhibiting adaptation	States that are not highly constraining and are easy to *align* with
Technology	Organisation possesses a single complex technology that is rapidly becoming outdated and that requires large amounts of capital for equipment	Organisation possesses the most advanced technologies for its products, services, and administrative systems along with a number of alternative technologies it might need in the future
Social system	Key norms are not supportive of organisational flexibility; little trust found in relationships; total power in the system is low; morale is low; little sense of shared purpose	Key norms are supportive of organisational flexibility; high trust found in relationships; total power in the system is high; morale is high; high degree of shared purpose
Employee and other tangible assets	Plant and equipment is run down; employees, especially middle managers, are unskilled; organisation has some highly specialised human skills and equipment it doesn't need anymore	Plant and equipment in top notch shape; employees, especially middle managers, are highly skilled; organisation possesses equipment and people with skills it doesn't need now but may need in the future
Organisational arrangements	Formal systems are not very sophisticated but are applied in great detail, uniformly across the organisation	Different kinds of formal system exist for structuring, measuring, rewarding, selecting and developing different types of people working on different tasks; formal systems also exist to monitor change in the organisation and its environment and to change the formal systems accordingly
Dominant coalition	A small, homogeneous, reasonably untalented group with no effective leadership; all about the same age	A large, reasonably heterogeneous yet cohesive group of very talented people who work together well and have plenty of effective leadership; members are of different ages.
External environment	The organisation is very dependent on a large number of externalities, with little or no countervailing power	The organisation has only a limited number of strong dependencies, with a moderate amount of countervailing power over all dependencies
	Demand for products and services are shrinking; supplies are hard to get; regulators behave with hostility and inconsistency	Demand for products and services is growing; supplies are plentiful; regulators behave consistently and fairly
	Public angry at the firm; economy in bad shape; political system isn't functioning well; overall, the environment is hostile	Public likes the organisation; economy is in good shape; political system is functioning well; overall, the environment is benevolent

Source: Adapted from Kotter (1980: 292–3). Reprinted with permission of John Wiley & Sons, Inc.

Adaptability is important because it is this that determines whether or not the organisation will be able to maintain the required degree of alignment over the long term. Over the longer term, therefore, the focus of change management needs to be ensuring that the structural elements of the organisation are as adaptable as possible.

A congruence model of organisations

An alternative open systems model, proposed by Nadler and Tushman (1982), also highlights the effect of the congruency of the component parts of the organisation on organisation effectiveness. In addition, it elaborates the relationship between the organisation and its wider environment and focuses more explicit attention on the role of strategy.

The model identifies four classes of input:

1 *Environment*   This includes any larger 'suprasysem' (such as a large corporation) that the focal organisation is a part of, markets, financial institutions, supplies, etc., and the wider environment that include the culture(s) within which the organisation operates. It is this environment that provides the opportunities and constraints that the organisation has to contend with.
2 *Resources*, such as liquid capital, physical plant, raw materials, technologies and labour.
3 *History*   This is important because past strategic decisions and the development of core values and patterns of leadership can affect current patterns of organisational behaviour.
4 *Strategy*   This involves determining how the organisation's resources can be used to the best advantage in relation to the opportunities, constraints and demands of the environment. Effective organisations are those that are able to align themselves with the external environment and, as required, reposition themselves to take advantage of any environmental changes such as shifts in markets, technologies, etc. Nadler and Tushman argue that strategy (and associated goals and plans) defines the task (purpose) of the organisation and is the most important input to the organisation's behavioural system. They suggest that effectiveness can be assessed in terms of how well the organisation's performance meets the goals of strategy.

Nadler and Tushman define the major components of the transformation process as:

1 *Task,* which can be viewed in terms of complexity, predictability, interdependence and skill demands.
2 *Individuals* who are members of the organisation and their response capabilities, intelligence, skills and abilities, experience, training, needs, attitudes, expectations, etc.

3 *Formal organisational arrangements* that include all the mechanisms used by the organisation to direct, structure or control behaviour.
4 *Informal organisation*, including informal group structures, the quality of inter-group relations, political processes, etc.

Like Kotter, Nadler and Tushman argue that any useful model of organisations must go beyond merely providing a simple description of the components of the organisation and consider the dynamic relationships that exist between the various components. They define 'congruence' as the degree to which the needs, demands, goals, objectives and/or structures of any one component of the organisation are consistent with the needs, demands, goals, objectives and/or structures of any other component. Their general hypothesis is that, other things equal, the greater the total degree of congruence between the various components the more effective will be the organisation's behaviour. Figure 3.3 summarises the congruence model and the bold double-headed arrows indicate the six 'fits' between the components of the transformation process (the internal organisation).

These are:

1 *Individual – formal organisation*   For example, to what extent are individual needs met by the formal organisational arrangements?
2 *Individual – task*   For example, to what extent do individuals have the skills necessary to meet task demands and to what extent do the tasks satisfy individual needs?

Figure 3.3   Congruence model

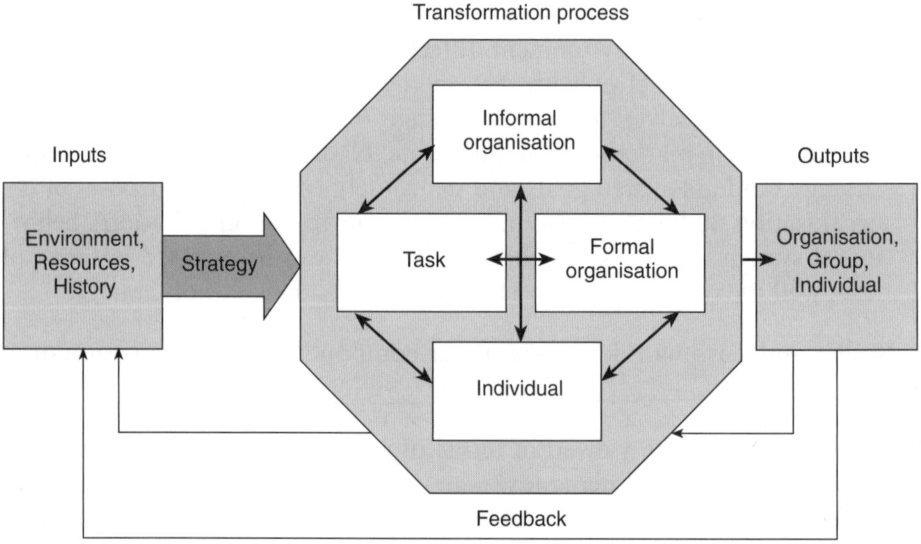

Source: Nadler and Tushman (1980: 274). Reprinted with permission of John Wiley & Sons, Inc.

3 *Individual – informal organisation* For example, to what extent does the informal organisation satisfy the needs of individuals or make best use of their talents?

4 *Task – formal organisation* For example, to what extent are the formal organisational arrangements adequate to meet the demands of the task?

5 *Task – informal organisation* For example, to what extent does the informal organisation facilitate task performance?

6 *Formal – informal organisation* For example, to what extent are the goals, rewards and structures of the informal organisation consistent with those of the formal organisation?

Many of the components that Nadler and Tushman choose to focus on are different to those that figure in Kotter's model. All models are simplifications of the real world, and the utility of any particular model, in the context of change management, needs to be judged in terms of whether or not it provides a helpful conceptual framework for managing the change process. The four components of the transformation process in Nadler and Tushman's congruence model are derived from Leavitt (1965). The basic hypothesis underpinning congruence would still be valid if these four components were replaced with the five sub-systems (production, supportive, maintenance, adaptive and managerial) identified by Katz and Kahn (1966). It is the congruence or alignment between the organisation and the environment and between the internal components of the organisation that is the key concept that can aid organisational diagnosis and the development of change strategies.

Internal and external alignment promotes organisational effectiveness because the various elements of the system reinforce rather than disrupt each other, thereby minimising the loss of system energy and resources (Schneider *et al.*, 2003). However, a state of perfect alignment is rarely achieved. Miles and Snow (1984) suggest that rather than viewing alignment as a state it might be better to think of it as a process – a dynamic search that seeks to align the organisation with its environment and the various internal elements of the organisation with each other. Higgins (2005) observes that one reason why alignment is becoming a greater challenge for many organisations is that, in a fast-moving business environment, organisations are forced to revise their strategies more frequently than in the past. As noted in Chapter 1, organisations that recognise or anticipate shifts in their external environment may be better placed to initiate actions to manage this process of alignment than those that are slow to recognise the need for change. But even where a need to improve alignment is recognised, forces for inertia within the organisation can make this difficult to achieve. This is especially the case in what Greenwood and Hinings (1996) and Levinthal (1997) refer to as 'tightly coupled systems', because the tighter the fit the more difficult it is to modify individual elements of the system through a process of incremental change.

The utility of the concept of alignment

The concept of alignment has been criticised on the grounds that it is difficult to apply in practice. Wilson (1992) refers to difficulties relating to problems of definition. Some view the organisation and the environment as 'objective' fact, readily open to description and definition, whereas others view them as 'subjective' fact. Problems can arise because managers, and others, perceive them from their own subjective point of view. This makes it difficult to establish any shared understanding of the current or desired level of alignment. Even when people can agree, there is no guarantee that this shared perception will be a reliable indicator of the conditions that will lead to organisation effectiveness.

Another criticism is that alignment might be a more valid concept when the focus is the management of incremental change. When faced with discontinuous change alignment might be a less helpful concept because the need is to break with the past and introduce radical innovation before seeking to re-establish a new state of alignment around a new task and/or new structural elements.

These criticisms may have some validity, but an understanding of systems models, alignment and the concept of 'fit' can make an important contribution to effective change management.

Summary

This chapter has considered the attributes of holistic (as opposed to component) models of organisation functioning.

It was noted that while component theories are useful for diagnosing specific problems, combining their assessments of different aspects of organisation functioning mayt not provide an adequate view of organisation effectiveness. Open systems models of organisations were seen to provide a useful over-arching conceptual framework for assessing organisational functioning and effectiveness.

This chapter summarises the main features of open systems models of organisations and:

- draws on contingency theory to illustrate the embeddedness of organisations within a larger system and the importance of alignment
- elaborates Kotter's integrative model of organisational dynamics and considers the relative importance of alignment and adaptability as determinants of organisation effectiveness over the medium and long term
- reviews Nadler and Tushman's congruency model of organisations and highlights the importance of strategy in achieving and maintaining alignment.

It concludes with a discussion of the utility of the concept of alignment.

Exercise 3.1   Checking alignment between steps in the transformation process

This exercise draws together some of the issues considered in this chapter and Chapter 2.

Think of your department or unit in terms of a process that transforms inputs into outputs.

Step 1   Identify the major inputs and outputs and make a note of them in the space provided below.

Depending on the time available, focus on one or more inputs *and* one or more outputs.

Step 2   Select one *input* and identify the department, unit or external supplier that provides it.

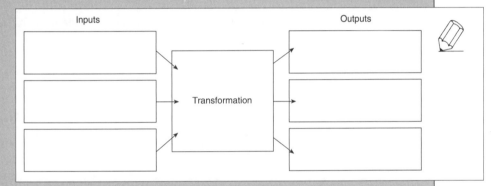

Step 3   Assess how effective you think this supplier is:

- List the indicators that *you* use to assess the effectiveness of the supplier.
- Against each indicator note *your* assessment of how effective the supplier is (use a five-point scale, where 1 = very ineffective and 5 = very effective).

Step 4   Think about how members of the supplying department or unit rate their own effectiveness:

- List the indicators that you think *they* use to assess their own effectiveness.
- Against each indicator note how you think *they* rate their own effectiveness.

Indicators *I* use to assess the effectiveness of the supplier	My assessment	Indicators *they* use to assess their effectiveness	Their assessment

Step 5   Compare the two lists. Do they suggest any actual or potential problems that could undermine organisational effectiveness? If so, specify below.

Now repeat steps 2–5 for one of your *outputs*.

Step 6   Select one *output* and identify the department, unit or external customer that receives it.

Step 7   Assess how effective you think your department or unit is:

- List the indicators that *you* use to assess the effectiveness of *your* department (with respect to the supply of the focal output).
- Against each indicator note *your* assessment of how effective you think your unit is (use a five-point scale where 1 = very ineffective and 5 = very effective).

Step 8   Think about how members of the receiving unit or department rate the effectiveness of *your* department.

- List the indicators that you think *they* use to assess your department's effectiveness.
- Against each indicator note how you think *they* rate the effectiveness of your department.

Indicators *I* use to assess the effectiveness of my unit	My assessment	Indicators customers use to assess the effectiveness of *my* unit	Their assessment

Step 9   Compare the two lists. Do they suggest any actual or potential problems that could undermine organisational effectiveness? If so specify below.

Potential problems with alignment between steps in the transformation process

References

Burnes, B. (2004) *Managing Change: A Strategic Approach to Organisational Dynamics*, Harlow: Pearson.

Burns, T. and Stalker, G.M. (1961) *The Management of Innovation*, London: Tavistock.

Greenwood, R. and Hinings, C.R. (1996) 'Understanding Radical Organizational Change: Bringing Together the Old and the New Institutionalism', *Academy of Management Review*, 21, pp. 1022–54.

Higgins, J.M. (2005) 'The Eight "S's" of Successful Strategy Execution', *Journal of Change Management*, 5 (1), pp. 3–13.

Katz, D. and Kahn, R.L. (1966) *The Social Psychology of Organisations*, New York: Wiley.

Kotter, J.P. (1980) 'An Integrative Model of Organisational Dynamics', in E.E. Lawler, D.A. Nadler and C. Cammann, *Organizational Assessment*, New York: Wiley, pp. 279–299.

Lawrence, P.R. and Lorsch, J.W. (1967) *Organization and Environment*, Boston: MA: Harvard Business School.

Leavitt, H.J. (1965) 'Applied Organizational Change in Industry', in J.G. March (ed.), *Handbook of Organizations*, Chicago: Rand-McNally.

Levinthal, D. (1997) 'Adaptation on Rugged Landscapes', *Management Science*, 43, pp. 934–50.

Miles, R.E. and Snow, C.C. (1984) 'Designing Strategic Human Resource Systems', *Organizational Dynamics*, 13, pp. 36–52.

Nadler, D.A. and Tushman, M.L. (1980) 'A Congruence Model for Organisational Assessment', in E.E. Lawler, D.A. Nadler and C. Cammann, *Organizational Assessment*, New York: Wiley.

Nadler, D.A. and Tushman, M.L. (1982) 'A Model for Diagnosing Organisational Behavior: Applying a Congruence Perspective', in D.A. Nadler, M.L.Tushman and N.G. Hatvany, *Managing Organisations*, Boston: Little, Brown.

Schneider, B., Hayes, S.C., Lim, B., Raver, J.A., Godfey, E.G., Huang, M., Nishii, L.H. and Ziegert, J.C. (2003) 'The Human Side of Strategy: Employee Experiences of Strategic Alignment in a Service Organisation', *Organizational Dynamics*, 32 (2), pp. 122–141.

Siggelkow, N. (2001) 'Change in the Presence of Fit: The Rise, the Fall, and the Renaissance of Liz Claiborne', *Academy of Management Journal*, 44 (4), pp. 838–57.

Wilson, D. (1992) *A Strategy for Change*, London: Routledge.

Organisational learning and organisational effectiveness

Organisations strive to avoid entropy. The ultimate criterion of effectiveness is survival and the dominant coalition/senior managers seek to achieve this by aligning the organisation with the environment. They do this in order to minimise waste and promote competitiveness.

It was noted in Chapter 3 that Nadler and Tushman (1982) highlight the importance of strategy as a vehicle for managing the organisation's alignment with its environment and that Kotter (1980) points to the importance of adaptability as a determinant of long-term effectiveness. The quality of individual and organisational learning has also been identified as another important determinant of organisation effectiveness (Lank and Lank, 1995) and De Geus (1988) argues that the ability to learn faster than competitors may be the only sustainable competitive advantage. Miles (1982), argues that organisations have leeway and choice in how they adjust to a changing environment, and that it is this choice that offers the opportunity for learning.

This chapter will provide a brief overview of strategic change management before moving on to review the role of individual and organisational learning in the quest for organisation effectiveness.

The nature of strategy and strategic change management

Strategy, according to Nadler and Tushman, is a set of key decisions about matching the organisation's resources with the opportunities, constraints and demands in the environment. Strategic change management is concerned with the formulation and implementation of strategy.

There are different views about how strategy is formulated. One view (the planning approach) is that strategy formulation *is an intentional and rational process*, whereas a competing view (the emergent approach) is that it is the *outcome* of a complex cultural and political process.

The planning approach

Those who subscribe to the first school of thought emphasise the logical nature of a process that involves analysis, forecasting and planning. Industrial economists and business planners have developed a range of models and tools that strategic planners can use to determine how the organisation should be developed in order to ensure that it remains aligned with its environment, or stretched to take advantage of perceived opportunities

Quinn (1993) observes that the strategies produced by managers who rely on a rational approach to planning often fail to be implemented successfully. He suggests that in organisations that have developed expensive and elaborate rational planning systems it is not uncommon for senior managers to behave as though they regard strategy formulation and strategy implementation as separate and sequential processes. Problems can arise when strategies are well developed before implementation starts. This is because those who have developed the strategies may not always have the power to execute them. Higgins (2005) argues that successful organisations are those that realise that executing is at least as important as formulating strategy.

Logical incrementalism

Quinn contrasts the rational planning approach with logical incrementalism. This approach falls somewhere between the planning and emergent approaches. It acknowledges that in complex environments it is difficult for any one group to be aware of all the factors that can impact on the organisation's success, and that different stakeholders will have different priorities that need to be recognised. Quinn argues that organisations require strategies that will work in practice, even if this involves some sort of political compromise. He also argues that successful senior managers tend to be those who have a view of where they want the organisation to be, but deliberately decide to act incrementally when leading the organisation. They take small steps and build on the experience gained. This incremental approach is more effective, according to Quinn, because it improves the quality of the information used in key decisions; helps overcome the personal and political pressures resisting change; copes with the variety of lead-times and sequencing problems associated with change; and builds the overall awareness, understanding and commitment required to ensure implementation. Based on his observations of senior managers in Xerox, GM and IBM, Quinn concludes that often, in practice, by the time strategies begin to crystallise, elements of them have already been implemented. He reports that through the incremental processes that successful senior managers consciously use to formulate their strategies, they are able to build sufficient organisational momentum and identity with the strategies 'to make them flow towards flexible and successful implementation'.

The emergent approach

The view of those who subscribe to the emergent approach is that the key decisions about matching the organisation's resources with the opportunities, constraints and demands in the environment evolve over time and are the outcome of cultural and political processes in organisations. The nature of the cultural processes will be elaborated below but they manifest themselves in the taken-for-granted assumptions and routines that influence strategic decisions. These processes are bound up with the bargaining and negotiation that occurs between different stakeholders, such as functional or professional groups, because each have their own world views and taken-for-granted assumptions.

While the models and tools associated with the planning approach can be a useful aid to change management (and some of these, such as SWOT and PEST, will be considered in more detail in Chapter 7) the apparent objectivity of the analyses they provide needs to regarded with some degree of caution. Pettigrew and Whipp (1993) argue that no matter how sophisticated they are, they have to be applied by someone. They note that managers rarely collect 'clean' data about the environment. All data has to be perceived and constructed: this process of perception and construction is influenced by the perceiver's values and norms and by the 'shared beliefs' that characterise the cultures of which they are a part.

Johnson (1993) argues that while individuals and groups within organisations may hold varying sets of beliefs there is likely to exist, at some level, a core set of beliefs and assumptions held relatively in common and taken-for-granted by all managers. He refers to this as the *organisational paradigm* (also referred to by others as the 'shared mental model') and argues that it is this paradigm that influences how managers perceive, interpret and make sense of their environment. He also argues that it is the shared mental model/paradigm that determines whether changes in the environment are perceived as relevant, and if so whether they are perceived to pose threats or offer opportunities. While outsiders may view a change in the environment as a threat to the organisation, members of the organisation, viewing the environment through their shared mental model, may fail to recognise the change or the potential threat it may pose.

Organisational learning and strategy formulation

Exponents of the emergent approach to strategy formulation, such as Pettigrew and Whipp (1993), argue that strategy emerges from the way organisations, at all levels, process information, especially information about the relationship between the organisation and its environment. The quality of this information processing is influenced by the relevance of the shared mental model or taken-for-granted paradigm. If organisations are to develop strategies that will ensure alignment and a strong competitive position the shared mental model needs to be subject to revision.

This is particularly the case if conditions change in ways that could affect the assumptions and beliefs on which the shared mental model is based. If organisations are to formulate effective strategies they need to have the capacity to learn from their experience and to use this learning to modify the shared mental model that guides the way they manage strategic change.

Organisational learning

Organisational learning involves enhancing the collective ability to act more effectively. The quality of collective/organisational learning is important because it affects both strategy formulation and strategy implementation. The collective nature of learning is especially important in complex and turbulent environments, because in such circumstances senior managers may not be the best-placed individuals to identify opportunities and threats. Organisational members, at all levels, who are involved in boundary-spanning activities – such as procurement, technical development or sales – may have data that could provide a valuable input to strategy formulation. Furthermore, the quality of response to any threats or opportunities that are identified may require individuals and groups located in different functions to collaborate and learn from each other in order to design and produce high-quality products or services in ever-shorter time frames.

Shared mental models, rules and behaviour in organisations

Swieringa and Wierdsma (1992) conceptualise organisations as a set of explicit and implicit rules that prescribe the way members behave (see Figure 4.1). These rules are based on insights which represent what is known and

Figure 4.1   Individual and collective learning in organisations

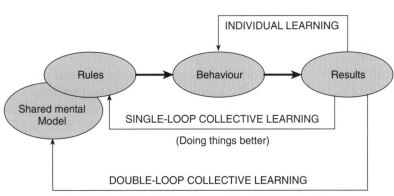

Source: Adapted from Swieringa and Wierdsma (1992).

understood. They relate to everything that happens in the organisation. For example, there are rules about the structure of the organisation that prescribe how activities will be grouped and responsibilities allocated, and there are rules about how resources are procured and used and about how people are managed and rewarded. These rules reflect the mental models (subjective theories, shared meanings or beliefs) through which organisational members examine and make sense of their experience. The shared mental model represents the basic assumptions that underpin the organisation's culture. Schein (1990: 111) defines culture as (a) the pattern of basic assumptions, (b) invented, discovered or developed by a group, (c) as it learns to cope with its problems of external adaptation and internal integration, (d) that have worked well enough in the past to be considered valid and, therefore, (e) are taught to new members as the (f) correct way to perceive, think, and feel in relation to these problems.

Learning to behave in accordance with the rules

So long as the rules lead to behaviours that produce desired results, there will be no need to change the rules. The only requirement will be for individual learning. Organisational members will have to learn to behave in accordance with the rules. For example, if an individual is promoted into a position that involves being responsible for a budget, he or she will not only have to develop an understanding of the rules relating to the management of budgets, but will also have to acquire the knowledge and skills necessary to behave in accordance with these rules.

This kind of learning, however, may not always be sufficient to guarantee organisational success. In today's turbulent and complex environment old ways of behaving may fail to produce the required results and the organisation may be faced with the need to change, to modify the rules and encourage new behaviours in order to ensure its continued competitiveness and survival.

Collective learning and the modification of rules

Organisational (collective) learning occurs when a group recognises something that offers a more effective way of functioning. It has already been noted that organisations will be more effective when their major components (such as structure, technology, systems and people) are congruent with each other and when there is a good 'fit' between the organisation and the environment. Organisational learning involves achieving and maintaining this 'fit', or when confronted by discontinuities in the external environment, finding a new and more productive one. This, in turn, involves organisational members diagnosing the organisation's predicament (including the consequences of their past behaviour), integrating this understanding into their shared mental models and using it as a basis for modifying, as required, the rules that guide decision making and action. This process is similar to that referred to by Daft and Weick (1984) when they describe organisations as 'open social systems' that seek and interpret information about their environment in order to provide a basis for action.

Modifying the rules via single- and double-loop learning

Argyris and Schon (1978) distinguish between two different kinds of organisational (collective) learning:

- *Single-loop learning* entails the detection and correction of errors leading to a modification of the rules within the boundaries of current thinking. It involves organisational members collectively *refining* their mental models about how the world operates in order to do things better. It does not offer any fundamental challenge to current thinking. The effect of single-loop learning is to promote an incremental approach to strategy formulation and change management.
- *Double-loop learning* is a more cognitive process; it occurs when the assumptions and principles that constitute the governing variables or shared mental model are examined and challenged. This kind of learning challenges accepted ways of thinking and can produce a new understanding of situations and events which, in turn, can lead to the development of new rules that require organisational members to change their behaviour and do things differently, or even do different things.

While double-loop learning is often seen as a desirable goal, it can be difficult to attain in practice, a point that will receive further consideration below.

Triggers for double-loop learning

When there is a good 'fit' between the organisation and its environment and when this leads to the achievement of desired levels of performance, there is a high chance that the prevailing shared mental model will be reinforced. The only collective learning in these circumstances will be the single-loop learning associated with the detection and correction of errors. This kind of learning is often associated with continuous improvement.

Double-loop collective learning is most likely to occur when desired performance levels are not achieved and when feedback signals a need to re-examine the relevance of the shared mental model. Leroy and Ramanantsoa (1997) refer to incongruous events that violate conceptual frameworks as triggers for this kind of learning, and Fiol and Lyles (1983) assert that some type of crisis is necessary to trigger higher-level or double-loop learning. Triggers are often associated with discontinuities such as the appointment of a new leader, or dramatically altered market conditions.

Can organisations learn or is it only individuals that learn?

The approach to organisational learning presented here focuses on the development of supra-individual or shared mental models that provide a basis for effective action. These shared mental models furnish organisations with a conceptual framework for perceiving and interpreting new information and for determining how stored information can be related to any given situation. They persist over time, despite changes in organisational membership. This implies that organisations have *collective memories* that are not wholly dependent on the knowledge stored in the minds of current members. It is assumed that knowledge can also be stored in files, procedural manuals, routines, traditions and conventions and that this collective memory enables past experience to be applied to current problems.

Douglas (1986) challenges the view that organisations can learn. She concedes that *institutional thinking* can exist in the minds of individuals and she accepts that much of the learning that goes on in an individual's head is influenced by what other organisational members know and by the kinds of information present in the organisational environment. She refers to this process as the 'squeezing' of each others' ideas into a common shape. However, she does not go along with the view that organisations, as collective entities, can learn.

Daft and Weick (1984) are more comfortable with the concept of collective or organisational learning. They base their view of organisations as interpretation systems on the assumption that they have both cognitive systems and memories. While they recognise that it is individuals who send and receive information and in other ways carry out the interpretation process, they argue that the organisation interpretation process is something more than that which is undertaken by individuals. Individuals come and go, but there is an order and regularity in the way that organisational members continue to respond. The implication is that organisations, as well as individuals, develop mental models.

March (1991) appears to support this view. He presents learning in organisations as a mutual process that leads to a convergence between organisational and individual beliefs. While there may be an external reality that is independent of beliefs about it, both individuals and organisations develop their own mental models and beliefs about reality. The organisation stores the knowledge that it accumulates, over time, from the learning of its members in the form of an organisational code of received truth. This code or mental model (which influences the explicit and implicit rules and procedures that regulate behaviour in the organisation) is modified by the beliefs of individuals, and at the same time individual organisational members are socialised into the beliefs about reality that are associated with the shared mental model or organisational code. Thus, over time, the organisation's mental model affects the beliefs of individuals while it is being affected by those beliefs.

Although March argues that this convergence is generally useful for both the individual and the organisation, he recognises a potential threat to the effectiveness of organisational learning if individuals adjust to the shared mental model or organisational code before the code can learn from them. This threat is most likely to manifest itself and undermine organisational learning when a group develops a strong ideological commitment to the code or shared mental models and dismisses or suppresses deviant thinking as either irrelevant or potentially dangerous. De Holan and Phillips (2004) argue that the failure to unlearn old dominant logics can inhibit collective learning and organisational change.

The revision of shared mental models: the key to collective learning

Shared mental models need to be fluid and open to modification if they are to provide an effective basis for assessing the environment and planning action. Unfortunately, once established, they may be resistant to change. Johnson and Scholes (1999) refer to the *strategic drift* that can occur when the need to modify the paradigm/shared mental model is not recognised and when managers, blinkered by an outdated set of taken-for-granted beliefs and assumptions, fail to detect changes in the organisation's competitive position. It may not be until this strategic drift manifests itself in an unacceptable poor level of performance that the need to modify the paradigm is eventually recognised.

Shared mental models are one of the main sources of inertia identified by Gersick (1991). Unless they are open to revision they can seriously limit an organisation's ability to adapt and change, and can promote an episodic rather than a continuous response to threats and opportunities.

The role of knowledge transfer in organisational learning

Organisational learning involves the acquisition of knowledge, the recognition of its potential and its application to improve organisational performance.

Knowledge may exist within an organisation, but it may not be available to those who can make best use of it. Huber (1991) draws attention to the importance of distributing information. As organisational members gain access to new information they may be better able to create new knowledge by piecing together patterns that had not previously been apparent or they may be able to identify and apply superior practices that are being used elsewhere in the organisation. But information does not always flow freely and consequently valuable learning opportunities are missed. In many organisations innovative work practices that are a great success in one location often remain 'islands of innovation'. Walton (1975) notes that the failure to diffuse innovation often forces organisations to invest in costly duplication of effort in order to reinvent similar practices in other locations. Zell (2001) reports that best practices often linger in isolated locations within companies for years, unrecognised and unshared. Szulanski (1996) also observes that in many organisations there are surprising performance differences between different units, suggesting that knowledge is not being utilised as effectively as it could be. For example, IBM had only limited success transferring reengineering logistics and hardware design processes between business units and General Motors experienced problems trying to transfer manufacturing processes between divisions. These observations prompted Szulanski to study 122 best-practice transfers in eight companies in order to better understand the 'internal stickiness' that impedes the transfer of knowledge. He found that, contrary to conventional wisdom (that attributes internal stickiness to poor motivation), the major barriers to internal knowledge transfer are a lack of capacity to value, assimilate and apply new knowledge; ambiguity regarding the precise reasons for the success or failure in replicating a practice in a new setting; and the quality of relationships.

Intra- and inter-organisational learning

Most of the literature on organisational learning focuses on collective learning (including knowledge transfer) within a single organisation. There is, however, a growing awareness of the importance of inter-organisational learning.

Knowledge transfer between unrelated organisations

Leseure *et al.* (2004) examine the use of superior knowledge and adoption of best or 'promising' practices from unrelated or competing organisations. They prefer to use the term 'promising' rather than 'best' practice because while a collection of ideas, values, procedures, techniques and tools may work well in some organisations, they may not be 'best practice' in all. Imported practices may not be aligned with the organisation's culture, structure and other practices and, if they are to work at all, may need to be customised before they can offer any benefit. They refer to Total Quality Management (TQM), JIT practices, Business Process Reengineering (BPR) and High-Performance Management as examples of some of the promising practices organisations may wish to adopt.

    Leseure *et al.* developed a model that posits that both *need pull* (associated with a performance gaps) and *institutional push* (normative pressures applied by customers, suppliers and regulators) can trigger efforts to adopt promising practices. Based on earlier work by Szulanski (1996) and Bessant, Kaplinsky and Lamming (2003) they suggest that the adoption process involves several steps:

1 *Initiation*   The process may start with the discovery of a need for performance improvement that prompts a search for superior knowledge (and promising practices) which address this need. Szulanski (1996) also suggests the possibility that the discovery of superior knowledge may cause organisational members to reframe as unsatisfactory a situation that, hitherto, was regarded as satisfactory.

2 *Set up and adaptation*   Following the decision to proceed, attention is focused on pre-empting implementation problems by exploring the feasibility of adapting the promising practice to suit the identified need. There are indications that this step in the process often receives insufficient attention.

3 *Implementation*   Launching the change programme with attention being given to short-term actions such as training, modifying structures, writing new procedures and the like.

4 *Ramp-up*   This begins when the organisation starts to use the new practices.

5 *Integration*   This involves the embedding of superior knowledge and the routinisation of the new practices.

Knowledge transfer within networks of related organisations

Bessant, Kaplinsky and Lamming (2003) discuss the importance of learning and development across networks of related organisations. These networks can take many forms – for example, strategic alliances, shared product development projects and regional small-firm clusters. Bessant, Kaplinsky and Lamming focus their attention on supply chains and assert that 'The competitive performance of the value stream depends upon the learning and development of the whole system, not just the leading players' (2003: 167). A common pattern in such networks is that learning is championed by a leading firm or by some external institution such as a government department or a trade association. Inter-firm learning is often facilitated by a sense of shared crisis or a shared perception of a common opportunity. Based on a study of six UK supply chains, Bessant, Kaplinsky and Lamming report that learning does not typically cascade throughout the supply chain and that it tends to be confined to lead firms and first-tier suppliers.

Impediments to organisational learning

The essence of collective learning is the *joint construction of meaning*. This occurs through sharing and dialogue. However, this process is rarely problem-free. Several sources of difficulty will be considered.

Poor appreciation of the systemic qualities of organisations and wider systems

Many individuals and groups have a parochial and limited view of their role, and this restricts their ability to contribute to collective learning. Often they focus all their attention on the immediate task and fail to appreciate how this relates to the overall purpose of the organisation or network of related organisations. Egan (1988) discusses the need to promote 'business thinking' that relates to the system's overall mission and the importance of markets, competitors, customers and the products and services that satisfy customers' needs and wants. 'Organisation thinking' is more blinkered and is essentially inward-looking, concerned about the way a firm organises its structures and processes to engage in its business. This type of thinking is important but, sometimes, people become too preoccupied with the details of their bit of the system and ignore how what they do affects others, and how this impacts on the overall effectiveness of the business.

Lack of accessible channels for dialogue and the sharing of meaning

When learning is shared, the data on which it is based are open to challenge. Others can reassess the reasoning and logic that led to conclusions. In other words, meanings are not just exchanged; Dixon (1997) argues that shared meaning is *constructed* in the dialogue between organisational members. She believes that in the process of articulating one's own meanings and comprehending the meanings others have constructed, people alter the meanings they hold. This joint construction of meaning is the essence of organisational learning. Unfortunately, the conditions that facilitate this process are often lacking. This has prompted many organisations to experiment with interventions designed to overcome some of the barriers to understanding between individuals and groups. Some of these interventions are referred to by Dixon (1997), and include: 'whole system in the room' processes such as General Electric's Work Out, Weisbord's Strategic Search Conferences, Beer's Team Syntegrity and Emery's Conference Model; and team approaches such as Revans' Action Learning. The active participation of others is a critical element in collective learning. Bessant, Kaplinsky and Lamming (2003) highlight the importance of feedback and the challenge and support that others can provide. They note that while Revans' (1980) concept of action learning was originally applied at the interpersonal level it can contribute to intra- and inter-organisational learning.

The context in which sharing and dialogue must occur

Brown and Eisenhardt (1997) illustrate the importance of context when describing the characteristics of firms that are able to manage change as a continuous process. They refer, for example, to organisational structures (semi-structures) that facilitate improvisation and the modification of work practices through mutual adjustments. Szulanski (1996) also reports that formal structures and systems, sources of coordination and expertise, and behaviour-framing attributes of the organisational context affect the quality of knowledge transfer.

The acquisition of knowledge, the recognition of its potential and its application to improve organisational performance often requires numerous individual exchanges. Reference has already been made to the availability of channels for communication but the quality of relationships between organisational members can also affect the quality of organisational learning. Szulanski suggests that this is particularly important in those situations where knowledge has *tacit* components (see Nonaka, 1994) and where the reasons for the success or failure of knowledge transfers are ambiguous.

Attitudes towards mistakes and failures can have an important impact on the quality of learning. Husted and Michailova (2002) argue that they are often the result of exploring unknown territory and can be a vital source of new insights, but they are often buried and kept secret. This happens when organisational members are uncertain about how others will react, and especially when they fear that they will be blamed for wasting resources. 'Blame cultures' limit information-sharing and increase the possibility of the same mistake being made repeatedly. They also inhibit creativity and learning, because people are motivated to play safe and avoid experimentation.

Characteristics of the sources and recipients of knowledge

An important factor that can influence an organisation's ability to learn is the willingness of individual organisational members to share with others the meaning they have constructed for themselves as they encountered new experiences and ideas. Issues of confidentiality may prevent some sharing, but there are occasions where knowledge is withheld for what Dixon (1997) describes as political and logistical reasons. These include gaining a personal competitive advantage, or a perceived lack of interest, on the part of others, in what the individual might want to share. Trust is also an issue. Lines *et al.* (2005) argue that whether change agents and others gain access to the knowledge and creative thinking they need to solve problems depends largely on how much people trust them.

Husted and Michailova (2002) cite organisational members' reluctance to spend time on knowledge-sharing as an impediment to organisational learning. This reluctance may arise because people are overwhelmed with other tasks or believe that their time can be invested more profitably elsewhere. They may also be reluctant to share information because they fear that this will encourage 'knowledge parasites' (who fail to invest much effort in acquiring their own knowledge) benefiting at their expense.

A related problem, referred to by Dixon, is that some organisational members may be reluctant to consider the relevance of knowledge that others are willing to share with them. Individuals and groups may prefer to develop their own ideas and knowledge and reject knowledge that is 'not-invented-here'. They may also reject knowledge because they have reservations about the source's reliability or trustworthiness.

Motivation to consider and utilise knowledge from other sources is not the only problem. Cohen and Levinthal (1990) suggest that lack of absorptive capacity (which manifests itself in the ability to value, assimilate and apply new knowledge) might render recipients incapable of exploiting the knowledge available to them. Szulanski (1996) also refers to a lack of retentive capability (the ability to institutionalise the utilisation of new knowledge) as a block to organisational learning, because it undermines persistence.

The management of knowledge transfer

Knowledge transfer and learning can be hindered by 'top-down' efforts to spread best practice. Zell (2001) suggests that forcing an innovation on to a new host unit may be ineffective because this approach may fail to develop employee commitment and the competencies necessary for the innovation to persist. Bessant, Kaplinsky and Lamming (2003) also report that in the context of inter-firm learning, attempts by a lead or coordinating firm to drive others down a particular path may affect the extent to which other members of a supply chain are willing to 'buy-in' to the process. They report that small and medium-sized organisations (SMEs) often feel excluded from decision making and planning.

Ideologies

Reference has already been made to how ideology can distort the free flow of meaning. Walsh (1995) notes how shared mental models can be detrimental to organisational learning. He cites a number of case studies which link 'organisational blunders' to dysfunctional-information processing among the organisations' top leadership groups – e.g. the Facit Corporation's inability to recognise the electronic calculator as a threat to its mechanical calculator business and the Allied commanders' unwillingness to accept the futility of the saturation bombing of Europe in the Second World War. In both these examples, the group could be seen as holding a supra-individual schema that distorted its understanding of the information world in a way that made it blind to certain important aspects of its environment. In terms of Swieringa and Wierdsma's model, the consequence was that the 'rules' used to guide behaviour were based on an inadequate understanding of the environment and they failed to promote behaviours that would contribute to the organisation's success

Weick (1979: 52) points to the phenomenon of *groupthink* (Janis, 1972) as an example of the dysfunctional consequences when people are dominated by a single self-reinforcing schema:

Having become true believers of a specific schema, group members direct their attention towards an environment and sample it in such a way that the true belief becomes self-validating and the group becomes even more fervent in its attachment to the schema. What is underestimated is the degree to which the direction and sampling are becoming increasingly narrow under the influence of growing consensus and enthusiasm for the restricted set of beliefs. (1979: 52)

Janis describes groupthink as a deterioration of mental efficiency, reality testing and moral judgement that is the result of in-group pressure. He defines eight symptoms of groupthink:

1   The group feels invulnerable. There is excessive optimism and risk taking.
2   Warnings that things might be going awry are discounted by the group members in the name of rationality.
3   There is an unquestioned belief in the group's morality. The group will ignore questionable stances on moral or ethical issues.
4   Those who dare to oppose the group are called evil, weak, or stupid.
5   There is direct pressure on anyone who opposes the prevailing mood of the group.
6   Individuals in the group self-censor if they feel that they are deviating from group norms.
7   There is an illusion of unanimity. Silence is interpreted as consent.
8   There are often self-appointed people in the group who protect it from adverse information. These people are referred to by Janis as mind guards.

All too often individuals and organisations fail to exploit the full potential for learning because they are unaware of the extent to which their mental models filter out important information. Covey (1992) contends that while people think they are objective and see things as they are, they actually see what they have been conditioned to see. He argues that:

The more aware we are of our basic paradigms, maps or assumptions, and the extent to which we have been influenced by our experience, the more we can take responsibility for those paradigms, examine them, test them against reality, listen to others and be open to their perceptions, thereby getting a larger picture and a far more objective view. (1992: 29)

Dysfunctional interactions between competing ideologies

Schein (1996) argues that in almost every organisation there are three important cultures that have a major impact on the organisation's capability to innovate and learn. These are the *operator* culture, the *engineering* culture and the *executive* culture. The operator culture is essentially an internal culture but the engineering and executive cultures have their roots outside the organisation in wider occupational communities. CEOs, for example, share common problems that are unique to their role and engineers have common educational backgrounds and are influenced by the external professional bodies that license them to practice.

Operations managers value people as human assets. They tend to be very sensitive to the interdependencies between the separate elements of the production process and recognise that, regardless of how carefully engineered a process is, its effective functioning will be determined by the quality of *human interaction*. Openness, mutual trust, commitment and the ability of people to learn and adapt to unanticipated circumstances are highly valued.

According to Schein, engineers, systems designers and technocrats (very broadly defined) are attracted to their profession because it is abstract and impersonal. They are pragmatic perfectionists who prefer people-free solutions. They 'recognise the human factor and design for it, but their preference is to is to make things as automatic as possible'.

The CEO and his or her immediate subordinates tend to be preoccupied with the financial survival and growth of the organisation, and focus much of their attention on boards, investors and the capital markets. Schein argues that their self-image tends to be the embattled lonely warrior championing the organisation in a hostile economic environment. They develop elaborate management information systems to stay in touch with what is going on in the organisation and impose control systems to manage costs. People tend to be viewed as 'resources' and are regarded as a cost rather than human assets.

Dysfunctional interactions arise when the three cultures are mis-aligned. Schein provides examples from a range of different organisational contexts. One relates to how the managers of operational units in a nuclear power generating company had their various plans for performance improvement over-ruled by the corporate engineering community who wanted to find standard solutions to common problems and the executive culture that were anxious to control costs. Another focused on teachers (operators) who valued human interaction with their students, and the advocates of computer-based learning (engineers), on the one hand, and school managers, on the other, who wanted to control costs by increasing class size (and consequently reducing the human interaction valued by the teachers).

Schein argues that a root problem is that we have come to accept conflict between the three cultures as 'normal' and this has encouraged members of each culture to devalue the concerns of the other cultures rather than looking for integrative solutions. As noted above, an organisation's ability to learn is largely determined by the receptiveness of organisational members to the concerns and knowledge presented by others and their willingness to be open and share their knowledge and concerns with others. All three cultures are valid and can be a source of valuable learning. CEOs do need to worry about the financial health of the organisation and engineers can make a valuable contribution by developing systems or solutions that eliminate human error. The way forward, therefore, is not to allow one of the three cultures to define reality for the others, but to seek greater alignment by developing sufficient mutual understanding to allow members to develop and implement integrative solutions.

However, because members of the executive and engineering cultures belong to wider occupational communities, even when organisations make great efforts to align these three cultures the effect may be short-lived. Schein suggests that executive succession, for example, might lead to the appointment of a new CEO who may take the organisation back to where it used to be.

Schein concludes that until executives, engineers and operators realise that they use different languages and make different assumptions about what is important, and until they come to accept that the assumptions of the other cultures are valid and worthy of attention, organisational learning efforts will continue to fail.

Exercise 4.1   Assessing the quality of organisational learning in your organisation

Consider the quality of organisational or collective learning in your organisation, or in a part of the organisation you are familiar with. When making your assessment, reflect on the following:

- What is the balance between single- and double-loop collective learning, and how does this relate to the kinds of change (continuous or discontinuous) confronting the organisation or unit?
- Do people fully appreciate the systemic nature of the organisation, and are they aware of how what they do affects overall organisational effectiveness?
- Are people motivated to share experiences and ideas, and seek a more effective way of operating?
- Is there an ideological commitment to an established way of doing things that discourages innovation and the exploration of new possibilities?

Notes

Summary

This chapter opened with a discussion of the nature of strategy and strategic change management. Three different approaches to strategy formulation and implementation were considered, and the effect of factors such as culture and organisational politics on the quality of information processing was highlighted.

The second section of the chapter examined the nature of organisational learning and how it can contribute to strategic change management. Different kinds of collective learning were discussed. Single-loop learning is concerned with continuous improvement through doing things better. Double-loop learning involves challenging current thinking and exploring the possibility of doing things differently, or doing different things.

The third section considered the role of knowledge transfer within and between organisations.

The final section focused on impediments to intra- and inter-organisational learning such as a failure to appreciate the systemic nature of organisations, the lack of accessible channels for dialogue and the sharing of meaning and pressures for conformity that constrain creative thinking.

References

Argyris, C. and Schon, D. (1978) *Organizational Learning*, London: Addison-Wesley.

Bessant, J., Kaplinsky, R. and Lamming, R. (2003) 'Putting Supply Chain Learning into Practice', *International Journal of Operations and Production Management*, 23 (3), pp. 167–85.

Brown, S.L. and Eisenhardt, K.M. (1997) 'The Art of Continuous Change: Linking Complexity Theory and Time-Paced Evolution in Relentlessly Shifting Organizations', *Administrative Science Quarterly*, 42, pp. 1–34.

Cohen, W.M. and Levinthal, D. (1990) 'Absorptive Capacity: A New Perspective on Learning and Innovation', *Administrative Science Quarterly*, 35 (1), pp. 128–52.

Covey, S.R. (1992) *The Seven Habits of Highly Effective People*, London: Simon & Schuster.

Daft, R.L. and Weick, K.E. (1984) 'Toward a Model of Organisations as Interpreting Systems', *Academy of Management Review*, 9 (2), pp. 284–95.

De Geus, A (1988) 'Planning as Learning', *Harvard Business Review*, 66 (2), p. 71.

De Holan, P.M. and Phillips, N. (2004) 'Remembrance of Things Past? The Dynamics of Organizational Forgetting', *Management Science*, 50 (11), pp. 1603–13.

Dixon, N. (1997) 'The Hallways of Learning', *Organizational Dynamics*, Spring, 23–34.

Douglas, M. (1986) *How Institutions Think,* Syracuse, NY: Syracuse University Press.

Egan, G. (1988) *Change-Agent Skills: Assessing and Designing Excellence*, San Diego: University Associates.

Fiol, C.M. and Lyles, M.A. (1983) 'Organizational Learning', *Academy of Management Review*, 10 (4), pp. 803–13.

Gersick, C.J.G. (1991) 'Revolutionary Change Theories: A Multilevel Exploration of the Punctuated Equilibrium Paradigm', *Academy of Management Review*, 16, pp. 10–36.

Higgins, J.M. (2005) 'The Eight "S's" of Successful Strategy Execution', *Journal of Change Management,* 5 (1), pp. 3–13.

Huber, G. (1991) 'Organizational Learning: The Contributing Processes and the Literature', *Organizational Science*, 2 (1), 88–115.

Husted, K. and Michailova, S. (2002) 'Diagnosing and Fighting Knowledge-Sharing Hostility', *Organizational Dynamics*, 31 (1), 60–73.

Janis, I.L. (1972) *Victims of Groupthink: A Psychological Study of Foreign Policy Decisions and Fiascos*, Boston, MA: Houghton-Mifflin.

Johnson, G. (1993) 'Processes of Managing Strategic Change', in C. Mabey and B. Mayon-White (eds), *Managing Change*, London: Paul Chapman, in association with the Open University, pp. 58–64.

Johnson, G. and Scholes, K. (1999) *Exploring Corporate Strategy*, 5th edn, London: Prentice Hall Europe.

Kotter, J.P. (1980) 'An Integrative Model of Organizational Dynamics', in E.E. Lawler, D.A. Nadler and C. Cammann, *Organizational Assessment*, New York: Wiley.

Lank, A.G. and Lank, E.A. (1995) 'Legitimising the Gut Feel: The Role of Intuition in Business', *Journal of Managerial Psychology*, 10 (5), 18–23.

Leroy, F. and Ramanantsoa, B. (1997) 'The Cognitive and Behavioural Dimensions of Organizational Learning in a Merger Situation: An Empirical Study', *Journal of Management Studies*, 34 (6), pp. 871–894.

Leseure, M.L., Bauer, J., Birdi, K., Neely, A. and Denyer, D. (2004) 'Adoption of Promising Practices: A Systematic Review of the Evidence', *International Journal of Management Reviews*, 5/6 (3 and 4), pp. 169–90.

Lines, R., Selart, M., Espedal, B. and Johansen, S.T. (2005) 'The Production of Trust during Organizational Change', *Journal of Change Management*, 5 (2), pp. 221–45.

March, J.E. (1991) 'Exploration and Exploitation in Organisational Learning', *Organizational Science*, 2 (1), pp. 71–87.

Miles, R.H. (1982) *Coffin Nails and Corporate Strategies*, Englewood Cliffs, NJ: Prentice-Hall.

Nadler, D.A. and Tushman, M.L. (1982) 'A Model for Diagnosing Organisational Behaviour: Applying a Congruence Perspective', in D.A. Nadler, M.L. Tushman and N.G. Hatvany, *Managing Organizations*, Boston, MA: Little, Brown.

Nonaka, I. (1994) 'A Dynamic Theory of Organizational Knowledge Creation', *Organizational Science*, 5 (1), pp. 14–37.

Pettigrew, A. and Whipp, R. (1993) 'Understanding the Environment', in C. Mabey and B. Mayon-White (eds), *Managing Change*, London: Paul Chapman, in association with the Open University, pp. 5–19.

Quinn, J.B. (1993) 'Managing Strategic Change', in C. Mabey and B. Mayon-White (eds), *Managing Change*, London: Paul Chapman, in association with the Open University, pp. 64–84.

Revans, R. (1980) *Action Learning*, London: Blond & Briggs.

Schein, E. H. (1990) 'Organisational Culture', *American Psychologist*, 45 (2), pp. 109–19.

Schein, E.H. (1996) 'Three Cultures of Management: The Key to Organizational Learning', *Sloan Management Review*, Fall, 9–20.

Swieringa, J. and Wierdsma, A. (1992) *Becoming A Learning Organisation*, Reading, MA: Addison-Wesley.

Szulanski, G. (1996) 'Exploring Internal Stickiness: Impediments to the Transfer of Best Practice within the Firm', *Strategic Management Journal*, 17, special issue, pp. 27–43.

Walsh, J.P. (1995) 'Managerial and Organisational Cognition: Notes from a Trip Down Memory Lane', *Organisational Science*, 6 (3), pp. 280–321.

Walton, R. (1975) 'The Diffusion of New Work Structures: Explaining Why Success Didn't Take', *Organizational Dynamics*, Winter, pp. 2–22.

Weick, K.E. (1979) 'Cognitive Processes in Organizations', in B.W. Staw (ed.), *Research in Organizational Behaviour*, 1, Greenwich, CT: J.A. Press, pp. 41–7.

Zell, D. (2001) 'Overcoming Barriers to Work Innovations: Lessons Learned at Hewlett-Packard', *Organizational Dynamics*, 30 (1), pp. 77–86.

5

Process models of change

This chapter opens with an activity designed to explore the issues and choices involved in developing an approach to managing organisational change. It then moves on to consider the main features of some frequently cited models for conceptualising the change process and presents a generic model that will provide the structure for Chapters 6–23 of this book.

Exercise 5.1   Managing a branch closure programme: an exercise in planning and managing the process of change

The aim of this activity is to explore the issues and choices involved in developing an overall strategy for large-scale change.

The scenario

A long-established bank is facing strong competition from new entrants into the retail banking market. The new entrants specialise in the provision of telephone and internet banking services and have a lower cost base because they do not carry the overheads associated with a large branch network.

A director of the branch network in the traditional bank has proposed a strategy for responding to this competition. It involves closing down 20 per cent of the branch network in order to reduce overheads and increase net revenue per customer. At this stage, the details of the strategy have not been finalised. For example, the branches targeted for closure could be city centre branches occupying expensive properties or small rural branches occupying low-cost premises but with relatively few customers of high net worth to the bank.

Imagine that you are a consultant who has been engaged by the director who initiated the proposal. Your role is to help her:

- explore the feasibility of the proposal to increase profitability by contracting the branch network
- design a change plan that could be implemented if it is decided to go ahead with the closures.

Step 1

The director, her immediate colleagues and you have brainstormed a list of possible actions that could provide the basis for a strategy for managing this change. These are listed below.

You are invited to review the list of actions presented in Table 5.1 and use your experience to:

- Delete any items that, on reflection, you feel are unimportant or irrelevant.
- Add, in the space provided in Table 5.1, any other actions that you feel should be included. You are allowed to add up to four additional actions.
- Think about how the actions might be sequenced from start to finish. For each action, identify whether you think it should occur early or late in the change management process. You can record this view in the space provided on the right-hand side of Table 5.1.

Table 5.1   Possible actions

		Early	Late
1	Identify key stake holders who might be affected by the change		
2	Provide counselling service and retraining for those who are to be displaced		
3	Inform staff how they, personally, will be affected by the closure plan		
4	Persuade those who are in a position to champion the favoured closure plan to support it in order to help ensure that the Bank maintains its competitive position		
5	Identify a project leader and set up a branch closure team		
6	Announce the scope and scale of the closure plan to all staff		
7	Brief key managers about the closure plan		
8	Identify which branches are to be closed		
9	Review success (or otherwise) of the closure programme and disseminate throughout the organisation any lessons learned about change management		
10	Identify the information that will be required in order to decide the number and location of branches to be closed in order to achieve targeted benefits		
11	Announce closure plan to existing customers		
12	Train members of the branch closure team in change management skills		
13	Identify (and quantify) benefits sought from closures		
14	Develop a personnel package for displaced staff		
15	Assess effects of the closures on other aspects of the Bank's functioning		
16	Plan any training that may be required for staff who are to be re-assigned to other work		
17	Hold team meetings to brief staff about how the closure plans will affect staff and indicate when they will be informed about how they (personally) will be affected by the change		
18	Identify what steps could be taken to retain high-value customers affected by the closures		
19	Provide training for managers and supervisors to assist them help others (and themselves) cope with change		
20	Issue newsletter outlining progress towards full implementation		
21	Decide who should be involved in analysing the information relating to whether a closure plan will deliver sufficient benefits to justify the costs involved		
22	Seek views of customers who might be affected by the closures about what issues should be given attention		
23	Seek views of branch staff about the issues that will have to be given attention if the closure plan is to be successfully accomplished		

		Early		Late	
24	If it decided to implement the closure plan, decide who should be involved in identifying which branches are to be closed				
25	Initiate programme to make properties suitable for disposal (e.g. remove vaults)				
26	Celebrate successes and build on them in order to motivate people to continue working to improve the Bank's competitive position				
27	Decide on date for first closures				
28	Identify any personal gains or losses that might be perceived by those employees who will be affected by the closures				
29	Specify a timetable for implementing the closure plan				
30	Consider what might be done to motivate employees to accept the change				
31	Issue a press release about the closure plan				
32	Monitor progress against timetable and anticipated benefits				
33	Explore the best way of disposing of redundant properties				
34	Identify social banking issues raised by the closures (e.g. what will happen to customers without transport when their local branch closes)				
35	Plan what will happen to displaced staff (redeployment, early retirement, redundancy)				
36					
37					
38					
39					

Step 2

Consider your list of action statements and assemble them into a plan:

- Identify the sequence of actions from start to finish, recognising that some actions may occur in parallel, or be repeated.
- Identify relationships between actions in your plan, and consider how different actions might be categorised as separate steps or distinctive parts.
- Summarise your plan (on a separate sheet or in the space provided below) as a flow diagram, including descriptive labels for the main aspects or stages of your plan.

You may find it helpful to print all of the actions listed in Table 5.1 on to separate post-it notes so that it will be easier to move them about and experiment with different ways of:

- sequencing them, and
- grouping them into categories that reflect the mains steps in your approach to managing the change process.

Your model, showing the main steps in the process of managing change

The next part of this chapter will consider some process issues associated with the management of change and will conclude by presenting a generic model that can be used as a guide when thinking about the best way to manage a particular change.

You may find it useful to compare this generic model with the model you developed to manage the branch closures.

As you read the remaining chapters of this book you may also find it helpful to reflect on how the content of each chapter might influence your approach to managing this kind of change.

The nature of change as a process

Weick and Quinn (1999) distinguish between change that is *continuous* and *episodic* (discontinuous). They note that a common presumption is that continuous change is emergent: 'The distinctive quality of continuous change is the idea that small continuous adjustments, created simultaneously across units, can cumulate and create substantial change.' Where interdependencies between organisational units are loose these same continuous adjustments may be confined to smaller units, but they can still be 'important as pockets of innovation that may prove appropriate in future environments'.

Discontinuous or episodic change, according to Weick and Quinn, occurs during periods of divergence when organisations are moving away from their equilibrium conditions and when there is 'a growing misalignment between an inertial deep structure and perceived environmental demands'. This misalignment is often a consequence of the poor quality of organisational learning. The failure of organisational members to create a continuously adaptive organisation leads to a failure that can be the trigger for planned change (see Dunphy, 1996).

The intentional management of change

Ford and Ford (1995) argue that the intentional management of change occurs when a change agent 'deliberately and consciously sets out to establish conditions and circumstances that are different from what they are now'.

Lewin (1951) provided some useful insights into the nature of change that are very relevant for those who seek to intentionally change the status quo. He argued that the state of 'no change' does not refer to a situation in which everything is stationary. It involves a condition of 'stable quasi-stationary equilibrium' comparable to that of a river which flows with a given velocity in a given direction. A change in the behaviour of an individual, group or organisation can be likened to a change in the river's velocity or direction. In a work situation, for example, certain hostile and friendly actions may occur between two groups. If the level of hostile behaviour is defined as a problem, a desired change may involve a new pattern of behaviour that involves less conflict, in other words in a move from one state of stable quasi-stationary equilibrium to another.

Lewin argued that any level of behaviour is maintained in a condition of quasi-stationary equilibrium by a force field, comprising a balance of forces pushing for and resisting change. This level of behaviour can be changed by either adding forces for change in the desired direction or by diminishing the opposing or resisting forces.

Both of these approaches can result in change but, according to Lewin, the secondary effects associated with each approach will be different. Where change is brought about by increasing the forces pushing for change, this will result in an increase in tension. If this rises beyond a certain level it may be accompanied by high aggressiveness (especially towards the source of the increased pressure for change), high emotionality and low levels of constructive behaviour. On the other hand, where change is brought about by diminishing the forces that oppose or resist change the secondary effect will be a state of relatively low tension.

This argument led Lewin to advocate an approach to managing change that emphasised the importance of reducing the restraining forces in preference to a high-pressured approach that only focused on increasing the forces pushing for change. He argued that approaches which involve the removal of restraining forces within the individual, group or organisation are likely to result in a more permanent change than approaches which involve the application of outside pressure for change.

Achieving a lasting change

Lewin highlighted the concept of *permanency*. He suggested that successful change requires a three-step procedure that involves the stages of unfreezing, moving and refreezing.

Burnes (2004a, 2004b) has observed a tendency in recent years to play down the significance of Lewin's work for contemporary organisations. For example, Dawson (2003) and Kantor, Stein and Jick (1992) argue that the notion of refreezing is not relevant for organisations operating in turbulent environments. They argue that organisations need to be fluid and adaptable and that the last thing they need is to be frozen into some given way of functioning. Lewin's point, however, is that all too often change is shortlived. After a 'shot in the arm', life returns to the way it was before. In his view, it is not enough to think of change in terms of simply *reaching* a new state – for example, a new pattern of behaviour between groups. He asserted that permanency, for as long as it is relevant, needs to be an important part of the goal. This state may be very brief and involve little more than taking stock before moving on to yet more change. It is, however, important to think in terms of consolidation in order to minimise the danger of slipping back to the way things were before.

Managing change, therefore, involves helping an individual, group or organisation:

- unfreeze or unlock from the existing level of behaviour
- move to a new level
- refreeze behaviour at this new level.

Hendry (1996) testifies to Lewin's lasting contribution to change management. He notes that 'Scratch any account of creating and managing change and the idea that change is a three stage process which necessarily begins with a process of unfreezing will not be far below the surface' (1996: 624). However, as Burnes (2004a) has observed, the strength of Lewin's contribution to the theory and practice of organisational change is when this three-step model is viewed as part of an integrated theory that includes field theory, group dynamics (see Chapter 17) and action research (see Chapter 18).

Stages in the process of managing change

This section briefly reviews three other process models of change that can be viewed as elaborations of Lewin's basic model.

- **Lippitt, Watson and Westley (1958)** expanded Lewin's three-stage model. After reviewing descriptions of change in persons, groups, organisations and communities they felt that the moving phase divided naturally into three sub-stages. These were:

  (a) The clarification or diagnosis of the client's problem
  (b) The examination of alternative routes and goals, and establishing goals and intentions for action
  (c) The transformation of intentions into actual change efforts.

  They also argued that change managers can be effective only when they develop and maintain an appropriate relationship with those involved in or affected by the change. This led them to introduce two further stages into the helping process, one concerned with the formation and the other with the termination of relationships.
- **Egan (1996)** developed a model that is based on Lewin's three stages of unfreezing, moving and refreezing, but it focuses most attention on the moving phase, with detailed consideration being given to the assessment of the current scenario (diagnosis), the creation of a preferred scenario (visioning) and the design of plans that move the system from the current to the preferred scenario (planning for change). The essential elements of each of these three stages are as follows:

(a) The *current* scenario: assessing problems and opportunities, developing new perspectives, and choosing high-impact problems or opportunities for attention

(b) The *preferred* scenario: developing a range of possible futures, evaluating alternative possibilities to establish a viable agenda for change and gaining commitment to the new agenda

(c) Strategies and plans for *moving to the preferred scenario*: brainstorming strategies for getting there, choosing the best strategy or 'best-fit' package of strategies and turning these strategies into a viable plan.

- **Beckhard and Harris** (1987) present a three-stage model that focuses on defining the present and the future, managing the transition and maintaining and updating the change. Special consideration is given to some of the issues associated with the moving or transitional stage, including the need for management mechanisms, the development of activity plans and the gaining of commitment from key stakeholders.

An overview of the change process

These models highlight the importance of:

- *Diagnosis* – change managers need to give attention to where the organisation is now and to what a more desirable (and attainable) state would look like
- *Strategies and plans* to move the organisation towards the desired state.
- *Implementation* – translating intentions (strategies and plans) into actual change efforts; implementation also involves managing the interpersonal and political issues associated with change.

Key steps in the change process

Change is often managed less effectively than it might be because those responsible for managing it fail to attend to some of the critical aspects of the change process. The model (Hayes and Hyde, 1998) presented below provides a conceptual framework for thinking about the management of change. It incorporates many of the features of the process models reviewed above. While the context here is organisational change, the same model can be applied to change at the level of the individual and the group.

At first glance, this model suggests that change is a neat, rational and linear process. This is rarely the way that it unfolds and is experienced in practice. Sometimes a desired end state is not obvious at the beginning of the process, a point that will be elaborated later. The dotted lines in Figure 5.1 represent feedback loops and possible iterations or repetitions in the process. The loop between 'review' and 'external factors' signals that change rarely involves moving from one steady state to another. Typically, it is an on-going

Figure 5.1   Steps in the change process

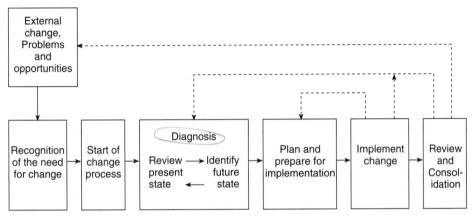

Source: Hayes and Hyde (1998).

process. Often new pressures for change emerge before the current change initiative has been completed.

Recognition

The start of the process is the recognition that external events or internal circumstances require a change to take place. Recognition involves complex processes of perception, interpretation and decision making that, if not managed carefully, can lead to inappropriate outcomes – for example the organisation might fail to change when it needs to, or it may change when change is not required.

Start of the change process

The start of the change process involves translating the need for change into a desire for change, deciding who will manage the change and, especially where an external change agent is introduced to help with this process, establishing a workable and effective change relationship.

The change may start with a formal announcement or it may be less explicit, but, at some point, it typically involves a review, feasibility study or project. Critical questions that need to be considered at this stage are:

● Who to involve?
● What to make public (if anything)?
● Who should have management responsibility?

It is also important to begin thinking about how to 'unfreeze' others, and gain acceptance that change is needed.

Diagnosis – reviewing the present state and identifying the preferred future state

Although reviewing the present and identifying the future state may seem at first sight to be separate and distinct activities, in practice they are often integrated. These two steps frequently go through several iterations, progressing from broad concepts towards something that is sufficiently concrete and detailed to be implemented.

There is also some debate about whether the process should in fact start with looking at the present or the future. The argument for starting with the present is to ensure that the change is not a 'utopian leap' to an unrealistic future which cannot be reached from the current situation. On the other hand, focusing too heavily on the present may limit horizons and lead to the goals of change being too cautious and constrained by current experience. Where radical or transformational change is needed it may be better to consider the direction of change than to concentrate on the start point. For these reasons, Figure 5.1 shows these two elements interacting in the same box.

Reviewing the present state

The present state of the organisation can often be understood only in terms of the context of its past history and its external environment. The precise objectives for reviewing the present state will depend upon the type of change that is being managed. Common reasons are to:

- help identify the required change by diagnosing the cause of a problem, identifying current deficiencies or clarifying opportunities
- establish a baseline so that it is clear what is changing
- help define the future direction.

Data gained from this kind of review can also be used to help assess how organisational members and other stakeholders will react, and to prepare people for change.

Identifying the future state

What is required when identifying the future state depends on the kind of change that is being undertaken, and on the role of the change managers in the overall process. If the change managers are responsible for initiating the change their task is likely to involve developing a view or 'vision' of what they (and others involved in the diagnostic process) think the organisation ought to look like in the future. If, on the other hand, their role is to implement a change that is being imposed from elsewhere, their task may be more limited to thinking through and visioning the likely impact of the change.

The way the diagnostic stage is managed can affect the way that the need for change is (or is not) translated into a desire for change. Organisational members are more likely to be motivated to let go of the status quo and seek a more desirable state if:

- the diagnostic process disconfirms their view that all is well with the existing state of affairs
- this challenge produces a sufficient level of anxiety to motivate organisational members to search for new possibilities
- the vision of what might be offers sufficient promise to make the effort of changing worthwhile.

Lewin refers to this as 'unfreezing'. Schein (1996) argues that unless the unfreezing process offers a promise of psychological safety any disconfirmation provided by the diagnostic phase will be denied or defended against and those involved will not be motivated to change.

Prepare and plan for implementation

Detailed analysis of the future and present state will lead to the identification of a long list of things which could be done in order to make the proposed change a reality. Burnes (2004a) illustrates the links between three aspects of Lewin's work (field theory, action research and the three-step model of change) when he refers to Lewin's assertion that following unfreezing one should seek movement (change) by taking into account all the forces at work and identifying and evaluating, on a trial and error basis, all of the available options.

There will be different lead-times associated with the various tasks, interdependencies between them and resource and other constraints. All of these things need to be taken into account when developing an implementation plan. However, it is important that implementation is not viewed as only a technical activity. Implementation has an important political dimension. It needs to address the extent to which people are ready for and accepting of change, and whether the process threatens them in any way. Choices need to be made, such as which method to adopt to implement the change and whether to proceed to full implementation or start with a trial or pilot. In Chapter 4, the dangers of separating planning and implementation were discussed and the benefits of adopting a more integrated and incremental approach were explored.

Implement change

Whatever has been planned now needs to be implemented and the focus shifts from planning to action. Attention also needs to be given to monitoring and control to ensure that things happen as intended. There are two

A → B
planned

A → ?
emergent
evolutionary

basic approaches to implementing change. Sometimes change involves moving from A to B, where, before implementation, the nature of B is known and clearly defined. This kind of change is sometimes referred to as a 'blueprint' change. Typical examples of a blueprint change include relocation, computerisation of a business process, or the introduction of a new appraisal or grading system. In these circumstances it is easier to view the management of change from the perspective of 'planned change' that involves a predetermined linear process (following step by step the successive stages in the models of change reviewed above).

Often, however, it is not possible to specify the end point (B) of a change in advance of implementation (see the discussion of logical incrementalism and the emergent approach to the formulation of strategy in Chapter 4). While a need for change might be recognised (because, for example, the organisation is losing market share or is failing to innovate as fast as its competitors), it may be less obvious what needs to be done to improve matters. There may be a broadly defined goal and a direction for change (for example, improving competitiveness), but it may not be possible to provide a very detailed specification of what this end state will look like. In some situations, it may not even be very helpful to think in terms of specific end states because the rate of change in the operating environment may be such that the precise definition of a desirable end state may be subject to constant revision.

In these circumstances, a 'blueprint' approach to change is inappropriate. Change needs to be viewed as a more open-ended and iterative process that emerges or evolves over time. Buchanan and Storey (1997) argue that this is not unusual and that change often unfolds in an iterative fashion and can involve much backtracking. Burke (2002) echoes this view and argues that the change process is often more like a series of loops than a straight line, reflecting the reality that things rarely progress as planned, and even when plans are implemented as intended there are often unanticipated consequences. Managers frequently report that for every step forward they seem to fall back two steps and that they are constantly having to 'fix things' to keep the change on track.

An emergent or evolutionary approach to change involves taking tentative incremental steps in, what it is hoped is, the right direction. After each step, the step itself and the direction of the change are reviewed to establish if the step worked and if the direction still holds good. As the process unfolds, it may be possible to define the end state a bit more precisely or to take future steps with more confidence. The dotted lines on Figure 5.1 illustrate the process of *feedback and review* which is an essential part of this approach to change.

Even with blueprint changes, this feedback loop is important because feedback from implementation can lead to the identification of new problems and possibilities. It may have implications for the planning of further activities to bring about change and may even affect the definition of a more desirable end state, thus leading to a revision of the 'blueprint'. Sometimes the feedback may also alert change managers to the possibility that what was originally perceived as a blueprint change might be more appropriately approached and managed as an evolutionary change.

Review and consolidate

The 'review' part of this heading is sometimes taken to imply some form of post-implementation review, but in practice monitoring and reviewing progress are on-going activities, as progress is measured against key milestones. Consolidation refers to the 'refreezing' aspect of Lewin's model. It involves, among other things, ensuring that there are feedback mechanisms and reward systems in place that will monitor and reinforce desired new behaviours. However, rather than attempting to simply ossify the new state, it also involves building on and updating the change as required.

Managing the people issues

As well as the steps described in the model and presented in Figure 5.1, a strategy for managing change must also address a number of 'people issues' that are on-going throughout the process. Some of these are:

- Power, politics and stakeholder management
- Leadership
- Communication
- Training and development
- Motivating others to change
- Support for others to help them manage their personal transitions.

These issues will be considered later in Chapters 9–14.

Change managers need to address these 'people issues' at all stages of the change process and not just when designing a strategy for implementation. A common mistake is to treat the stages of reviewing the present state and designing the future state as purely technical activities. Consequently, little attention is given to the political and motivational issues associated with the plan for change. Diagnosing what needs to be changed is often viewed as a precursor to the 'real business' of managing change. This is a dangerous attitude to adopt. In Chapter 4, a distinction was made between the planning and emergent approaches to formulating and implementing strategy that is relevant to this discussion. It was noted that the successful implementation of strategies can be threatened when the stages of formulation and implementation are separated, and when there is an over-reliance on rational approaches that neglect cultural and political issues. Diagnosing and visioning are not benign activities. Nadler

(1987) refers to the importance of shaping the political dynamics of change and motivating constructive behaviour. Stakeholders may resist any attempt to even consider the possibility that change might be required.

A change strategy is essentially a plan to make things happen. It needs to address all of the things that have to be done to bring about the change. When developing a strategy change managers need to attend to each step in the change process and to the way the overall process is to be managed. However, all of this needs to be regarded as something that is dynamic and evolving, and not a grand plan that can be 'set in stone' from the start. It is

Figure 5.2   The relationship between Chapters 6–23 and the generic process model of change

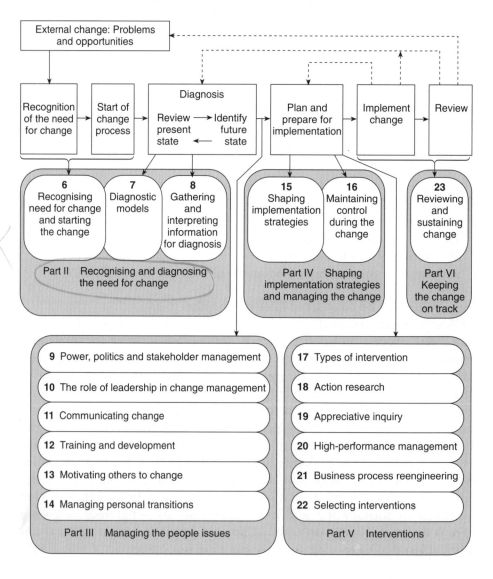

also important to recognise that there is no one recipe, or prescription, about how change 'should' be managed, that can be applied to all situations. Managing change is a complex process. Change managers need to contextualise their approach and develop bespoke strategies that accommodate the cultural and political dynamics that can undermine or facilitate any attempt to manage change. Other actions are associated with issues such as stakeholder management, communication, etc., which need to be attended to throughout the whole process.

Summary

This chapter opened with an exercise that invited you to think about how you might go about managing the process of change associated with contracting the branch network of large traditional bank.

A generic model of the change process has been presented, against which you can compare, assess – and, if necessary, revise – your own approach to change management. This generic model provides the framework for Chapters 6–23. The way in which Chapters 6–23 relate to the generic model is illustrated in Figure 5.2.

References

Beckhard, R. and Harris, R. (1987) *Organizational Transitions: Managing Complex Change*, 2nd edn, Reading, MA: Addison-Wesley.

Buchanan, D.A. and Storey, J. (1997) 'Role Taking and Role Switching in Organizational Change: The Four Pluralities', in I. McLoughlin and M. Harris (eds), *Innovation, Organisational Change and Technology*, London: International Thompson.

Burke, W.W. (2002) *Organization Change: Theory and Practice*, Thousand Oaks, CA: Sage.

Burnes, B. (2004a) 'Kurt Lewin and the Planned Approach to Change: A Re-Appraisal', *Journal of Management Studies*, 41 (6), pp. 977–1002.

Burnes, B. (2004b) 'Kurt Lewin and Complexity Theory: Back to the Future?' *Journal of Change Management*, 4 (4), pp. 309–25.

Dawson, P. (2003) *Organisational Change: A Processual Approach*, London: Paul Chapman.

Dunphy, (1996) 'Organisational Change in Corporate Settings', *Human Relations*, 49 (5), pp. 541–2.

Egan, G. (1996) *Change Agent Skills B: Managing Innovation and Change*, Englewood Cliffs, NJ: Prentice Hall.

Ford, D.J. and Ford, L.W. (1995) 'The Role of Conversation in Producing Intentional Change in Organizations', *Academy of Management Review*, 20 (3), pp. 571–600.

Hayes, J. and Hyde, P. (1998) 'A Process Model of Change', unpublished workshop handout.

Hendry, C. (1996) 'Understanding and Creating Whole Organisational Change through Learning Theory', *Human Relations*, 48 (5), pp. 621–41.

Kantor, R.M., Stein, B.A. and Jick, T.D. (1992) *The Challenge of Organizational Change*, New York: Free Press.

Lewin, K. (1951) *Field Theory in Social Science*, New York: Harper & Row; see also Lewin (1947) 'Frontiers in Group Dynamics', *Human Relations*, 1, pp. 5–41.

Lippitt, R., Watson, J. and Westley, B. (1958) *The Dynamics of Planned Change*, New York: Harcourt Brace Jovanovich.

Nadler, D.A. (1987)' The Effective Management of Organizational Change', in J.W. Lorsch (ed.), *Handbook of Organizational Behaviour*, Englewood Cliffs, NJ: Prentice Hall.

Schein, E.H. (1996) 'Kurt Lewin's Change Theory in the Field and in the Classroom: Notes Towards a Model of Management Learning', *Systems Practice*, 9 (1), 27–47.

Weick, K.E. and Quinn, R.E. (1999) 'Organisational Change and Development', *Annual Review of Psychology*, 50 (1), pp. 361–86.

Recognising and diagnosing the need for change

Part II reviews some of the issues that need to be addressed in the early stages of the change process.

Chapter 6 Recognising the need for change and starting the change process

This chapter considers some of the issues associated with starting the change process, including:

- recognising the need for change
- translating this need into a desire for change
- deciding who will facilitate the change
- establishing a working relationship between the change manager(s) and those who might be affected by the change.

After reading this chapter you will be asked to:

- think of an occasion when a need for change in your department was recognised in good time, and an occasion when it was never recognised, or only very late in the day
- identify some of the factors that might have contributed to these different outcomes.

Chapter 7 Diagnostic models

This chapter is divided into three sections. The first examines the role of models in organisational diagnosis and introduces an exercise designed to help raise your awareness of the implicit models you use when thinking about organisations and assessing the need for change.

The second section presents a range of diagnostic models that are commonly used by consultants and managers.

The final section invites you to compare your implicit model with some of the explicit models that are widely used by others. It provides an opportunity for you to reassess the utility of your implicit model and, if shortcomings are identified, to revise it.

Chapter 8   Gathering and interpreting information for diagnosis

This chapter considers some of the issues associated with gathering, analysing and interpreting information about individual, group and organisational functioning.

After reading this chapter you will be invited to think about a recent occasion when you (or somebody working close to you) attempted to introduce and manage a change in your part of the organisation, and:

1   Reflect on the extent to which this change initiative was based on an accurate diagnosis of the need for change.
2   Consider the extent to which this was related to the:

   (a) appropriateness of the (implicit or explicit) diagnostic model used
   (b) nature of the information collected
   (c) way in which it was interpreted.

3   Reflect on what steps *you* might take to help improve the quality of the way that the need for change is diagnosed in your unit or department.

Recognising the need for change and starting the change process

This chapter considers some of the issues associated with starting the change process. These include recognising the need for change, translating this need into a desire for change, deciding who will facilitate the change and establishing a workable and effective change relationship.

Recognising the need for change

It was noted in Chapter 1 that some organisations (or units) are good at anticipating the need for change and this gives them time to investigate the emerging problem or opportunity and decide how best to respond. Others lack this ability. Some may fail to recognise the need for change until they have little choice but to react quickly to an unanticipated set of circumstances. Others may never recognise the problem or opportunity at all. In some circumstances such failures can threaten the organisation's long-term survival, but often the change may not be so critical or the organisation may have sufficient 'fat' to survive. Nevertheless the cost may be that it ends up performing at a level much below what it might have been.

Organisations may fail to recognise the need for change because members pay insufficient attention to what is happening in the wider environment. Even where organisational members are aware of what is going on outside they may fail to recognise its implications for the organisation. In Chapter 4 (on organisational learning and organisational effectiveness) reference was made to how ideologies and inappropriate shared mental models can undermine an organisation's ability to interpret and understand what is going on in the environment. At the level of the organisation this can lead to strategic drift and at the level of the unit or sub-system it can lead to a similar lack of alignment and consequent inefficiencies.

Nadler and Shaw (1995) illustrate this with their argument that one of the paradoxes of organisational life is that success often sets the stage for failure. This is because when organisations are successful,

Figure 6.1   The trap of success

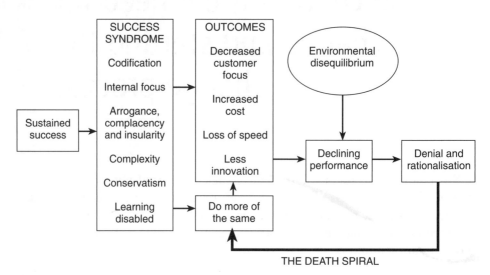

Source: Nadler, D.A., Shaw, R. and Walton, A.E., *Discontinuous Change* (1995: 11). Reprinted with permission of John Wiley & Sons, Inc.

managers become locked into the patterns of behaviour that produced the original success. These patterns become codified or institutionalised and are rarely questioned. Nadler and Shaw elaborate their argument with the proposition that success often leads to growth and growth leads to complexity and greater differentiation. As this happens, attention shifts away from how the organisation relates with the environment (it is taken for granted that this relationship will be successful) and attention is switched to managing the new and more complex relationships within the organisation. Customers and supplies receive less attention and competitive gains of rival organisations (for example, in terms of reduced costs or shorter time to market) are ignored. Where this complacency and internal focus leads to declining performance, the organisation may behave as if the solution is to do more of what led to success in the past. Nadler and Shaw refer to the organisation becoming 'learning disabled'. It becomes incapable of looking outside, reflecting on success and failure, accepting new ideas and developing new insights. If unchecked the ultimate outcome of this trap of success can be what they refer to as the 'death spiral' (see Figure 6.1).

Improving the organisation's ability to sense the need for change

Sensing a need for change and formulating a change agenda begins when individuals notice and respond to what they perceive to be significant external or organisational events. Pitt, McAulay and Sims (2002) observe that sometimes the signals or events that cause them to sense that an issue is important or urgent may be relatively weak but, based on their intuition and context-particular experience, some individuals are able to anticipate the implications of these signals. It is often argued that when top teams are populated by executives with diverse backgrounds they are more likely to be sensitive to a wider range of internal and external issues that could impact on future performance than when they are drawn from similar backgrounds, and therefore will be less likely to be learning disabled and caught in the trap of success. This proposition is based on the assumption that functional conditioning (current and past functional experience) affects cause and effect beliefs and directs attention to issues related to these beliefs. Various studies support the validity of this view. For example, Cohen and Ebbesen (1979) found that goals that are salient during a task amplify the salience of information related to these goals, suggesting that executives who work or have worked in various functional areas will be influenced by the information and issues related to their various and different past experiences. However, Chattopadhyay *et al.* (1999), in a study of 371 executives working in fifty-eight businesses across twenty-six industrial sectors, found little support for this view. A key finding of their study was that the beliefs of other members of the top team had a much greater effect on collective sense-making than members' functional experience. This raises the possibility that 'groupthink' (discussed in Chapter 4) could undermine the top team's ability to recognise the need for change.

According to Pitt, McAulay and Sims (2002), issues emerge and are shaped to form the *agenda for change* through various forms of individual initiative. While agenda-forming initiatives are often restricted to very senior managers at the top of the organisation, people located at multiple levels in the hierarchy can take action to influence the agenda for change. However, such personal actions may not be sufficient to guarantee that the organisation will address the issues identified by individuals. Pitt, McAulay and Sims assert that if ideas and concerns are to have any impact on what the organisation does they must receive some minimal level of collective attention and be recognised as having sufficient priority to deserve further consideration. Personal concerns compete for collective attention and interpretation. 'Whether, and how fast a concern crystallizes into an issue or item *on the agenda* depends on who is involved and the opportunities they have to interact and construct the issue through conversation and debate' (2002: 157, emphasis in the original). Political behaviour to promote self-interest and strong ideologies that marginalize minority or dissenting views (and promote 'groupthink') are some of the factors that can affect which issues emerge as part of the agenda for change.

The role of playmakers

The individuals who influence the organisational agenda are referred to by Pitt, McAulay and Sims as '*playmakers*', a term they borrow from football where it refers to the restless, energetic, midfield role that links play, energises the team and 'makes things happen'. They argue that these playmakers do not always have to form an exclusive elite. Top managers can encourage other organisational members to perform playmaker roles by seeking out relevant opinion from those who are close to the realities of the operating environment (however, in many organisations this does not happen – see the discussion of 'organisational silence' in Chapter 11).

Based on a study in a manufacturing company Pitt, McAulay and Sims identified three roles that people from various parts of the organisation can play to influence the agenda for change:

- *Upward-facing advocates* are those who promote ideas and concerns via rational arguments. Those who opt to play this kind of role are most effective when they are perceived as experts and are able to present persuasive technical evidence and well-crafted arguments. Describing his approach to influencing the top team, a systems manager who acted as an upward-facing advocate said: 'Senior people like to measure things. Arguments about change are easier to sustain if you can quantify things. If you want to justify something, get clear measurements of feasibility and benefits, proof on paper' (2002: 161).

- *Upward-facing emotive champions* are those who use emotion and polemics rather than rational arguments to manage impressions and champion issues. Those who adopt this approach are often motivated by self-interest allied to a genuine concern for the future of the organisation. Pitt, McAulay and Sims cite a manager who adopted this approach to influencing the change agenda: 'I went to a meeting and really stirred it up. I told them what they were saying was ludicrous. I came back and said to my manager that lunatics have taken over the asylum. I created a major issue.' This approach can involve risks but the person quoted above felt so strongly about the issue that he was prepared to speak up.

- *Democratic brokers* facilitate lateral communication among peers. They tend to be respected organisational members with perceived expertise who function as interpreters, ideas brokers and opinion canvassers. They use their nodal position in communication networks to originate and trade concerns with peers. Because they bring together different groups and interests, brokers can make a particularly valuable contribution by promoting diverse interpretations of situations that can point to opportunities or threats that might not be identified by a narrow group of senior managers acting alone. Pitt, McAulay and Sims note a planning manager who described a situation in which he acted as broker with his peers in various departments: 'We bounce problems off each other all the time. What's expected of us and how it fits in with where the company's going. How we want to restructure it, where people actually fit in. A lot is about communication . . . trying to . . . influence our peers. Its about networking . . . talking to people, bouncing ideas off them' (2002: 165).

Pitt, McAulay and Sims report that in the company they studied, not withstanding the examples referred to above, the locus of playmaking was narrowly demarcated and tended to be confined to a select few. 'Although newcomers and junior staff were in theory free to contribute to issue debates, older and wiser hands tended to be ambivalent or dismissive when they did so, thereby limiting interpretive diversity in practice' (2002: 164). Widening the opportunity for organisational members to engage in playmaking can greatly improve an organisation's ability to recognise the need to take action to either minimise threats or exploit new possibilities.

The Active Sports Equipment Company (Case study 6.1) provides a good example of how people located at different points in the organisation can make a valuable contribution to the formulation of the change agenda.

Case study 6.1 The Active Sports Equipment Company

The Active Sports Equipment Company (as it will be referred to here) is a small-to medium-sized manufacturer of high-quality sports equipment. It was founded thirty years ago and currently employs around fifty people to manufacture a specialist piece of sporting equipment. 65 per cent of output is exported world-wide. Current turnover is £4 million.

The founder of the company is a mechanical engineer. He established Active Sports Equipment (ASE) to produce a specialist piece of sports equipment based on his own original and highly innovative design. He is still the managing director and his obsessive concern with the details of design and engineering excellence dominate the culture of the company.

This concern for engineering excellence has served the company well, and it has built itself an enviable reputation as *the* standard by which all other sporting equipment in this specialist category is judged, despite the fact that the basic design of ASE's product has evolved little over the years. Recently, however, a number of challenges to this dominant position have emerged as other sports equipment manufacturers have sought to enter what they regard as an attractive market with newer designs. These newcomers compete effectively on price, many aspects of performance and specification, though they still fail to match ASE's product on ease and speed of assembly and the compactness of the fold when the equipment is collapsed for transportation. Much of the success of the ASE product is based on its well-engineered and robust construction that enables it to be folded and unfolded easily and quickly. However, it is with such challenges in mind that ASE introduced its biggest-ever number of innovations in April 2005, the most significant of which was the option of a number of titanium parts that deliver important weight-saving advantages.

But what about the future? ASE might continue to focus on its core competence and seek to retain its current competitive advantage by further improving the design of its product. Product and production engineering are highly valued within the company. There is no doubt that it is engineering that has created the ASE brand and made it what it is today. There is, however, the risk that engineering alone may not guarantee that the current record of success will be sustained.

In addition to continuing to engineer an improved product there are a number of other possibilities that might deserve attention. For example, some managers see opportunities for improving the effectiveness of the company by reviewing the way it functions. Like many SMEs, it appears to have pursued a rather informal approach to the development of its own internal organisation. This reflects the priority given to the development of product and production processes in the early years. Since then, staff roles have been redefined and new ones created on an ad hoc basis to reflect changing demands on the business. There maye, for example, be advantages to be gained from improving internal communication and planning processes, or reviewing the way the organisation is structured. Such changes might lead to superior performance by improving internal alignment. Other managers are aware of opportunities in the market place. A marketing manager was recruited two years ago but this appointment has not had much impact on the company's overall culture, which continues to be engineering-led. More attention to marketing issues might help ensure that if and when customer needs change this will be recognised by those who control the strategic agenda. Related opportunities might involve building alliances between product engineering and marketing to extend the product range and exploit the ASE brand. People working in the production departments are also aware of opportunities to reduce manufacturing costs, but they may be reluctant to voice some of these because they could lead to job losses.

If you were a manager in ASE aware of some of these issues would you actively try to influence the company's strategic agenda? If no, why not. If yes, how would you attempt to do this?

Source: This case study is based on contributions from Andy Shrimpton.

Problems relating to the recognition of the need for change are more likely to arise in those organisations where alternative perspectives and interpretations are ignored or suppressed than in those organisations where they are actively sought out and debated. Such debates will not necessarily lead to major changes, but they at least ensure that the possibility of new threats or opportunities is properly considered. There are many examples of companies that have continued to exploit, for many years, whatever it is that has provided them with a competitive advantage. This can be a healthy state of affairs so long as care is exercised to avoid complacency and the trap of success. Organisations that are most likely to sustain their success over long periods are those that engage in the process of double-loop collective learning discussed in Chapter 4. They identify and question basic assumptions and take nothing for granted. Sometimes this process points to the need for major change but sometimes it confirms the validity of the existing strategy and way of operating, and points to little more than the kind of change that fine tunes the existing way of working.

Recognising the need for change is an essential step in starting the change process. You may want to reflect on your own experience and consider whether those who are best placed to recognise the need for change are able to influence those responsible for formulating the change agenda.

Exercise 6.1   Recognising the need for change

Think of an occasion within the last three years when your unit (or your organisation) recognised the need for change in good time, and think of another occasion when it failed to do this.

In the space below list those factors that you suspect may have contributed to these different outcomes.

Factors that contributed to the recognition of the need for change	Factors that contributed to the failure to recognise the need for change

Reflect on your unit or organisation's past record of recognising the need for change. Note anything that you or others could do to help ensure that in the future your unit or organisation will be more alert to the need for change.

Notes

Translating recognition of need for change into desire for change

There are many issues that can affect whether a need for change is translated into a desire for change.

Self interest

Organisational members may recognise a problem or opportunity but this recognition may not be translated into a desire for change because they fear that, while a change will benefit the organisation, it may disadvantage them or their unit.

Lack of confidence in self or others

Another problem may be that those who recognise the need for change may have little confidence in their own ability or the ability of others to implement the change and achieve a more desirable state. (See the section on beliefs about change agency in Chapter 2 and the discussion on how leadership can affect these beliefs in Chapter 10.) This lack of confidence may be related to a history of failures to bring about change or to a feeling that the competencies, commitment and other resources required for change will not be available in the current situation.

Pugh (1993) argues that those who are most likely to want to change are those who are basically successful but who are experiencing tension or failure in some particular part of their work. This group will have both the confidence and the motivation to change. The next most likely to change are the successful because they will have the required confidence. However, because of their success they may be satisfied with the status quo and lack the motivation to change. The least likely to understand and accept the need for change are the unsuccessful. While they may be the ones who need to change most, they are also the ones who are likely to lack confidence in their own ability to improve their predicament. Consequently, they may prefer the status quo (the devil they know) to the possible outcome of a failed effort to change (the devil they don't know).

This has implications for deciding where to initiate the change effort. When faced with the possibility of alternative start points, the change agent might decide to start working with those who have the confidence and motivation to engage in the change process because early successes can inspire others to get involved (Case study 6.2).

Case study 6.2   Failure to convince others of the need for change at AT&T

There are many instances where those who recognise the need for change want to embrace it but cannot because they are unable to convince others that the change is necessary. Werther (2003) illustrates this with the example of AT&T's telephone manufacturing division (Western Electric) following deregulation of the telecommunications sector in the US. Prior to deregulation consumers had no choice other than to lease their telephones from one of the Bell operating companies (another part of AT&T). These local operating companies were regulated monopolies, allowed to earn up to a set maximum return on their assets. This regulated monopoly situation encouraged AT&T to pursue a high-reliability–high-cost strategy for the manufacture of its telephone instruments. This strategy was attractive for a number of reasons. First, the cost of the phones was included as part of the asset base on which the local operating company's returns were calculated. This offered no incentive for them to persuade Western Electric to reduce its manufacturing costs. Secondly Western Electric's market was protected from the threat of low-cost phones produced elsewhere because customers had to lease their phones from the local Bell Company. Finally, high-quality–high-cost phones were more reliable. This reduced the cost of repairs and service for the operating company and also reduced the number of complaints to the Regulator about the quality of service.

All this changed after deregulation. Customers were allowed to purchase and install their own telephones and they were very attracted to the many low-cost instruments that began to flood the market.

This had a dramatic effect on Western Electric's share of the market and convinced senior management of the need to switch from a high-reliability–high-cost manufacturing strategy to one that focused on producing low-cost phones. Werther reports that this proposed switch was fiercely resisted by engineers, managers and assemblers across the company because they believed that the company should remain committed to its traditional policy of producing high-quality, if expensive, telephones. Their resistance was so strong that the company was forced to outsource the production of low-cost phones overseas. This case study illustrates the importance of translating the need for change into a desire for change on the part of all those who can affect the success of the change project. Is there anything that senior managers could have done to overcome the resistance from engineers, managers and assemblers?

Pitt, McAulay and Sims (2002) refer to how senior managers can adopt a downward-facing evangelist playmaker role to win subordinates' attention and commitment. In their study they found evidence to suggest that spreading a message via potent, emotive symbols could be more effective than rational appeals. They cite the case of a technical director who needed to win support for a proposed change to improve hygiene standards. His message was that the company is in a high-risk business (producing ingredients for the processed food industry) and that 'the bottom line is life and death – if you get it wrong you are going to kill people'. There are, however, circumstances where alternative ways of winning support might be more effective. These are considered in Chapter 13.

Doing something about it: starting the change process

After persuading others of the need for change it is necessary to decide *who* will, at least in the first instance, facilitate the change. The change agent could be an insider, a member of the system or sub-system that is the target for change, or an outsider. An insider might be chosen in situations where:

- the person responsible for managing the unit or sub-system that is to be the (initial) target for change is committed to acting as change agent
- it is agreed that a particular insider has the time, knowledge and commitment to manage the change more effectively than an outsider
- the system does not have the resources to employ an outsider
- issues of confidentiality and trust prohibit the use of an outsider
- it proved impossible to identify a suitable outside consultant.

An outsider might be chosen where:

- there is nobody on the inside who has the time or competence to act as facilitator/change agent
- it is felt that all of the competent insiders have a vested interest in the outcome and therefore might be less acceptable to other parties than a neutral outsider.

Establishing a change relationship

Where the change agent is a member of the target system, entering the change relationship may simply involve agreeing with members of the target system that:

- there is a problem or opportunity that requires attention
- there is a need to engage in some form of preliminary data gathering in order to determine what further action is required.

A brand manager who is unhappy with the time it takes to introduce a change in the way a product is packaged may enlist the support of others to bench mark their performance against that of leading competitors. Similarly, a manager of a sports centre might set up a meeting with staff to consider possible reasons why an increasing proportion of existing members is failing to renew their membership.

Since the change agent is an insider and known to others, many of the issues that can be problematical and require careful attention when introducing an external consultant/change agent can often be managed informally and without too much difficulty.

Where the change agent is an outsider (coming from another part of the organisation or from outside) the establishment of a change relationship can be a more complex, and sometimes a more formal, process.

Issues that can affect the quality of the relationship

One of the key issues is building trust and confidence. Some individuals and groups are less comfortable than others when it comes to being open and discussing their affairs with outsiders. This may be because they fear that it might be difficult to communicate the nature of their problem (or opportunity) to others or that others may view them as incompetent or foolish. Alternatively, it may be because they fear that seeking help will threaten their autonomy and make them too dependent on others.

The early stages of the relationship-building process can be critical because clients quickly form impressions about the change agent's competence, ability to help, friendliness and inferred motives.

In terms of competence and ability, some clients want a consultant/change agent who has sufficient expertise to be able to 'see a way through' and tell them what to do. They may expect the change agent to undertake a diagnostic study and prepare a written report. In these circumstances the competence they are seeking from the consultant is related to the *content* of the problem or opportunity. Others may want a more collaborative relationship and expect the change agent to work with them to help them solve their own problems. The competence that is valued in this type of relationship is related more to the *process* of problem solving and managing change rather than to the *content* of a problem. The important point to make at this stage is that both parties need to reach some agreement about the role of the external consultant/change agent.

In terms of friendliness and approachability, what many clients want is a helper who is, on the one hand, sympathetic to their needs and values but, on the other hand, is sufficiently neutral to offer objective comment, feedback and other assistance.

In terms of inferred motives, where clients feel that they can trust the consultant/change agent and believe that they are 'on their side' and are 'working for them' they will be more likely to share sensitive information and be receptive to feedback or suggestions about helpful processes, etc. However, where the change agent is seen as untrustworthy, incompetent or 'not for them' the clients will be much more likely to react defensively and resist any attempt to influence their thinking. The development of an appropriate helping relationship receives more detailed consideration in Chapters 24 and 25.

Developing a relationship with an external change agent can take time and sometimes clients test the helper's competence, attitudes, perceived role and trustworthiness by presenting them with what they regard as a safe or peripheral problem. If they are satisfied with the change agent's performance the client may move on to present what they believe to be the real problem.

Identifying the client

From the perspective of the change agent, an issue that must be managed carefully is the identification of the client. The person who invites an outsider into a situation may not be the person or group that ends up as the focal client. The change agent needs to be ready to amend the definition of the client if a preliminary diagnosis suggests that the problem is not confined to one group or unit, but involves multiple units, several levels of the hierarchy, or people outside the organisation, such as customers, suppliers, trade associations or unions.

Problems can arise when external change agents define the client as the person/group who invited them into the situation. If they are blind to the need to redefine who the client is they may end up, inadvertently, working to promote or protect a sectional interest rather that the effectiveness of the whole organisation.

One way of defining the client is in terms of the person (or persons) who 'owns' the problem and is responsible for doing something about it. Thus, for example, the client might be either the manager who seeks help to improve the effectiveness of his or her department, or the organisation as a whole. Cummings and Worley (2001) define the client as those organisational members who can directly impact the change issue, whether it is solving a particular problem or improving an already successful situation. This definition is more likely to identify the client as a group or the members of a sub-system rather than as an individual. Cummings and Worley specify the client in terms of all those who can directly impact on the change, because they argue that if key members of the client group are excluded from the entering and contracting process they may be reluctant to work with the change agent.

The author learned about this from direct experience. He was invited by the personnel director of an international oil company to help with a problem in a distant oil refinery. He was flown to the nearest major airport, put up in a hotel and, next morning, flown by a small plane to the refinery's own airstrip. Eventually he found himself in a meeting room in the refinery with all the senior managers. After some brief introductions the refinery manager started the meeting by asking the consultant why he was there. It was clear that the personnel director had not involved the refinery manager in the decision to engage an external consultant. This was strongly resented and by the time the consultant had arrived at the refinery there was little he could do to build an effective working relationship with the management team. However, some months later, the same refinery manager approached the consultant and invited him back to the refinery to work on a different problem. On this occasion it was his problem, and his decision to involve an outsider. The rejection first time round had nothing to do with the consultant's competence. The refinery manager had been very unhappy that somebody else had decided that he had a problem and that, without any consultation, had decided that he needed external help to resolve it.

Clarifying the issue

Reference has already been made to the possibility that the symptoms or problem presented may not be related to the issue that the client is most concerned about. There are other problems associated with deciding what the real issue is.

Those who seek help from consultants to resolve a problem often present the difficulty as somebody else's problem. The head of human relations (HR) of a manufacturing company invited the author to meet the finance director over lunch. The problem that the finance director (who was also the deputy chairman of the board) wanted to talk about was to do with the poor state of communications between the board and senior management. He defined the problem in terms of the quality of the senior managers. Eventually, after the consultant had met with the board, they redefined the problem as something to do with the board itself, about conflicting views regarding the board's role and political issues that affected how the board functioned.

Another issue is that problems are often presented to others in terms of implied solutions. For example, 'We need help to:

- improve the appraisal system
- build a more cohesive team
- improve communications.'

The communications problem might be further defined in terms of improving the communicating skills of certain individuals. However, a preliminary investigation may suggest that while communications are a problem, an important factor contributing to the problem is the structure of the organisation and the effect this has on communication networks. In such a situation, improving the communication skills of selected individuals or replacing existing members with others might do little to resolve the underlying structural problem.

Change agents need to keep an open mind about the nature of the problem until there has been some kind of preliminary investigation. However, it is important that the change agent pays careful attention to the felt needs of the client.

Exercise 6.2   Starting the change process

Think of an occasion when you acted as a change agent. It might have been at work or elsewhere (home, a club, etc.) and it might have involved an individual, group or larger system. Did it go smoothly from the start or did you hit problems initiating the change process?

If you did hit problems, did they relate to any of the issues considered in this chapter? Reflect on this experience and make a note of any learning points that might help you to avoid similar problems in the future.

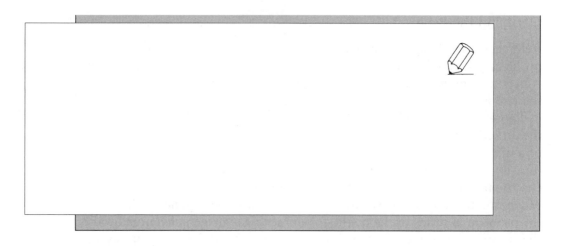

Summary

This chapter has considered some of the issues associated with starting the change process. These include recognising the need for change, translating this into a desire for change, deciding who will manage the change and, especially where an external consultant is introduced to help with this process, establishing a workable and effective change relationship. Associated issues for the change agent include being clear who the client is, and keeping an open mind about the precise nature of the problem while seeking to clarify the issues that are of concern to the client.

References

Chattopadhyay, P., Glick W-H., Miller, C.C. and Huber, G.P. (1999) 'Determinants of Executive Beliefs: Comparing Functional Conditioning and Social Influence', *Strategic Management Journal*, 20 (8), pp. 763–89.

Cohen, C. and Ebbesen, E. (1979) 'Observational Goal and Schema Activity: A Theoretical Framework for Behavior Perceptions', *Jurnal of Experimental and Social Psychology*, 15, pp. 305–29.

Cummings, T.G. and Worley, C.G. (2001) *Organization Development and Change*, 7th edn, Cincinnati, OH: West.

Nadler, D.A. and Shaw, R.B. (1995) 'Change Leadership: Core Competency for the Twenty-First Century', in D.A. Nadler, R.B. Shaw and A.E. Walton (eds), *Discontinuous Change: Leading Organisational Transformation*, San Francisco: Jossey-Bass, pp. 3–14.

Pitt, M., McAulay, L. and Sims, D. (2002) 'Promoting Strategic Change: "Playmaker" Roles in Organizational Agenda Formulation', *Strategic Change*, 11, pp. 155–72.

Pugh, D. (1993) 'Understanding and Managing Organisational Change', in C. Mabey and B. Mayon-White (eds), *Managing Change*, London: Paul Chapman in association with The Open University, pp. 108–12.

Werther, W.B. (2003) 'Strategic Change and Leader-Follower Alignment', *Organizational Dynamics*, 32 (1), pp. 32–45.

Diagnostic models

Chapters 7 and 8 are concerned with identifying *what* it is that needs to be changed in order to move towards a more desirable state and improve organisational effectiveness. The first part of this chapter examines the role of models in organisational diagnosis, and introduces an exercise designed to help raise your awareness of the implicit models you use when thinking about organisations and assessing the need for change. The second part presents a range of diagnostic models that are commonly used by consultants and managers. In the final section you are invited to compare your implicit model with some of the explicit models that are widely used by others. This will provide an opportunity to reassess the utility of your model and, if shortcomings are identified, to revise it.

The role of models in organisational diagnosis

Organisational behaviour, at all its different levels, is a very complex phenomenon. It is impossible for anyone to pay attention to, or understand the interactions between, all the many elements or variables that can have an effect on how an organisation functions. Consequently we simplify the real world by developing models that typically focus attention on:

- a limited number of *key elements* that are seen to offer a good representation of the real world
- the ways these elements interact with each other, sometimes referred to as *causal relationships* or laws of effect
- the *outputs* produced by these interactions.

Models that include explicit reference to outputs offer the possibility of evaluating performance and assessing effectiveness.

We all develop our own implicit theories or conceptual models about how organisations function, and we use these models to:

- guide the kind of information that we attend to
- interpret what we see
- decide how to act.

We develop these models on the basis of our personal experience, either as organisational members or external observers of organisational behaviour. Sometimes these models provide a good basis for understanding what is going on and predicting what kind of actions or interventions would produce desired change. Often, however, they are very subjective and biased, they over-emphasise some aspects of organisational functioning and completely neglect others. Consequently they do not always provide a useful guide for management practice and the management of change.

The aim of Exercise 7.1 is to help you develop a greater level of aware-ness of your own model of organisational functioning. This will help you assess whether your own personal model is consistent with or relevant to the problems or opportunities that you need to address. It will also help you compare you model with alternatives and modify it to improve its utility.

Making personal models more explicit can be of benefit to all of the people involved in managing a change. It can provide an opportunity for them to share their models, debate their relative merits and move towards the development of a collective model that can be used to provide a basis for joint diagnosis and concerted action.

Exercise 7.1   Raising awareness of your implicit model of organisational functioning

This exercise is based on a procedure for collaborative model building devised by Tichy and Hornstein (1980) and involves four steps. Step 1 requires you to prepare a short assessment of the current state of your organisation. Steps 2–4 involve reflecting on how you arrived at this assessment to tease out the main features of your implicit model of organisational functioning.

Step 1   Assess the current state of your organisation

Prepare a short note that describes your organisation (either the total organisa-tion or an important unit that you are familiar with) and assesses or diagnoses its current state. Make reference to the issues that you feel require attention. These issues might be problems or opportunities. If you feel that there is a need for some kind of change to ensure that these issues will be managed more effec-tively, justify this view.

Do *not* explain the kind of interventions that you think may be necessary to bring about any required changes. The aim of this exercise is to diagnose the *current state* of the organisation (and assess whether it is performing and will continue to perform, effectively), not to provide a prescription of actions required to improve matters.

Step 2   Identify the information you used to make this assessment

Think about the things that you considered when making your assessment in Step 1 of this exercise. Identify and list the 'bits of information' that you attended to. Focus on the information that you actually attended to. Try not to let the kind of information that you think you 'should' have considered influ-ence your list.

Identify, if possible, at least twenty-five different bits of information and record them in the space provided. Table 7.1 provides some examples of the bits of information that people might attend to when assessing the state of their organisation. These are offered only as examples to stimulate your thinking; your own list may not contain any of these.

Table 7.1   Examples of the kind of information that might be attended to when assessing the state of an organisation

Quality of boss–subordinate relationships	Production/operations systems	The way activities and staff are grouped together	Awareness of competitive threats
Effectiveness of co-ordinating mechanisms	Quality of communications	Level of commitment to the organisation	Training and staff development
Knowledge management	Reward systems	Costs	Inventory levels
Margins	Staff turnover	Customer satisfaction	Cash flows
The extent to which people feel challenged in their present jobs	Match between staff competencies and task requirements	Extent to which staff understand the central purpose of the organisation	Awareness of possible future sources of income/revenue
The way the business is financed	Attitudes towards quality assurance	The way conflicts are managed	Level of bureaucracy
Effectiveness of IT system	Number of levels in the hierarchy	Marketing procedures and policies	Management accounting systems

Step 3   Developing categories for organising your diagnostic information

Some of the bits of information that you used to make your assessment might be related and it might be possible to group them together into a number of more inclusive categories:

● Do this by grouping related bits of information into the category boxes provided below. (Typically people identify between four and twelve categories, but there are no restrictions on the number of categories you might identify.)
● When you have categorised your bits of information, describe the rationale you used for including information in each category.

These categories reflect the main elements or variables of your diagnostic model.

Category name	**Category name**
Items included in category:	Items included in category:
Briefly state rationale for including items in this category:	Briefly state rationale for including items in this category:

Category name	**Category name**
Items included in category:	Items included in category:
Briefly state rationale for including items in this category:	Briefly state rationale for including items in this category:

Category name	Category name	✎
Items included in category:	Items included in category:	
Briefly state rationale for including items in this category:	Briefly state rationale for including items in this category:	

Category name	Category name	✎
Items included in category:	Items included in category:	
Briefly state rationale for including items in this category:	Briefly state rationale for including items in this category:	

Use additional category boxes if required.

Step 4   Specifying relationships between categories/elements

The categories identified above reflect the elements of your implicit diagnostic model. Step 4 of the model-building process focuses on *interdependencies* and *causal relationships* between the elements. These can be identified by considering whether a change in any one element will have an effect on any other element:

- Using the format of Table 7.2, list the elements (categories) identified in Step 3 down the left-hand column and across the top of the table.
- Take each element down the left-hand column in turn and assess the impact a change in this element might have on every other element, using a three-point scale where 0 = no or slight impact; 1 = moderate impact; 2 = high impact.

Table 7.2   Interdependencies between elements

Elements: \ Effect of change on	1	2	3	4	5	6	7	8	9	10	11	12
1	–											
2		–										
3			–									
4				–								
5					–							
6						–						
7							–					
8								–				
9									–			
10										–		
11											–	
12												–

Note: Even though elements might be inter-related and affect each other, one element (e.g. **A**) can have a greater effect on another (e.g. **B**) than vice versa. This is illustrated in Table 7.3.

Table 7.3   An example of a matrix of interdependencies

Categories	A	B	C	D	E
A	–	2	1	0	2
B	1	–	1	0	0
C	0	1	–	0	1
D	0	0	1	–	2
E	2	0	1	2	–

Your implicit model can be represented diagrammatically:

- Draw a circle for each of the elements that you identified in Table 7.1.
- Label each circle with the name of the element it represents.
- Draw lines between those elements that have any impact on each other. Use a solid line to show a *strong* relationship between elements (with the arrow-head indicating the direction of a cause and effect relationship) and a dotted line to show a *moderate* link. (Do not join elements that have only a slight or no impact on each other.)

The model represented by Table 7.3 is presented diagrammatically in Figure 7.1.

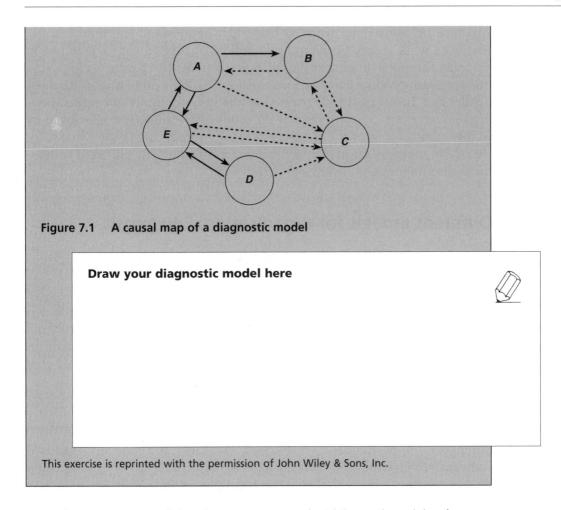

Figure 7.1   A causal map of a diagnostic model

Draw your diagnostic model here

This exercise is reprinted with the permission of John Wiley & Sons, Inc.

In the next section of this chapter a range of widely used models of organisational functioning is presented; you may wish to compare your own model with these alternatives.

Using models for diagnosis

Postma and Kok (1999) describe organisational diagnosis as a process of research into the functioning of an organisation that leads to recommendations for improvement. In practice, it is usually a multi-stage iterative process that begins with change managers using the kind of holistic model of organisational functioning elicited by Exercise 7.1 to look at the organisation as a whole before moving on to investigate particular aspects of organisational functioning in more detail. Sometimes, however, this process is reversed. Change managers focus their attention on specific components of organisational functioning (such as motivation, group processes, leadership, task design, information systems, organisational structure or culture) in order to help them understand the total picture. However, while it may be tempting to build a picture of what is going on in an organisation by looking at the various components separately, the picture this approach produces may be incomplete or in some other way misleading. Nadler and Tushman (1980) argue that 'the systems nature of organisations implies that there are properties of the whole that cannot be understood by simply adding together the component parts. Indeed, part of the dynamic of the whole concerns the nature of the interaction among the different components of organisational behavior' (1980: 262).

Different models for organisational diagnosis

In Chapter 2, reference was made to how organisations can be conceptualised from a number of different perspectives. Each of these emphasises different elements, different causal relationships and different definitions of effectiveness. In Chapter 3, a distinction was made between component models that provide insights into the functioning of components of an organisation, and models that provide an overview of the total system. In this section, all the models that are considered are holistic models that provide an overview of the total organisation.

The first set of models to be considered is primarily concerned with diagnosing the 'fit' between the organisation and its environment. Examples include PEST (Political, Economic, Social, Technological), SWOT (Strengths, Opportunities, Weaknesses, Threats) and Strebel's cycle of competitive behaviour. The second set is mainly concerned with diagnosing the organisation's internal alignment. Examples include Weisbord's six-box organisational model, and Pascale and Athos' 7S model. The third set is concerned with open-systems models that give greater attention to both internal and external alignment. Examples include Kotter's integrative model of organisational dynamics and Nadler and Tushman's congruence model of organisations (both considered in Chapter 3) and the Burke–Litwin causal model of organisational performance and change.

Diagnosing organisation–environment 'fit'

There are a number of models that focus on assessing the environment and how environmental changes might affect organisational performance.

PEST analysis

This approach can be used by managers to examine the organisation's environment and search for evidence of change that might signal a problem or opportunity. The mnemonic refers to Political, Economic, Socio-cultural and Technological factors.

Political factors include new legislation in areas such as environmental management, consumer protection and employment; regulation of markets in areas such as telecommunications and broadcasting; fiscal policies; and so forth. Organisations that operate in international markets need to be aware how legislative changes or changes in the level of political stability in different parts of the world might influence their operations.

Economic factors include issues such as exchange rates, cost of borrowing, change in levels of disposable income, cost of raw materials, and the trade cycle.

Socio-cultural factors include demographic trends such a fall in the birth rate or an ageing population. They also include shifting attitudes towards education, training, work and leisure which can have knock-on effects on the availability of trained labour, consumption patterns and so on. Cultural factors can also affect business ethics and the way business is done in different parts of the world.

Technological factors include issues such as the levels of investment competitors are making in research and development (R&D) and the outcome of this investment; the availability of new materials, products, production processes, means of distribution and so forth; the rate of obsolescence and the need to reinvest in plant and people.

SWOT analysis

This approach focuses on *S*trengths, *W*eaknesses, *O*pportunities and *T*hreats. In addition to assessing the opportunities and threats that a PEST analysis might reveal, it also includes an assessment of the organisation's strengths and weaknesses and its capability of responding to the threats and opportunities that confront it.

Strebel's (1996) evolutionary cycle of competitive behaviour

Strebel's model can be used to anticipate technological and economic changes in the environment and initiate planned organisational changes that will enable a company to remain one step ahead of the competition. Strebel posits that there is an evolutionary cycle of competitive behaviour and that different phases of the cycle are marked by break points. He also suggests that, given proper attention to competitive trends, these break points can be predicted in advance. The two phases of the cycle are innovation and efficiency.

The start of the innovative phase of the cycle (the bottom left of Figure 7.2) is characterised by a sharp increase in divergence and begins when an innovation by one competitor is seen to create a new business opportunity. This triggers others to innovate and gives rise to a greater variety in the offerings (products and services) available to customers. This process continues until there is little scope for further innovation that offers suppliers or customers much in the way of added value. At this point the divergence of

Figure 7.2   Strebel's cycle of competitive behaviour

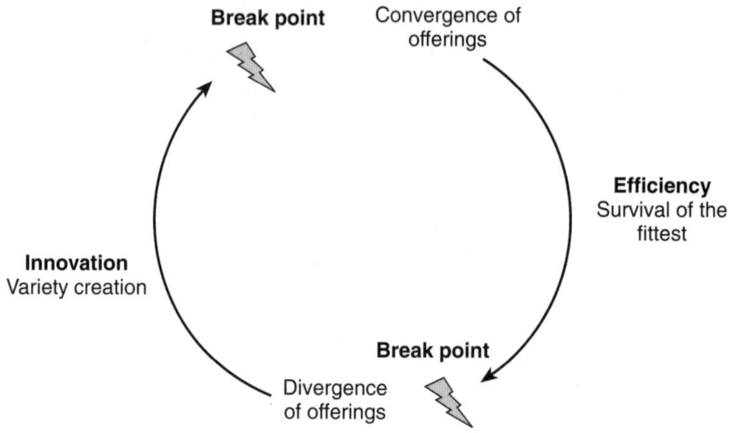

Source: Strebel, P., 'Breakpoint: How to Stay in the Game', *Mastering Management*, 1996, Part 17, *Financial Times*. Reprinted with permission of Pearson Education Ltd.

offerings begins to decline as the best features of past innovations are imitated by competitors.

The next phase of the cycle begins when one or more providers begin to turn their attention to efficiency rather than innovation: cost reduction is seen as the route to maintaining market share and increasing profit. They achieve this by improving systems and processes to reduce delivered cost. While each phase of the cycle can present opportunities for some, it can also pose threats for others. In the efficiency phase of the cycle only the fittest survive and inefficient competitors are driven out of business.

When most of the opportunities for gaining competitive advantage from improving efficiency have been exploited, attention might switch once again to innovation, and the cycle will repeat itself. Strebel (1996) suggests indicators that can be used to anticipate break-points. He also notes that convergence is usually easier to anticipate than divergence because it involves a move towards greater similarity in existing products and services, whereas divergence is based on potential new offerings and their existence might not be known until a competitor offers them to customers.

Diagnosing internal alignment

Two examples of models that are widely used to diagnose internal alignment are Pascale and Athos' 7S model and Weisbord's six-box organisational model.

Pascale and Athos' (1981) 7S model

This model highlights seven elements of organisations that are seen to make an important contribution to organisational effectiveness. While it considers strategy it does not make explicit reference to outcomes or to the external environment. The 7S framework points to a range of useful diagnostic questions, such as:

1 *Strategy* Purpose of the business; nature of the competition; relationship between espoused and actual strategy.
2 *Structure* Division of activities; integration and coordination mechanisms; nature of informal organisation.
3 *Systems* Formal procedures for measurement, reward and resource allocation; informal routines for communicating, resolving conflicts and so forth.
4 *Staff* Demographic, educational and attitudinal characteristics of organisation members.
5 *Style* Typical behaviour patterns of key groups such as managers and other professionals and of the organisation as a whole.
6 *Shared values* Core beliefs and values and how these influence the organisation's orientation to customers, employees, shareholders and society at large.
7 *Skills* The organisation's core competencies and distinctive capabilities.

Higgins (2005) has elaborated this model to provide senior managers with an 8S heuristic that, he suggests, offers a more effective basis for monitoring and assessing cross functional alignment.

Weisbord's (1978a) six-box model

Weisbord presents his systemic model as a 'practice theory' that synthesises knowledge and experience for change agents. It provides a conceptual map of six elements or boxes that can be used to apply any (component) theories to the assessment of these elements in a way that can reveal new connections and relationships between elements. It is an open-systems model that recognises the importance of organisation–environment relationships but focuses most attention on what needs to be done internally to ensure that the organisation becomes/remains a high-performance organisation able to adapt to external changes.

The six boxes are presented in Figure 7.3. Weisbord argues that the effectiveness of an organisation's functioning depends on what goes on *in and between* the six boxes. There are two aspects of each box that deserve attention: the *formal* and the *informal*. Weisbord argues that the formal aspects of an organisation (for example, stated goals or the structure as represented by an organisation chart) may bear little relation to what actually happens in practice. Attention needs to be given to the frequency with which people take certain actions in relation to how important these actions are for organisational performance. This leads to a consideration of why people do what they do, and what needs to be changed to promote more effective behaviour.

Figure 7.3   Weisbord's six-box model

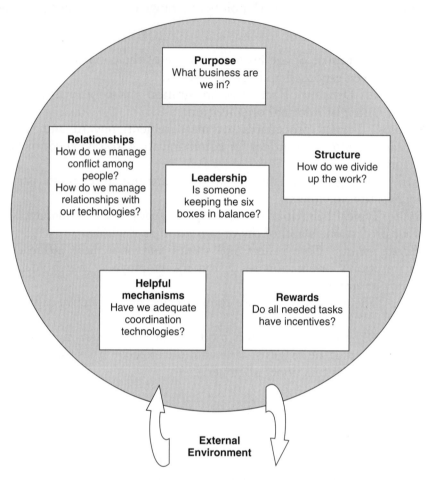

Source: Weisbord, M.R., *Organizational Diagnosis* (1978b: 9). Reprinted with permission of Sage Publications, Inc.

Leadership is seen to have a role to play in coordinating what goes on in the other five boxes.

Weisbord suggests that a useful starting point for any diagnostic exercise is to:

- focus on one major output (of a unit or the total organisation)
- explore the extent to which the producers and the consumers of the output are satisfied with it
- trace the reasons for any dissatisfaction to what is happening in or between the six boxes that represent the unit or organisation under consideration.

Models that attend to both internal and external alignment

Kotter's (1980) integrative model of organisational dynamics and Nadler and Tushman's (1980) congruence model of organisations have been the focus of attention in Chapter 3. Both will be summarised here, but most attention will be reserved for the Burke–Litwin causal model of organisational performance and change.

Kotter's (1980) integrative model of organisational dynamics

This model comprises seven elements, as summarised in Figure 7.4. A distinctive feature of this model, as noted in Chapter 3, is the important role played by the key organisational processes such as information gathering,

Figure 7.4   Kotter's integrative model of organisational dynamics

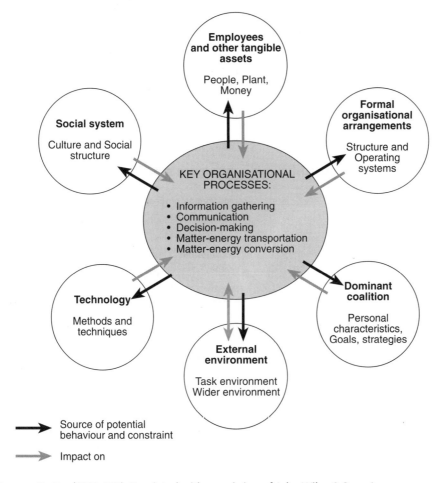

Source: Kotter (1980: 282). Reprinted with permission of John Wiley & Sons, Inc.

communication, decision making and matter–energy transformation. Another is that it offers three perspectives on effectiveness. *Short-run* effectiveness is determined by the quality of the processes and cause and effect relationships that link all the elements of the system together. Medium-term-effectiveness is influenced by the organisation's ability to sustain its short-term effectiveness. This is determined by the degree of alignment of its main elements. Longer-term-effectiveness is determined by the organisation's ability to adapt to internal and external changes.

Nadler and Tushman's (1980) congruence model

Nadler and Tushman's model conceptualises the organisation as a transformation process that takes inputs from the environment and transforms them into individual, group and organisational outputs. The transformation process includes four major elements: task, individuals, formal organisational arrangements and the informal organisation (see Chapter 3 for a more detailed description).

Effectiveness is determined by the degree of congruence (alignment) that exists between the organisation and its environment and between the four internal elements of the organisation. Strategy is presented as an input that manages the organisation's alignment with the wider world (see Figure 7.5). Congruence (alignment) is defined as the degree to which the needs, demands, goals, objectives and structures of any one element are consistent with the needs, demands, goals, objectives and structures of any other element.

Figure 7.5   Nadler and Tushman's congruence model

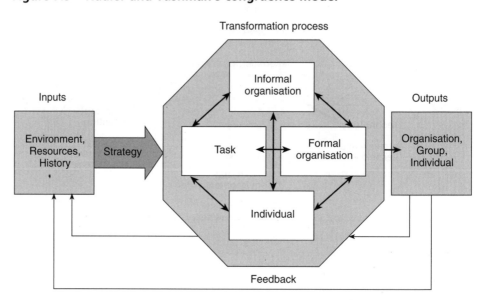

Source: Nadler and Tushman (1980: 274). Reprinted with permission of John Wiley & Sons, Inc.

PB 33   Barham

The Burke–Litwin (1992) causal model of organisational performance and change

This model points to causal linkages that determine the level of performance and affect the process of change. It also differentiates between two types of change: *transformational* change that occurs as a response to important shifts in the external environment, and *transactional* change that occurs in response to the need for more short-term incremental improvement. These features distinguish this model from the others considered in this section.

The model, illustrated in Figure 7.6, comprises twelve inter-related elements. It is an open-systems model in which the inputs are represented by the external environment element at the top of the figure, and the outputs by the individual and organisational performance element at the bottom. Feedback loops go in both directions: the organisation's performance affects its external environment and the external environment affects performance. The remaining ten elements represent the process of transforming inputs into outputs, and reflect different levels of this process. Strategy and culture, for example, reflect aspects of the whole organisational or total system. Work unit climate is an element associated with the local unit level, and motivation, individual needs and values, and the nature of tasks and individual roles are individual-level elements.

The model is presented vertically (rather than across the page from left to right, like the Nadler and Tushman, 1980, model) to reflect causal relationships and the relative impact of elements on each other. Burke and Litwin posit that those elements located higher in the model, such as mission and strategy, leadership and organisational culture, exert greater impact on other elements than vice versa. In other words, even though elements located lower down in the model can have some impact on those above them, position in the model reflects 'weight' or net causal impact.

This said, the model does not prescribe that change *should* always start with elements at the top of the model. It is a predictive rather than a prescriptive model. It specifies the nature of causal relationships and predicts the likely effect of changing certain elements rather than others. The decision about where to intervene first might be influenced by whether the aim is to secure transformational or transactional change. The model elaborates these two distinct sets of organisational dynamics. One is associated with organisational transformation and the need for a fundamental shift in values and behaviour, and the other is associated with behaviour at the more everyday level.

Transformational change is required when an organisation has to respond to the kind of environmental discontinuities that were considered in Chapter 1. This kind of change involves a paradigm shift, and completely new behaviours. Instead of changes designed to help the organisation do things better (incremental change) the organisation needs to do things differently or do different things. As noted in Chapter 4, this calls for the

Figure 7.6   The Burke–Litwin causal model of organisational performance and change

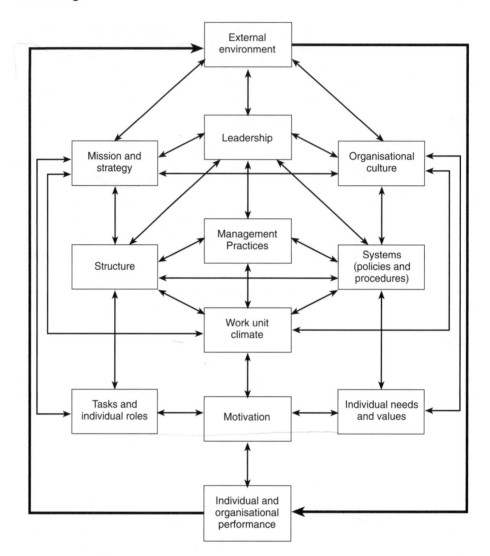

Source: Burke, W.W. and Litwin, G.H., 'A Causal Model of Organizational Performance and Change', *Journal of Management* (1992: 528). Reprinted with permission of Elsevier Science, Inc.

principles, assumptions and values that underpin the implicit and the explicit rules that guide behaviour to be revised. It involves a change in the organisation's culture. It also calls for a change in the organisation's mission and strategy, and for managers especially, but not only senior managers, to provide a lead and to behave in ways that clarify the new strategy and encourage others to act in ways that will support it. Where the need is for this kind of change, attention needs to be focused on the transformational elements highlighted in Figure 7.7.

Figure 7.7   The transformational factors

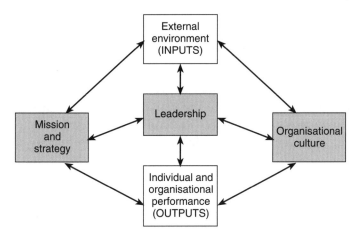

Source: Adapted from Burke and Litwin (1992: 523).

Transactional change is associated with 'fine tuning', with how the organisation functions within the existing paradigm. It emphasises single- rather than double-loop learning, as in the model of organisational learning discussed in Chapter 4 (see Figure 4.1, p. 61). The focus of attention needs to be the structures, management practices and systems that affect the work climate, which in turn impact on motivation and performance (at both the unit and the individual level).

Interventions designed to bring about organisational transformation that target 'higher-level' elements in the model will eventually and inevitably have an impact on all other elements in the system because of their weight and relative impact. If, however, the target of interventions is primarily the elements in the lower part of the model, aimed at achieving what Burke and Litwin refer to as 'transactional change', the impact is more likely to remain at local unit level. Interventions targeted at this type of element may have relatively little, if any, impact on overall organisational culture and strategy. Burke and Litwin (1992) also present an impressive (if selective) summary of studies that provides empirical support for the causal linkages hypothesised by their model.

Revising your personal model of organisational functioning

The previous section has presented a brief summary of some widely used models of organisational functioning and has identified some of the main differences between them. You are advised to develop a 'healthy scepticism' towards the utility of different models and to constantly reassess which is most appropriate for the purpose at hand.

Characteristics of a good model

All the models considered above are simplifications of the real world. None is guaranteed to accommodate all circumstances and provide a reliable basis for understanding why things are the way they are, or identify actions that can be taken to produce a desired outcome. Depending on circumstances and purpose, some theories or models may have greater utility than others.

The three characteristics of 'good' diagnostic models are that they:

- are relevant to the particular issues under consideration
- help change agents recognise cause and effect relationships
- focus on elements that they can influence.

Points to consider when refining your own model

When identifying a model that you might use to guide your diagnosis and planning you might usefully reflect on two points:

- How do the available models relate to your *personal experience*? For example, to what extent do the models considered above (or other models that you are aware of) accommodate or ignore elements and causal relationships that your experience has led you to believe are important? It might be unwise to slavishly apply a model that ignores aspects of organisational functioning that your own experience tells you are significant.
- Do any of the available models include elements and/or relationships that you have never previously considered but which, on reflection, might help you make better sense of your own experience? You need to be alert to the danger of *rejecting alternative models* too hastily. You may find that a model that is quite different from your own personal model can provide useful new insights. Even if you decide not to adopt an alternative model in its entirety, you may decide to incorporate some aspects of it into your own model.

Giving proper consideration to these issues can prompt you to refine and improve your own personal model of organisational functioning. Before moving on to Chapter 8, you might find it useful to reflect on the model you articulated in Exercise 7.1 (p. 108).

The Site Security and Secure Escorts case (Case study 7.1) illustrates how a change manager's subjective model of organisational functioning provided a basis for developing a better understanding of the organisation and identifying targets for change.

Case study 7.1 Site Security and Secure Escorts

This case illustrates a 'funnel' approach to diagnosis which began with a newly appointed CEO using his own model of organisational functioning to diagnose 'the big picture' and then moving on to use component models to develop a better understanding of particular issues.

Site Security and Secure Escorts (SSSE) is a company wholly owned by (what will be referred to here as) CP Security Services. The parent company provides a wide range of security services in the UK and abroad, including risk assessment and management; site security and secure escort services; cash transit and high-value courier services; detention centres and prison escorts; and technical security systems. SSSE provides manned guard and secure escort services across a range of sectors including pharmaceuticals, financial services, telecommunications, defence and utilities to provide protection from theft, vandalism, industrial espionage, terrorism and attacks from radical activists motivated by issues such as animal rights. A new CEO was appointed to SSSE in April 2005 and tasked to grow the business and improve profitability.

His first task was to familiarize himself with the current state of affairs and to identify what could be done to improve the situation. He spent a lot of time out of his office meeting people. He had almost daily conversations with most managers at head office and, with his director of operations, visited clients and met with SSSE staff working on client's premises. His aim, using conversations, observations and management reports, was to identify key issues and begin to formulate an agenda for change. He did not embark on this process with a 'clean sheet'. When he joined SSSE he brought with him his own subjective model of how organisations work and the key cause and effect relationships that determine effectiveness (see Figure 7.8) and used this to direct his attention and interpret what he saw, heard and read about the organisation.

Figure 7.8 The CEO's model of causal relationships affecting the performance of SSSE

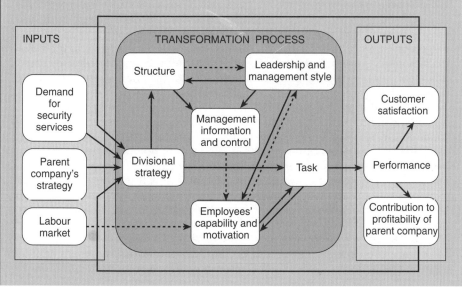

He quickly realized that a number of clients were unhappy with the quality of service provided by SSSE. This not only threatened to undermine his plan to grow the business and increase margins but also raised the possibility that SSSE would lose existing business as and when contracts came up for renewal. His initial diagnosis (informed by the model presented in Figure 7.8) pointed to several factors that appeared to be contributing to this state of affairs:

- *Staff shortages* Following 9/11 and the aggressive tactics employed by some animal rights activists there had been a sharp increase in the demand for site security. This was accompanied by a related demand for new recruits to be more thoroughly vetted. This was a time-consuming process that reduced supply just when the demand for new staff was growing.
- *Management style* The company's management style was 'top-down' command and control. While this had been effective in the past when management could easily impose sanctions for poor performance, it was proving less effective in the current tight labour market. There was evidence that it was having a negative impact on motivation and some employees were paying less attention to performance standards and were ignoring operating procedures because they were confident, given the rising demand for staff, that they would not be dismissed.
- *Management structure* The number of supervisors had not increased in line with the number of new contracts. Consequently supervisors were over-stretched. This situation was exacerbated because, in order to fulfil immediate contractual requirements for guards and escorts, supervisors had to stand in and personally cover for staff shortages.
- *Ineffective management information systems* Decision making was highly centralized but inadequately supported by the quality of available management information. For example, managers located at headquarters (HQ) did not have access to up-to-date information on operations, making it very difficult for them to schedule work effectively.

This assessment was shared and debated with other senior managers and produced a number of suggestions for improvement. One of these was to explore ways of improving the performance of existing staff. The operations director and a site supervisor conducted two focus groups with guards and escorts drawn from several sites. While the guards and escorts raised different points specific to their roles a number of common themes emerged. For example, both groups indicated that most of their job was boring and lacked any meaningful challenge, and some remarks hinted that when not directly supervised they read newspapers or did puzzles rather than give full attention to their duties. They also felt under-valued. They realized that there was a growing demand for personnel who had the level of security clearance required by SSSE's clients, but they felt that this 'scarcity factor' was not reflected by their rates of pay. These finding prompted a more detailed diagnosis of the roles people were required to perform with a view to redesigning their jobs in ways that would improve their motivation and the quality of their work. Managers were introduced to Hackman and Oldham's (1980) job characteristics theory and used the Job Diagnostic Survey to gather more information.

Another suggestion for improvement was to take a detailed look at the way the organisation was structured and to consider alternatives that might address some of the issues uncovered by the initial diagnosis. A consultant was brought in to facilitate a workshop on organisation design. This led the senior management team to explore the possible impact of introducing team working on client sites, with self-managed teams being delegated responsibility for monitoring their own performance as well as executing the task. Hackman's book on *Leading Teams* (2002) guided much of this work.

Diagnosis is not a one-off activity: it is on-going and often begins with a review of the total system. The use of component models to investigate specific aspects of organisational functioning elaborates and helps to build a richer picture of the organisation as a whole, and because this 'big picture' exists it is possible to align efforts to improve particular aspects of organisational performance. For example, in the SSSE case there were obvious opportunities for synergy between the redesign of jobs and efforts to restructure the organisation that involved the introduction of team working. Both of these initiatives also had implications for the development of new management information systems, and so on.

Summary

This chapter has:

- Examined the role of models in organisational diagnosis
- Presented an exercise designed to help you raise awareness of your implicit model of organisational functioning
- Provided an overview of some widely used diagnostic models that you can use as a bench-mark when assessing the validity and utility of the model you currently use
- Suggested some guidelines for revising your current model or selecting an alternative that might improve the quality of your diagnosis.

Chapter 8 examines some of the issues that you need to consider when deciding how to collect information for diagnosis.

References

Burke, W.W. and Litwin, G.H. (1992) 'A Causal Model of Organizational Performance and Change', *Journal of Management*, 18 (3), pp. 523–45.

Hackman, J.R. (2002) *Leading Teams*, Boston, MA: Harvard School Press.

Hackman, J.R. and Oldham, G.R. (1980) *Work Redesign*, Reading, MA: Addison-Wesley.

Higgins, J.M. (2005) 'The Eight "S's" of Successful Strategy Implementation', *Journal of Change Management*, 5 (1), pp. 3–13.

Kotter, J.P. (1980) 'An Integrative Model of Organizational Dynamics', in E.E. Lawler, D.A Nadler and C. Cammann (eds), *Organizational Assessment*, New York: Wiley, pp. 279–99.

Nadler, D.A. and Tushman, M.L. (1980) 'A Congruence Model for Organisational Assessment', in E.E. Lawler, D.A. Nadler and C. Cammann, *Organizational Assessment*, New York: Wiley, pp. 261–78.

Pascale, R. and Athos, A. (1981) *The Art of Japanese Management*, New York: Warner Books.

Postma, T. and Kok, R. (1999) 'Organizational Diagnosis in Practice: A Cross-Classification Analysis Using the DEL-Technique', *European Management Journal*, 17 (6), pp. 584–97.

Strebel, P. (1996) 'Breakpoint: How to Stay in the Game', *Mastering Management*, Part 17, London: *Financial Times*.

Tichy, N.M and Hornstein, H.A. (1980) 'Collaborative Organisation Model Building', in E.E. Lawler, D.A. Nadler and C. Cammann, *Organizational Assessment*, Chichester: Wiley, pp. 300–16.

Weisbord, M.R. (1978a) 'Organisation Diagnosis: Six Places to Look for Trouble With or Without a Theory', *Group and Organization Studies*, December, pp. 430–47.

Weisbord, M.R. (1978b) *Organizational Diagnosis*, Reading, MA: Addison-Wesley.

Gathering and interpreting information for diagnosis

Diagnosing the need for change involves a process of gathering, analysing and interpreting information about individual, group and organisational functioning. The five main steps in this process are:

1 Selecting a conceptual model for diagnosis.
2 Clarifying information requirements.
3 Information gathering.
4 Analysis.
5 Interpretation.

In those circumstances where the information is collected by an internal or external change agent working on behalf of a client group the information will need to be feed back to the other organisational members who will be involved in the diagnosis. This often occurs after those who have collected the data have completed a preliminary analysis but before the information has been interpreted.

Selecting a diagnostic model

It was noted in Chapter 7 that organisational behaviour, at all its different levels, is a very complex phenomenon and that it is impossible for managers to pay attention to every aspect of organisational functioning. We cope with this complexity, sometimes unconsciously, by developing or adopting conceptual models that simplify the real world and focus attention on a limited number of elements and relationships. Some of the explicit models of organisational functioning that are available to change agents relate to how the organisation functions as a total system. Others (component models) focus on selected elements of the overall system, such as leadership, structure, job design, competencies, etc.). A range of total system models was considered in Chapter 7 and most good texts on organisational behaviour critically review a wide range of component models.

Conceptual models play a key role in the diagnostic process because they help us decide which aspects of organisational behaviour require attention and they provide a focus for information gathering. They also provide a basis for interpreting the information that has been collected.

When selecting a model for diagnosis the obvious first point that has to be considered is the extent to which the model is relevant to the issue(s) under consideration – for example, loss of market share, dysfunctional inter-group conflict, high labour turnover, etc.

An effective model is one that identifies specific elements and/or cause and effect relationships that contribute to the problem or opportunity, and indicates which of these have most weight (or effect) on other aspects of organisational functioning and performance. Evidence, from personal experience or published research, about the ability of a conceptual model to explain and predict cause and effect relationships can help the change manager select an appropriate model for diagnosis. However, the ultimate aim of organisational diagnosis is more than improving our understanding of why something is the way that it is. It also involves using this understanding to plan action to improve organisation effectiveness.

Consequently, if a diagnostic model is to have any practical utility, it needs to highlight aspects of organisational functioning that, either directly or indirectly, the change manager can do something about.

Clarifying information requirements

Exercise 7.1 invited you to think about the information you would use in order to diagnose the current state of your organisation. This information was then categorised and used to help you make explicit your personal model of organisational functioning.

This process can be reversed. When a diagnostic model has been selected, the change manager can identify the items of information that will be required to assess how an organisation (unit or group) is performing and to distinguish what is going well and what is going not so well.

In Chapter 7 the Burke–Litwin causal model of organisational performance was presented. The twelve elements of the model are defined in Table 8.1,

Table 8.1   Examples of questions asked in a 1993 BBC staff survey

Elements	Indicative questions
External environment Any outside condition or situation that influences the performance of the organisation, these conditions include such things as market-places, world financial conditions, political/governmental circumstances, etc.	Regarding the pace of change, what would you say the organisation as a whole is experiencing (from static to very rapid change)?
Mission/strategy What organisational members believe is the central purpose of the organisation and how the organisation intends to achieve that purpose over an extended time	How widely accepted are the organisation's goals among employees?

Elements	Indicative questions
Leadership Executive behaviour that encourages others to take needed actions	To what extent do senior managers make an effort to keep in touch with employees at your level in the organisation?
Culture 'The way things are done around here.' The collection of overt and covert rules, values and principles that guide behaviour and that have been strongly influenced by history, custom and practice	To what extent are the standard ways of operating in the organisation difficult to change?
Structure The arrangements of functions and people into specific areas and levels of responsibility, decision making authority, and relationships	To what extent is the organisation's structure clear to everyone?
Management practices/action What managers do in the normal course of events to use human and material resources to carry out the organisation's strategy	To what extent does your manager communicate in an open and direct manner?
Systems Standardised policies and mechanisms that facilitate work; they typically manifest themselves in the organisation's reward systems and in control systems such as goal and budget development and HR development	To what extent are the following communication mechanisms in the organisation effective (e.g. grapevine)?
Climate The collective current impressions, expectations, and feelings of the members of local work units, these affect members' relations with supervisors, with one another and with other units	Where you work in the organisation, to what extent is there trust and mutual respect among employees?
Task requirements and individual skills The behaviour required for task effectiveness, including specific skills and knowledge required for people to accomplish the work assigned and for which they feel directly responsible (often referred to as the job–person match)	How challenged do you feel in your present job?
Motivation Aroused behavioural tendencies to move towards goals, take needed action and persist until satisfaction is attained.	To what extent do you feel encouraged to reach higher levels and standards of performance in your work?
Individual needs and values The specific psychological factors that provide desire and worth for individual actions and thoughts	(From disagree strongly to agree strongly) I have a job that matters
Performance The outcomes or results, with indicators of effort and achievement. Examples include productivity, customer or staff satisfaction, profit, and service quality.	To what extent is the organisation currently achieving the highest level of employee performance of which they are capable?

together with examples of the kind of question that might be used to elicit information about each element. The examples are taken from an instrument used in a diagnostic exercise in the BBC. The survey instrument included a minimum of four questions relating to each element of the model. Respondents were invited to respond to the questions on a five-point scale.

Information gathering

This stage of the process begins with a series of planning decisions relating to which methods of data collection to employ and whether data can/should be collected from every possible source or from a representative sample of the total population of sources.

Method for collecting information

There are a number of different techniques or methods that can be used to collect information. They include individual and group interviews, questionnaires, projective methods such as drawings and collages, observation and the use of secondary data, sometimes referred to as 'unobtrusive measures'. Cummings and Worley (2001) provide a useful discussion of most of these methods. Only their main features are summarised in this chapter.

Interviews

Individual and group interviews are a rich source of information about what is going on in an organisation. People can be asked to *describe* aspects of the organisation and how it functions, and they can also be asked to make *judgements* about how effectively the organisation, or an aspect of it, functions and how they feel about this (their *affective reaction*). For example, after describing how the appraisal system operates in an organisation, some employees might judge it to be ineffective but indicate that they are quite happy about this because the ineffective system works to their personal advantage.

Individual interviews have some added advantages. Respondents might be persuaded to share private views that they may be reluctant to express in a more open forum. The interaction between interviewer and respondent can offer the possibility that respondents might be stimulated to articulate and make explicit vague feelings and views that they had not previously formulated at a conscious level.

Interviews are adaptive. If respondents raise issues that the interviewer had not anticipated the interview schedule can be modified to allow these emerging issues to be explored in more detail. The interview also offers the opportunity for the interviewer/change agent to build rapport and develop trust with respondents and motivate them to develop a constructive attitude towards the change programme.

Interaction between respondents in a group interview can generate information that might not be forthcoming in an individual interview. For example, if individuals from different units or levels in the organisation express different views, these differences might promote a useful discussion of why the conflicting perceptions exist and what problems or opportunities they might point to.

There are, however, a number of potential problems associated with using the interview to collect information:

- Interviews can be very time-consuming and costly, although group interviews are less so than individual interviews.
- Coding and interpreting responses can be a problem, especially when interviews are unstructured. Coding and interpretation can be simplified by adopting a more structured approach, asking all respondents the same set of predetermined questions and limiting the use of open-ended questions. However, the gains from adopting a more structured approach need to be balanced against the potential loss of rich data that can be gleaned from a more unstructured conversation – for example where the interviewer leads off with some general open-ended questions and then follows the respondent's chain of thought.
- Bias is another problem that can arise from the way interviewers organise the order of topics to be covered and from the way they formulate questions. Especial care needs to be taken to avoid the use of leading questions that signal to the respondent that there is a desired response.

Questionnaires

These are sometimes referred to as 'self-administered interviews'. They are designed to obtain information by asking organisational members (and others) a predetermined set of questions about their perceptions, judgements and feelings. Using questionnaires to collect diagnostic information can be more cost-effective than using interviews because they can be administered simultaneously to large numbers of people without the need to employ expensive interviewers. They can also be designed around fixed-response-type questions that ease the burden of analysis.

However, they do have a number of disadvantages:

- They are non-empathic. When using questionnaires to collect information it can be difficult for change managers to build rapport and communicate empathy with respondents. This can have an adverse effect on respondents' motivation to give full and honest answers to the questions asked.
- Questionnaires are also much less adaptive than interviews. Interviewers can modify their approach in response to the interviewee's reaction to

questions and can explore unanticipated issues. The format of the questionnaire, on the other hand, has to be decided in advance. Problems can arise because respondents fail to understand or mis-interpret the meaning of questions. Important questions may also be omitted, a problem that is difficult to resolve once the questionnaire has been administered.

● Another problem is self-report bias. Questionnaires (like interviews) collect information from people who may, either deliberately or otherwise, bias their response. Responses to questions are based on the respondents' perceptions of what is going on. These perceptions may be based on incomplete or false information. There is also a tendency for respondents to present their own behaviour in the most positive light and to protect their own interests. The design of the questionnaire can also bias responses. For example, people may fall into a pattern of answering co-located questions in a similar manner or their attention may wander and they may take less care when answering questions towards the end of the questionnaire.

Projective methods

Methods such as drawings and collages can be a useful way of collecting information about issues that people may find difficult to express in other ways. Fordyce and Weil (1983) suggest that by asking sub-groups to (a) prepare a collage around themes such as 'how do you feel about this team?' or ' what is happening to the organisation?' and (b) to present and explain it to the total group in a plenary session, organisational members can be helped to express and explore issues at a fairly deep and personal level. A similar procedure is to invite individuals to prepare and share drawings that show certain aspects of organisational life. For example, individuals might be asked to draw a circle for each member of their group, making the circles larger or smaller depending on the influence they have over the way the group works. They may also be asked to elaborate their drawing by locating the circles for different members of the group in terms of how closely they need to work together to get the job done. A further elaboration might be to ask them to join the circles with blue lines where the people they represent have a personally close relationship and with red lines if they are far apart in terms of communication, rapport and empathy.

These kinds of approaches to surfacing information can be good icebreakers and can provide an easy route to the discussion of sensitive issues that are rarely discussed openly. However, while they may be well received by some groups, others may reject them as childish games.

Observations

Observing behaviour as it occurs is one approach to collecting information that avoids self-report bias. One of the key issues associated with this

approach is deciding how the observation can be organised to focus attention on required behaviour and avoid being distracted or swamped by irrelevant information. When collecting information about behaviour in a group
setting, for example, the degree of structure for observing and recording can
vary from using broad categories such as leadership or communication to
the use of detailed category sets such as the Interaction Process Analysis
framework developed by Bales (1950):

- An advantage of this approach to information collection is that the
  observer may recognise patterns of behaviour that those being observed
  may be unaware of and, therefore, are unable to report in interviews or
  in their responses to questionnaires.
- Another advantage is that observations relate to current behaviour and
  are less likely than self-reports to be contaminated by historical factors.
- Observation is also an adaptive approach to collecting information.
  What is observed might cue the observer to explore connected aspects of
  current practice.
- Some of the disadvantages of this approach include problems associated
  with coding and interpretation, cost and possible observer bias.

Unobtrusive measures

In many organisational settings there are large amounts of information that
are collected as a normal part of day-to-day operations. This can relate to
various aspects of organisational functioning such as costs, down-time,
wastage rates, absenteeism, labour turnover, delivery times, margins,
complaints, number and type of meetings, etc. This kind of information is
referred to as 'unobtrusive' because the fact that it is being collected for
diagnosis is unlikely to prompt any specific response bias. It is also likely to
be readily accepted by organisational members and, because of the nature of
many of the records that contain this kind of information, it may be easy to
quantify.

However, even when records are maintained, it may be difficult to access
information in the required form. For example, information about individuals, such as the outcome of performance appraisals, increments awarded,
absenteeism and sickness rates may all be contained in each individuals'
personal record but may not be available in any aggregate form for all
members of a particular department.

Sampling

Sometimes – for example, when collecting information from members of a
relatively small work group – it may be possible to include every member of
the group in the survey. However, when a diagnostic exercise involves
collecting information about a whole department, or the total organisation,

it may be necessary to consider ways of sampling people, activities and records in a way that will provide sufficient information to provide a representative picture of what is going on.

Important issues that need to be considered when drawing a sample relate to sample size (relative to the total population), and composition. For example, how many people should be interviewed, events observed or records inspected, and which individuals, events or records should be included in the sample? The answer to the size or 'how many' question depends on the degree of confidence in the findings that is required and, if the information is to be subjected to statistical analysis, the type of analysis that is to be used. The answer to the composition or 'which' question depends on the complexity of the total population. If the total population is relatively homogeneous the selection of members to be included in the sample might be done on a random basis, using random number tables, or by selecting every nth member of the total population. If, however, the total population contains different sub-groups it might be important to ensure that all of them are represented in the sample. This involves segregating the total population into a number of mutually exclusive sub-populations and drawing a sample from each. The composite sample that results from this process is referred to as a 'stratified sample'.

Analysis

Once information has been collected, it needs to be analysed. For example, in response to a question such as 'How challenged do you feel in your present job?' only some of those surveyed might have offered a positive response. The change agent may want to know what proportion of the sample responded in this way compared to those who responded in the same way in other organisations in order to be able to assess whether lack of challenging work is a problem. It might also be useful to consider whether there is any relationship between those who do not feel challenged and the unit they work in or their level in the hierarchy. Analytical procedures organise information in ways that can provide answers to diagnostic questions.

Analytical techniques are often classified as qualitative or quantitative.

Qualitative techniques

These tend to be more concerned with meaning and underlying patterns than with scientific tests. Cummings and Worley (2001) refer to content analysis and force-field analysis as two qualitative analytical techniques that are frequently used in organisational diagnostic exercises:

● *Content analysis* attempts to summarise respondents' comments into meaningful categories. This involves identifying the comments or answers that tend to recur most frequently and grouping them in ways that provide a set of mutually exclusive and exhaustive categories or themes. For example, in response to a question such as 'What do you like best about your work?' a number of responses might refer to working with friendly colleagues, considerate supervisors and having the opportunity to communicate with co-workers while doing the job. All of these comments might be regarded as referring to a common theme, the *social aspects* of the job. A different set of comments might refer to the degree of challenge offered by the work, the opportunity to be creative and the freedom to experiment with new methods. All of these comments might be regarded as referring to different aspects of the *nature of the work itself*. These two categories might then used as a basis for analysing the content of all the information collected from respondents. When a category set is exhaustive it is possible to allocate every response to a category, and when it is mutually exclusive each item of information will fall into one particular category. After all responses have been classified, one way of determining the importance of the different categories is to identify those that have been referred to most often.

NUDist is a software tool that can be used for coding and analysing qualitative data, and provides a relatively easy method of comparing the responses from different respondents to particular questions.

- *Force-field analysis*, based on Lewin's (1951) three-step model of change discussed in Chapter 5 (on process models of change), also involves categorising information. The distinctive feature of force-field analysis, however, is that it involves organising the categories into two broad types; those relating to forces or pressures *for change* and those relating to forces or pressures supporting the (problematic) *status quo and resisting change*.

It was noted in Chapter 5 that Lewin viewed the level of behaviour in any situation as the result of a force field comprising a balance of the forces pushing for change (for some different level of behaviour) and the forces resisting that change. Diagnosing situations in terms of 'driving' and 'restraining' forces can provide a useful basis for developing action plans to secure desired change. When the forces pushing in one direction exceed the forces pushing in the opposite direction the dynamic equilibrium changes. The level of behaviour can be changed towards a more desirable state by increasing the strength of forces for change in the desired direction (increasing the driving forces) or by diminishing the strength of restraining forces (Figure 8.1).

Exercise 8.2, at the end of this chapter, provides a step-by-step approach that you can use to apply force-field analysis to an opportunity development or problem management issue that you might have to deal with.

Figure 8.1   A force-field

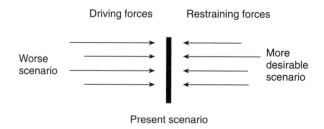

Present scenario

Quantitative techniques

Some of the very basic techniques most frequently used by change agents when analysing quantitative information are means, standard deviations, correlation coefficients and difference tests. The mean is a measure that indicates the average response or behaviour. For example, over the last year, the eight employees in department X might have averaged five days' sick leave. The standard deviation indicates the extent to which there is high or low variation around this mean, for example six members of the department may have had no sick leave whereas the other two may have had twenty days each. Correlation coefficients measure the strength of the relationship between variables – for example sick leave might be inversely related to job satisfaction. Difference tests indicate whether the scores achieved by one group (for example, an average of five days' sick leave for members of department X) are significantly different from those achieved by members of other groups (different departments in the same organisation or some bench mark score or industry norm). More details on these and other techniques can be found in any standard text on statistics.

Interpretation

Conceptual models provide a basis for interpreting diagnostic information and identifying what needs to be changed to achieve a more desirable state of affairs. The results of the 1993 staff survey in the BBC, which was designed around the Burke–Litwin causal model of organisational performance (see Figure 7.6, p. 122), indicated some priorities for change. The elements most in need of change were structure, leadership and factors affecting motivation, but there was also evidence that there was scope for improvement in many other areas. A very brief summary of the results of this survey is presented in Figure 8.2.

Figure 8.2 Results of the 1993 BBC staff survey

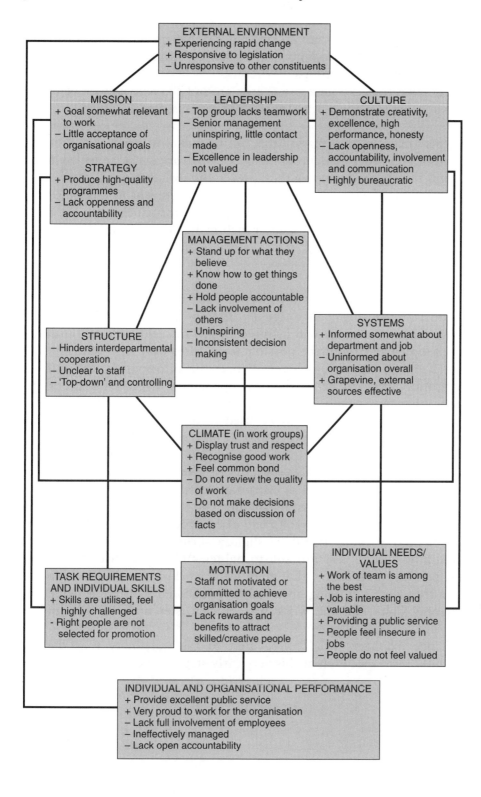

Political considerations

Collecting information is not an innocuous or benign activity. Nadler (1977) argues that the collection and distribution of information can change the nature of power relationships.

Data collection can generate energy around the activities or behaviours that are being measured, for a number of reasons. For example:

- It may result in information that an individual or group has previously withheld in order to secure some political advantage being widely distributed, thereby undermining their power and influence.
- It opens up the possibility of comparing the current performance of an individual or group with their own past performance, with the performance of others or with some bench-mark. These possibilities may be perceived as threatening, especially where there is a link between performance and rewards.

The energy generated by data collection can be directed towards assisting or undermining the change agent's attempt to diagnose the need for change. How the energy will be directed will be influenced by the perceptions people have about the possible future uses that may be made of the data. If, for example, employees expect the information collected in a diagnostic survey to be used in an open, non-threatening and helpful manner they may be motivated to provide accurate information. If, on the other hand, they expect it to be used in a punitive manner they may attempt to withhold or distort data. This point is illustrated in a case reported by Porter, Lawler and Hackman (1987). They refer to a group of employees who worked together to assemble complicated large steel frameworks. Their method of working varied depending on whether or not they were being observed by anyone who might influence the rate they were paid for the job. The group had discovered that by tightening certain bolts first, the frame would be slightly sprung and all the other bolts would bind and be very difficult to tighten. When they used this method they gave the impression that they were working hard all of the time. When they were not being observed they followed a different sequence of tightening bolts and the work was much easier and the job could be completed in less time.

Change managers need to be alert to the possibility that they will encounter resistance even at this very early stage in the change process.

Exercise 8.1   Evaluating your use of diagnostic information

Think about a recent occasion when you (or somebody working close to you) have attempted to introduce and manage a change in your part of the organisation:

1   Reflect on the extent to which this change initiative was based on an accurate diagnosis of the need for change.
2   Consider to what extent this was related to:
    ● The appropriateness of the (implicit or explicit) diagnostic model used
    ● The nature of the information collected
    ● The way in which it was interpreted.
3   Reflect on what steps *you* might take to help improve the quality of the way the need for change is diagnosed in your unit or department.

Notes

Summary

This chapter has examined the process of gathering and interpreting information for the purpose of diagnosis. Attention has been focused on five main steps:

1   Selection of an appropriate conceptual model for diagnosis.
2   Clarification of information requirements.
3   Information gathering.
4   Analysis.
5   Interpretation.

Attention has also been drawn to the political issues associated with data collection that can frustrate attempts to gain an accurate impression of organisational functioning.

Exercise 8.2   A force-field approach to opportunity development or problem management

1 Think about a problem you have to manage or an opportunity you could develop in terms of what a more desirable scenario would look like. Use this as a basis for identifying a concrete goal you wish to achieve, and write it in the box down the right-hand side of the page.

   (An alternative might be to apply force-field analysis to Case study 9.2 presented in Chapter 9).

2 List the driving forces that are pushing towards the more desirable scenario down the left-hand side of the page. Down the right-hand side list the restraining forces which are blocking the achievement of your goal.

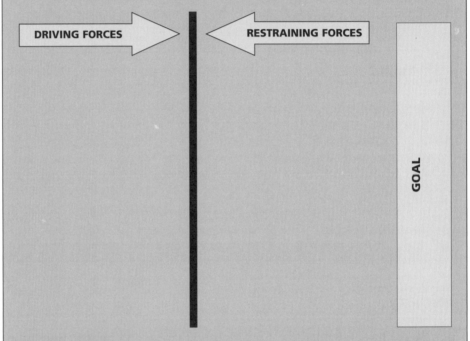

3 Review your list of driving and restraining forces and highlight those that are both powerful (in terms of either pushing for or resisting change) and manageable (i.e. you anticipate that you will be able to affect the power of the force).

DRIVING FORCES   Review each of the driving forces that you have highlighted (starting with the most important) and brainstorm all the steps you could take to *increase* the effect of the force. Do not confine yourself to 'sensible' ideas. List everything that comes to mind.

DRIVING FORCE . . . .
Brainstorm action steps to *increase* the effect of this force

DRIVING FORCE . . . .
Brainstorm action steps to *increase* the effect of this force

DRIVING FORCE . . . .
Brainstorm action steps to *increase* the effect of this force

DRIVING FORCE . . . .
Brainstorm action steps to *increase* the effect of this force

DRIVING FORCE . . . .
Brainstorm action steps to *increase* the effect of this force

*Do not evaluate any of these action steps until you have brainstormed action
steps to reduce the effect of the restraining forces.*

RESTRAINING FORCES   Now do the same for the most important restraining
forces, but this time brainstorm all the steps you could take to *reduce* the effect
of each restraining force.

RESTRAINING FORCE . . . .
Brainstorm the steps you could take to *reduce* the effect of this force

RESTRAINING FORCE . . . .
Brainstorm the steps you could take to *reduce* the effect of this force

RESTRAINING FORCE . . . .
Brainstorm the steps you could take to *reduce* the effect of this force

RESTRAINING FORCE . . . .
Brainstorm the steps you could take to *reduce* the effect of this force

RESTRAINING FORCE . . . .
Brainstorm the steps you could take to *reduce* the effect of this force

Now review *all* the action steps:

1   Eliminate those action steps that are totally impractical (but only after you are sure that they cannot be 'tweaked' or adapted to provide a useful contribution).
2   Identify the 'best of the rest'. Consider whether some action steps can contribute to the strengthening of more than one driving force or the erosion of more than one restraining force. An alternative approach to distilling the most useful action steps is to group similar actions together and identify those from each group that seem most practical.
3   Finally, list those action steps that deserve serious consideration below.

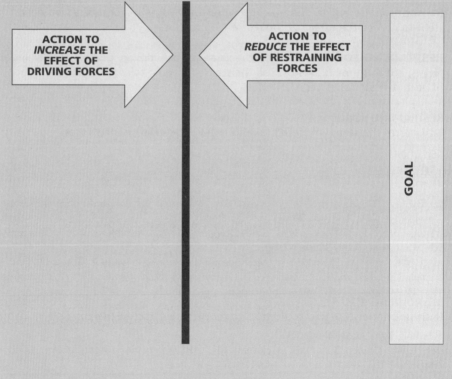

ACTION TO *INCREASE* THE EFFECT OF DRIVING FORCES

ACTION TO *REDUCE* THE EFFECT OF RESTRAINING FORCES

GOAL

The final step involves re-evaluating the action steps from a cost–benefit perspective. The plan has to be practical and some of the proposed action steps may be too expensive in terms of time or other resources. It may be necessary to amend the plan at this stage in order to improve its viability. However it may also be necessary to include new elements to mould individual action steps into an integrated plan. Give some thought to time scale and milestones against which progress can be assessed. Milestones are important because they provide early warning if the plan is not working and signal the need for renewed effort or the implementation of contingency plans.

Summary of action plan

Action plans that are only concerned with increasing the effect of driving forces may be less effective than plans that include reducing the effect of restraining forces. If restraining forces are weakened the balance of the remaining forces may push the situation towards the desired scenario.

An example of how a change agent can use force-field analysis is presented in Chapter 25.

References

Bales, R.F. (1950) *Interaction Process Analysis: A Method for the Study of Small Groups*, Cambridge, MA: Addison-Wesley.

Cummings, T.G. and Worley, C.G. (2001) *Organisational Development and Change*, 7th edn, Cincinnati, OH: South Western.

Fordyce, J.K. and Weil, R. (1983) 'Methods for Finding Out what is Going On', in W. French, C.H. Bell and R. Zawacki (eds), *Organisation Development: Theory, Practice and Research*, Plano, TX: Business Publications, pp. 124–32.

Lewin, K. (1951) *Field Theory in Social Science*, New York: Harper & Row.

Nadler, D. (1977) *Feedback and Organization Development: Using Data-based Methods*, Reading, MA: Addison-Wesley.

Porter, L.W., Lawler, E.E. and Hackman, J.R. (1987) *Behavior Organizations*, London: McGraw-Hill.

Managing the people issues

It was noted in Chapter 5 that there are a number of issues that have to be attended to throughout the change process. These are considered in Chapters 9–14.

Chapter 9   Power, politics and stakeholder management

This chapter explores the politics of organisational change and the need to enlist the support of key stakeholders. An instrumental theory of stakeholder management is elaborated with reference to resource dependence theory, prospect theory and lifecycle models. It provides a conceptual framework for identifying which stakeholders are likely to be most important at various stages of a change project and for selecting appropriate ways of managing relationships with different types of stakeholders. After completing an exercise designed to help you explore some of the issues involved in stakeholder management, you will be invited to think about a recent change in your organisation and, with the advantage of hindsight:

- identify the stakeholders involved in the change
- classify them according to their power to influence and their attitude towards the change
- assess the extent to which the change manager was aware of these stakeholders and took proper account of them when managing the change.

Chapter 10   The role of leadership in change management

This chapter examines the role of leadership in change management. Special attention is given to the leader's role in terms of creating a vision, aligning relationships around the vision and inspiring others to achieve the vision. Leadership is also considered as a collective process and some of the issues associated with maintaining coherence in the leadership group and between the group and internal and external stakeholders are reviewed. The chapter closes with a review of Kotter's eight-point checklist of what leaders can do to promote change and an invitation to test the validity of this list in relation to the way change managers have behaved in your organisation when leading change.

Chapter 11   Communicating change

This chapter considers the role of communication in the management of change. Often the focus is exclusively on the 'what, when, who and how' of communicating from the perspective of the change manager communicating to others. In this chapter, attention is also given to issues associated with change managers perceiving, interpreting and using information communicated to them by others.

After studying this chapter you will be invited to consider how the quality of communication has helped or hindered change in your organisation.

Chapter 12   Training and development

Organisational change is typically associated with some degree of individual change. Often this individual change is the outcome of an informal and natural process of learning and development. However, there may be occasions when those responsible for managing an organisational change decide that some form of deliberate training intervention is required in order to help individuals develop new knowledge, skills, attitudes and behaviours. Such interventions can be highly structured and very focused on the achievement of closely specified outcomes, or they can be designed to help organisational members learn how to learn and encourage them to actively involve themselves in a self-directed process of professional development.

This chapter considers the main elements of an effective training strategy and how training can contribute to the successful implementation of a change plan.

After reading this chapter, you will be invited to critically assess the way training has been used in your organisation to help achieve organisational change.

Chapter 13   Motivating others to change

This chapter considers how the general level of commitment in an organisation can affect the level of support for change, and identifies some of the most common sources of resistance to change. The utility of expectancy theory for assessing and managing resistance to change is explored.

The second half of the chapter involves an exercise designed to help you use expectancy and equity theory to motivate others to change.

Chapter 14   Managing personal transitions

This chapter addresses the way organisational members experience change. It examines the response to change (irrespective of whether the change is viewed as an opportunity or a threat) as a progression through a number of stages of psychological reaction. It also considers how an understanding of the way individuals react to change can help managers plan and implement organisational change in ways that will maximise benefit and minimise cost for both the organisation and those affected by the change.

Before reading this chapter, you will be invited to reflect on how you reacted to a change that was lasting in its effects, took place over a relatively short period of time and affected a number of key assumptions that you made about how you related to the world around you. The information generated by this exercise will be used to validate a generic stage model of transition.

Overview

These six 'people issues' are considered at this point for convenience. While they must be attended to when developing, implementing and managing a change programme (the focus of Parts IV, V and VI), they are also relevant at the very early stages of the change process. For example, at the start of the process, only some of the constituencies that have a stake in the future of the organisation may have been involved in (a) recognising the need for change and (b) undertaking a preliminary diagnosis.

At some point, decisions will have to be made about whether and when to involve others in the diagnostic and visioning process. Related decisions will include which others to involve and how to involve them. Associated with this issue of stakeholder management is the development of a communications strategy. It may not be possible to keep the likelihood of change secret. Consequently, even in the early stages of the process (well before the details of an implementation strategy have been worked out) it may be necessary to decide who is to be told what, and when they should be told.

Those involved in managing the early stages of the change process may also require some training in diagnostic methods or they may need to participate in a team-building exercise to ensure that they can work effectively as a change management group. It is also possible that some of those who become involved in the early stages of the process may be hostile to the prospect of change and attention may need to be given to how they can be motivated to make a constructive contribution. Even when people support the change they may experience problems 'letting go' of the status quo and they need some help to cope with the process of transition.

Part VII of the book deals with people management issues, change agent skills and the development and maintenance of a helping relationship between the change agent and the client system.

Power, politics and stakeholder management

This chapter explores the politics of organisational change and considers the role of stakeholder management in change management.

When thinking about managing change, some people assume that organisations are well-integrated entities within which everybody works harmoniously together. Some also believe that decisions are made logically and rationally, that people share similar views of the world around them and that they act to promote the interests of the organisation as a whole. This is rarely the case.

Organisations as political arenas

In Chapter 2, organisations were conceptualised as a collection of internal (and external) constituencies, each pursuing their own objectives. This view presents organisations as *political arenas* within which individuals and groups attempt to influence each other in the pursuit of self-interest. Those who adopt this political perspective argue that when there is a conflict of interest it is the power and influence of the individuals and groups involved that determine the outcome of the decision process, not logic and rational argument. This perspective submits that those responsible for managing change cannot afford to ignore issues of power and influence.

Nadler (1987) argues that political behaviour tends to be more intense in times of change because individuals and groups perceive the possibility of upsetting the existing balance of power. Some may be motivated to defend the status quo whereas others may perceive change as an opportunity to improve their position (see McNulty, 2003). Pettigrew (1972) also argues that some may engage in political action for ideological reasons, especially when they fear that a change may be inconsistent with their values.

Change managers need to be alert to these political dynamics, and especially to the possibility that others may be motivate to act in ways that undermine their efforts to bring about change. These others may not only resist change because they feel threatened by the anticipated future state, but also because they feel threatened by the processes used to secure change. For example, some organisational members may be very concerned that the collection of information for diagnosis could weaken their position because they may be asked to disclose information that they had previously protected in order to secure some political advantage (this point is discussed in Chapter 8).

Given that different constituents or stakeholders are likely to act in ways that maximise their power and their ability to secure preferred outcomes, change managers need to be alert to the identity of important stakeholders and to their predisposition to either support or resist the change.

Power

McClelland (1975) defines power as the ability to change the behaviour of others. It is the ability to cause others to perform actions that they might not otherwise perform.

Power and authority

Those in authority are those who are seen to have a legitimate right to influence others, but power is not always legitimate. Sometimes individuals and groups who do not have legitimate authority are able to exercise considerable influence and may even have more power than legitimately appointed managers. Change managers need to ensure that they do not overlook or ignore powerful individuals or groups just because they do not have any formal authority to influence a proposed change.

Exercise 9.1   Consider the following questions:

- Who are the most powerful people/units in your organisation?
- Why? What is the basis of their power?

Sources of power

Power acquisition is not just a matter of chance or personality. McCall (1979) argues that it is possible to predict where power will reside in an organisation. He suggests that power accrues from position, timing, resources and past actions. The constituencies or stakeholder groups that are most powerful are those that:

- are in a position to deal with important problems facing the organisation
- have control over significant resources valued by others
- are lucky or skilled enough to bring problems and resources together at the same time
- are centrally connected in the work flow of the organisation
- are not easily replaced
- have successfully used power in the past.

In order to ensure the successful introduction of change it is essential that change managers secure the assistance of powerful stakeholders and build a critical mass of support for the change.

Stakeholders

Freedman (1984) defines a stakeholder as any individual or group who can affect, or is affected by, the achievement of the organisation's objectives. Clarkson (1995), in the context of evaluating corporate performance, widened the traditional definition to include the government and the communities that provide infrastructure and markets (whose laws must be obeyed, and to whom taxes and other obligations may be due) as well as traditional stakeholder groups such as employees, shareholders, investors, customers and suppliers. Stakeholders other than employees can exercise considerable influence over the outcome of many strategic change initiatives, but often the success of a project is highly dependent on support from other organisational members. Several examples illustrate this point.

McNulty and Ferlie (2002) attribute the lack of success of a project to change the care process for patients in the accident and emergency (A&E) department of large UK hospital to the change agents' failure to generate sufficient support for the change from senior doctors and nurses. Clinical staff viewed the attempt to introduce change as interference from 'outside' by people who lacked adequate experience and understanding of the work of the department. They were suspicious of the change agents' objectives, and believed that the project failed to address the core problems of the department and was more concerned with achieving cost savings rather than improving the services provided to patients. McNulty and Ferlie also report that A&E doctors viewed the process-based philosophy behind the initiative as a threat both to the established function of the A&E department in the broader context of the hospital and to the roles of doctors within the department.

In a large manufacturing company a change was blocked by a senior manager who was not immediately involved in any of the departments directly affected by the change but was pursuing a separate agenda that was inconsistent with the proposed change. The proposal was to drive down costs by centralising procurement in order to gain economies of scale. It had many supporters but the senior manager who opposed it favoured the company adopting a more decentralised structure.

While internal stakeholders can exercise considerable influence, external stakeholders can also be very important. Local residents in a UK city were offended (to the point of rioting in the streets) when a large leisure company decided to re-brand its bingo halls 'Mecca Bingo'. The problem arose because the company failed to recognise the impact of demographic changes which resulted in many of its bingo halls being located in neighbourhoods that had predominantly Islamic populations. Another example involved the Bank of Scotland when some customers (including the West Lothian Council with a £250 million account) threatening to close their accounts in protest at the Bank's proposed joint business venture with US evangelist Pat Robertson. Customers were unhappy with the proposal after he proclaimed that Scotland was a 'dark land' and a stronghold of homosexuality. These examples illustrate the point that it is not always easy to identify all the individuals and groups who may be affected by a change or who have the power to influence the outcome of the change.

Which stakeholders should be taken into account by change managers?

Jones and Wicks (1999) identify two divergent theoretical positions regarding stakeholder management.

Normative theories

According to normative or ethics-based theories of stakeholder management the interests of all stakeholders have intrinsic value and should be taken into account when formulating strategy and planning and implementing change. Berman et al. (1999) note that ethics-based theories hold that many stakeholders' claims are based on fundamental moral principles unrelated to the stakeholders' instrumental value to the organisation. Those who subscribe to normative theories argue that moral commitments should provide the basis for managing stakeholder relationships rather than the desire to use stakeholders to promote managerial interests.

Instrumental theories

The basic premise of instrumental theories is that managers will attend to the interests of stakeholders only to the extent that those stakeholders can affect their interests. They posit that managers are selective in who they attend to and are not motivated by a concern for the welfare of stakeholders in general. Managerial interests vary, and may range from parochial concerns such as status or the end-of-year bonus, to more strategic concerns such as market place success and organisational survival. In most formulations of the instrumental approach, however, managerial interests are equated with the firm's financial performance and the satisfaction of shareholders. Schein (1996) refers to a tacit set of assumptions that CEOs and their immediate subordinates appear to share world-wide:

> This executive worldview is built around the necessity to maintain an organization's financial health and is preoccupied with boards, investors, and capital markets. Executives may have other preoccupations but they cannot get away from having to worry about the financial survival and growth of their organisation. (1996: 15)

At lower levels in the organisation, however, many managers may be more concerned with managing relationships with different stakeholders who can have a more immediate impact on the performance of their department.

Implicit in the instrumental perspective is the assumption that change managers will abandon modes of dealing with stakeholders that prove to be unproductive. Berman *et al.* (1999) argue that while a firm might try to improve sales by adopting a TQM approach that involves investing considerable effort in improving relationships with workers and suppliers, it might reassess its commitment to this strategy if it fails to deliver results. Similarly, an organisation might adopt an employee share ownership scheme in the hope that it will motivate organisational members to work more effectively, but might abandon the scheme if it has little effect on performance.

The instrumental approach to stakeholder management is highly pragmatic. In the context of change management, regardless of the purpose of the change, it dictates that the change manager will focus attention on those relationships that will affect the success of the change.

A lifecycle approach to stakeholder management

Jawahare and McLaughlin (2001) offer an approach to managing stakeholders that draws on resource-dependence theory, prospect theory and organisational lifecycle models. The underlying premise is that an organisation faces different pressures and threats at different stages in its lifecycle. Consequently, over time, certain stakeholders will become more important than others because of their ability to satisfy critical organisational needs.

Jawahare and McLaughlin's theory identifies which stakeholders will be important at different stages in the organisational lifecycle and indicates how the organisation will attempt to deal with each of its primary stakeholders at every stage. Although Jawahare and McLaughlin focused their attention on stakeholder management at different stages of an organisation's lifecycle, their theory offers many insights into the management of stakeholders at different stages of the lifecycle of specific change projects within this broader context.

The contribution of resource-dependence theory

Resource-dependence theory conceptualises the organisation as being dependent on the resources in its environment for survival and growth. Jawahare and McLaughlin extend this theory to stakeholder management and propose that organisations will pay most attention to those stakeholder groups who control resources critical to the organisation's survival. The different levels of attention that they devote to different groups of stakeholders are manifest in the form of different stakeholder management strategies. Others (Carroll, 1979; Clarkson, 1995) have identified these strategies as:

- *proaction* – doing a great deal to address stakeholder issues
- *accommodation* – a less active approach for dealing with stakeholder issues
- *defence* – doing only the legally minimum required to address stakeholder issues
- *reaction* – ignoring or refusing to address stakeholder issues.

The contribution of prospect theory

Prospect theory posits that, relative to whatever reference point is used to evaluate an outcome (which might be the current position or a level of benefit that an individual hopes to achieve), outcomes that are evaluated as losses are weighted more heavily than similar amounts of outcome that are evaluated as gains. Central to prospect theory is the notion that actual (objective) and psychological (subjective) values attributed to an outcome can and do differ. Kahneman and Tversky (1979) argue that the relationship between the actual and psychological value of an option can be depicted by an 'S-shaped' value function that is concave in the domain of gains and convex in the domain of losses. Bazerman (2001) illustrates the effect of this relationship by suggesting that the pain associated with losing $1,000 is generally perceived to be greater than the pleasure associated with winning a similar amount. Kahneman and Tversky hypothesised that individuals will be risk- seeking in the loss domain and risk averse in the gain domain, and that their choice between 'certain' (no risk) and risky options will depend on whether the outcome of the choice is framed in positive terms (e.g. jobs *saved*) or negative terms (e.g. jobs *lost*).

Table 9.1 Positive frame

Plan A		Plan B
'Certain' (no-risk) outcome *Selected by the majority*		High-risk outcome
Save one of three plants and 2,000 (of 6,000) jobs	*versus*	1/3 chance of saving all three plants and all 6,000 jobs, but 2/3 chance of saving no plants and no jobs

Table 9.2 Negative frame

Plan C		Plan D
'Certain' (no-risk) outcome		High-risk outcome *Selected by the majority*
Lose two of the three plants and 4,000 jobs	*versus*	2/3 chance of losing all three plants and all 6,000 jobs, but 1/3 chance of losing no plants and no jobs

Bazerman (2001) provides an example of how this might work in practice. He describes a plant closure problem. When managers are presented with a positively framed version of the problem the majority select plan A, the option with the 'certain' outcome (tinted area in Table 9.1).

However, when managers are presented with a negatively framed version of the same problem the majority select plan D, which is the risky option (tinted area in Table 9.2).

Both sets of alternative plans are *objectively* the same. Plan A (saving one of three plants and 2,000 of 6,000 jobs) offers the same objective outcome as plan C (losing two of the three plants and 4,000 of the 6,000 jobs), and plan B offers the same objective outcome as plan D.

Jawahare and McLaughlin point to the essence of prospect theory. 'in the context of gains, individuals will be risk averse and choose the option with a certain outcome over a risky option, whereas in the context of losses, individuals will be risk seeking and choose the risky option over the option with a certain outcome' (2001: 404). They go on to argue that addressing the concerns of all stakeholders in a proactive or accommodating manner is a 'certain' or risk averse option because it is likely to persuade all stakeholders to provide the organisation with the resources it requires for survival and prosperity. However, using strategies of proaction and accommodation to address the concerns of only some stakeholders and using the strategies of defence and reaction to respond to others is a more 'risky' option.

Based on these contributions from resource-dependence theory and prospect theory Jawahare and McLaughlin take the first step towards the development of their descriptive stakeholder theory, by proposing two theorems:

1 In the absence of threats to organisational survival, a gain frame will be adopted, and the organisation will follow a risk averse strategy and actively address *all* stakeholder issues.

2 In the presence of threats to organisational survival, a loss frame will be adopted, and the organisation will pursue a risky strategy that involves addressing the concerns of only those stakeholders who are relevant to the immediate loss threat, while at the same time defending or denying any responsibility for the concerns of other stakeholders. For example, if a firm is in danger of being forced into administration, senior managers might do everything possible to address the concerns of creditors while giving little attention to the concerns of employees.

The contribution of organisational lifecycle models

Most organisational lifecycle models point to four overlapping phases in the life of an organisation: start-up, emerging growth, maturity, and decline/revival. The pressures, threats and opportunities, internal as well as external, that confront firms vary with the stages of the organisational lifecycle. Consequently the resources required by the firm will also vary with lifecycle stage.

Jawahare and McLaughlin argue that if, at any stage in the organisational (or change project) lifecycle, the fulfilment of critical resource requirements is threatened, organisational decision makers will adopt a loss frame and interact with those stakeholders who control the critical resources in a proactive or accommodative manner and with other stakeholders in a defensive or reactive manner. In those stages where the flow of resources is not threatened, decision makers are likely to adopt a gain frame, pursue a risk averse strategy and actively address the concerns of all stakeholders.

Jawahare and McLaughlin's stakeholder theory

Drawing on organisational lifecycle, resource-dependence and prospect theories, Jawahare and McLaughlin argue that:

1 At any given lifecycle stage certain stakeholders become more important than others because of their potential to satisfy critical organisational needs.

2 It is possible to identify which stakeholders are likely to be more or less important at each stage of the lifecycle.

3 The strategy that will be used to deal with each stakeholder will depend on the importance of that stakeholder relative to other stakeholders.

This stakeholder theory is based on the premise that organisations have finite resources and at times they are in short supply. Consequently, managers have to decide how best to allocate them in order to manage stakeholders in the most effective way possible. Jawahare and McLaughlin's theory suggests that different individuals and groups might need to be the focus of the change managers' attention at different points in the lifecycle of a particular change project. Change managers must not assume that if they engage in the kind of stakeholder analysis suggested below they will have identified, once and for all, the key constituents who require attention. Power relationships and the ability of various individuals and groups to influence events will change over time and therefore it may be necessary to review and manage stakeholder relationships on a continuing basis.

Managing stakeholders

Grundy (1998), building on the key player matrix developed by Piercy (1989), suggests a useful approach for managing stakeholder relationships. The first part of the process involves a stakeholder analysis to identify important stakeholders and appraise their power to influence and their attitude towards the proposed change. The second part involves developing a strategy for persuading influential stakeholders to support the change.

Case study 9.1   Hospital merger: stakeholder brainstorm

Familiarise yourself with this departmental merger case and list all the individuals and groups who can affect or might be affected by the outcome of the change.

You are the recently appointed HR director of a newly merged Acute Hospital Trust in West Yorkshire. You have been in post four weeks. The new Trust has been formed from the merger of two co-located Hospitals (*A* and *B*). The new Chief Executive (CEO) was appointed five months ago. He was previously CEO of *B*. You moved to your post from elsewhere in the Health Service.

You were the last of the directors to be appointed. The Board is in place but, as yet, the structure of the new Trust has not been finalised. The two parts of the new Trust continue to operate much as they did before the merger. However, the CEO feels that the HR and Finance functions need to be reorganised as quickly as possible. He also expects that the HR and Finance functions will help facilitate the merger of other parts of the new Trust.

You have been tasked with merging the HR departments of the two former Hospitals and achieving an annual saving of £100k on the HR budget.

It is obvious that the HR staff have very high expectations about what you will deliver. Almost everybody wants the merger of the two departments to be completed quickly, but with minimum disruption to the status quo.

There are important differences in the culture and structure of the two original Hospitals and these differences are reflected in the way their HR departments operate. A potential problem is that the staff in both HR departments (and line managers in their respective former Hospitals) appear to be very happy with the way things are operating at present and would like their way of working to be the template for the new merged department.

The members of staff who work in the two HR departments are located in hospitals that are approximately fifteen miles apart. Irrespective whether the way forward will involve bringing all staff together, the staff working in what was Hospital *B* will have to move (even if only to a new location on their present site) because their existing accommodation has been reallocated. Your impression is that people will be reluctant to move between sites.

Some of the main differences between the two original Hospitals are shown in Table 9.3:

Table 9.3   Differences between original Hospitals

Hospital *A*	Hospital *B*
Decentralised structure, two big and largely autonomous directorates (surgery and medicine) each with its own operational director	Centralised structure, many small departments led by general managers who report direct to the CEO
Fragmented culture, medical staff and managers are separate groups	Collaborative culture, medical staff and managers work very closely together
The HR department is only responsible for personnel information and employee relations, training and development is located under Nursing	All the HR functions, including training and development are centralised within one department
The HR department employs a small group of staff who tend to stay within their own department and act as professional advisors to the operational managers, operational managers are responsible for much of the HR management within their own departments	The HR department is 'staff rich', HR staff work very closely with operational managers, accompany them to meetings, take notes for them and assume responsibility for much of the day-to-day HR activity
Line managers hold personnel files in operational departments	HR holds personnel files centrally

You recognise that it may be necessary to slim down the HR establishment if you are to achieve the £100k cost savings.

Additional issues that might influence your approach to managing this change are:

1   The two former heads of the HR functions (who are still leading the two departments) have very different philosophies about the nature of HR.
2   Since the two Hospitals were merged there has been a rapid rise in the number of grievances registered by staff across the new Trust, especially from staff required to work alongside colleagues from different former Hospitals. Most of these grievances relate to the differences in terms and conditions that apply across the new Hospital. For example, there are differences in the

protection agreements that safeguard an individual's pay and conditions when their work is regraded and there are differences in holiday entitlements that lead to problems when members of the two former Hospitals start working together. This has had a marked effect on the day-to-day workload of sections of your staff.

3 Managers across the new Hospital are seeking help from HR on issues related to the merger. This presents you with two related issues. First, it adds to the HR workload problem. At a time when HR needs to allocate resources to managing its own internal merger it has to respond to new demands from client departments. Second, managers across the new Hospital, depending on where they worked previously, have different expectations regarding the support HR should provide.

You are required to develop a plan to bring together the two HR departments in order to:

● create a new HR function that will promote excellent HR practice and
● deliver efficiency gains of £100k p.a.

Task: brainstorm a list of stakeholders

Identifying the power and commitment of stakeholders

The first part of Grundy's process involves three steps:

1 He refers to the first step as the 'stakeholder brainstorm'. It involves identifying all those who might be affected by and/or could affect the outcome of the proposed change.

2 The second step involves assessing how much power and influence each group of stakeholders has. This can be quite difficult in practice:

(a) There may be people with little influence over organisational issues in general but who have considerable influence over a particular issue related to the change

(b) There may be individuals who express support for the change but who cannot be relied on because their supportive efforts are undermined by other people in their departments

(c) There may be people who have exercised little influence in the past but who have more power than anticipated or who have recently acquired the ability to influence others.

3 The third step involves assessing stakeholders' attitudes towards the proposed change. Again, this can be difficult. For example:

(a) There may be individuals or groups who appear to support the proposal in public but who work against it behind the scenes

(b) There may be others who misunderstand the proposed change but who would be supportive if they were better informed.

Attitudes can range from positive, through neutral to negative. Shaw and Maletz (1995) describe those who proactively work to prevent the change effort from succeeding as 'blockers', and those who proactively work to ensure that it succeeds as 'sponsors'.

The two dimensions of 'attitude' and 'power' are brought together in the stakeholder grid presented in Figure 9.1.

Case study 9.2   Hospital merger: stakeholder mapping

Developing the merger case presented in Case Study 9.1, imagine that your initial vision for the new HR function is one where:

- There will be a core group of HR professionals working on strategic HR issues. Most day-to-day operational matters will be devolved to line managers. The HR department will work on operational issues only where there are clear benefits from providing a centralised service. These benefits could be cost savings or service quality.
- Training and development will be moved from Nursing to HR, but some delivery – especially the day-to-day aspects of work-based training – will be based in operational departments.
- The HR function will be restructured. Instead of the two existing departments (based on the former Hospitals) each providing a full range of services, work will be reallocated into two broad portfolios and will be managed on a new Trust-wide basis. You (the new HR director) will manage one of these portfolios and the other will be managed by one of the heads of the two former HR departments.
- While you feel that it necessary for HR to have a 'presence' on each of the two major sites, you feel that on one of the sites this should be limited to a small number of staff who will work alongside line mangers as advisors.
- You want to co-locate most staff on a single site but you feel that this might be easier to achieve if everybody moved to a new location on one of the

existing sites in order to avoid the feeling that one of the former departments has been 'taken over' by the other.

Before you begin to test out this vision with others, or start to develop a plan to move from the current situation to your vision for the HR function, think about others who may have a stake in the change and how they might react.

Locate all the stakeholders who can affect or might be affected by the outcome of the change on to the stakeholder grid presented below

Figure 9.1   Stakeholder grid

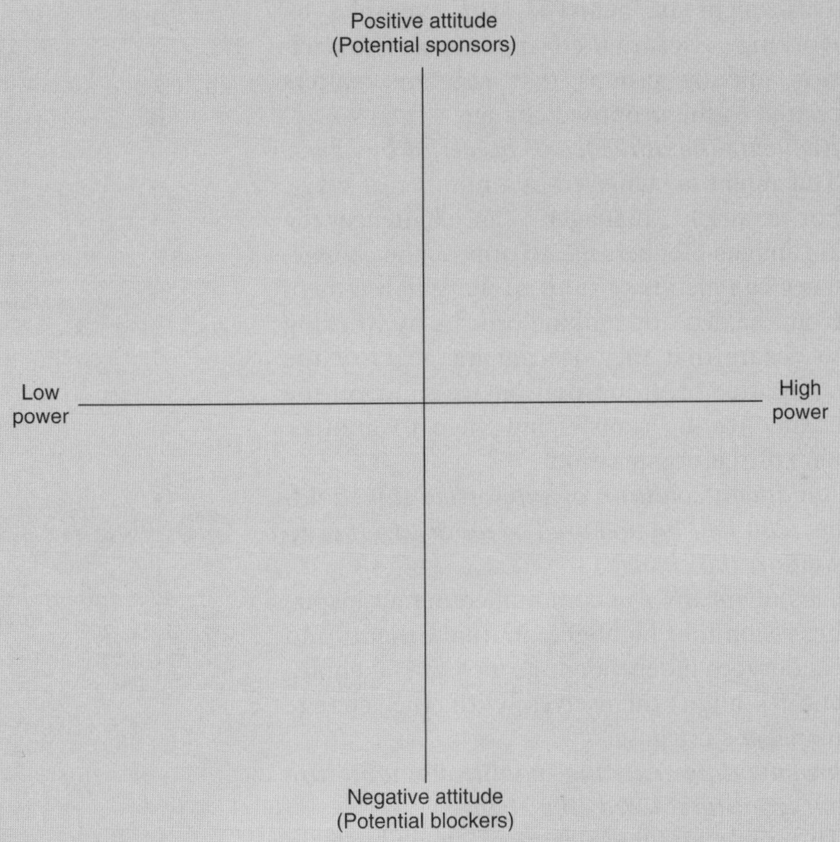

Positive attitude
(Potential sponsors)

Low
power

High
power

Negative attitude
(Potential blockers)

Influencing stakeholders to support the change

The second part of the process described by Grundy involves the change manger acting in ways that will ensure maximum support for the change. This might involve:

1 *Winning the support of those who oppose the change and who have the power to influence the outcome*
Changing powerful blockers into sponsors might be achieved by providing them with information that could persuade them to be more supportive, involving them in the change process in order to give them more control over the outcome, or bargaining with them to win their support.

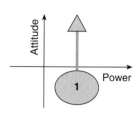

2 *Increasing the influence of those stakeholders who are already supportive*
This might be achieved, for example, by working to secure their appointment to decision making groups that regulate matters related to the proposed change.

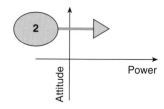

3 *Reducing the influence of powerful blockers*
This might be achieved in a number of ways. For example, managers can challenge the arguments blockers use to oppose the change. They can also take steps to marginalise them from the decision making process by working to ensure that they are not members of the committee or group that has to sanction the change, or by transferring them to another part of the organisation.

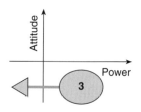

4 *Building a coalition of supportive stakeholders who will be prepared to work together to support the change*
This might involve communicating an inspiring vision that highlights mutual benefits and encourages independent groups of stakeholders to align themselves with the change manager's purpose.

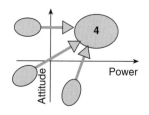

5 *Fragmenting existing coalitions who are antagonistic towards the change*
This might involve 'picking off' key players in the coalition and providing them with information that could persuade them to be more supportive, involving them in the change process in order to give them more control over the outcome, or bargaining with them to win their support (as suggested in **1** above) or undermining their case (as suggested in **3** above).

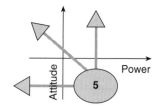

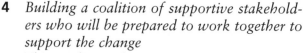

6 *Bringing new sponsors or champions into play*
This could involve persuading 'players' who have not been proactive to take a more active part in influencing events. It may also involve publicising the proposed change within the company or, via the media, in the wider community in order to seek support from powerful individuals or groups who may be unknown to the change manager. However, this kind of intervention is not without risk, because it could also attract the attention of unknown others who may be opposed to the change.

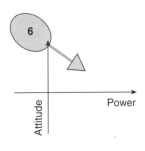

Another possibility that the change manager might consider is reformulating the change in a way that will make it more acceptable to a wider range of stakeholders.

Case study 9.3   Hospital merger: managing stakeholder relationships

1 Review the stakeholder map you produced on page 163 and indicate how you would attend to the concerns of stakeholders. Which stakeholder would you:

- *Address proactively* – do a great deal to address their concerns (indicate with a '*P*' on your stakeholder map)
- *Accommodate* – take a less active approach to dealing with their concerns (indicate with an '*A*' on your stakeholder map)
- *Ignore* – do the legal minimum or refuse to address their concerns (indicate with an '*I*' on your stakeholder map).

Reflect on how the project might unfold and consider whether any of the stakeholders you decided to ignore might become more important at a later date.

2 What steps would you take to increase support or reduce opposition for your proposed way of managing the merger?

An important point to remember is that as a change project unfolds and as circumstances change the identity of key stakeholders may also change. This can have implications for how you decide to manage stakeholder relationships over the short term because some stakeholders who may be unimportant today could become much more important in the future. If they feel that their interests have been disregarded in the past they may be reluctant to support the change manager in the future.

Reflect on the issues discussed in this chapter and addressed in Case Studies 9.1–9.3 and consider how they apply to the management of stakeholders in your organisation.

Exercise 9.2   Stakeholder analysis

Think about a recent change in your organisation and, with the advantage of hindsight:

- identify the stakeholders involved in the change
- classify them according to their power to influence and their attitude towards the change
- assess the extent to which the change manager was aware of these stakeholders and took proper account of them when managing the change.

Notes

Summary

This chapter explores the politics of organisational change and points to the importance of enlisting support from key stakeholders.

An instrumental theory of stakeholder management is elaborated with reference to resource-dependence theory, prospect theory and lifecycle models. It provides a conceptual framework for identifying which stakeholders are likely to be most important at various stages of a change project and for selecting appropriate ways of managing relationships with different types of stakeholder.

References

Bazerman, M. (2001) *Judgement in Managerial Decision Making*, 5th edn, Chichester: Wiley.

Berman, S.L., Wicks, A.C., Kotha, S. and Jones, T.M. (1999) 'Does Stakeholder Orientation Matter? The Relationship between Stakeholder Management Models and Firm Financial Performance', *Academy of Management Journal*, 42 (5), 488–506.

Carroll, A.B. (1979) 'A Three Dimensional Conceptual Model of Corporate Social Performance', *Academy of Management Review*, 4, 497–505.

Clarkson, M.B.E. (1995) 'A Stakeholder Framework for Analyzing and Evaluating Corporate Social Performance', *Academy of Management Review*, 20, pp. 92–117.

Freedman, R.E. (1984) *Strategic Management: A Stakeholders Approach*, Boston, MA: HarperCollins.

Grundy, T. (1998) 'Strategy Implementation and Project Management', *International Journal of Project Management*, 16 (1), pp. 48–50.

Jawahare, M. and McLaughlin. G.L. (2001) 'Toward a Descriptive Stakeholder Theory: An Organizational Life Cycle Approach', *Academy of Management Review*, 26 (3), 397–414.

Jones, T.M. and Wicks, A.C. (1999) 'Convergent Stakeholder Theory', *Academy of Management Review*, 24 (2), 206–21.

Kahneman, D. and Tversky, A. (1979) 'Prospect Theory: An Analysis of Decisions under Risk', *Econometrica*, 47, 263–91.

McCall, M.W. (1979) 'Power, Influence and Authority', in S. Kerr (ed.) *Organizational Behavior,* Columbus, OH: Grid Publishing, pp. 185–206.

McClelland, D.C. (1975) *Power: The Inner Experience*, New York: Irvingston.

McNulty, T. (2003) 'Redesigning Public Services', *British Journal of Management*, supplement 1, 14, pp. 31–45.

McNulty, T. and Ferlie, E. (2002) *Reengineering Health Care: The Complexities of Organisational Transformation*, Oxford: Oxford University Press.

Nadler, D.A. (1987) 'The Effective Management of Organizational Change', in J. Lorsch (ed.), *Handbook of Organizational Behavior*, Englewood Cliffs, NJ: Prentice Hall.

Pettigrew, A.M. (1972) 'Information Control as a Power Resource', *Sociology*, 6 (2), pp. 187–204.

Piercy, N. (1989) 'Diagnosing and Solving Implementation Problems in Strategic Planning', *Journal of General Management*, 15 (1).

Schein, E.H. (1996) 'The Three Cultures of Management: The Key to Organizational Learning', *Sloan Management Review*, Fall, pp. 9–20.

Shaw, B.R. and Maletz, M.C. (1995) 'Business Processes: Embracing the Logic and Limits of Reengineering', in D.A. Nadler, R.B. Shaw and A.E. Walton (eds), *Discontinuous Change: Leading Organizational Transformation*, San Francisco: Jossey-Bass, pp. 169–89.

10

The role of leadership in change management

Tichy and Devanna (1986) and Kotter (1990) draw attention to a tension between leadership and management. They argue that management is concerned with maintaining the existing organisation. Leadership, on the other hand, is more concerned with change. This creates a tension between 'doing things right' and 'doing the right things'. This chapter explores the propositions that managerial work, in times of change, is increasingly a leadership task and that leadership needs to be viewed as a collective process.

Differences between leadership and management

Kotter (1990) argues that both managers and leaders have to attend to three functions: deciding what needs to be done, developing the capacity to do it, and ensuring that it is done. However, there is a marked difference in the way that managers and leaders attend to these functions.

Deciding what needs to be done

1   *Managers* decide what needs to be done through a process of goal setting, establishing detailed steps for achieving these goals and identifying and allocating the resources necessary for their achievement (through planning and budgeting).
2   *Leaders*, on the other hand, focus on setting a direction and developing the strategies necessary to move in that direction (creating a vision).

  In terms of the ideas discussed in Chapter 4 (on organisational learning) management is more focused on developing plans to do things better, whereas leadership involves more double-loop thinking about what is the right thing to do. It involves attending to a wide range of cues that might signal emerging opportunities or problems and setting a direction that will maximise future benefit. However, visions need to serve the interests of key stakeholders. Kotter argues that visions that ignore the legitimate needs and rights of some stakeholders, favouring certain stakeholders over others, may never be achieved. Bruch, Gerber and Maier (2005) also argue that leadership decisions about the 'right thing to do' need to be made before the management decisions about 'how to do the change right', otherwise ongoing debates about 'Does the change make sense?' will rob the project of its energy and weaken the implementation process.

Developing the capacity to do it

1   *Managers* develop the capacity to accomplish their agenda by organising and staffing.
2   *Leaders* focus on aligning people, communicating the new direction and creating coalitions committed to getting there. Successful leaders empower others to make the vision happen. Kotter (1995) argues that a central feature of modern organisations is interdependence, where no one has complete autonomy, and where most members of the organisation are tied to many others by their work, technology, management systems and hierarchy. Kotter argues that these linkages present a special challenge when organisations attempt to change: 'Unless many individuals line up and move together in the same direction, people will tend to fall all over one another.' Kühl, Schnelle and Tillman (2005) argue that managers throughout the organisation have to engage in 'lateral leadership' to create a shared understanding, influence the political process and develop trust. Transformational leaders have the ability to identify those who might be able to support or sabotage an initiative, network with them and communicate in a credible way what needs to be done. Aligning people in this way empowers them, even people at lower levels of the organisation. When there is a clear (and shared) sense of direction, committed stakeholders, including subordinates, are more likely to feel able to take action without encountering undue conflict with others or being reprimanded by superiors.

Ensuring that it is done

1   *Managers* ensure that people accomplish plans by controlling and problem-solving.
2   *Leaders* are more concerned with motivating and inspiring. Kotter believes that inspiring others and generating highly energised behaviour can help them overcome the inevitable barriers to change that they will encounter as the initiative unfolds. He identifies four ways in which leaders can do this:

   (a)   Articulating the vision in ways that are in accord with the values of the people they are addressing

(b) Involving people in deciding how to achieve the vision, thereby giving them some sense of control
(c) Supporting others' efforts to realise the vision by providing coaching, feedback and role modelling
(d) Recognising and rewarding success.

Managerial work, in times of change, is increasingly a leadership task

Kotter (1990) argues that managers are the people who, typically, are in the best position to provide the leadership required to ensure that a change will be successful. However, if they are to provide this leadership they need to recognise that their role involves a dual responsibility, for *management* (keeping the system operating effectively) and for *leadership* (revitalising and renewing the system to ensure that it will remain effective over the longer term).

The thrust of the argument developed in Chapter 1 (on the nature of change) is that not only is the pace of change increasing, but that there is also a shift in emphasis away from incremental towards transformational change. An implication of this is that leadership and the provision of a sense of direction is becoming a more important part of managerial work.

In the first instance, the initiator of change might be an individual or a small group of individuals. These people might be viewed as the ones who are leading the change, but Kotter (1999) argues that this leadership has to be multiplied and shared if the change is to be successful. Managers, throughout the system, have to accept that they have a leadership role to play. They have to contribute to creating a vision, aligning relationships and inspiring others. Oxtoby, McGuiness and Morgan (2002) support this view, and argue that not only does a system of leadership need to cascade down the organisation in a form of a distributed network of key players, each providing leadership in their part of the organisation, but also that, to be effective, this network needs to share a common vision of the organisation's purpose that is clear, consistent and inspiring. Developing and maintaining this common approach is not always easy.

The collective nature of leadership

In much of the literature on organisational change the role of the CEO as leader receives considerable attention. Pascale and Sterin (2005) point out that when individuals stand out as champions of change there is a danger that this will generate unconstructive dependence from other members of the organisation. They argue that leadership needs to come from *within* a community. Denis, Lamothe and Langley (2001) also caution against this glorification of individual heroes. Organisations are becoming more complex and pluralistic, their external boundaries are becoming increasingly blurred as they engage in a variety of collaborative arrangements and as they outsource many of their operations. Within organisations the growth of matrix and network structures and the move from functional to more process-oriented organisational forms is creating circumstances where traditional command and control cultures are being eroded and where managers are increasingly having to collaborate with others (over whom they have no direct authority) in order to get things done.

One of the key problems associated with managing change in pluralistic settings is the development of sufficient *coherence*. Denis, Lamothe and Langley argue that in situations where power is diffused and where there are divergent objectives, change initiatives need to be led by a collective leadership group rather than by a single individual.

On the basis of their research in health care organisations Denis, Lamothe and Langley argue that major change in pluralistic organisations is more likely to be achieved under unified collective leadership in which members of a 'leadership constellation' play complementary roles and work harmoniously together. In many countries there are conventions or legally binding codes of practice that explicitly formalise the collective nature of strategic leadership by separating the posts of CEO and president or chair of the company's board of directors, but often the membership of the leadership constellation is wider than this, with members having different but complementary roles. For example, some may focus their attention on the management of external relations whereas others may manage relationships with particular internal constituencies. Collective leadership is essential in those circumstances where a single individual is unable to formulate and implement a vision that is acceptable to a sufficient body of powerful stakeholders. Collective leadership offers the possibility of bringing together the range of skills and experience required to formulate an acceptable vision as well as the ability to influence others in a manner that is perceived to be legitimate.

While Denis, Lamothe and Langley argue that unified collective leadership is necessary in pluralistic settings, they find that leadership constellations are always fragile. They define 'fragility' in terms of three types of 'coupling':

- *Strategic coupling* is the internal harmony between members of the leadership constellation. Constellations can become disconnected when divergent views emerge about what is important and when these differences lead to conflicts within the constellation. Internal harmony can also be threatened if some members feel that their position is threatened by a proposal to introduce new members who have different skills and experiences that will help the constellation respond to new external challenges.
- *Organisational coupling* reflects the relationship between members of the leadership constellation and their organisational constituencies, which in

turn relates to the perceived conformity between the objectives of leaders (as reflected by their behaviour) and the interests of constituents. If members of the leadership constellation lose touch with their constituents the constituents will begin to feel that their views are not being properly represented by their leaders. This can reduce the leaders' ability to influence constituents and may even threaten their membership of the leadership constellation. The reason for this is that leaders rule, at least in part, by the consent of the led. Denis, Lamothe and Langley argue that:

> In a context of fluid power relationships, the judgements of others concerning the appropriateness of one's behaviour are crucial for long term survival in a leadership position. Actions that tend to enhance survival prospects are called credibility enhancing, and those that tend to diminish it are credibility draining. Changes in credibility directly or indirectly affect the capacity of an individual or leadership group to act in the future. Increased credibility widens the scope for action. Reduced credibility diminishes it and may lead to leader turnover (2001: 825–6).

This has implications for the effectiveness of different leadership styles. Denis, Lamothe and Langley suggest that if a constellation is tightly coupled and covers all power bases, members of the constellation may find that behaving in an aggressive, secretive and authoritarian manner is an effective way of getting things done in the short term, but they suggest that in the long term these tactics can be credibility draining. There may be a need, especially over the long term, to balance forceful leadership action with maintaining a necessary level of approval from those who are being led.

- *Environmental coupling* refers to the degree of coherence between the leadership constellation's vision and aspirations and the demands and constraints imposed by powerful external stakeholders. Constellations can break down if they become so detached from their environments that performance begins to decline. This happens when concerns about performance lead to pressures from the company's board or other powerful external stakeholders for members of the constellation to be replaced.

Denis, Lamothe and Langley argue that it can be difficult to maintain harmony at all three levels. Sometimes too much attention is directed towards developing a close alignment between the aspirations of internal stakeholders (organisational coupling) and insufficient attention given to the impact of external demands (environmental coupling). Accommodating different interests is easier when there is a degree of organisational slack, but when resources are limited there is less opportunity for accommodations and compromises. In these circumstances the stability of leadership constellations and their ability to deliver change may depend on some of the personal and interpersonal skills of members. Denis, Lamothe and Langley refer to the importance of a *tacit knowledge* of how things can be done in the organisation (social embeddedness) and *creative opportunism* (the ability to see opportunities to reconcile a range of aspirations with environmental pressures). Hollenbeck and Hall (2004) highlight the effect of self-efficacy (leader self-confidence) on leader performance, and while Ferris *et al.* (2000) agree that tacit knowledge and self-efficacy are important they also point to the importance of a number of other social skills such as social intelligence, emotional intelligence, ego-resilience and self-monitoring.

A checklist for leading change

In a much-cited paper, Kotter (1995) adopts a process perspective on change management and highlights, in terms of leadership, what needs to be done to ensure success at each stage in the process. These eight actions can be easily mapped on to the process model of change presented in Chapter 5:

1 *Establishing a sense of urgency*
   Change managers often underestimate how hard it can be to drive people out of their comfort zones. 'Unfreezing' involves alerting organisational members to the need for change and motivating them to let go of the status quo. Many factors can make this difficult to attain. These include a history of past success and the lack of an immediate crisis. After British Gas was privatised many senior managers refused to recognise that there was any real threat to the organisation's monopoly position. Those attempting to lead change in the business had to work very hard to convince colleagues that they should begin to prepare for major discontinuities. Chapter 6 (on recognising the need for change and starting the change process) considers a range of issues that require the leader's attention at the beginning of a change.

2 *Forming a powerful coalition*
   This point relates to the collective nature of leadership discussed above. Kotter (1995) argues that unless those who recognise the need for change can put together a strong enough team to direct the process, the change initiative is unlikely to get off the ground. He suggests that while this 'guiding coalition' might not include all the senior managers it is much more likely to succeed if, in terms of titles, information, experience, reputations and contacts, it is seen to signal a real commitment to change.

3 *Creating a vision*
   The guiding coalition needs to develop a shared vision that can be easily communicated to others affected by the change. In his book *Leading Change*, Kotter (1996) summarises six criteria for an effective vision:

   (a) *Imaginable*: conveys a picture of what the future will look like
   (b) *Desirable*: appeals to the long-term interests of employees, customers, stockholders, and others who have a stake in the enterprise
   (c) *Feasible*: comprises realistic, attainable goals

(d) *Focused*: is clear enough to provide guidance in decision making
(e) *Flexible*: is general enough to allow individual initiatives and alternative responses in the light of changing conditions
(f) *Communicable*: is easy to communicate; can be successfully explained within five minutes.

Sometimes interventions such as visioning workshops (see Chapter 17 on types of intervention) can be helpful in developing a vision that satisfies these criteria.

4 *Communicating the vision*
Communication is considered in more detail in Chapter 11. However, in terms of communicating the vision, people – all those affected by the change – need to hear the message repeatedly. Kotter asserts that in many change programmes the vision is under-communicated by a factor of ten! He also emphasises that communicating a vision involves more that the spoken and written word. Organisational members (and other stakeholders) watch those responsible for managing the change for indications of their commitment. It is important that they 'walk the talk' and communicate the vision by example.

5 *Empowering others to act on the vision*
Transformational leadership involves identifying and removing obstacles that can stop people acting to implement the vision. Some of these obstacles might include tangible aspects of the organisation such as reward systems that penalise valued behaviour, restrictive rules and regulations or inflexible organisational structures. Others may be less tangible and involve beliefs and assumptions that stifle initiative. Empowering others to act includes creating a climate in which people believe in themselves and are confident that they have the support of others to make things happen. The importance of beliefs about change agency is considered in Chapter 2 and some practical examples of empowering others to act in Chapter 15.

6 *Planning for and creating short-term wins*
Kotter argues that achieving major change can take time. The danger with this is that the change effort can slow down as people lose the initial sense of urgency and their attention drifts elsewhere, possibly to pressing operational matters. One way of minimising this risk is for those leading the change to seek out short-term wins and plan for visible (interim) performance improvements that can be celebrated along the way.

7 *Consolidating improvements and producing still more change*
This involves capitalising on early wins. However, while Kotter advocates celebrating early wins, he cautions against declaring victory too soon because this can kill momentum. Leaders should capitalise on early wins to motivate others to introduce further changes to systems and structures that are consistent (aligned) with the transformation vision.

8 *Institutionalising new approaches*

Leaders need to ensure that changes are consolidated. They can help achieve this by showing others how the changes have produced new approaches, behaviours and attitudes that have improved performance. Kotter argues that leaders should take every opportunity to demonstrate benefit and reinforce these changes until they become an accepted part of the culture and the 'way things are done around here'.

Many of these points will be referred to again in other chapters of this book.

Exercise 10.1   Validating Kotter's (1996) checklist

Identify two change managers (or 'constellations' of change managers) who have been key figures in attempting to introduce and manage change in your organisation. One should be a person(s) who you judge to have been very successful at managing change. The other should be someone who you judge to have been much less successful.

Assess their approach to managing change using Kotter's checklist for leading change.

Consider whether there is any evidence to suggest that successful change managers are those who attend to Kotter's eight points.

Summary

The role of leadership in change management is summarised as creating a vision, aligning relationships around the vision and inspiring others to achieve the vision. Leadership is also considered as a collective process, and some of the issues associated with maintaining coherence in the leadership constellation and between the constellation and internal and external stakeholders are reviewed. The chapter closes with an eight-point checklist of what leaders can do to promote change.

References

Bruch, H., Gerber, P. and Maier, V. (2005) 'Strategic Change Decisions: Doing the Right Change Right', *Journal of Change Management*, 5 (1), pp. 97–107.

Denis, J.-L., Lamothe, L. and Langley, A. (2001) 'The Dynamics of Collective Leadership and Strategic Change in Pluralistic Organizations', *Academy of Management Journal*, 44 (4), 809–37.

Ferris, G.R., Perrewe, P., Anthony, W.P. and Gilmore, D.C. (2000) 'Political Skills at Work', *Organizational Dynamics*, 28 (4), 25–37.

Hollenbeck, G.P. and Hall, D.P. (2004) 'Self-Confidence and Leaders Performance', *Organizational Dynamics*, 33 (3), 254–69.

Kotter, J.P. (1990) 'What Leaders Really Do', *Harvard Business Review*, 73 (3), reproduced in Kotter (1999), *On What Leaders Really Do*.

Kotter, J.P. (1995) 'Leading Change: Why Transformation Efforts Fail', *Harvard Business Review*, 73 (2), pp. 59–68.

Kotter, J.P. (1996) *Leading Change*, Boston, MA: Harvard Business School Press.

Kotter, J.P. (1999) *On What Leaders Really Do*, Boston, MA: Harvard Business School Press.

Kühl, S., Schnelle, T and Tillmann, F.J. (2005) 'Lateral Leadership: An Organisational Change Approach', *Journal of Change Management*, 5 (2), pp. 177–89.

Oxtoby, B., McGuiness, T. and Morgan, R. (2002) 'Developing Organisational Change Capability', *European Management Journal*, 20 (3), 310–20.

Pascale, R.T. and Sterin, J. (2005) 'Your Company's Secret Change Agents', *Harvard Business Review*, 83 (5), pp. 72–81.

Tichy, N.M. and Devanna, M.A. (1986) *The Transformational Leader*, Chichester: Wiley.

Communicating change

The quality of communications can have an important impact on the success or otherwise of a change programme. It was noted in Chapter 3 that communication is a key process that can influence how effectively an organisation adjusts to a change. It was also noted in Chapter 4 how the nature of collective learning is affected by the structures and processes that facilitate or inhibit individuals and groups sharing the meanings they construct for themselves as they encounter new experiences and ideas. And in Chapter 10 it was noted that communicating the vision has a vital role to play in leading change. This chapter briefly considers the features of communication networks that relate to the management of change, reviews some alternative communication strategies, discusses the effect of interpersonal relations on the quality of communication and explores some of the factors that can deprive change managers of access to vital information.

Features of communication networks

Four features of communication networks will be considered: directionality, role, content and channel.

Directionality

The management of change is often experienced as a 'top-down' process, with those responsible for managing the change informing others lower down the organisation about the need for change, what is going to happen and what is required of them. However, it also requires a stream of upward communication that provides change managers with the information they require in order to clarify the need for change, and develop and implement a change programme. Beer (2001) identifies the poor quality of upward communication as one of his six 'silent killers' that block change and learning.

O'Reilly and Pondy (1979) list some of the consequences of directionality on the content of messages. Senders transmitting messages up the organisation hierarchy send information that they perceive to be relevant *and* which reflects favourably on their (or their unit's) performance. Where possible, they screen out information that reflects unfavourably on them. Consequently people further up the organisation may not receive all the information that may be relevant to the issues they have to manage.

Senders transmitting messages downwards have a tendency to screen out any information that they perceive to be not directly relevant to the subordinates' task. This 'need-to-know' attitude can lead to problems when change managers fail to pass on information that might have helped others understand the need for change or helped them feel more involved in the change process.

The quality of lateral communication can also have a powerful impact on an organisation's level of performance and its ability to innovate and change. Orlikowski (1996), Brown and Eisenhardt (1997) and Tjosvold (1998) all argue that intense and open communication between people within and between teams is an essential requirement for continuous improvement. This information-sharing contributes to the identification of issues and the development of new possibilities. Hargie and Tourish (2000) assert that when groups work in isolation, with people sharing minimal information, 'the locomotive of change slows to a crawl'. They report finding that poor inter-departmental communication is linked to feelings of isolation and dissatisfaction and to low levels of involvement in the decision making process. In their opinion, 'poor information exchange exacerbates uncertainty, increases alienation and produces a segmented attitude to work that is inimical to the spirit of innovation' (2000: 7).

Morrison and Milliken (2000) discuss how, in some organisations, there is a widespread withholding of opinion and concerns that deprives change managers of vital information. This will be considered later in this chapter under the heading 'organisational silence'.

Role

The nature of what is communicated can be affected by the roles that organisational members occupy. The nature of an *inter-role relationship* is important; a person might communicate certain things to a colleague that she would not communicate to an external consultant, an auditor, a member of another department, their boss, a subordinate, or a customer. This issue will be discussed in more detail when the effect of trust and power on the quality of interpersonal relationships is considered.

The nature of a role can be an important determinant of whether the role occupant will be an *isolate* or a *participant* in the organisation's affairs. Some roles are potentially more isolated than others: a finance officer may be better networked within the organisation than a salesperson who is responsible for a remote territory; an employee on an assembly line may have relatively few opportunities to communicate with others and therefore may be deprived of opportunities to contribute to collective learning. This may be much less of a problem for somebody located in an open-plan office who is constantly interacting with colleagues. Some of the interventions that will be considered in Chapter 17 are designed to create opportunities for the dialogue, sharing and provision of feedback that are so important in situations characterised by uncertainty and change. When planning to communicate with people about a proposed change it is important to take account of those who occupy isolated roles. People who feel that they have been neglected or excluded are more likely to be alienated than those who feel that they are in a position to participate in the change.

Some members of the organisation occupy *boundary-spanning roles* that enable them to transfer information from one constituency to another. For example, people in sales, customer support and product development occupy roles that link the organisation with the wider environment. Within the organisation there are also roles that straddle the boundaries between internal constituencies; the occupants of these boundary-spanning roles may have access to important information that could be used to identify emerging problems or opportunities. MacDonald (1995) argues that critical information is often imported into organisations through informal and individual contacts and that the persons who are the boundary-spanners who acquire this information may not be the people who can use it as a basis for managing change. They may have to pass their information on to others who are in a better position to respond. However, these 'others' may not recognise the importance of the information or may receive a message that is different to that which the originator of the message intended to convey.

Distortion can occur because information is passed on to others by *gatekeepers*. Gatekeepers are those who are in a position to interpret and screen information before transmitting it to others. Almost everybody in the organisation is to some extent a gatekeeper, but some roles offer their occupants considerable power to control the content and timing of the information that is passed on to decision makers. Change managers need to be aware of who controls the flows of information that are important to them. One way of reducing dependence on some gatekeepers is to build an element of redundancy into the communication network in order to provide the possibility of obtaining information from more than one source.

Content

MacDonald (1995) distinguishes between internal and external information and draws attention to the importance of attending to information from outside the organisation and integrating this with the information that is routinely available to organisational members in order to facilitate organisational learning. A common problem, however, is that this external information is often unfamiliar, and responding to it frequently leads to disruption and uncertainty. Consequently, organisational members tend to prefer the more familiar internal information that is easier to integrate into the prevailing mental models and paradigms that are used for making sense of the situation that confronts them.

Other important aspects of content are whether it is perceived as good news or bad news, and how senders expect it to be received. Change managers need to be alert to content issues and especially to the need to give careful consideration to the potential relevance of information that at first sight may appear to be of little consequence.

Channel

Information and meaning can be communicated in many different ways: written communication via hard copy, electronic communication via email, video-conferencing, telephone, face-to-face communication on a one-to-one, one-to-group or group-to-group basis and so on. O'Reilly and Pondy (1979) suggest that written communication may be effective when the sender and receiver have different vocabularies or problem orientations, and that oral communication may be most effective when there is a need to exchange views, seek feedback and provide an immediate opportunity for clarification. They note, however, that while organisation members may prefer certain media and while certain forms of communication may have clear advantages in specific circumstances, external factors may limit the freedom to select a particular mode of communication. For example, distance may prohibit face-to-face interaction, budget constraints may demand the use of written communication rather than video-conferencing, and time constraints may rule out the use of lengthy meetings. Clampitt, DeKoch and Cashman (2000) echo this efficiency/effectiveness dilemma. They note that while it may be more efficient to send an email to all employees outlining a major change it may not be the most effective way to create employee buy-in. They argue that face-to-face communication is a more persuasive channel because it provides a dynamic and effective way for dealing with people's concerns. However, face-to-face communication costs the organisation more in terms of time and energy than a 'lean medium' such as email.

Communication strategies

These features of communication networks provide a useful backcloth for comparing the advantages and disadvantages of various communication strategies. As Clampitt, DeKoch and Cashman (2000) have observed, managers can communicate about anything but they cannot communicate about everything – so, implicitly or explicitly, they make choices about communication content. They also take decisions or unconsciously act in ways that impact on the shape of communication networks. For example, they may communicate with some organisational members but not with others and they may authorise or encouraged certain others to communicate with each other. They may also influence, if only by example, preferred channels for passing on particular kinds of information.

Communication plays a vital role in the change process. It is an essential prerequisite for recognising the need for change, and it enables change managers to create a shared sense of direction, establish priorities, reduce disorder and uncertainty and facilitate learning. However change managers often give insufficient attention to the role of communication. Clampitt, DeKoch and Cashman (2000) suggest that communication strategies emerge from existing practices with little hard thinking about communication objectives or processes and little, if any, attention to reviewing the consequences of their approach to communicating with others. On the basis of their experience in several organisations and a review of the literature they identified five basic strategies. Sometimes the communication strategy in any particular setting closely resembles one of these, but sometimes it is a hybrid and includes a blend of elements from more than one. The five basic strategies are:

- *Spray and pray*   Clampitt, DeKoch and Cashman use this term to describe a communication strategy that involves showering employees with all kinds of information in the hope that they will feel informed and have access to all the information they require. It is based on the assumption that more information equals better communication, which in turn contributes to improved decision making. It is also based on an implicit assumption that all organisational members are able to differentiate between what is significant and what is insignificant. In practice, some employees may attend only to the information that is related to their own personal agendas, while others may be overwhelmed by the amount of information they are confronted with – unable to sort the wood from the trees.
- *Tell and sell*   This approach involves change managers communicating a more limited set of messages that they believe address core issues related to the proposed change. They first of all tell employees about these key issues and then sell them the wisdom of their approach to managing them. Clampitt, DeKoch and Cashman observe that change managers who adopt this kind of strategy often spend a great deal of time planning sophisticated presentations but devote little time and energy to fostering meaningful dialogue and providing organisational members with the opportunity to discuss their concerns. They also assume that they possess much of the information they need and they tend to place little value on input from others.
- *Underscore and explore*   Like the tell-and-sell approach this strategy involves focusing attention on a limited set of fundamental issues linked to the change, but unlike the tell-and-sell approach change managers give others the creative freedom they need to explore the implications of these issues. Those who adopt this approach are concerned not only with developing a few core messages but also with listening attentively for potential misunderstandings and unrecognized obstacles.

- *Identify and reply*   This strategy is different from the first three in that the primary focus is the concerns of organisational members. It is a reactive approach that involves a lot of listening in order to identify and then respond to these concerns. It is essentially directed towards helping employees make sense out of the often-confusing organisational environment, but it is also attentive to their concerns because it is assumed that organisational members are in the best position to know what the critical issues are. However, this may not always be the case: Clampitt, DeKoch and Cashman suggest that often they may not know enough to even ask the right questions.
- *Withhold and uphold*   This strategy involves withholding information until necessary. When confronted by rumours, change managers uphold the party line. There may well be special circumstances where commercial or other considerations require information to be shared on a need-to-know basis but there are also change managers whose implicit values are secrecy and control whatever the circumstances. Some of those who adopt this strategy assume that information is power and they are reluctant to share it with anyone. Others assume that most organisational members are not sophisticated enough to grasp the 'big picture'.

Clampitt, DeKoch and Cashman use a crescent-shaped continuum to compare the effectiveness of the different strategies. At the left-hand end, the 'spray-and-pray' strategy provides employees with all the information they could possibly desire, while at the other end the 'withhold-and-uphold' strategy provides the absolute minimum information. Both these strategies make it very difficult for employees to frame and make sense of the intended change, and its consequences. The strategies toward the middle of the continuum pay more attention to prioritizing and managing content to provide guidance for those involved in the change and, to varying degrees, attend to employee concerns. Clampitt, DeKoch and Cashman argue that the strategies at the extreme are the least effective and that the most effective is 'underscore and explore'. This is because it incorporates elements of the 'tell-and-sell' strategy and allows change managers to shape the change agenda, and it also incorporates aspects of the 'identify-and-reply' strategy that responds to the concerns of employees.

Hargie and Tourish (2000) recommend the regular auditing of communications. This requires change manages to have a clear idea about their communication objectives in order to assess the extent to which they are being achieved. Some of the questions they might need to ask are:

- Who is communicating with whom?
- What issues are they talking about?
- Which issues receive most attention and arouse most anxiety?
- Do people receive all the information they require?
- Do people understand and use the information they receive?

- Do people trust and have confidence in the information they receive?
- From what sources do people prefer to get their information?
- Which channels are most effective?

Organisational silence: a major barrier to change

Morrison and Milliken (2000) argue that many organisations are caught in an apparent paradox in which most employees know the truth about certain issues and problems but are afraid to voice that truth to their superiors. They refer to the widespread withholding of opinions and concerns as 'organisational silence' and assert that it can be a major barrier to organisational change and development. In Chapter 6 the importance of ensuring that multiple and divergent views contribute to the decision making process was highlighted in the context of formulating the agenda for change but Morrison and Milliken refer to several studies (e.g. Moskal, 1991; Ryan and Oestreich, 1991) indicating that in practice employees often feel compelled to remain silent and refrain from voicing their views. The dynamics that give rise to organisational silence are summarized in Figure 11.1.

According to Morrison and Milliken, a climate of silence in organisations will develop when:

1 Senior managers fear negative feedback from subordinates and try to avoid it – or, if this is not possible, dismiss it as inaccurate or attack the credibility of the source.
2 Senior managers hold a particular set of implicit beliefs about employees and the nature of management that make it easy for them to ignore or dismiss feedback. These beliefs are that:

   (a) employees are self-interested, untrustworthy and effort averse
   (b) management knows best and therefore subordinates should be unquestioning followers (especially since they are self-interested and effort averse and therefore unlikely to know or care about what is best for the organisation)
   (c) dissent is unhealthy and should be avoided and unity, agreement and consensus are indicators of organisational health.

Conditions that foster these beliefs

Morrison and Milliken (2000) argue that top management teams that are dominated by members with economic or financial backgrounds are more likely to subscribe to the belief that employees are self-interested because this belief is rooted in economic models of behaviour. They also argue that dissent will be less welcome by top teams that are homogeneous with respect to functional training and experience, and by teams that have experienced

Figure 11.1   Dynamics giving rise to organisational silence

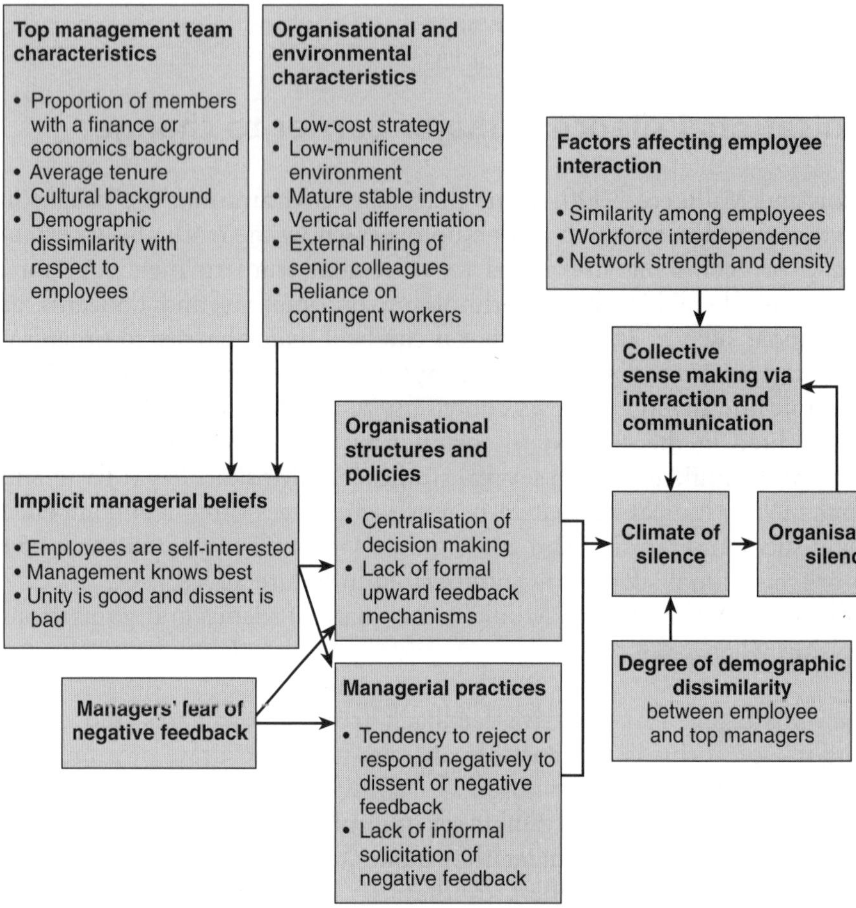

Source: Adapted from Morrison, E.W. and Milliken, F.J., 'Organisational Silence: A Barrier to Change and Development in a Pluralistic World', *Academy of Management Review*, 2000, 25, 4, p. 709.

low turnover. This is because such teams are likely to be more cohesive and share entrenched assumptions. Distrust is also fostered when top teams are highly dissimilar to lower-level employees in terms of demographic characteristics such as age, gender and race.

Organisational and environmental variables can also foster these beliefs. For example, Morrison and Milliken argue that when organisational strategies emphasise control in order to maximise economic value (see the discussion of economic change strategies in Chapter 15) managers may view negative feedback and dissent as a threat to their authority. Furthermore, organisations operating in stable and mature environments are more likely to subscribe to beliefs that foster silence than organisations in high-velocity environments because, in stable environments, a lack of upward communication is less likely to threaten their survival. They also argue that these beliefs are more likely to be fostered in organisations that have many levels in the hierarchy, hire top managers from outside and make heavy use of temporary and agency workers. These conditions limit interaction across the hierarchy and do little to build senior managers' trust in their subordinates.

The effect of managerial beliefs and the fear of feedback on structures, polices and practices

Morrison and Milliken argue that in those organisations where the dominant ideology reflects the beliefs that employees are self-interested, management knows best and disagreement is bad, it will give rise to structures, policies and managerial behaviours that create an environment that discourages upward communication. Examples include centralised decision making procedures that exclude most employees, an absence of formal feedback mechanisms for soliciting employee feedback on decisions after they have been made, a tendency to reject employees' concerns about a proposed change because they are viewed as 'resistance' motivated by self-interest rather than a true concern that the change may be bad for the organisation, and a general unwillingness on the part of managers to seek informal feedback from subordinates.

They point out that these barriers to upward communication can exist at many different levels in the organisation. While it may only be top management that can impose company-wide structures and polices that foster organisational silence, managers at all levels can discourage upward communication by the way they design their bit of the organisation and by reacting negatively to unsolicited inputs from subordinates and failing to seek feedback from employees on issues that affect performance. However, even when middle managers do not share the implicit beliefs held by their superiors, top management attitudes can encourage middle managers and many other supervisors to behave in ways that foster silence. For example, middle managers may choose to respond to senior managers' lack of openness to dissenting views by filtering out some of the information they receive from their subordinates before passing it up the organisation. Their subordinates, in turn, notice this apparent disregard for their views and respond by not voicing their own concerns and those reported to them by their subordinates. In this way, the conditions that encourage a climate of silence trickle down the organisation.

The creation of shared perceptions that lead to organisational silence

The management beliefs outlined above promote the development of structures, polices and practices that foster a climate of organisational silence. A climate of silence exists when employees believe that (a) speaking up about problems is not worth the effort and (b) voicing one's problems and concerns is dangerous.

Morrison and Milliken adopt an interactionist perspective and argue that it is through the sharing of perceptions and experience that employees engage in a process of collective sense making and develop a common understanding and a set of shared beliefs. They go on to argue that centralised decision making, lack of upward feedback mechanisms, managerial resistance to employee input and a lack of downward feedback-seeking behaviour are more likely to lead to a climate of silence when there is a relatively high level of interaction and communication between mid-to-lower-level employees. The amount of interaction that takes place is related to several factors. These include:

- similarity between direct co-workers, because there is evidence that people are more open when communicating with people they perceive to be similar to themselves
- relatively stable organisational membership, because this increases the likelihood that shared perceptions will persist over time
- workflow interdependence that necessitates regular communication, coordination and teamwork
- informal social networks and strong ties that promote intense and frequent contact.

This collective sense making process can be flawed, and inaccurate perceptions may develop as employees share and collectively interpret their observations and experience. Sources of bias include the reliance on second-hand information (because many people prefer to learn vicariously than to risk finding out first-hand) and the tendency to exaggerate the riskiness or futility of voicing dissent. However, even if they are inaccurate, these shared perceptions have a strong impact on employees' attitudes and behaviour.

The implications of organisational silence

Organisational silence can compromise decision making and elicit undesirable reactions from employees.

Organisational silence deprives decision makers of the opportunity to consider alternative perspectives and conflicting viewpoints. There is considerable evidence that this can adversely effect creativity and undermine the quality of decision making. Blocking negative feedback can also inhibit organisational learning because it affects the ability of managers to detect and correct the causes of poor performance. Morrison and Milliken also suggest that decision makers may not receive important information because employees pass on only the information that they think their managers want to hear.

Organisational silence can have destructive outcomes for employees, with knock-on effects for the organisation:

- Employees may feel undervalued, and this may affect their commitment and lead to lower motivation, satisfaction, psychological withdrawal or the decision to quit.
- When discouraged from speaking up employees may feel that they lack sufficient control over their working environment. This can also lead to low motivation, low satisfaction and, possibly, attempts to regain some control through acting in ways that are destructive to the organisation, such as engaging in sabotage.
- Employees may also experience cognitive dissonance because of the discrepancy between their beliefs and behaviour, leading to anxiety and stress.

Morrison and Milliken argue that when top management adheres to the assumptions that foster silence it makes it difficult for organisations to respond to the diversity of values, beliefs and other characteristics that are the features of pluralistic organisations. The more these differences 'pull' the organisation in divergent directions the more senior managers may 'push' against these forces because they view differences as a threat that has to be suppressed. They argue that 'despite "knowing" that they should encourage upward communication, organisations' dominant tendency may be just the opposite – namely, to create a climate of silence' (2000: 720)

Interpersonal effects on the quality of communication

Factors such as *trust* and *influence* can have an important effect on the quality of the information that is exchanged. Lines *et al.* (2005) argue that whether change agents gain access to the knowledge and creative thinking they need to solve problems depends largely on how much people trust them. O'Reilly and Pondy refer to studies that show that lack of trust is associated with a tendency for senders to withhold unfavourable but relevant information while passing on favourable but irrelevant information. There is also evidence that senders are guarded in what they are prepared to share with those others who are able to influence what happens to them.

Change managers often have to seek out information from others, but this is not always an easy task. Interpersonal interactions are complex social encounters in which the behaviour of each party is influenced by the other. An often-used model of information gathering presents the process solely in terms of an information-seeker (change manager) getting information from respondents (organisational members). This model is an over-simplification, because it fails to take full account of the interactive nature of the encounter (see Figure 11.2).

Organisational members are aware that the change managers are observing what they say and do and that they may be making judgements about them and their future role. Consequently they may not openly and honestly

Figure 11.2   An over-simplified model of the interview

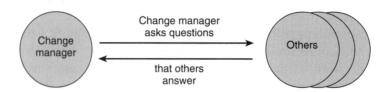

answer all the questions they are asked. They may attempt to manage the way they respond so as to maximise their personal benefit from the interaction rather than help the change managers achieve their purpose. (Note that this example could just as easily be presented in terms of organisational members 'interviewing' a change manager.)

Goffman (1959), Mangham (1978) and others have used drama as a metaphor for describing and explaining a wide range of interactions, and this metaphor can usefully be applied to this kind of social encounter. Goffman talks about putting on a performance for an audience and argues that people's portrayal of action will be determined by their assessment of the audience. He also notes that actors use mirrors so that they can practise and become an object to themselves, backstage, before going 'on-stage' and becoming an object to others. Similarly, organisational members may anticipate the nature of their audience, the change managers, and rehearse the way they want to present themselves.

A better representation of the interaction between change managers and organisational members is illustrated in Figure 11.3. The change managers are likely to structure the situation and behave in ways that they feel will best project their definition of the purpose of the encounter and the role they want to assume in the interaction. This behaviour not only says a lot about how the change managers wish to be seen, but also about who they take the other organisational members to be and the role they are expected to play. The change managers attempt to influence the others' interpretation of the situation and to focus their attention on those issues which they (the change managers) regard as important, and much of what takes place at this stage involves cognitive scene setting.

At stage **2** in Figure 11.3, the organisational members seek to understand what it is that the change managers are projecting and what implications this has for them. Do the change managers, for example, appear to see the encounter as an information gathering exercise designed to provide them with the information they need to determine what has to be changed? Alternatively, do they see it as the first step towards involving organisational members in the management of the change process?

Organisational members might detect a difference between the performance the change managers consciously and deliberately give, and what Mangham (1978) refers to as the information they 'give off'. The change

Figure 11.3   The interaction between change agents and organisational members

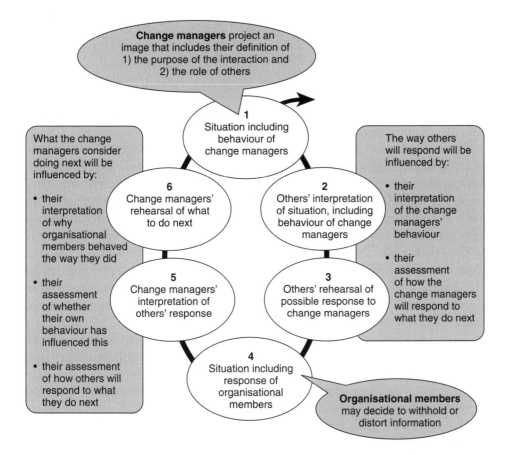

managers may attempt to perform in a way that gives the impression to others that they are committed to a shared approach to the management of change; however, they may actually 'give off' signals, verbal and non-verbal, that contradict this intended impression. Thus, as the interaction progresses through stages **3** and **4** the organisational members may decide to cooperate and give the change managers the information they are seeking, or they may decide to distort or withhold information until they are more confident about the change managers' intentions.

Reference has already been made to rehearsal of action. At stage **3**, organisational members have to decide, on the basis of their interpretation of the situation, how to respond to the change managers. Farr (1984) discussing the work of Mead, notes that Man not only acts but 'reacts' to his own actions. He reacts to his own behaviour on the basis of the actual or *anticipated* reaction of others. He can anticipate their reactions through simulation or rehearsal. He can try out, in his own mind, a few pieces of behaviour and test them for 'fit'. Mangham even suggests that he can simulate several stages into alternative futures for an interaction, a form of mental chess in which various moves and their consequences are tested.

Once the organisational members have decided what to do and have responded to the change managers' initial behaviour, the situation changes. Both parties, at stage 4 on the circle, are faced with a situation that includes the most recent behaviour of the organisational members. If the change managers failed to make their purpose explicit (at stage 1), the organisational members may misinterpret their behaviour and act in ways that the change managers either did not anticipate or feel are inappropriate to the situation. (They may, for example, decide to withhold or distort information).

The change managers have to assess this situation (stage 5) and attempt to understand the meaning of the organisational members' behaviour. Their interpretation of the organisational members' response offers a basis for assessing the relevance and validity of any information communicated by them. Good interviewers/information gatherers have the ability to empathise with the other party; they can assume the other's role in the interaction, putting themselves in the other's shoes and replaying in their mind the situation the other organisational members' face. They can interpret the others' behaviour, including their answers to questions, from this perspective. Unfortunately this is a skill that many change managers have not developed and it can lead to many misunderstandings.

On the basis of their interpretation of the situation, including the organisational members' behaviour, the change managers can rehearse their next move (stage 6) before deciding what to do and/or say. This then forms part of the unfolding scene to which the other organisational members will have to respond, and so the process continues.

The point of this example is that the nature of the encounter will influence how *both parties* will interpret what they see and hear. It will also influence the quantity and quality of the information that each is prepared to offer. Change managers need to give careful thought to how others will interpret their actions. Their interpretation will be an important determinant of what others are prepared to communicate to them and how they will behave in response to information passed to them by the change managers. All of this is very relevant to the process of developing and maintaining helping relationships, which will be discussed in Part VII.

Summary

Often the discussion of communication issues associated with the management of change tends to focus exclusively on the 'what, when, who and how' of communication from the perspective of the change manager communicating to others. The discussion in this chapter has also emphasised issues associated with change managers perceiving, interpreting and using information provided by others.

There are no magic formulae about the 'what, when, who and how' of communication that can provide ready answers for all situations. In some circumstances change agents may advocate a policy of complete openness about all issues to everybody as soon as possible. In other circumstances, information might be highly restricted because it is deemed to be commercially sensitive, or it might be decided that information should not be widely shared until after certain high-level decisions have been made. Counter-arguments might focus on the difficulty of keeping the need for change secret and the importance of not losing control of communications to the informal grapevine. The alternative strategies, considered earlier, highlight some of the options available to change managers.

What is important is that adequate attention be given to ensuring that all relevant information is sought and is attended to by change managers, and that they pay careful attention to the information that they need to communicate to others.

Exercise 11.1 Assessing the quality of communications

Think about a recent attempt to introduce and manage change in your organisation or a particular part of the organisation that you are familiar with, and reflect on how the quality of communication helped or hindered the change process:

- Did the change manager(s) communicate effectively to all those involved in or affected by the change?
- If not, to what extent was this related to 'network factors' such as directionality, role, content, or channel, or to interpersonal factors that interfered with the quality of communication?

What could the change manager(s) have done differently that might have improved the quality of communications?

References

Beer, M. (2001) 'How to Develop an Organization Capable of Sustained High Performance: Embrace the Drive for Results–Capability Development Paradox', *Organizational Dynamics*, 29 (4), pp. 233–47.

Brown, S.L. and Eisenhardt, K.M. (1997) 'The Art of Continuous Change: Linking Complexity Theory and Time-Paced Evolution in Relentlessly Shifting Organizations', *Administrative Science Quarterly*, 42, pp. 1–34.

Clampitt, P.G., DeKoch, R.J. and Cashman, T. (2000) 'A Strategy for Communicating about Uncertainty', *The Academy of Management Executive*, 14 (40), pp. 41–57.

Farr, R. (1984) 'Interviewing: The Social Psychology of the Inter-View', in Cary L. Cooper and Peter Makin (eds), *Psychology for Managers*, London: British Psychological Society.

Goffman, E. (1959) *The Presentation of Self in Everyday Life*, New York: Doubleday.

Hargie, O. and Tourish, D. (2000) *Handbook of Communication Audits for Organisations*, London: Routledge.

Lines, R., Selart, M., Espedal, B. and Johansen, S.T. (2005) 'The Production of Trust During Organizational Change', *Journal of Change Management*, 5 (2), pp. 221–45.

MacDonald, S. (1995) 'Learning to Change: An Information Perspective on Learning in the Organisation', *Organizational Science*, 6 (5), pp. 557–68.

Mangham, I.L. (1978) *Interactions and Interventions in Organizations*, Chichester: Wiley.

Morrison, E.W. and Milliken, F. J. (2000) 'Organizational Silence: A Barrier to Change and Development in a Pluralistic World', *Academy of Management Review*, 25 (4), pp. 706–25.

Moskal, B.M. (1991) 'Is Industry Ready for Adult Relationships?' *Industry Week*, January 21, pp. 18–25.

O'Reilly, C.A. and Pondy, L.R. (1979) 'Organisational Communication', in S. Kerr (ed.), *Organisational Behavior*, Columbus, OH: Grid Publications, pp. 119–49.

Orlikowski, W.J. (1996) 'Improvising Organisational Transformation Over Time: A Sustained Change Perspective', *Information Systems Research*, 7 (1), pp. 63–92.

Ryan, K.D. and Oestreich, D.K. (1991) *Driving Fear out of the Workplace: How to Overcome the Invisible Barriers to Quality, Productivity and Innovation*. San Francisco: Jossey-Bass.

Tjosvold, D. (1998) *Team Organisation: An Enduring Competitive Advantage*, New York: John Wiley.

Training and development

O rganisational change is typically associated with some degree of individual change. Often this individual change is the outcome of an informal and natural process of learning and development. However, there may be occasions when those responsible for managing an organisational change decide that some form of deliberate training intervention is required in order to help individuals develop new knowledge, skills, attitudes and behaviours. Such interventions can be highly structured and very focused on the achievement of closely specified outcomes, or they can be designed to help organisational members learn how to learn and encourage them to actively involve themselves in a self-directed process of professional development.

Training and development is considered here rather than in Part V (on interventions) because it is one of the 'people issues' identified in Chapter 5 (on process models of change) that require constant attention at every stage of the change process.

Training interventions tend to be targeted at two main types of organisational member. On the one hand, there are those who are required to perform new roles associated with managing the change. They may require training, for example, in order to lead a task force charged with diagnosing organisational problems and identifying what needs to be changed. On the other hand there are those who, as a result of the change, will be required to behave differently and may require training in order to be able to achieve new standards of performance.

This chapter will consider, briefly, how training can help to re-establish alignment between the competencies of organisational members and other elements of the system such as task and structure. Attention will also be given to the main aspects of a systematic approach to the development of effective training interventions. The final section will review some Australian studies that have investigated recent trends in the provision of training.

Achieving a 'match' between organisational members and changing task demands

When change calls for new behaviours on the part of organisational members, a number of factors will determine whether or not these new behaviours will be forthcoming. These include the quality of the 'match' between competencies and task demands, the effect of reward systems on the motivation to deliver revised performance outcomes and the availability of feedback to enable individuals and their managers to assess whether the new performance standards are being achieved. This chapter is concerned with the first of these.

Sometimes organisational members will already possess all the competencies they require in order to achieve the new performance standards. All that such people will need (in terms of their ability to perform in new ways) is information about the revised performance outcomes that they will have to achieve.

At other times the people affected by the change may not posses the competencies they will need. In these circumstances, a number of options may be available to those managing the change. They may explore ways of redesigning the task to match the existing competencies of organisational members, they may replace existing staff with others who already have the required competencies, or they may help existing staff to acquire the required new competencies.

A systematic approach to training

Goldstein (1993) and others argue that effective training involves three main steps: the analysis of training needs, the design and delivery of training and the evaluation of training effectiveness.

Training needs analysis

A training needs analysis starts with a system-level review to determine how the proposed change will affect organisational goals, objectives and task demands. This overview provides the information necessary to identify where more specific task and person analyses are required. For example, the move from an optical to a digital scanning technology in the reprographics equipment sector changed the nature of the tasks performed by many organisational units. In this case, a system-level review might have pointed to a need for a more detailed analysis in departments such as product design, assembly, technical support, sales, etc. However, in other departments, such as finance, the system-level review might have identified few implications for the nature of the task performed and the competencies required.

The next step, a task analysis, focuses on specific jobs or roles and examines how modifications to the task of a unit will affect the nature of the performance that will be demanded from members of that unit. It also points to the competencies (knowledge, skill, attitude or behaviour) that people performing these new or modified roles will require in order to perform to the new standard. Elaborating the example of the reprographics equipment manufacturer, a task analysis of, for example, the selling function might have revealed how the introduction of digital scanning technology changed the nature of the performance required by sales persons to sell digital as opposed to optical reprographics equipment.

The person analysis seeks to identify discrepancies between the required competencies, as determined by the task analysis, and the existing competencies of the organisational members available to perform these revised tasks. This analysis provides the information necessary to (a) identify which individuals or groups will require training and (b) specify training objectives in terms of what trainees need to know and how they will be required to behave.

The most useful way of expressing training objectives is in terms of *behavioural objectives* that specify what trainees will be able to do after training. For example, one of the training objectives for the reprographics equipment sales representatives might be 'to be able to accurately describe how the new technology affects the performance of the new range of copiers produced by the company'. Another might be 'to be able to demonstrate to customers how to maintain the equipment to keep it operating at peak efficiency'.

The design and delivery of training

M. Smith (1991) suggests that choice of training method should, at least in part, be determined by the kind of competencies that the training is designed to impart. For example, training methods that are good at imparting knowledge and information include lectures, and reading books and manuals. Where the focus is on attitudes, role play or informal discussion groups might be selected. Where the aim is to develop cognitive strategies, case studies, simulations, projects or mentoring might be used, and where the focus is perceptual and motor skills a variety of methods might be considered. These could include the discrimination method that is designed to help trainees detect differences between items that are very similar, and the progressive parts method which is a schedule for organising the practice of complex motor skills.

Reid and Barrington (1999) classify training strategies under five main headings: training on-the-job; planned organisation experience; in-house courses; planned experience outside the organisation; and external courses. They also recommend four criteria that can be used to determine which of these strategies will be most appropriate:

- Compatibility with training objectives
- Estimated likelihood of transfer of learning to the work situation
- Availability of resources (such as time, money and skilled staff)
- Trainee-related factors.

Reid and Barrington illustrate how these factors can influence choice of training method with an example that can easily be adapted to apply to preparing managers to participate in an organisation-wide change programme. The change agent might be required to set up and manage a project team to develop a strategy to implement a series of changes agreed by the company's management committee. It may be decided that the team should include managers representing a range of departments that will be affected by the changes.

The objectives of the training for team members might include:

1 *Imparting knowledge* (so that trainees will understand, be able to describe to others and recognise actions that will help achieve the aims of the change programme).
2 *Developing positive attitudes* (so that trainees will be committed to the aims of the programme and to working constructively with other members of the team to achieve these aims).
3 *Developing group process skills* (so that trainees will be able to diagnose what is going on in the group and act in ways that will contribute to group effectiveness).

In terms of compatibility with training needs, the change agent might quickly reject some strategies, such as on-the-job training, because there may be no project teams currently operating in the company that could provide the required work experience. External courses, such as outward bound-type team training, might offer a good way of developing positive attitudes towards colleagues and developing group process skills. However, in order to satisfy some to the other training needs, the change agent or somebody else from the company would have to be involved and the course would have to be adapted to provide some sessions that dealt with the aims of the change programme. This would also require the external course to be restricted to managers from the same company who are to work together in the new project team. A specially designed in-company course might be an attractive option. It could include a mix of formal inputs on the aims of the change programme, informal discussion sessions to explore trainees' reactions to these aims and group activities that could be used as a vehicle for developing group process skills.

In terms of the transfer of learning, both the external course, if it were restricted to prospective members of the project team, and the in-house course could facilitate the transfer of group process skills and positive attitudes towards other trainees to the work situation. The in-house course could also score high on the transfer of learning if the group activities involved working on real issues that the team would have to deal with once it 'went live'.

In terms of availability of resources, time might be a factor that would preclude the use of internal or external planned work experience. Cost, in terms of money in the budget rather than the opportunity cost of the change agent's time, might also be a factor that would work against the external course. The in-house course might cost less but the change agent would have to find the time to develop the training materials and the work-related group activities. The change agent may be confident that she has the necessary skills to design and deliver the in-house programme. She might also be aware of an external consultant who could be employed to help at a fee that would be considerably less than the cost of the external course.

In terms of trainee-related factors, from a business perspective, it may be impossible to release all the managers at the same time to participate in a week-long external course. Also, for domestic reasons, some members of the proposed project team may also find it very difficult to be away from home for a whole week.

Taking into account all these factors the change agent may opt for the in-house course.

The evaluation of training effectiveness

The role of evaluation in the context of change management will be discussed in some detail in Chapter 23, together with some of the issues that can affect the validity of evaluation exercises. The focus of attention here is the kind of criteria that can be used when evaluating the effectiveness of training interventions. Kirkpatrick (1983) argues that training can be evaluated at four levels:

- At level one, the criterion is how trainees *reacted* to the training. Did they feel it was relevant, interesting, demanding, etc.?
- At level two, the criterion is *what they learned*. It is not unknown for trainees to react favourably to the training but to learn relatively little, or achieve acceptable standards of learning in respect of only some, but not all, of the learning goals. This kind of feedback has obvious implications for those responsible for selecting the training strategy and designing the details of the learning activity.
- At level three, the criterion is *behaviour*. Trainees may have reacted positively to the training and learned what it was intended they should learn. However, back on the job their behaviour may have changed little, if at all. In other words, what was learned on the course may not have been transferred to the work situation. It is relatively easy to apply the relevant principles of learning to design a training activity that will encourage learning. It is much more difficult to design a training activity that will ensure that the learning is transferred and used in the work situation. A common problem that inhibits transfer is the social pressure that trainees are subjected to after they return from training. While they may have learned best practice when on the course, back on the job colleagues often pressure them to revert back to the traditional ways of working.
- At level four, the criterion is *results*. It is possible for the training to produce the intended changes in behaviour, but this behaviour change

may not produce the intended results. Sales representatives may have started to call more regularly on customers but this may not produce the increase in sales that had been anticipated. This kind of feedback indicates a need for a fundamental rethink of the training strategy.

Training for change: the Australian experience

Studies in several countries have found that organisational change is closely associated with the level of training activity in organisations (Cappelli and Rogovsky, 1994; Osterman, 1995). A. Smith (2005) reviewed two major studies of enterprise-level training in Australia that confirm this relationship.

Smith and Hayton (1999) investigated the drivers of enterprise-level training. Their research involved forty-two case studies in five industry sectors (construction, electronic manufacturing, food processing, retail and financial services) and a national survey of 1,760 organisations across all sectors.

In terms of the systematic approach to training outlined in this chapter there was evidence that organisations did adopt some form of training needs analysis and in many cases this was based on a system of performance appraisal. However, the evaluation of training was relatively underdeveloped. None of the case study organisations went much beyond the use of traditional end-of-course evaluation forms.

Senior managers in some organisations adopted a proactive strategic approach to training and viewed it as a vehicle for building skill sets that could provide the basis for a sustainable competitive advantage, but attitudes towards training were often fragmented and middle and junior managers tended to be more reactive and viewed training as a short, sharp and focused response to immediate operational problems. Because training responsibilities were often devolved to operational managers, it appeared that the real drivers for training were the changes that were introduced as part of the strategic response. These included workplace change, quality improvement and new technology.

Workplace change was the most important of these drivers. New technology was less important than anticipated. The introduction of new products frequently required only minimum changes to existing production processes and could be introduced with little additional training. New production processes, on the other hand, often involved fundamental changes to the way work was carried out and therefore triggered a more extensive need for training. However, the required training was often short and simple and was frequently outsourced to the vendors of the new process technology. New forms of work organisation and structural change accounted for most of the increase in training activity and emphasised behavioural rather than traditional technical skills. Smith and Hayton suggest that this shift towards behavioural skills training reflects a growing concern in Australian enterprises to develop adaptability to changes in work organisation rather than technology.

The second study (Smith *et al.*, 2003) investigated in more depth the relationship between enterprise-level training and organisational change. It involved a survey of 3,415 HR managers and follow-up interviews with seventy-eight of them. While training activity was clearly associated with the introduction of new management practices (such as TQM, team working and BPR), few of the managers surveyed felt that training had played a major role in the implementation of change. Typically training played a 'catch-up role' dealing with the *consequences* of change rather than playing a major role in its planning or implementation (Smith *et al.*, 2003: 41).

Findings relating to the kind of training associated with the introduction of new management practices confirm the move away from technical skills to a new training paradigm that emphasises the development of broad sets of generic behavioural skills. For example, the introduction of TQM involves the implementation of team working, the development of interpersonal and problem solving skills and, especially in service industries, customer service skills. There is also a requirement to train large numbers of staff in specific TQM skills such as data collection and analysis. Experience from Australia and elsewhere indicates that the scale of the training input often requires the use of non-training specialists, which in turn requires the provision of trainer training programmes.

Team working had been introduced by about two-thirds of the organisations included in the survey and was clearly linked to an increase in training activity. This was focused on team working skills for team members and management training for more senior staff. Banker *et al.* (1996) found that training is a key determinant of the success and longevity of teams. Team working often changes the role of the supervisor or involves people being appointed to a new role of team leader. This calls for training to help leaders facilitate their teams. Team members may also receive training in group process skills and training to cover jobs other than their own and/or to take on greater responsibility for their work.

One new management practice that was not always associated with an increase in training activity was the introduction of *lean production*. Smith *et al.* (2003) found that lean production was consistently associated with cost cutting and this included measures to cut the cost of training. Typically the level of formal training and the level of training infrastructure (training facilities and dedicated training staff) were reduced. Most of the training that was undertaken tended to be on-the-job and skewed in favour of managers.

The studies undertaken by Smith and Hayton (1999) and Smith *et al.* (2003) provide an overview of enterprise-level training in Australia over a period of ten years from 1994 to 2003. This was a period of rapid change because from the early 1980s companies operating in Australia have been exposed to increasing levels of international and domestic competition. A number of trends in the development of enterprise-level training emerged from these studies.

The first relates to the link between *training* and *business strategy*. Notwithstanding the finding reported by Smith *et al.* (2003) that training did not play a major role in the planning and implementation of change, A. Smith (2005) reports that there has been an increase in the number of organisations that are conscious of the need to link training to business strategy if they are to capitalise more effectively on their investment in training. He notes that where enterprises have made this link the result has been a substantial increase in all forms of training, and a greater embedding of training into the management of the enterprise.

The second trend relates to the *individualisation of training*. There has been a shift away from delivery methods that impose uniform training programmes on large groups of employees towards a more focused training provision linked to individual performance management. This trend has been associated with the demise of large centralised training departments and the devolution of responsibility for training to line managers.

Finally, much of the growth in training activity has involved the development of broad sets of *generic behavioural skills* rather than technical skills, and has been linked to the introduction of new management practices.

Summary

This chapter has considered how training can contribute to the change process. Attention has been directed towards the main elements of an effective approach to training. These are:

1   A training needs analysis, which involves three steps:

   • A system-level review to determine which parts of the organisation will be affected by the change
   • A more focused task analysis to determine how the pattern of task demands and required competencies will change
   • A person analysis to identify the extent to which existing organisational members posses the required competencies.

2   The design and delivery of training.
3   The evaluation of the training.

The final section of this chapter has reviewed the development of training practice in Australia over a ten-year period and highlighted a number of trends in training provision.

Exercise 12.1   Assessing the way training is used in the change process

Reflect on either an organisation-wide change or a change targeted at a particular department or unit in your organisation.

Consider the following points and then make a brief assessment of the way training was used to help achieve change:

- Was there any evidence indicating that the organisation and/or particular change managers were prepared to invest in training to support change?
- Was the attention given to training inadequate, about right, or 'over the top'?
- Was the training targeted at the individuals and groups most in need of training?
- Was the training that was provided compatible with training requirements and delivered in a way that maximised the transfer of learning to the work situation?

Assessment of the way training was used to help achieve change

References

Banker, R.D., Field, J.M., Schroeder, R.D. and Sinha, K.K. (1996) 'Impact of Work Teams on Manufacturing Performance: A Longitudinal Field Study', *Academy of Management Journal*, 39 (4), pp. 867–90.

Cappelli, P. and Rogovsky, N. (1994) 'New Work Systems and Skill Requirements', *International Labour Review*, 133 (2), pp. 205–20.

Goldstein, I.L. (1993) *Training in Organisations*, 3rd edn, Monterey, CA: Brooks/Cole.

Kirkpatrick, D.L. (1983) 'Four Steps in Measuring Training Effectiveness', *Personnel Administrator*, 28 (11), pp. 19–25.

Osterman, P. (1995) 'Skill, Training and Work Organisation in American Establishments', *Industrial Relations*, 34 (2), 125–46.

Reid, M. and Barrington, H. (1999) *Training Interventions*, London: Institute of Personnel and Development.

Smith, A. (2005) 'The Development of Employer Training in Australia', Discussion Paper, Charles Sturt University, Australia.

Smith, A. and Hayton, G. (1999) 'What Drives Enterprise Training? Evidence from Australia', *International Journal of Human Resource Management*, 10 (2), pp. 251–72.

Smith, A., Oczkowski, E., Noble, C. and Macklin, R. (2003) 'New Management Practices and Enterprise Training in Australia', *International Journal of Manpower*, 24 (1), pp. 31–47.

Smith, M. (1991) 'Training in Organisations', in M. Smith (ed.), *Analysing Organizational Behaviour*, London: Macmillan, pp. 49–76.

Motivating others to change

It was noted in Chapter 3 that organisations, like all open systems, seek to maintain a state of equilibrium; they tend to gravitate to a condition where all the component parts of the system are aligned with each other. Intentionally intervening to change the organisation by modifying one component of the system can disturb this state of equilibrium and can create pressure to restore it. Restoration can be achieved by re-aligning other components with those that have been changed or by resisting the change and seeking to re-establish the status quo.

In all organisational systems, there is a natural tendency to resist change. This chapter will:

- consider how the general level of commitment in an organisation can affect the extent to which organisational members will support new initiatives
- review and synthesise some of the views on resistance to change presented by Zaltman and Duncan (1977), Kotter and Schlesinger (1979), Nadler (1993) and Pugh (1993)
- assess the utility of expectancy theory as a basis for assessing the motivation of an individual or group to support or resist change
- consider how change strategies can be designed to motivate individuals and groups to change.

Organisational commitment and the level of support for change

People's past experience of change can affect their level of commitment to the organisation and their willingness to support further change.

Over forty years ago, Argyris (1964) first defined the psychological contract as the perceptions of both parties to the employment relationship of their obligations implied in the relationship. More recently, Guest *et al.* (1996) referred to it in terms of perceptions of fairness, trust and the extent to which the 'deal' is perceived to have been delivered. It is an unwritten set of expectations between every member of an organisation and those who represent the organisation to them, and it incorporates concepts such as fairness, reciprocity and a sense of mutual obligation. For example, organisations may expect employees to be loyal, keep trade secrets, work hard and do their best for the organisation. In return, employees may expect that they will receive an equitable level of remuneration, will be treated fairly and with dignity, will have some level of security of employment and, possibly, some level of autonomy and an opportunity to learn and develop. If employees feel that their employer/managers have kept their side of the psychological contract, they are likely to respond by displaying a high level of commitment to the organisation. If, on the other hand, they feel that the organisation has failed to keep its side of the bargain they may respond by redefining their side of the psychological contract. They may invest less effort in their work, be less inclined to innovate and less inclined to respond to the innovations or changes proposed by others.

Exercise 13.1   Violations of the psychological contract

Think of an incident at work when the organisation/management fell short of what might have been reasonably expected of them in their treatment of an individual or group of employees.

In the space below, list any effects this incident had on the level of commitment of the individual or group and on their willingness to support change.

 Notes

You might also consider the effect on others. People observe how colleagues are treated, and this affects their views about how they may be treated in the future if they are involved in some kind of change. Note, in the space below, any 'ripple effect' that this incident had on the commitment of others and on their willingness to support change.

 Notes

Managers often expect that those who have been retained after a programme of redundancies will be relieved and grateful and will respond with higher levels of commitment and performance. Research on the 'survivor syndrome' (see Doherty and Horsted, 1995) suggests that this may not be the case. Survivors may respond in a number of ways, ranging from shock, anger, animosity towards management, guilt, concern for those gone, and anxiety, to relief that they still have a job or fear of losing their job in the future. The evidence suggests that survivors often display less confidence in and a lack of commitment, trust and loyalty to the organisation.

As Bob Worcester, chair of MORI, once said:

> Don't worry about those staff who turn off and go: worry about those who turn off – and stay!

Reasons for resisting specific changes

Kotter and Schlesinger (1979) identify four main reasons why people resist change.

Parochial self-interest

People resist change when they think that it will cause them to lose something of value. It is not uncommon for stakeholders to focus on their own best interests rather than those of the organisation.

Pugh (1993) suggests that all too often managers fail to anticipate resistance because they consider change only from a rational resource allocation perspective and fail to appreciate that many organisational members are much more concerned about the impact it will have on them personally. They will assess its impact in terms of how it might affect ways of working, job opportunities, career prospects, job satisfaction, and so on, and in terms of how it might undermine or enhance their power and status, and the prestige of the groups to which they belong.

Zaltman and Duncan (1977) view threats to power and influence as one of the most important sources of resistance to change. They observe that the prospect of a merger often gives rise to fears on the part of individuals, groups and even entire organisations that they will lose control over decision making. They also note that managers, even very senior managers, may resist the use of certain approaches to the management of change if they feel that they may undermine their power and authority. They illustrate this with an example of head teachers who were resistant to the use of a survey feedback approach to organisation development because it enabled teachers and district-level personnel to have access to data and to use it, along with the heads, to propose solutions to problems. Some of the head teachers were concerned that this approach would increase the power of the teachers and undermine their own power to influence how the schools were managed.

Misunderstanding and lack of trust

Misunderstandings can be a frequent source of resistance. Stakeholders often resist change because they do not understand the implications it may have for them. Such misunderstandings may lead them to perceive that the change will cost them more than they will gain.

Misunderstandings are most likely to arise when trust is lacking between the person(s) initiating the change and the stakeholders who feel that they will be affected by it. Lines *et al.* (2005) note that several studies have linked trust to levels of openness in communication and information-sharing, levels of conflict and the acceptance of decisions or goals. When organisational members do not trust change managers, they are likely to resist any change they propose.

Managers and change agents often fail to anticipate this kind of resistance, especially when they are introducing a change that they perceive will be of benefit to those involved, because they assume that people only resist changes that undermine their best interests. The author was asked by the CEO of a chemical company to investigate why the work-force had rejected a productivity agreement that senior management believed offered considerable advantage to both the organisation and process workers. It turned out that the message that had been communicated to the work-force was, in some important respects, different to the proposal that the senior management team had agreed to make (see Chapter 11 on communication problems). These differences had arisen as the proposal had been passed down the management chain. However, this communication problem had been compounded by the fact that the process workers felt that the offer was too good to be true and that management was intent on manipulating them in some way.

Different assessments

Kotter and Schlesinger (1979) suggest that another common reason why some stakeholders resist change is that they assess the situation differently from those initiating the change and see more costs than benefits resulting from it, not only for themselves but also for the organisation or other constituencies that are important to them. They argue that managers who initiate change sometimes assume that (a) they have all the relevant information required to conduct an adequate organisation analysis and that (b) those that will be affected by the change have the same facts. Often neither assumption is correct. Those initiating change also often fail to take account of how the change might affect stakeholders who are not organisational members. External stakeholders can be an important source of resistance. This problem was discussed in Chapter 9.

Zaltman and Duncan (1977) point to how selective attention and retention can prevent individuals or groups appreciating that the current state of affairs is unsatisfactory. The mental models that influence how they perceive, interpret and make sense of their environment (referred to in Chapter 4 on organisational learning) can have a strong effect on how organisational members assess their circumstances and whether or not they perceive any problems that require remedial action. Their mental models can also affect the kind of solution that will be favoured if a problem is perceived to exist. It is not unusual for resistance to occur, even when organisational members and their managers have a shared view of the nature of a problem, because both parties have conflicting views about what should be done to resolve it.

Low tolerance for change

Stakeholders also resist change when they are concerned that they will not be able to develop the new skills and behaviours that will be required of them. All people are limited in their ability to change, but some are much more limited than others. In Chapter 1 reference was made to Toffler's view that people respond to the increasing rate of change in different ways and that some are more able than others to internalise the principle of acceleration, modify their durational expectancies and make an unconscious compensation for the compression of time. Toffler also considers the phenomenon of adaptive breakdown, which he refers to as 'future shock'.

Even when stakeholders intellectually understand the need for change they, sometimes, are emotionally unable to make the transition (see Chapter 14 on the management of personal transitions). The change may involve a grieving process similar to that which occurs when a person loses a loved one. Perceived loss can affect people in different ways but often this involves some element of denial and a reluctance to 'let go'.

Expectancy theory and the motivation to support or resist change

Expectancy theory considers how expectations influence motivation. It offers a useful conceptual framework for assessing whether a stakeholder is likely to support or resist an impending change. Expectancy theorists (e.g. Vroom, 1964; Porter and Lawler, 1968) argue that behaviour is a function of two factors – the attractiveness of outcomes and expectancies about the future:

- *Outcomes* can be evaluated in terms of their value or attractiveness. Vroom refers to this as 'valence'. If stakeholders expect the change to reduce the availability of valued outcomes they are likely to offer resistance. If, on the other hand, they expect it to increase the availability of valued outcomes they are more likely to offer support.

- *Expectancies*. It is not only the potential availability of valued outcomes that will determine whether a stakeholder will support or resist a change. Stakeholder motivation will also be influenced by expectancies about the likelihood that they will actually receive valued outcomes in practice. The theory focuses attention on two expectancies about the future:

  (a) *Effort to performance expectancy* This refers to the person's expectation (subjective probability about the likelihood) that she can perform at a given level (in other words, that effort will lead to successful performance).

  (b) *Performance to outcome expectancy* This refers to a person's expectation that some level of performance will lead to desired outcomes (or the avoidance of negative outcomes).

From a motivational perspective it is the expectation or belief about the relationship between effort, performance and valued outcome that will determine whether a stakeholder will be motivated to support or resist a change. The basic elements of this theory are illustrated in Figure 13.1.

Equity of treatment

The model can be extended to include the stakeholder's expectations about equity of outcome in the changed situation. If stakeholders believe that comparable others will receive more favourable treatment (in terms of valued outcomes) as a result of the change this will affect their assessment of the attractiveness of the outcomes they expect to receive. Some stakeholders who expect, in absolute terms, to receive a net increase in valued outcomes may resist the change because they feel that they are being treated unfairly relative to comparable others.

Figure 13.1   The expectancy model of motivation

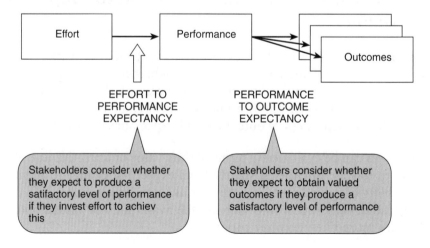

Understanding and competence

The model can also be extended to include key factors that may affect effort–performance expectancies. These include the stakeholder's understanding of the nature of the required performance (and the rules that govern how a performance should be produced) and the competencies required to deliver a satisfactory level of performance. These will be discussed below. This is illustrated in Figure 13.2.

Figure 13.2   An expectancy model of the motivation to support or resist change

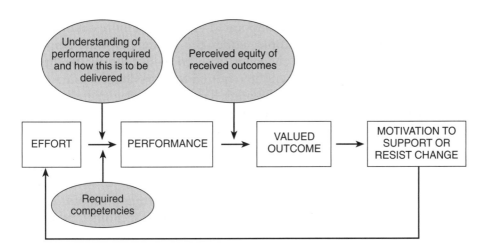

Assessing the availability of valued outcomes

The first step in assessing how stakeholders will respond to change is to identify how the change will affect the availability of valued outcomes in the changed situation.

In order to do this the change manager needs to:

- Be aware of the kinds of outcome that are valued by the stakeholders who will be affected by the change
- Have some understanding of the extent to which the current situation provides these outcomes
- Have some understanding of the extent to which valued outcomes will be (at least potentially) available in the changed situation.

This assessment will provide a useful first indication of the extent to which stakeholders will support or resist the change. It will also indicate the extent to which they are likely to be motivated to perform in ways that will contribute to organisational effectiveness in the changed situation.

When people are confronted by an impending change they often fear that they will lose some of the outcomes that they value in the existing situation. However, they may also anticipate some gains. These gains might be more of the outcomes that they already enjoy or some completely new benefits. In order to anticipate how stakeholders will feel about a change it is necessary to empathise with them in order to construct a balance sheet of (what we think) they will perceive as gains or losses.

Different people value different outcomes. Even the same person may value different outcomes at different points in time. The more that we know about stakeholders, the better placed we will be to construct a balance sheet of their gains and losses. Listed in Table 13.1 are some broad headings that might suggest the kinds of outcomes that could be important to stakeholders.

Each of these headings can be elaborated to include a more detailed list of associated outcomes. For example, under the heading of pay, employees might feel that the impending change is likely to reduce the availability of a valued outcome because they will be required to work longer hours or at a faster rate for the same pay. On the other hand, the change might be viewed as enhancing valued outcomes if it leads to a re-grading that will boost pay. This might also be the case if it offers a shift to annualised hours that will eliminate unpredictable variations in weekly pay and provide a guaranteed annual income that can be used, for example, to secure a bank loan or a mortgage.

The broad headings listed in Table 13.1 are intended as prompts. They do not provide an exhaustive list. Different kinds of stakeholder may value different kinds of outcome.

Table 13.1   Types of outcome that could be important to stakeholders

Pay
Working conditions
Interesting/meaningful work
Autonomy
Opportunity for competition or collaboration
Opportunities to be creative
Power and influence
Belonging/involvement
Location
Security
Working with considerate supervisors
Satisfaction
Challenge
Achievement
Recognition
Status
Openness/sharing
Opportunity to use knowledge and skills

Exercise 13.2   Assessing the availability of valued outcomes

1   Think about a recent or impending change at work or elsewhere (home, church, etc.), and identify a key stakeholder affected by the change.
2   List all the *valued outcomes* that you believe the stakeholder receives in the *current situation*. Review the list and indicate whether you feel that the change will produce a gain (✔), no change (**?**), or a loss (✘) for each outcome.

Valued outcome in existing situation	✔	?	✘	Rank

3   Next, extend the list by adding any *new outcomes* that you anticipate will be available to the stakeholder in the *changed situation* and indicate your assessment of whether the stakeholder will view them as a gain (✔), neutrally (**?**), or as a loss (✘) for each outcome.

New outcome in changed situation	✔	?	✘	Rank

4   Finally, review the content of the full table and *rank* how you think the stakeholder will value the outcomes. In the column headed 'Rank', enter the figure 1 next to the most valued outcome, 2 next to the second most valued, and so on.
5   *Assess net gain or loss.* In order to make an overall assessment of the potential net gain or loss for the stakeholder it is necessary to take account of both the number of gains and losses identified in the table, and also the relative importance of the different valued outcomes to the stakeholder.

The ranking is intended to provide a basis for weighting the significance of each gain and loss.

Is the stakeholder likely to view the net effect of the change as a:

GAIN	
LOSS	

6   Consider whether those responsible for managing the change were/are aware of how the change was/is likely to affect the availability of outcomes that are valued by the selected stakeholders.

7   Consider whether this information might have improved the way the change was/is being managed.

 Notes

Expectancies about effort–performance and performance–outcome relationships and equity of net benefits

Although the change manager may see potential net gains for the people affected by the change, the individuals concerned may not share this assessment.

Whether stakeholders will be motivated to support or resist the change will depend on *their* expectations about:

- their ability to deliver a satisfactory level of performance in the changed situation

- whether a satisfactory (or even exceptional) level of performance will lead to the achievement of valued outcomes in the changed situation
- whether the net benefits accruing to them will be equitable when compared to the net benefits accruing to comparable others in the changed situation.

In order to understand better the extent to which stakeholders will resist or support change the change manager needs to consider these three issues.

> **1. Anticipate stakeholder expectations regarding whether they will be able to produce a satisfactory level of performance in the changed situation**

There will be less resistance (more support) in those situations where stakeholders expect to be able to deliver a satisfactory level of performance in the changed situation. Individuals or groups are more likely to resist a change when they expect that, irrespective of how hard they work, the change will undermine their ability to produce a satisfactory level of performance.

Diagnosis

In order to anticipate how the change might affect stakeholder expectations about their ability to produce a satisfactory level of performance in the changed situation the change manager needs to:

- Consider whether any misunderstandings might arise about the processes and procedures that will apply in the changed situation. Stakeholders may assume that any new rules that define the nature of a satisfactory level of performance, or new rules that regulate working practices may undermine their ability to produce a satisfactory level of performance.

  ### Example
  Individuals may assume that in the changed situation they will have less autonomy and that they will be required to work in a group setting. They may also fear that in this group setting their performance will be dependent on inputs from others who are poor or unreliable performers. Their fears may be well founded, but they may also be based on misunderstandings about the nature of the change or the other people they may have to work with.

Possible action

The change manager may be able to reduce resistance from this source by:

- helping people develop a clear understanding of how the change will affect the way they will be required to work (*education*)
- helping them understand the consequences that these new processes and procedures may have for their ability to deliver a performance (*education and persuasion*)
- providing them with an opportunity to be involved in the planning of the change; this might reassure them that the change will be managed in a way that will minimise those factors that could undermine their ability to deliver a satisfactory level of performance (*participation and involvement*).

- Consider the relevance of existing core competencies in the changed situation.

Example
In those situations where a stakeholder's core competencies become more highly valued the individual is more likely to support the change. However, where core competencies are perceived to be less relevant (or even redundant) the change is more likely to be resisted because stakeholders may fear that they will not be able to produce a satisfactory level of performance.

Possible action

The change agent may be able to reduce the resistance from this source by:

- considering possibilities for re-deploying people to roles that will better utilise existing competencies (*planning*)
- involving people in identifying possibilities for redeployment, (*participation*)
- providing training to develop more relevant competencies (*training and development*).

---

2. Anticipate stakeholder expectations about the relationship between performance and the achievement of valued outcomes in the changed situation

There will be less resistance (and more support) for a change in those situations where stakeholders expect that the delivery of a satisfactory level of performance will be linked to the achievement of valued outcomes. In those situations where they expect the change to undermine the achievement of valued outcomes they are more likely to resist the change and to be less motivated to perform in the changed situation.

Diagnosis

In order to anticipate how the change might affect stakeholder expectations about the relationship between performance and the achievement of valued outcomes change agent needs to:

- Empathise with the stakeholders affected by the change in order to develop a better understanding of how they might expect the change to affect the link between performance and the achievement of valued outcomes.

  ### Example
  If an individual values promotion and expects that in the changed situation there will be a closer link between advancement and level of performance, s/he may support the change and be motivated to perform well in the changed situation. If, however, the individual expects the change to weaken this link then it will increase the possibility that the change will be resisted.

Possible action

The change agent may be able to reduce resistance from this source by:

- considering ways of modifying the change to strengthen the links between performance and the achievement of valued outcomes (planning)
- persuading individuals that the change will actually strengthen these links (persuasion)
- Involving stakeholders in the diagnosis, planning and implementation of the change. This might reassure them that the change will be managed in a way that will strengthen links between performance and valued outcomes (participation).

---

3. Anticipate stakeholder perceptions of their net benefits (or losses) compared to those enjoyed by comparable others

There will be less resistance (and more support) in those situations where stakeholders feel that they are being treated equitably relative to others. Where they feel that they are being treated unfairly they may be more likely to resist the change.

Diagnosis

In order to anticipate the effects of perceived equity on the level of resistance or support for change the change agent needs to:

- Identify those who may regard themselves as being treated inequitably.

Possible action

The change agent may be able to reduce resistance from this source by:

- helping people who feel this way recognise all the potential gains available to them and ensuring that they fully understand the possible losses if the change is not implemented (*education and persuasion*)
- exploring the possibilities for improving the availability of valued outcomes for those who feel they have received inequitable treatment (*planning*)
- exploring the possibility of redistributing costs and benefits between those affected by the change in order to produce greater equity (*planning*)
- Involving stakeholders in the diagnosis, planning and implementation of the change. This might reassure them that the change will be managed in a way that will maximise equity of treatment (*participation*).

Resistance and the need to motivate people to change

Attempts to introduce change often founder because the new initiative is resisted. Earlier sections of this chapter have considered why resistance might be encountered and presented an expectancy based model for diagnosing resistance and identifying possible ways of managing it. This section provides a more detailed discussion of how change strategies can be designed to motivate individuals and groups to change.

Kotter and Schlesinger (1979) identify six methods for dealing with resistance to change:

Education and persuasion √

One of the most frequently used ways of minimising resistance is to educate people about the need for change. Zaltman and Duncan (1977) refer to 'educative strategies' as those that provide a relatively unbiased presentation of the facts in order to provide a rational justification for action. This approach is based on the assumption that organisational members and other stakeholders are rational beings capable of discerning fact and adjusting their behaviour accordingly when the facts are presented to them.

A related approach is the *persuasive strategy* that aims to motivate people to change by biasing the message to increase its appeal. Most advertising is persuasive in nature. When the level of commitment to change is low, persuasive approaches are likely to be more effective than rational educative strategies. Persuasive approaches can increase commitment by stressing (realistically or falsely) either the benefits of changing or the costs of not changing. If the message is so false/biased as to deceive the change target, the approach is better classified as manipulative (see below).

Nadler (1993) builds on Lewin's notion of 'unfreezing' and argues that one of the most effective ways of motivating people to change is to expose or create a feeling of dissatisfaction with the current state. This can be accomplished via education or persuasion, but there is evidence to suggest that focusing attention on the weaknesses of the change target's current practice is less effective than informing them of the potential benefit associated with the adoption of alternative practices. Confronting people about problems associated with current practice can be interpreted as criticism and blame, and can provoke a defensive reaction. Instead of motivating people to change, the effect can be to motivate them to save face by justifying current practice and denying the need to change.

Participation and involvement

Nadler (1993) argues that another effective way of surfacing and creating dissatisfaction with the current state and motivating people to change is to involve them in the collection, analysis and presentation of information. Information that people collect for themselves is more believable than information presented to them by external experts or other advocates of change.

A potential benefit of participation and involvement is that it can *excite, motivate and help create a shared perception of the need for change* within a target group. When change is imposed, the change target is likely to experience a lack of control and feel the 'victim' of change. The more people are involved the more likely they are to feel that the change is something that they are helping to create. In addition to increasing motivation, participation and involvement can also produce better decisions because of the wider input and can help to sustain the change once implemented because of a greater sense of 'ownership'.

The classic study by Coch and French (1948) demonstrated that workers are much more accepting of a change in work practices when they are involved in the planning of the change. Their findings suggested that participation led to the *acceptance of new practices* because it encouraged the group to 'own' them as a group goal. Group ownership offered the bonus that group norms developed that helped to implement and sustain the changes. Acceptance (and the effect of acceptance on productivity) was most marked when the basis of participation was the whole group. When participation was by representation there was an initial decline in productivity. This suggests that when people are not personally involved it can take them longer to understand and accept the new practices. Lines (2004) reports a study of change management in a national telecommunications firm that demonstrates a link between participation and the acceptance of change. The findings indicate a strong positive relationship between participation, goal achievement and organisational commitment and a strong negative relationship with resistance.

Involvement can be encouraged at any stage of the change process and can include all of a target group or only a representative sample. Organisational members might be invited to participate in the initial diagnosis of the problem, in the development of solutions and the planning of implementation strategies, in the actual implementation of the change plan and/or in the evaluation of the effectiveness of the change. Some of these possibilities will be discussed in more detail in Chapter 17, when different types of intervention are considered.

Some managers have an ideological commitment to participation and involvement whereas others feel that it threatens their power and authority and is almost always a mistake. Kotter and Schlesinger (1979) maintain that both attitudes can lead to problems because neither is very realistic. They argue that where change initiators do not have all the information they need to design and implement a change, or when they need the wholehearted commitment of the change target, involving others can make very good sense. However, involvement does have some costs. It can be very time-consuming and, if those who are involved have less technical expertise than the change initiators, it can result in a change plan that is not as good as it might be.

Facilitation and support

Kotter and Schlesinger (1979) suggest that when fear and anxiety lie at the heart of resistance an effective approach to motivating change is to offer facilitation and support. They suggest that this might involve the provision of training in new skills, giving time off after a demanding period, or simply listening and providing emotional support.

Nadler (1993) refers to the need to provide time and opportunity for people to disengage from the current state. This can be especially helpful when they feel a sense of loss associated with the 'letting go' of something they value or something they feel is an important part of their individual or group identity. Nadler also refers to the value of group sessions that provide organisational members with the opportunity to share their concerns about the change. However, he acknowledges the possibility that such sessions might also have the effect of increasing rather than reducing resistance.

Ceremonies and rituals that mark transitions can also help people 'let go' of the past and begin to think constructively about the future.

The provision of emotional support can be particularly effective in circumstances where feelings and emotions get in the way and undermine people's ability to think clearly and objectively about a problem. Some examples of facilitation and support will be considered in Chapter 14, the management of personal transitions.

Negotiation and agreement

People can be motivated to change by rewarding those behaviours that will facilitate the change. The explicit provision of rewards is a useful approach when the change target is unlikely to perceive any obvious gains associated with the original change proposal.

Kotter and Schlesinger suggest that negotiated agreements can be a relatively easy way to avoid resistance when it is clear that someone, who has sufficient power to resist a change, is going to lose out if the change is implemented. The problem associated with this approach is that others who may have been content to go along with the change may now see the possibility of improving their lot through negotiation. The long-term effect can be to increase in the cost of implementing changes and to increase the time required to negotiate the change with all the interested parties.

Manipulation and cooptation

Manipulation is the covert attempt to influence others to change and it can involve the deliberate biasing of messages, as considered above in the discussion of persuasive communications. It can also involve cooptation. Kotter and Schlesinger (1979) note that coopting usually involves giving an individual or group leader a desirable role in the design or implementation of the change. The aim is not to seek access to any expertise they may have; rather, it is to secure their endorsement.

While this approach may be quicker and cheaper than negotiation it runs the risk of those who are coopted feeling that they have been 'tricked' into supporting the change. Those who are coopted may also exercise more influence than anticipated, and steer the change in a direction not favoured by the change initiators.

Direction and a reliance on explicit and implicit coercion

The ability to exercise power exists when one person or group is dependent on another for something they value. Coercive strategies involve change managers using their power to grant or withhold valued outcomes in order to motivate people to change. While the result may be a willingness to comply and go along with the change, the change target's commitment to the change may be low. Consequently, compliance may be sustained only so long as the change manager continues to monitor the situation and maintains the threat of withholding valued outcomes.

In spite of the risks of long-term resentment and the possibility of retaliation that are often associated with coercive change strategies, there may be occasions where their use is appropriate. These may include situations where the target group has a low perceived need for change, where the proposed change is not attractive to the target group and where speed is essential.

Summary

This chapter has considered how the general level of commitment in an organisation can affect the level of support for change. It has also considered the utility of expectancy theory for assessing resistance to change, and has examined six methods for dealing with resistance to change.

References

Argyris, C. (1964) *Integrating the Individual and the Organization*, New York: Wiley.

Coch, L. and French. J.R. (1948) 'Overcoming Resistance to Chage', *Human Relations*, 1, pp. 512–32.

Doherty, N. and Horsted, J. (1995) 'Helping Survivors Stay on Board', *People Management*, 1, pp. 26–31.

Guest, D., Conway, N., Briner, R. and Dickman, M. (1996) *The State of The Psychological Contract in Employment*, London: Institute of Personnel and Development.

Kotter, J.P. and Schlesinger, L.A. (1979) 'Choosing Strategies for Change', *Harvard Business Review*, 57 (2), pp. 106–114.

Lines, R. (2004) 'Influence of Participation in Strategic Change: Resistance, Organisational Commitment and Change Goal Achievement', *Journal of Change Management*, 4 (3), pp. 193–215.

Lines, R., Selart, M., Espedal, B. and Johansen, S.T. (2005) 'The Production of Trust during Organizational Change', *Journal of Change Management*, 5 (2), pp. 221–45.

✝ Nadler, D. (1993)' Concepts for the Management of Organisational Change', in C. Mabey and B. Mayon-White (eds), *Managing Change*, 2nd edn, London: Paul Chapman, in association with the Open University, pp. 85–98.

Porter, I. and Lawler, E.E. (1968) *Managerial Attitudes and Performance*. New York: Irwin.

Pugh, D. (1993) 'Understanding and Managing Organisational Change', in C. Mabey and B. Mayon-White (eds), *Managing Change*, 2nd edn, London: Paul Chapman, in association with the Open University, pp. 108–12.

Vroom, V.H. (1964) *Work and Motivation*, London: Wiley.

Zaltman, G. and Duncan, R. (1977) *Strategies for Planned Change*, chapter 3, London: John Wiley.

Two other useful references are:

Arnold, J. (1996) 'The Psychological Contract, A Concept in Need of Closer Scrutiny', *European Journal of Work and Organisational Psychology*, 5 (4), pp. 511–20.

Herriot, P., Manning, W. and Kidd, J. (1997) 'The Content of the Psychological Contract', *British Journal of Management*, 8, pp. 151–62.

Managing personal transitions

Chapter 13 (on motivating others to change) considered some of the factors that determine whether stakeholders will view a change as an opportunity that promises personal benefit or a threat that may reduce access to valued outcomes. It also considered some of the steps that change managers can take to motivate stakeholders to support a change.

This chapter addresses the way that organisational members experience change (irrespective of whether they view it as an opportunity or threat). It examines the individual's response to change as a progression through a number of stages of psychological reaction. It also considers how an understanding of the way individuals react to change can help managers plan and implement organisational change in ways that will maximise benefit and minimise cost for both the organisation and individual stakeholders.

Organisational change involves a change in contextual or situational factors (such as technology, structures, systems and required competencies) *and* a series of personal transitions for all those affected. Bridges (1980) suggests that while many managers are wise about the mechanics of change, they are often unaware of the dynamics of transition.

Personal transitions are important because, even though some situational factors can be changed relatively quickly, the new organisational arrangements may not work as planned until the people involved 'let go' of the way things used to be and adjust to the new situation. Commenting on the factors that can undermine the successful implementation of change Bridges (1991) claims that: 'It isn't the changes that do you in, it's the transitions.'

The nature of personal transitions

Individuals, like organisations, can be confronted with *incremental* or *discontinuous* change. It was noted in Chapter 4 that a feature of discontinuous change is that it challenges taken-for-granted assumptions about how the organisation relates with the environment. It calls for a rethink about what business the organisation is in, and what needs to be done in order to ensure that it survives and grows.

Some changes are very gradual – for example – ageing, and individuals can adjust to them without experiencing any sudden personal disruption. Where the process of change is continuous and incremental it rarely presents any abrupt challenges to the assumptions individuals make about how they relate to the world around them. But this is not the case for all types of change. A sudden merger, and the announcement that key personnel will have to compete for senior posts in the new organisation, will raise many questions in the minds of those affected about what the future will hold for them. This is an example of a change that poses a serious challenge to an individual's assumptive world.

Parkes (1971) argues that this 'assumptive world' is the only world we are aware of. It includes everything we know or think we know. It affects our interpretation of the past and our expectations of the future, our plans and our prejudices. Any or all of these may need to change as a result of an organisational change, whether or not these changes are perceived as gains or losses.

When changes are lasting in their effects, take place over a relatively short period of time and affect large areas of the assumptive world, they are experienced as personal transitions.

The change manager may perceive the promotion of a team member to team leader as a simple and quickly accomplished organisational change. However, from the perspective of the individual who is promoted, the personal transition associated with this organisational change might be a much more protracted process. It may be difficult for the newly promoted team leader to 'let go' of his or her former role as team member, the close friendships this involved with some colleagues and the distant, business-like relationships it involved with others. The newly promoted team leader may feel isolated in the new role and unsure about how to behave towards others, especially subordinates who used to be both colleagues and close friends. It may take some time and quite a lot of experimenting to discover a style of managing that works. In some cases the individual may be so unhappy with the new role that he or she may give up the struggle and resign, leaving the change manager with the job of finding a new team leader.

Loss of employment, whether through redundancy or early retirement, is another example of a personal transition. Parkes (1971) suggests that loss of a job deprives a person of a place of work, the company of work mates and a source of income. It also removes a familiar source of identity, self-esteem and sense of purpose. Adjustment to this change will require, for example, new assumptions about the way each day will be spent and about sources of income. It may also affect the individual's faith in his or her capacity to work effectively and to earn a living. This kind of disruption to the assumptive world will cause an individual to set up a cycle of internal and external changes aimed at finding a new 'fit' between self and the changed environment.

Even the loss of a job that was wanted but not secured can be difficult to cope with because a person's assumptive world contains models of the world as it is and also as it might be. People who might be promoted to works manager rehearse in their mind the world they hope to create. They engage in a kind of anticipatory socialisation aided by the rich imagery of' their new comfortable office, efficient secretary, challenging assignments and respectful subordinates. It may be almost as hard to give up such expectations and fantasies as it is to give up objects that actually exist. Thus the people who are not promoted may actually lose something very important, and they may have to make new assumptions about how things will be in the future.

The personal cost of coping with transitions

Personal transitions require those affected to engage in some form of coping behaviour. Holmes and Rahe (1967) developed a Social Readjustment Rating Scale (see Table 14.1) that attributed mean values to the degree of adjustment required after individuals experience a series of life events. The scale was originally constructed by telling 394 subjects that marriage had been given an arbitrary value of 50 and asking them to attribute a score to 42 other life events, indicating whether each life event would require more or less adjustment than marriage. The mean values attributed to the 43 events included in the Social Readjustment Rating Scale ranged from 100 for death of spouse to 11 for a minor infringement of the law. 'Social readjustment' was defined in terms of the amount and duration of change in one's accustomed pattern of life following a life event, irrespective of the desirability of the event. Various retrospective and prospective studies using the Social Readjustment Rating Scale, reported by Holmes and Masuda (1973), found that magnitude of life change is highly significantly related to the time of illness onset. An example of a prospective study of this relationship is one that involved recording the life changes experienced by 2,500 officers and enlisted men aboard three US Navy cruisers. It was found that there was a clear correlation between life changes experienced in a given period before the cruisers put to sea and the onset of illness during the period at sea. The studies reported by Holmes and Masuda indicate that the higher the score over the last twelve months the greater the likelihood of illness onset over the next twelve months.

This relationship may be moderated by individual differences in the ability to cope with personal transitions. People may perceive the same event and/or assess their ability to cope with it in different ways. This can be influenced by many factors, including past experience of the event and

Table 14.1   The Social Readjustment Rating Scale

Rank	Life event	Mean value
1	Death of spouse	100
2	Divorce	73
3	Marital separation	65
4	Jail term	63
5	Death of close family member	63
6	Personal injury or illness	53
7	Marriage	50
8	Sacked from work	47
9	Marital reconciliation	45
10	Retirement	45
11	Change in health of family member	44
12	Pregnancy	40
13	Sexual difficulties	39
14	Gain of a new family member (child or 'oldster' moving in)	39
15	Business readjustment	39
16	Change in financial state	39
17	Death of close friend	37
18	Change to a different line of work	36
19	Change in number of arguments with spouse	35
20	Taking on a large mortgage (e.g. for house purchase)	31
21	Foreclosure of mortgage or loan	30
22	Change in responsibilities at work	29
23	Son or daughter leaves home	29
24	Trouble with in-laws	29
25	Outstanding personal achievement	28
26	Spouse beginning or ceasing work	26
27	Begin or end school (formal education)	26
28	Change in living conditions	25
29	Revision of personal habits (dress, manners, associations etc.)	24
30	Trouble with boss	23
31	Change in work hours or conditions	20
32	Change in residence	20
33	Change in schools/college	20
34	Change in recreation	19
35	Change in church (mosque) activities	19
36	Change in social activities	18
37	Taking on medium level loan (for TV, computer, etc)	17
38	Change in sleeping habits (amount, time of day, etc.)	16
39	Change in number of family get-togethers	15
40	Change in eating habits	15
41	Holidays	13
42	Christmas	12
43	Minor violations of the law	11

Source: Adapted from Holmes, T. and Rahe, R. 'The Social Readjustment Rating Scale', *Journal of Psychosomatic Research*, 1967, vol. 11, table 3, p. 215. Reprinted with permission of Elsevier, Inc.

personality variables such as hardiness, self-esteem, self-reliance, and the like.

You may find it interesting to use the Social Readjustment Rating Scale in Table 14.1 to assess the amount of life change that you have experienced in the last twelve months. Total the values of the life change events that you have experienced over a twelve-month period. A 'life crisis' is defined as 150 or more life change units in any one year:

- A mild life crisis is defined as 150–199 life change units
- A moderate crisis is 200–299 life change units
- A major life crisis is defined as more than 300 life change units.

The relationship between life change and illness susceptibility highlights the personal cost associated with adjusting to change, irrespective of whether the change is viewed as desirable or undesirable. It also points to the possibility that different people may react to the same organisational change in different ways, because for some it is an isolated event whereas for others it is one of a number of changes, at work and elsewhere, that push them towards a major life crisis.

Adjusting to organisational change

When individuals adjust to organisational changes that:

- are lasting in their effects
- take place over a relatively short period of time
- affect large areas of the assumptive world

they experience a process of personal transition. Exercise 14.1 invites you to reflect on how you have reacted to a change that involved a personal transition. The information generated by this exercise will enable you to compare your reactions with the typical pattern of reaction described by the stage model of transition that is presented later in this chapter.

Exercise 14.1   Your experience of a transition

Think of a change that was lasting in its effects, took place over a relatively short period of time and affected the assumptions you made about how you related to the world around you.

Examples of this kind of change could be redundancy, job change, promotion, relocation, bereavement, marriage, birth of your first child or illness or accident that affected your mobility or some other aspect of your functioning.

For the purpose of this exercise, the change need not be an organisational change.

Answer the following questions:

Entry:

When did you realise that the transition was to take place?

How did you know?

What did you feel at the time?

What did you do/how did you behave?

During the transition:

Did your feelings and/or behaviour change during the transition? Are you able to identify any stages that highlighted differences in the way you reacted to the change? If so, what were these stages?

Exit:

When did you realise that your transition had ended? How did you know?

Think about your answers to the questions posed in Exercise 14.1 when the stages of psychological reaction to a change are considered below.

Organisational change and personal transition

Organisational change involves the ending of something and the beginning of something else. For example, it might involve the introduction of a new organisational structure, a more automated production process, revised procedures, the merger of two units, the closure of a plant, a redundancy programme, job transfers, a new project or a promotion. While these changes might be carefully planned and happen on a predetermined date it might be some time before those involved have adapted to these external events. Managers need to develop an understanding of how people *respond to change*. They need to know the course of events associated with the process of transition, and the kinds of action they can engage in to facilitate adaptation.

A model of change as a transition

The model presented in Figure 14.1 is based on the work of William Bridges (1980, 1991). It conceptualises transition as beginning with an ending and then going on to a new beginning via a neutral zone. These three phases are not separate stages divided by clear boundaries. Phases can overlap and an individual can be in more than one phase at any one time. Bridges sees the movement through a transition as being marked by a change in the dominance of one phase as it gives way to the next.

Figure 14.1 Bridges' model of transition

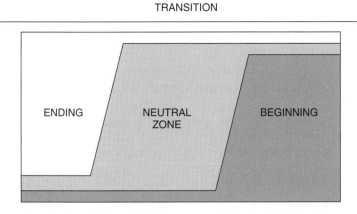

Source: Bridges, W., *Managing Transitions: Making the Most of Change* (1991: 70). Reprinted with permission of Da Capo Press, a member of Perseus Books, LLC.

Endings involve 'letting go' of the old situation, and the identity that went with it. It is impossible to fully engage in a new role or have a new purpose until those involved have let go of the old role or old purpose. For example, as noted above, a promotion, especially when it is in the same work group, involves letting go of the role of group member and internalising the new role of group leader. Fink, Beak and Taddeo (1971), drawing on the work of Lewin, argue that every human system has within it forces for maintenance of the status quo and forces for growth. While these forces tend to operate counter to each other, the balance between maintenance and growth is constantly shifting. Endings are often associated with a predominance of maintenance forces that manifest themselves in a resistance to change and a reluctance to let go.

The neutral zone is the in-between state. It involves a recognition of the need to change and uncertainty about the nature of more desirable end states. It is a period of disorientation, self-doubt and anxiety, but it can also be a period of growth and creativity in which new opportunities are identified. However, there is a danger that people may be so uncomfortable with the ambiguity and disorientation associated with this stage of transition that they push prematurely for certainty and closure. Consequently they may lock on to the first opportunity that offers any promise of a more satisfactory state of affairs and, in so doing, lock out the possibility of a creative search for better alternatives.

Beginnings involve reorientation to a new situation and the development of a new identity. Initially the forces for growth predominate but eventually, as the new situation is more clearly defined and a new identity is internalised, the forces for maintenance and growth achieve a new balance.

The stages of psychological reaction

People going through change experience a variety of emotional and cognitive states. Transitions typically progress through the cycle of reasonably predictable phases described below. This applies to all kinds of transition: voluntary and imposed, desirable and undesirable. There is a widely held view that in each case the person experiencing the transition will have to work through all of the stages if the transition is to be successfully completed. Understanding this process can help both individuals and managers.

The model presented below has been developed by John Hayes and Peter Hyde from an earlier version which originally appeared in *Transitions: Understanding and Managing Personal Change* by Adams, Hayes and Hopson (1976) (see Figure 14.2). The cycle reflects variations in the degree to which people feel able to exercise control over the situation.

Figure 14.2 Transition phases

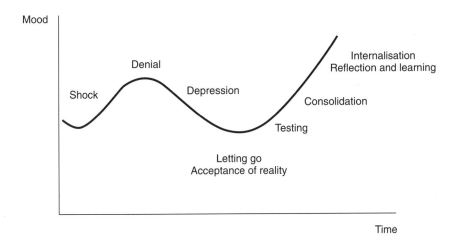

Awareness/shock

Often people have little warning of changes and they experience the initial phase of a transition as a shock. They feel overwhelmed, frozen, paralysed. Feelings of anxiety and panic can undermine their ability to take in new information, think constructively and plan. This leads to a state of immobilisation. People behave as though they are on 'auto-pilot' and show little response to new developments. While their mood may be more positive if the transition is perceived as a desirable gain (e.g. first prize on the lottery) they may still experience a state of immobilisation and have difficulty planning and taking constructive action. In those circumstances where people develop a gradual awareness of a pending change, they often focus on what they might lose and engage in 'worry work' that diverts their attention from other matters that might require their attention. The intensity of this phase will be influenced by the degree of preparedness and the desirability of the transition – immobilisation will be greater when the transition is unexpected and unwanted.

Denial

This phase is characterised by a retreat from the reality of change. Negative changes may be denied or trivialised and attention may be displaced onto other more immediate but less important matters. Energy and activity are devoted to the known and the familiar and any perceived threat to the status quo is managed by behaving in habitual ways. Clinging to the past and refusing to consider the need to change can lead to a reduction in anxiety. Anything or anyone who challenges this false sense of security is likely to provoke an angry response. Resistance to change is at its highest at this point. Positive changes may induce euphoria together with an unwillingness to consider any possible negative consequences. In some cases denial may be functional if it provides the opportunity to recharge 'emotional batteries' and helps a person face up to the need to change.

Depression

Eventually the reality of the change becomes apparent and the individual acknowledges that things cannot continue as they are. In terms of Bridges' model, this corresponds to the start of the neutral zone. This provokes a feeling of depression which is often associated with a feeling that the situation is beyond one's control. The phase may be characterised by anger, sadness, withdrawal and confusion. This depressed mood occurs even in changes which were initially embraced enthusiastically whenever practical difficulties are encountered. It is in the depression phase therefore that the change really starts to be experienced as stressful. If the change was a voluntary one, this may be the point at which the person gives up. In involuntary changes, the person may seek to leave the situation.

Letting go

This phase involves accepting reality for what it is. It implies a clear letting go of the past. This may be experienced as a 'little death' and often entails a process of mourning. It can help at this point to remember that the lowest ebb is the turn of the tide.

Testing

A more active, creative, experimental involvement in the new situation starts to take place. New ways of behaving and being are tried out. More energy is available but anger and irritability may be easily aroused if the new behaviour is not successful. This phase may involve trial-and-error behaviour or a more active cycle of experience–review–conclude–plan may be employed. As some patterns are found which seem to work, this phase gradually gives way to the next.

Consolidation

Out of the testing process come some new ways of being and behaving which are gradually adopted as new norms. This corresponds to the beginning stage in Bridges' model. This stage progresses in parallel with testing, but to begin with there is more testing than consolidation. It involves reflecting on new experiences and assessing whether they offer a basis for a constructive way forward. (Sometimes there is little consolidation. Early experiments with new roles and relationships are rejected and there is no learning from the experience.) When consolidation occurs it involves reflecting on the new experience and using any learning to build on it and inform the choice of further 'testing' experiences.

Internalisation, reflection and learning

The transition is complete when the changed behaviour is normal and unthinking and is the new natural order of things. Ideally the past has been left behind and little or no 'unfinished business' remains. Reflection and learning is a cognitive process involving reflecting on what all the activity and emotion has really meant. It is at this point that learning and personal growth, which may benefit future transitions, is recognised.

Validation of the model

You might find it interesting, at this point, to reflect on the answers you provided to the questions posed in Exercise 14.1. Does the stage model of psychological reaction presented above provide a useful conceptual framework for understanding the process of adjustment you went through?

Some observations on the stage model of transitions

Each individual's experience of a transition will be influenced by a number of factors. These include the importance of the transition, whether it is perceived as a gain or loss, the intensity of its impact, the existence of other simultaneous transitions (and the magnitude of any associated life crisis), personal resilience and so on. It follows therefore that there can be no absolutely standard pattern of reaction. Some possible variations are noted below:

- The wave can be shallower or deeper and the overall shape of the curve may be skewed one way or the other. For example, if the change is perceived as a desirable opportunity the individual might find it easier to let go of the past whereas if it is perceived as a threat or loss the individual might be reluctant to let go and resist the change for as long as possible.
- The time taken to pass through all the phases can vary greatly. Just as some people take longer than others to come to terms with the loss of a loved one, so organisational members can vary in terms of the time it takes for them to adjust to a work-related transition.
- Although presented as a purely linear process, people may regress and slip back to an earlier stage in the process.
- People can get 'stuck' at any phase and not complete the cycle. They may, for example, continue to deny the need to change or fail to recognise new opportunities associated with it.

Where multiple transitions are involved, people handle the situation in different ways. Some people keep the transitions firmly compartmentalised and deal with one at a time; others throw their energy into one as a displacement activity to get away from another (which is therefore held in denial); in other cases, one major transition predominates and swamps the others.

Implications for individuals and change managers

Hayes and Hyde (1996) summarise some of the implications for individuals and change managers.

For *individuals*:

- It takes time for people to make the adjustments required in transitions
- It can help them to know that their own experience is normal, that it will involve ups and downs and that it will eventually come to an end
- The process can be managed: there are things that they can do to facilitate their own transitions.

For *change managers*:

- It is important to recognise that there will often be a time lag between the announcement of a change and an emotional reaction to it: it is easy to mistake the apparent calm of the immobilisation and minimisation phases for acceptance
- Because any given change will have different implications for different individuals or groups, different parts of the organisation will progress through the cycle at different rates and in different ways
- Change managers need to beware of getting out of phase with their staff, they tend to know about the change before others and, therefore, it is not unusual for them to have reached an acceptance of change long before other organisation members, which can create great potential for ineffective communication
- The cycle cannot be avoided, but there is much that change managers can do to facilitate people's passage through it.

Facilitating progress through a transition

This final section outlines, briefly, some of the interventions that change managers can make to help facilitate the progress of other people through a transition. This kind of facilitation is particularly important where people have become 'stuck' at a particular stage in the process.

The interventions are presented in relation to each stage of the process of transition. What follows is not meant to be a prescriptive list of what the change manager should do. It is a set of suggestions, based on observations and anecdotal evidence of what seems to have worked in practice, supplemented by managers' reports (during workshops with John Hayes and Peter Hyde) about what they have done that appeared to help others manage their personal transitions. These suggestions may alert you to some of the issues that have to be managed and to possible ways of intervening that might be appropriate in a particular set of circumstances.

Shock associated with the announcement/discovery of a change that affects an individual's assumptive world

Sometimes the shock reaction can be minimised by:

- Preparing the ground and creating a climate receptive to change
- Consulting and involving people in the decision making.

If this is not possible, the change manager might consider possible ways of announcing the change. Anecdotal evidence suggests that the following points may be worth considering:

1 *Who should make the announcement* This might be a senior manager in order to signal the importance of the change and the organisation's concern for the people involved. Alternatively, it might be decided that a relatively junior manager should make the announcement because she has a better relationship with those affected.

2 *Timing* When should an announcement be made:

   (a) Should the announcement be made simultaneously to all staff, or should some be told before others?
   (b) Should people be told as soon as possible or should the announcement be delayed?

3 *Method* Should it be done face-to-face, via a video link, by email, or by letter?

   (a) In face-to-face encounters it is important to keep calm and avoid becoming defensive or aggressive in the face of questions.

4 *Content* Should a consistent message be given to all:

   (a) How much information should be communicated? Should the message be kept as simple as possible?
   (b) Should explanations be given about why the change is necessary?
   (c) It often helps to show empathy and understanding for how people will feel (e.g. 'I know this will be upsetting for you and I feel very sad about it myself, but . . .').

5 *Dialogue* Should questions be encouraged?

It is important to allow time for people to digest the information and share their feelings with others.

When people are in shock, the change manager needs to recognise that:

- Performance may be temporarily impaired and that in some circumstances this may lead to dangerous or costly consequences. This may influence the timing of the announcement.
- Some people may need more support than others.

Denial

The change manager needs to diagnose what it is that is being denied (e.g. the change isn't necessary, is not real, does not affect me, etc.) and then consider whether it would be helpful to:

- Confront what is being denied gently and supportively
- Repeat the message
- Draw people's attention to relevant examples, evidence and experience
- Arrange demonstrations of what the change will involve, if possible
- Establish and keep to a timetable to provide milestones and evidence of change
- Find ways to ensure that people have to engage with the reality of the change
- Take early action if at all possible: the longer the gap between the announcement of a change and the change taking effect the easier it is for an individual to ignore that the change is for real
- Get people to do practical things related to the change.

Depression

The change manager can intervene in order to help others understand and accept the situation by:

- providing support
- listening
- adopting an accepting and non-critical reaction to their expression of feelings.

The change manager can also help others to work on their feelings about the situation by:

- helping them get it off their chest
- providing space to grieve
- providing appropriate opportunities to vent emotion.

They can also help them identify opportunities to move on by:

- Not letting them wallow in feeling bad: be gently confronting and challenging
- Helping them identify other things they are good at
- Providing further information about the change to help people envisage what the future will be like
- Helping them identify options and possible benefits
- Helping them focus their attention on the things they can do or can influence
- Where possible, providing opportunities for the exercise of influence (e.g. consultation and involvement).

Letting go

The change manager can help people let go of the past by:

- Explaining the need for change in terms of benefits rather than problems associated with past practice: rubbishing the past can provoke a defensive reaction
- Providing challenging targets associated with the movement towards a more desirable state
- Drawing attention to deadlines
- Eliminating the symbols of the past
- Reminiscing in a way that leads to a process of taking the best forward from the past
- Marking the ending by rituals and ceremonies, wakes and leaving parties
- Letting people take souvenirs and mementoes.

Testing

Some of the ways in which the change manager can encourage testing include:

- creating the space, time and resources required to test
- promoting creative thinking
- helping people identify options
- encouraging risk taking and experimentation
- discouraging premature closure
- avoiding punishing those who make mistakes
- injecting new processes, tools and competencies that will help people help themselves
- eliminating the drivers of old behaviours
- acting as a mentor
- praising and supporting successes
- encourage networking and cross-fertilisation
- providing feedback.

Consolidation

This can be facilitated by:

- reviewing performance and learning
- helping others identify the characteristics of a more desirable state
- recognising and rewarding achievement
- getting them to help others and share their experience
- helping them to build on successes
- broadcasting their successes.

Reflecting, learning and internalisation

This can be facilitated by:

- helping them review the experience of change – asking questions, running review workshops, etc.
- conducting formal post implementation reviews
- getting them to help others and share their experience.

Summary

This chapter has addressed the way that organisational members experience change. Attention has been focused on those changes that are perceived to be relatively lasting in their effects, take place over a relatively short period of time and affect large areas of the assumptive world.

When confronted with this kind of change, people experience a process of personal transition that involves a number of stages of psychological reaction. These stages are awareness/shock, denial, depression, letting go, testing, consolidation, reflection and learning and internalisation.

The implications of this process of adjustment are considered from the perspective both of the individuals experiencing a transition and of the change managers. Attention has also been given to ways in which change managers can intervene to facilitate this process of adjustment.

References

Adams, J., Hayes J. and Hopson, B. (1976) *Transitions: Understanding and Managing Personal Change*, London: Martin Robertson.

Bridges, W. (1980) *Transitions*, Reading, MA: Addison-Wesley.

Bridges, W. (1991) *Managing Transitions: Making the Most of Change*, Reading, MA: Addison-Wesley.

Fink, S.L., Beak, J. and Taddeo, K. (1971) 'Organisational Crisis and Change', *Journal of Applied Behavioral Science*, 7 (1), pp. 15–37.

Hayes, J. and Hyde, P. (1996) *Transitions Workshop*, unpublished manual, Hyde Management Consulting, Woodvale House, Basingstoke Road, Reading RG7 1AE.

Holmes, T.H. and Masuda, M. (1973) 'Life Change and Illness Susceptibility', *Separation and Depression*, American Association for the Advancement of Science, pp. 161–86.

Holmes, T.H. and Rahe, R. (1967) 'The Social Readjustment Rating Scale', *Journal of Psychosomatic Research*, 11, p. 215.

Lewin, K. (1951) *Field Theory in Social Science*, New York: Harper & Row.

Parkes, C.M. (1971) 'Psycho-Social Transitions: A Field of Study', *Social Science and Medicine*, 5, pp. 101–15.

A further useful reference is:

Stuart, R. (1995) 'Experiencing Organisational Change: Triggers, Processes and Outcomes of Change Journeys', *Personnel Review*, 24 (2), pp. 1–87.

Shaping implementation strategies and managing the change

Part IV considers some of the issues that need to be examined when deciding how to manage the change process and how to maintain control during the transition phase.

Chapter 15   Shaping implementation strategies

This chapter considers the strengths and weaknesses of three approaches to managing change, explores some of the situational variables that need to be considered when shaping an implementation strategy and considers how and why this strategy may need to change over time. The chapter concludes with a brief review of some alternative start points for change.

   After reading this chapter you will be invited to critically assess the strategy used to manage a recent change within your organisation.

Chapter 16   Maintaining control during the change

It is not unusual for change programmes to disrupt normal work practice and undermine existing management systems. This chapter looks at issues of control and considers some of the steps change managers can take to maintain control during the period between the identification of a need for change and the achievement of a desired future state.

   After reading this chapter you will be invited to reflect on an occasion when you were involved in the management of a change and to consider what you or others might have done differently to maintain better control.

Shaping implementation strategies

This chapter considers the strengths and weaknesses of three approaches to managing change and explores some of the situational variables that need to be considered when shaping an implementation strategy.

Read the Asda case in Case study 15.1 before reviewing the content of this chapter and consider how you would have managed the situation if you had been the newly appointed CEO of Asda.

Case study 15.1   Asda

A winning formula

Asda was the first company in the UK to invest in large, edge-of-town superstores, with ample free car parking, selling food and related products.

Asda was created in 1965 as a subsidiary of Associated Dairies. It started business by opening a string of very large discount stores in converted mill and warehouse premises. In the early days shoppers were offered a limited range of very competitively priced products.

When Asda went public in 1978 it was the third largest food retailer in the UK, selling an ever-widening range of food and non-food products. Its success continued to be based on high volume, low margins and good value for money (Asda price).

A change of strategy: the pursuit of higher margins

In 1981 Asda began to shift towards a new strategy focused on raising margins. A range of new initiatives involved seeking efficiencies to reduce costs and introducing more high-margin products such as prepared foods and a wider range of non-food items.

There was also a drive to expand in the South of England where customers had greater spending power:

● This expansion policy was slow to get off the ground, partly because planning permissions for large retail developments were more difficult to secure in the South, the price of land was significantly higher and many of the best sites were already being developed by competitors.

- Sales were lower than anticipated because Asda's value-for-money image and its relatively austere store layouts tended to be unattractive to relatively wealthy southern customers who were used to shopping in more up-market stores. Asda attempted to brighten up some of its stores and further distance itself from its 'pile-them-high and sell-them-cheap' image but this did not generate the anticipated contribution to operating profits.
- Another (related) problem was that long-standing customers in the North appeared to be confused by what Asda was beginning to offer them and many switched their allegiance to new cut-price retailers who were more focused on offering value for money.

Diversification

Towards the end of the 1970s senior management began to consider the possibility that saturation might limit future growth in food retailing, and the decision was taken to diversify into non-foods.

Some of the most notable acquisitions included:

1977 Wades Department Stores (with over seventy prime high-street sites)

1978 Allied Retailers (Allied Carpets, Ukay Furniture and Williams Furnishings). Unfortunately this acquisition did not make the anticipated contribution to profitability because the recession in the early 1980s led to heavy discounting. Ukay furniture faired worst and was sold in 1982. While the recession hit Allied Carpets it continued to make modest profits and by 1985 had improved to the point where it was decided to expand this side of the business.

1985 Asda merged with the MFI furniture group. This merger, the biggest in British retailing up to that point, was another disappointment. Asda–MFI attributed the poor performance to one-off problems, such as a new range of kitchens that failed to sell. It was anticipated that the problems would be short-lived but performance failed to pick up as expected.

1986 Asda launched Asdadrive, a car-retailing business at sites adjacent to six of its superstores, with the intention of rolling it out to about 75 per cent of all sites.

Refocusing on the core business

Following the merger with MFI, Asda–MFI's shares significantly underperformed. In 1987 the company surprised the market with a major change of strategy. Instead of continuing with the policy of diversification it decided to refocus on the Asda superstores.

The Asda–MFI merger ended with a management buy-out of MFI (although Asda then bought a 25 per cent stake in this new company). Asdadrive and most of the Associated Fresh Foods business were also disposed of and it was intended to dispose of the Allied Carpets business. However, following the collapse of the equity market, it proved impossible to obtain the anticipated profit from the sale of Allied Carpets, so the business was retained (and later expanded with the acquisition of Marples in 1989).

In order to develop the core business it was decided to invest up to £1 billion over a period of three years. Most was earmarked for accelerating the opening of new stores, especially in the South, but there were also other demands. Asda had lagged behind its competitors in a number of areas:

1 *Own-label products* They had all invested heavily in own-label products (that offered higher margins and better value to customers) whereas Asda had only started to introduce them in the mid-1980s, and on a much smaller scale.
2 *Computerised point-of-sale (POS) equipment* Competitors had invested heavily in technology that improved stock control and provided better customer service at check-outs.
3 *Centralised distribution networks* The competition had also developed centralised distribution networks for fresh foods that pushed down costs, enabled stores to receive fewer 'JIT' deliveries from vehicles carrying full loads and reduced the requirement for store related warehousing space.
4 *Store refurbishment* Asda had neglected many of its stores, which were beginning to look very tired and in urgent need of refurbishing.

Asda recognised the need for investment in all these areas.

A leap forward that contributed to a major debt problem

In 1989 a consortium that was planning to buy Gateway agreed that, if their bid was successful, they would sell sixty-two superstores to Asda for £705 million. This was seen as a very attractive proposition. It offered Asda the possibility of making up for lost ground and regaining its old position as the third largest British food retailer. It also promised to double the number of Asda stores in the South of England and contribute an extra £1 billion to sales. Asda bought the stores in October 1989.

Asda's performance following the purchase of the Gateway stores was poor. Profits were down and Asda's stake in MFI contributed a loss. Allied–Marples was also in trouble. Asda had net debts of over £900 million. From the end of 1989 Asda's share price began to slide compared with major competitors and in September 1991 it dropped a further 29 per cent. The announcement of a rights issue at the end of the month led to another massive fall in the share price.

The appointment of Archie Norman

Archie Norman was offered the role of CEO in October 1991 and took up his appointment in December. By the time he arrived the company was fast running out of cash.

He found a company that was bureaucratic, hierarchical and highly centralised. There was a large headquarters staff located in the new custom-build Asda House. Directors had little contact with their subordinates. The culture was risk averse. People at all levels appeared to be intimidated by their bosses and told them what they thought they wanted to hear. They also seemed reluctant to take any initiatives that would call attention to themselves. Morale was low.

The trading department was dominant. Buyers, located at Asda House, determined what the stores would sell but they had little contact with store managers. The new CEO had concerns about both the quality of management and the apparent unwillingness, throughout the organisation, to make best use of the talent that existed.

Store managers felt ignored and found it impossible to have any meaningful input to thinking at Asda House. There were also problems within stores. Vertical communication was poor and customers were not valued.

 If you had been Archie Norman in December 1991, what would have been your strategy for change?

The trap of success

It was noted in Chapter 6 that one of the paradoxes of organisational life is that success often sets the stage for failure. This is because when organisations like Marks & Spencer continue to be successful year after year managers become locked into the patterns of behaviour that produced the original success. These patterns become codified or institutionalised (part of the 'deep structures' discussed in Chapter 1) and are rarely questioned. Successful firms can become complacent, internally focused, and caught in what Nadler and Shaw (1995) refer to as the 'trap of success'. They take their eyes off the competition and fail to pay enough attention to what is going on in their external environment. Even those organisations that invest heavily in continuous improvement can become victims of strategic drift. They may change, but fail to change fast enough to keep pace with the rate of change in their external environment. Part of the problem is that continuous improvement tends to focus attention on 'doing things better' and insufficient attention is given to the potential benefit of 'doing things differently' or even 'doing different things'. This argument supports the punctuated equilibrium paradigm and predicts that, at some point, almost all organisations will be faced with the need to transform themselves in order to survive.

Effective change strategies

How can companies transform themselves? Beer (2001), a leading US consultant and professor at the Harvard Business School, has identified two well-tried strategies *(Economic* and *Organisation Development),* but argues that the most effective strategy is a third way that combines the best of both. As you read this chapter, reflect on your own experience to test the validity of this proposition and consider which strategy you would have adopted if you had been Archie Norman at Asda.

Economic strategies

These focus on the drive for economic value through tough, 'top-down', results-driven action. These actions involve the imposition of technical solutions to those problems that are seen to undermine organisational effectiveness. There are a wide range of such solutions including restructuring, reengineering, drives for efficiencies and layoffs. Often large groups of consultants are employed to help top management drive them into the organisation. Sometimes a new CEO or other senior executive might be appointed to act as a 'turn-around' manager.

There are many examples where economic strategies have led to improved shareholder returns. Many believe that they made a major contribution to the success of Lord Hanson and his colleagues at Hanson Trust. However, economic strategies have been criticised on the grounds that they often destroy human commitment: they might deliver short-term results, but they may not guarantee longer-term success.

Organisation development (OD) strategies

These focus on creating the capabilities required to sustain competitive advantage and high performance. Beer and others identify some of these capabilities as:

- coordination and team work
- commitment and trust
- competence (technical and leadership)
- open communications
- creativity
- the capacity for constructive conflict
- learning.

OD strategies emphasise the importance of shared purpose, a strong culture, 'bottom-up' change and involvement rather than financial incentives as the motivator for change. This approach can improve shareholder value but it has been criticised on the grounds that it is too indirect and takes too long, especially when the need for change is urgent.

The BBC offers good examples of the implementation of both economic and OD strategies. During the 1990s the dominant strategy was economic but when Greg Dyke was appointed Director General in 2000 he began to pursue more of an OD strategy (Case study 15.3).

Case study 15.2   The implementation of an economic strategy at the BBC

After a long period of sustained success during which the BBC established itself as the world's leading public broadcaster the Corporation began to become complacent. It knew that it was the best in the field and, because of the way it was funded via a compulsory license fee, felt that it was financially secure. But then the world began to change and the BBC was faced with a range of pressing problems. These included:

1   *A new political climate*   In 1979 Margaret Thatcher and a Conservative government came to power with an agenda for change that included plans to transform the public sector. Although the BBC was not the new Government's first target, Thatcher viewed it as a bloated bureaucracy that was over-manned, inefficient and ripe for reform. The government was also unhappy with the Corporation's editorial policy and was particularly irritated by what it perceived as unpatriotic reporting of issues such as Northern Ireland and the Falklands' war.
2   *Wide-ranging technological change*   Possibly the biggest challenge came from the development of digital technologies that opened up the possibility of many more channels, better technical quality, video-on-demand and interactivity.
3   *Increased competition*   This came from new players and the launch of BSkyB.

In order to fend off the possibility of privatisation, protect the licence fee (which the government had reduced in real terms) and prepare the Corporation for the digital world, John Birt (Director General between 1992 and 2000) introduced a range of tough reforms. His mission was to make the BBC 'the best managed organisation in the public sector'. At the time he was appointed it was almost impossible to determine how much it cost to make a programme or to use an in-house facility such as a studio. The core values were about quality rather than cost.

Birt was determined to make the organisation more efficient. He introduced 'Producer Choice' and created an internal market that shifted the balance of power away from programme makers to managers and accountants. Departments became cost centres that had to break even, and producers were required to reduce the cost of programme making by using external suppliers whenever they could provide a more cost-effective service than in-house providers. This 'top-down' drive to introduce new structures and systems slashed the cost of making programmes, but the reorganisation led to nearly 10,000 people being made redundant or opting to leave the organisation.

By the time Birt retired in 2000 his strategy for change had delivered results that secured the future of the BBC. He had gained the confidence of the government and other opinion formers (the public sector equivalent of shareholders) and had successfully introduced a range of 'technical' solutions that helped secured the licence fee for a further six years, plus extra funding to develop new digital services. However, his change strategy had neglected the social system. He had done little to win the hearts and minds of the majority of staff. His reforms fragmented what had been a very collaborative organisation: people became much more focused on achieving their own targets, and were inclined to 'play safe' rather than take risks and innovate (Case study 15.3).

Case study 15.3   The implementation of an OD strategy at the BBC

When Greg Dyke took over as Director General he inherited a very efficient organisation but he detected a climate of fear and was worried about whether this increased efficiency had been won at the expense of other factors that would begin to have a negative impact on the Corporation's performance. Efficiency was still on his agenda but he pursued it via a more inclusive approach. He also began to pursue a 'bottom-up' strategy to identify what inspired people and to develop the capabilities required to ensure that the BBC retained its position as the world's leading public service broadcaster.

He introduced a new vision. In place of striving 'to make the BBC the best managed organisation in the public sector' his vision was 'to turn BBC into the most creative organisation in the world, where people enjoy their work and feel supported and powered to excel'.

In February 2002 he launched 'One BBC – Making it Happen'. While he had some ideas about how to make it happen he wanted the detailed plans to emerge from within the organisation.

The aims of Making it Happen were to:

- put audiences at the heart of the BBC
- inspire creativity
- develop current leaders and nurture those of the future
- provide an environment where people felt valued and encouraged to give of their best
- cut through the bureaucracy and build greater collaboration between divisions.

Dyke decided that he and the executive team would take every opportunity to demonstrate their commitment to the process. For example, they brought together the top 400 managers for two days to create a collective sense of responsibility for leading change. Dyke also led many discussions with staff and introduced the notion of the 'big conversation'.

He was determined to consult with a critical mass of employees. In order to promote buy-in and ownership this process was managed by in-house staff rather than external consultants. The first phase involved a search for 'quick wins'. These included modest changes such as refurbishments and reward schemes that recognised people when they made a special contribution. In the News Division, for example, one of the first winners was a travel desk clerk.

The second phase involved 10,000 staff (a third of the entire workforce) participating in 180 half-day workshops. Local managers and their staff were invited to 'Just Imagine' what the organisation could be like and to identify what needed to be changed in order to make it happen.

In each of the Corporation's seventeen divisions 'Make it Happen' teams were established to coordinate the 'Just Imagine' sessions and introduce change at the local level. For example, in the News Division various measures were introduced to improve the working climate and encourage staff to take risks and give of their best. The change plan also included a number of simple, inexpensive measures designed to address other issues that had emerged from the' Just Imagine' sessions. These included 'back-to-the-floor' days for managers and short secondments to enable staff to understand better what was happening in other departments.

In addition to what was happening within divisions there were organisation-wide initiatives that emerged from the *Making it Happen* process. These included giving more attention to providing a thorough induction to all new staff, a shift away from the extensive use of short-term contracts in an attempt to build more commitment and a big investment in leadership and management training.

The third way: a combined economic/OD strategy

Beer (2001) asserts that while both economic and OD strategies can produce improvements, neither of these strategies is as effective as one that combines 'top-down' results-driven change with the slower 'bottom-up' development of organisational capability. It could be argued (with the benefit of hindsight) that change at the BBC was successful because it did embrace Beer's combined strategy – but implemented it sequentially rather than simultaneously. However, change at the BBC was not planned as a combined strategy. This emerged because Dyke recognised a need to address issues that had not been addressed by his predecessor. The real challenge for change managers is simultaneously to implement a combined strategy.

Beer argues that change strategies that are capable of delivering sustained high performance require:

1   *The development of a compelling and balanced business and organisa-tion development direction*
   This requires the CEO to lead change at the top and create an effective executive team that can speak with one voice and articulate a coherent story about why and what type of change is needed.

   This story is more likely to win the support of key stakeholders if it not only provides an explanation of why the change is necessary but also offers an *inspiring vision* of a preferred future that includes (a) a business direction that will lead to the achievement of key results and (b) an overview of the organisational capabilities required to achieve and sustain this vision.

2 *The management of key stakeholders in order to buy time to develop organisation capability*
   Often, but not always, this will involve managing shareholder expectations. Making over-ambitious commitments about the achievement of economic results can push change managers into short-term cost-cutting strategies rather than longer-term strategies designed to create the capability required to generate revenue (or achieve the other outcomes that are required to sustain organisational success).

3 *The adoption of a socio-technical approach that involves the development of down-the-line managers*
   When tightly prescribed change programmes are rolled out across the organisation they typically focus on improving the technical system, and the interaction between the technical and social system tends to be ignored. Problems can arise when this type of programmatic change strategy fails to:

   (a) respond to local conditions
   (b) adequately involve local managers in a way that enables them to take real responsibility for moving the organisation forward
   (c) provide local managers with the opportunity to reflect on and learn from their experience of managing change.

Beer argues that 'top down initiatives undermine one of the key capabilities needed for sustained performance – down-the-line leaders who can lead a process of organisational learning' (2001: 242). He advocates the management of corporate change on a unit-by-unit basis with a high involvement of local staff because this:

- enables organisational members to engage with senior managers and contribute to shaping the change process
- facilitates the development of down-the-line leaders.

Top management's reluctance to adopt a combined 'drive and develop' approach

Beer's research suggests that CEOs and their top teams have a mind-set that promotes a 'top-down' drive for results. There are three key aspects of this mind-set:

The importance given to share holder interests

Shareholders have gained considerable power relative to employees (and even customers). Low share prices lead analysts, the financial community at large and board members to press CEOs for change. Those who do not respond risk being fired. Consequently the top team is very focused on the need to maximise economic value. This attention to shareholder interests echoes Schein's (1996) view that CEOs and their immediate subordinates tend to see themselves as embattled lonely warriors championing the organisation in a hostile economic environment. They develop elaborate management information systems to stay in touch with what is going on in the organisation and impose control systems to manage costs. They view people as 'resources' and regard them as costs rather than human assets: 'The well oiled organisation does not need "people", only activities that are contracted for.'

The assumption that it is the organisation's technical rather than its social system that is the prime determinant of performance

Change strategies are designed to improve the organisation as a technical system and interventions such as BPR, TQM and performance management tend to be viewed as technical solutions. Beer extends this argument to include the introduction of new human resource management (HRM) systems such as performance appraisal, succession planning and training programmes. They are implemented without too much thought being given to how they might affect roles, responsibilities, relationships and the power, status, self-esteem and security of individuals and groups across the organisation. This neglect can erode trust, commitment and communication.

The assumption that there is little to be gained from dialogue with employees

When top teams are planning and implementing transformational change they often over-rely on 'top-down' communication. Beer notes how the thoughts and feelings of the CEO and the top team can be shaped by pursuing a 'drive' strategy:

> To avoid the dissonance aroused by the opposites of tough, top-down action to lay off employees and sell businesses on the one hand, and the need to gain commitment to change on the other, they distance themselves from employees. They begin to assume that employees are part of the problem. (2001: 238)

Morrison and Milliken (2000) suggest that senior managers are more likely to discourage upward communication when they believe that employees are self-interested and effort averse and therefore unlikely to know or care about what is best for the organisation. This kind of thinking can lead to a situation where top managers are deprived of vital information that can signal a need for further change or provide feedback about the effectiveness of change initiatives that have already been implemented (see Chapter 11). It can also lead to a situation where the top team begins to rely on outside consultants and new managerial hires. Beer notes that when this happens it can further alienate people down-the-line, leading to an erosion of trust and the capabilities required for high performance such as coordination, commitment, communication and learning.

Beer (2000) and Beer and Nohria (2000) summarise the main differences between economic and OD strategies and highlight the main features of combined strategies:

1 *Leadership* Economic strategies involve 'top-down' leadership, OD strategies involve participative leadership and combined Economic and OD strategies involve senior managers setting the direction and then engaging people throughout the organisation.
2 *Focus* Economic strategies focus on changing structures and processes (the technical systems), OD strategies focus on changing the organisation's culture (the social systems) and combined Economic and OD strategies focus simultaneously on changing technical and the social systems.
3 *Process* Economic strategies are programmatic and involve the development and implementation of plans, OD strategies are more emergent and encourage experimentation and combined Economic and OD strategies involve plans that accommodate spontaneity.
4 *Reward systems* A feature of Economic strategies is a reliance on extrinsic motivation and the use of financial incentives, OD strategies rely on intrinsic motivation and the development of commitment and combined Economic and OD strategies use financial incentives and other extrinsic motivators but only to reinforce change rather than to drive it.
5 *Use of consultants* Economic strategies involve using consultants to analyse problems and prescribe solutions, OD strategies involve using consultants as facilitators to help managers diagnose problems and shape their own solutions and combined Economic and OD strategies involve using consultants who are experts but who are able to use their expertise to empower organisational members.

Reflect on the strategy you would have adopted if you had been Archie Norman at Asda. Would your strategy have been primarily an economic strategy that involved a drive to maximise economic value, a development strategy that focused on developing organisational capabilities or a combined drive *and* development strategy?

Situational variables that can shape an implementation strategy

The strategy Archie Norman implemented at Asda was a combined drive and development strategy. When he arrived the company was facing bankruptcy and there was an urgent need to generate cash to ensure short-term survival, but there was also a need to transform the business in ways that would ensure its long-term success. Norman's approach to managing change was 'tough', at times he was very directive and many people ended up leaving, but he also encouraged people at all levels to participate in the process of transforming the business. He went to great lengths to involve others and to ensure that managers down-the-line engaged with their subordinates. He also integrated careful planning with a willingness to let the details of the change strategy emerge over time.

There is no simple formula for designing implementation strategies based on Beer's 'third way'. Eriksson and Sundgren (2005), after studying the merger of the Swedish pharmaceutical company Astra AB with the British company Zeneca, concluded that while there are benefits from combining OD and Economic theories the ideal balance between the two may vary from case to case.

Kotter and Schlesinger (1979) argue that successful change strategies are those that are internally consistent and are compatible with key situational variables. In practice, many managers vary their approach to managing change at different stages of the change process. For example, some may decide not involve others in the preliminary diagnostic phase but might draw more people into the latter stages of problem definition and the specification of a more desirable future state. They may then move on to involve many more in the details of implementing the plan for change. Factors that might lead to a variation in approach over time will receive more attention below.

Situational variables

Some of the main situational variables that can influence the shape of an implementation strategy are illustrated in Figure 15.1:

1 *Urgency and stakes involved* The greater the short-run risks to the organisation if the current situation is not changed quickly the more the change managers may have to adopt a directive strategy towards the left-hand side of the continuum. Involvement and participation takes time, and this time may not be available if the need for change is urgent.

2 *Clarity of desired future state* Reference has already been made to two very different types of change – *blueprint* change and *evolutionary* change (see Chapter 5 on process models of change). Blueprint changes are those where the desired end state can be clearly specified from the start, whereas evolutionary changes are those where the need for change is recognised but it is difficult to anticipate what a more desirable future state will look like.

Depending on other factors, such as the power of the change managers relative to other stakeholders, it may be easier to adopt a more directive approach to implementation when confronted with a blueprint-type change than when the change involves an incremental process of

Figure 15.1 A continuum of intervention strategies

DIRECTIVE	COLLABORATIVE
Urgent requirement for change	Non-urgent requirement for change
Desired end state clearly specified from the start	Problem/opportunity recognised but what needs to be done to resolve problem or exploit opportunity not clear from the start
Little resistance anticipated	Great resistance anticipated
Change managers have access to all the information they need to diagnose the need for change, develop a change plan and monitor its implementation	Change managers need information from other stakeholders
Others have high trust in change managers	Others have low trust in change managers
Change managers do not have to rely on the commitment and effort of others to implement the change plan	Successful implementation of the change plan is highly dependent on the commitment and effort of others

action learning. Implementing an evolutionary change involves hypothesising about what might be a useful next step, planning how to achieve it, taking action to implement the plan, reflecting on what happened and then hypothesising about what needs to be done next. This process is more likely to be successful when change managers seek inputs and feedback from others, and adopt a more collaborative approach.

3 *Amount and type of resistance that is anticipated* All other factors being equal, the greater the anticipated resistance the more the change manager will have to work at persuading others to accept the need for change. This might require the adoption of a more collaborative approach towards implementation.

4 *Extent to which change managers have the required data for designing and implementing the change* The more the change managers anticipate that they will need information from others to help design and implement the change, the more they will have to adopt a collaborative approach and move towards the right-hand side of the continuum.

5 *Degree to which other stakeholders trust the change managers* The more the other stakeholders trust the change managers the more likely they are to be prepared to follow their direction. The lower the level of trust the more the change managers may have to involve others in order to win trust and build commitment to the change plan.

6 *Degree to which the change managers have to rely on the commitment and energy of others to implement the plan* The more the change

managers have to rely on the energy and commitment of others to engage in discretionary behaviours to make the change plan work, the more they may have to adopt a collaborative approach and involve them in the change process.

Kotter and Schlesinger (1979) argue that one of the most common mistakes made by change agents is that they often rely on a single approach to implementing change regardless of the situation. They refer to:

- the autocratic manager, whose only approach is to coerce people
- the people-oriented manager, who typically tries to involve and support people
- the cynical manager, who always tries to manipulate others
- the intellectual manager, who relies too much on education as an influence strategy
- the lawyer-type boss, who typically tries to negotiate and bargain.

The model presented here emphasises the need for change managers to adopt a contingent approach to the choice of implementation strategy that accommodates and balances a number of interdependent factors.

Variations over time

Balogun and Hailey (1999) suggest that the focus of the change strategy may need to change over time. For example, in the short term the critical requirement may be to secure the organisation's survival. In order to do this, it may be necessary to adopt a tough 'top-down' results-driven strategy that involves radical cuts and closures or it may be necessary to redefine the purpose of the organisation. Over the longer term the focus may switch to a more incremental strategy of tuning and the major concern may become continuous improvement. Associated with this change in focus may be a move towards a more collaborative approach to implementation.

   Zaltman and Duncan (1977) cite complexity, communicability, compatibility, relative advantage and divisibility as factors that might influence the way change managers attempt to influence others. These factors might also affect the *styles of influence* that will be most effective at different stages of the transition phase:

- *Complexity and communicability*   If the required change is very complex and difficult to communicate the initial style of influence might involve a high level of explanation and education. However, once people understand the problem and what is required, other means of influence might be more effective.
- *Compatibility and relative advantage*   Similarly, a change that is compatible with the change targets preferences and offers relative advantage over

current practice might lend itself to a persuasive strategy. In other cases negotiation or high levels of involvement might be the most effective way forward.

- *Divisibility* Where the change is divisible and where quick action is required, it might be decided to direct a part of the organisation to adopt a small-scale trial before making a decision about how to proceed. If it is decided to go ahead, speed may be less of an issue and commitment may be more important. Consequently, at this stage, a less directive approach might be adopted.

Alternative start points

Balogun and Hailey (1999) consider the advantages and disadvantages of different start points for change:

- *Pilot sites* A small-scale change might be introduced into a pilot site that might be a single unit or a completely new site. At Asda, for example, three stores were selected for the early experimental phase of the change. An alternative approach is to introduce changes in new sites, with new staff. They can provide effective 'test beds' for initiatives that might be resisted elsewhere because of ingrained traditional attitudes and practices. Once a change initiative has been proven on the pilot site, other parts of the organisation might find it more difficult to resist the change. However, care needs to be exercised when rolling out change to other parts of the organisation.
- *Pockets of good practice* Another type of small-scale change is the kind of development that is led by an individual or group who takes an initiative and promotes a pocket of good practice that, eventually, might be copied by others.
- *Top-down versus bottom-up* An advantage of a 'bottom-up' approach is that organisational members who are in a position to recognise problems long before they are obvious to top management can take initiatives and introduce changes at an early stage. 'Bottom-up' strategies also encourage commitment. However, they may not produce widespread action fast enough. In times of crisis, when a rapid organisation-wide response is essential, the most effective approach might be to adopt a 'top-down' approach. Coordination may also become a problem if a number of separate and incompatible change initiatives begin to emerge at different points across the organisation. In some cases coordination from the top may be an essential ingredient of an effective change strategy, even if many of the initiatives originate at lower levels in the organisation.

Summary

This chapter has considered the strengths and weaknesses of three approaches to managing change and explored some of the situational variables that need to be considered when shaping a change strategy and how these variables might have different implications for the strategy over time. The chapter concludes with a brief review of some alternative start points for change.

Exercise 15.1 Change strategy

1 In your experience, which is the most frequently used change strategy? What are the reasons for this?
2 In your opinion can a change strategy that combines a 'top-down' drive for results *and* the development of organisational capability offer a better best chance of achieving sustained high performance than one that focuses on either results or capability? Why might this be so?

 Notes

Exercise 15.2 Strategy for change

Identify a recent change in your organisation and critically assess the effectiveness of the strategy used to implement it.

 Notes

References

Balogun, J. and Hailey, V.H. (1999) *Exploring Strategic Change*, London: Prentice Hall.

Beer, M. (2000) 'Cracking the Code of Change', *Harvard Business Review*, 78 (3), pp. 133–41.

Beer, M. (2001) 'How to Develop an Organization Capable of Sustained High Performance: Embrace the Drive for Results-Capability Development Paradox', *Organizational Dynamics,* 29 (4), 233–47. ✓

Beer, M. and Nohria, N. (2000) *Breaking the Code of Change*, Boston, MA: Harvard Business School Press.

Eriksson, M. and Sundgren, M. (2005) 'Managing Change: Strategy or Serendipity – Reflections from the Merger of Astra and Zeneca', *Journal of Change Management*, 5 (1), pp. 15–28.

Kotter, J. and Schlesinger, L.A. (1979) 'Choosing Strategies for Change', *Harvard Business Review*, 57 (2), pp. 106–114.

Morrison, E.W. and Milliken, F. J. (2000) 'Organizational Silence: A Barrier to Change and Development in a Pluralistic World', *Academy of Management Review*, 25 (4), 706–25.

Nadler, D. and Shaw, R. (1995) 'Change Leadership', in D. Nadler, R. Shaw and A.E. Walton, *Discontinous Change*, San Francisco: Jossey-Bass.

Schein, E. H. (1996) 'The Three Cultures of Management: The Key to Organizational Learning', *Sloan Management Review*, Fall, pp. 9–20.

Zaltman, G. and Duncan, R. (1977) *Strategies for Planned Change*, London: Wiley.

16

Maintaining control during the change

Every stage of the change process raises issues of control. One of the reasons why managers are sometimes reluctant to call in external consultants is the fear that they may be difficult to control. This chapter focuses attention on the issues of control associated with the implementation stage of the change process.

Beckhard and Harris (1987) define the period of time between the identification of the need for change and the achievement of a desired future state as the *transition state*. Often key phases of this state are unique and different from either the state that exists before the change or the state that will exist after it. For example, if an organisation recognises that it needs to improve the way it manages information and, after exploring a number of possibilities, decides to move to an enterprise resource planning (ERP) integrated information system it will experience a period of transition. There will come a point when the organisation continues to rely on the old system while the new one is being developed, installed and debugged. During this period people affected by the change will have to (a) keep the old system going while learning how to work with the new system and (b) develop the work roles and relationships that will have to be in place when the new system is up and running.

It is not unusual for many types of change to disrupt normal work practices and undermine existing systems of management. Nadler (1993) argues that during this period one of the major challenges facing management is one of *control*. To abandon previous management systems before new ones have been developed can frustrate any attempt to manage the change unless some form of temporary management system is put in place. Nadler refers to the need for 'transition devices'. These include the appointment of a transition manager; the development of a plan for the period of transition between the old state and the proposed future state; the allocation of specific transition resources such as budgets, time and staff; and the development of feedback mechanisms to facilitate monitoring and control.

This chapter highlights seven steps that the change manager can take to help maintain control during the transition state.

Develop and communicate a clear vision of the future state

The first step in managing a transition is to provide a *sense of direction*. Nadler make the obvious point that it is difficult to manage toward something when people do not know what that 'something' is. People need a vision in order to recognise what kind of behaviour will be appropriate, helpful and constructive. This was identified as a key leadership task in Chapter 10.

With the 'blueprint' type of change, referred to in Chapter 5, this kind of vision is relatively easy to establish and communicate. However, it can be much more difficult to achieve in situations that involve more of an evolutionary process of change. In these circumstances, Nadler proposes an incremental approach that involves presenting change in terms of a *series* of short transitions, the first being defined in relatively concrete terms and subsequent steps towards the uncertain future being envisioned in less concrete and more flexible terms.

Appoint a transition manager

Should the person in charge of the pre-change state continue to be in charge during the transition or should management responsibility pass to the person who will be in charge post-transition? Beckhard and Harris (1987) suggest that there is no cut and dried answer to this question. Typically the transition state is one which is characterised by high levels of ambiguity and conflict and the individual (or group) tasked with managing the transition needs:

- The 'clout' to mobilise the resources necessary to keep the change moving (in situations where resources are scarce those responsible for keeping the old system going may resist giving up the staff time and other resources required to develop the new system; the transition manager needs the power and authority to ensure that resources are allocated as required)
- The respect of both the existing operational leadership and those who are working on the development of the new system
- The ability to get things done in ways that will win support and commitment rather than resistance and compliance.

Depending on the nature of the change, there may be several possible candidates for the transition management role. A very senior person in the organisation may step in and take control. A project manager may be appointed on a temporary basis. The person in charge of the pre-change state may be given responsibility for the transition in addition to his or her current operating role. A task force or temporary team may be established. Where a team approach is adopted consideration needs to be given to team composition. It might include representatives from the constituencies affected by the change; a diagonal slice of staff representing different levels of the organisation, 'natural leaders' (people who have the confidence and trust of large numbers of their colleagues), or a group who are drawn together because of their technical skills.

Develop a transition plan

Mention has already been made of the need to diagnose sources of resistance, identify who needs to be involved in the change, develop a critical mass of political support and establish temporary transition structures. There is also a need to develop a plan of how activities will be managed through the transition state. Beckhard and Harris (1987) identify seven characteristics of effective transition plans. Effective plans are:

- *purposeful* – the planned activities are clearly linked to the change goals and priorities
- *task specific* – the types of activities involved are clearly identified rather than broadly generalised
- *integrated* – the discrete activities are linked
- *temporal* – events and activities are timetabled
- *adaptable* – there are contingency plans for adapting to unanticipated opportunities and problems
- *agreed* – senior managers (and other stakeholders, as required) support the plan
- *cost-effective* – avoid unnecessary waste.

This list might be extended to include some of the issues considered below – for example, the provision of adequate resources and rewards for desired behaviours.

Provide the resources for the transition

There is always a cost associated with change. For example, there may be a need for training, new equipment, the development of software, the design of new structures and staff time for all of this. When the need to change is anticipated it is more likely that the resource requirements will have been foreseen. However, when change is imposed as an urgent response to a pressing problem the organisation may find itself stretched. In some circumstances it may be so stretched that it cannot resource the change and has no option but to go out of business. In less pressing circumstances it is not unusual for management to assume that much of the staff burden of change will be borne by employees working longer and harder. While people often rise to the challenge in the short term, goodwill cannot be relied on for ever. In situations where change is a constant feature of organisational life this needs to be recognised and the required resources made available.

Reward transition behaviours

In those situations where people are required to continue working in accordance with the pre-change system in order to 'keep the show on the road' and maintain operations while simultaneously developing the new system, they may give insufficient attention to the change. This can happen because existing control systems reward current practice and offer little incentive for development work. Consequently people are discouraged from investing their time in this work and from experimenting with new behaviours that might be required in the future. Steps need to be taken to ensure that transition behaviour is not penalised and every opportunity to reward this kind of behaviour needs to be explored.

Use multiple and consistent leverage points for change

It was noted earlier that organisations are equilibrium-seeking systems. If only one component of the system is changed this can trigger forces that seek to re-align all the components of the system by re-establishing the status quo. One way of avoiding this is to use multiple and consistent leverage points for achieving change. For example, if it is decided to change the structure of an organisation it may be necessary to modify other elements of the system (such as culture and career management systems) in order to secure the intended benefits (Case study 16.1).

> ### Case study 16.1   Matrix structures
>
> Managers in an auto-component manufacturing company decided that in order to improve performance they needed to introduce a new structure that would be more responsive to both the complex technical issues associated with production and the unique project requirements of their customers (see Figure 16.1). This kind of dual focus has long been recognised as a requirement in the aerospace industry where products are technically complex and customers very demanding.

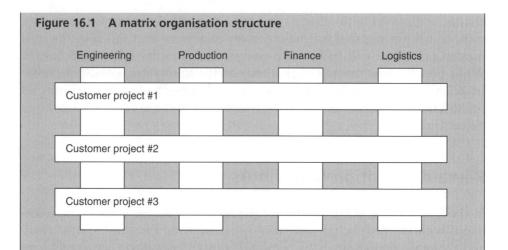

Figure 16.1 A matrix organisation structure

In this case the promise of improved performance was not realised because the transition plan did not incorporate multiple and consistent leverage points for change. It failed to recognise the need, when introducing the new structure, to adjust a range of other elements of the wider organisation, such as the organisation's systems and culture.

Matrix structures will only be effective if they are supported by organisational systems concerned with planning, controlling, appraising and rewarding that serve the needs of both the functional and customer-project dimensions of the new structure. If appraising and rewarding are left in the hands of functional managers (such as the heads of engineering and production) the managers responsible for the customer related projects might find that they have little influence over the members of their project teams who also report to a functional manager. In the example of the auto-components manufacturing company, team members gave priority to the demands of their functional managers because they continued to exercise most influence over their career and reward package. Systems were not modified to accommodate the new dual focus.

There was also no attempt to modify the pre-change organisation culture to ensure it would be compatible with the new matrix approach to management. In this case there was a rigid bureaucratic tradition, a belief in the sanctity of unity of command and a commitment to immediate departmental objectives. This culture undermined attempts to achieve the dual strength of technical competence and customer focus. A matrix organisation will only be effective when members are aware of and willing to work towards these broad goals and when they have the skills and competence to expand their contribution to embrace responsibility for managing the relationship between their sub-task and the broader organisational purpose.

Develop feedback mechanisms

A key requirement for maintaining control is the development and installation of new feedback devices and control systems that will facilitate the monitoring of progress towards the desired future state. Nadler (1993) is a particularly strong advocate of customised feedback mechanisms during the transition phase because the feedback processes that managers normally use to collect information about how the organisation is functioning might be less appropriate during over this period. Additional sources of feedback might include organisation-wide surveys, focus group discussions and feedback from individual organisational members. Bruch, Gerber and Maier (2005) argue that a comprehensive system for monitoring and reporting is essential to maintain peoples' attention on the change.

Summary

This chapter has considered some of the steps that can be taken to maintain control of the change process. These include:

- Developing and communicating a clear vision
- Identifying an individual or group who can lead the change and promote a vision of the desired future state
- Producing an implementation plan, with clear targets and goals, that can indicate progress and signal any need for remedial action
- Ensuring that adequate resources are allocated to the change and that an appropriate balance is maintained between keeping the organisation running and implementing the changes necessary to move to the desired future state
- Implementing reward systems that encourage experimentation and change
- Using multiple and consistent leverage points for change
- Developing feedback mechanisms that provide the information required to ensure that the change programme moves forward in a coordinated manner, especially where the plan calls for consistent change in a number of related areas.

Exercise 16.1   Maintaining control during the transition stage

Reflect on some of the changes that you have been responsible for managing at work or elsewhere.

- Did you lose control, or fear that you might lose control, during the transition stage?
- If so, why was this?
- What could you have done differently that might have helped you to maintain better control?

If you cannot identify an occasion when maintaining control was a problem for you, reflect on an occasion when you were aware of somebody else who had lost control of a change that they were responsible for managing. Identify what this other change manager might have done to maintain better control.

Make a note of what you/they might have done to maintain better control in the space provided below.

 Notes

References

Beckhard, R. and Harris, R.T. (1987) *Organizational Transitions: Managing Complex Change*, Reading, MA: Addison-Wesley.

Bruch, H., Gerber, P. and Maier, V. (2005) 'Strategic Change Decisions: Doing the Right Change Right', *Journal of Change Management*, 5 (1), pp. 97–107.

Nadler, D.A. (1993) 'Concepts for the Management of Organisational Change', in C. Mabey and B. Mayon-White (eds), *Managing Change*, London: Paul Chapman, in association with the Open University.

Interventions

Part V considers some of the interventions that change managers can use to help secure a desired outcome, and some of the issues that need to be considered when deciding which interventions to use in particular circumstances.

Chapter 17 Types of intervention

Chapter 17 opens with four case studies. Case study 17.1 is set in southwest India and involves improving the effectiveness of primary healthcare centres. Case study 17.2 involves designing an intervention to increase the motivation and flexibility of the workforce of a Danish dairy company operating in the UK. Case study 17.3 involves designing an intervention to improve the treatment offered by the trauma orthopaedic care department of a large UK hospital. Case study 17.4 involves reducing absenteeism in the elderly care sector of the Silkeborg Council in Denmark.

The chapter moves on to consider how different theoretical perspectives on change have influenced the development of interventions over the course of the last 100 years. A typology that classifies interventions according to the focal issues they are designed to address is then introduced. The main types of intervention are human process, techno-structural, strategic and human resource interventions.

After reading this chapter you will be invited to review some of the change programmes in your organisation (that you have witnessed or been involved in) and classify the types of interventions used.

Chapters 18–21 provide a more detailed examination of four widely used types of intervention.

Chapter 18 Action research

Action research is the basic model underpinning most organisational change interventions. It involves the application of scientific methods (fact-finding and experimentation) to organisational problems and underpins the generic process model of change presented in Chapter 5.

Chapter 19 Appreciative inquiry

Appreciative inquiry is a process that involves exploring the best of what is (or has been) and amplifying this best practice. It seeks to accentuate the positive rather than eliminate the negative; it focuses attention on what is good and working rather than on what is wrong and not working. This chapter examines appreciate inquiry from three perspectives; a philosophy of knowledge, an intervention theory and a methodology for intervening in organisations to improve performance and the quality of life.

Chapter 20   High-performance management

'High commitment', 'high involvement' and 'high performance' are terms that are often used interchangeably to refer to an approach to managing an organisation's HR that involves employing HR practices to achieve sustainable improvements in productivity and financial performance. Rather than focusing on separate HR practices, high-performance management involves developing and implementing a 'bundle' or system of HR practices that is internally consistent, aligned with other business processes and aligned with the organisation's business strategy. It is an approach to improving organisational performance that is consistent with open systems thinking and the concept of 'fit' discussed in Chapter 3.

Chapter 21   Business process reengineering

Business process reengineering (BPR) involves switching attention away from fragmented functional-based thinking towards cross-functional processes that create value for the organisation. It involves redesigning core processes in order to make them faster and more flexible, and to make organisations more responsive to changes.

Chapter 22   Selecting interventions

This chapter examines the factors that need to be considered when selecting which type of intervention to use. Consideration is also given to factors that can affect decisions regarding the sequencing of interventions. This is important because sometimes an inappropriate sequence can undermine the effectiveness of a change programme.

After reading this chapter you will be invited to critically assess the choice and sequencing of interventions in one or more of the change programmes that you have been involved in.

Types of intervention

Four case studies

Before reading this and the other five chapters of Part V, you are invited to complete at least two of the following four cases (Case studies 17.1–17.4). Imagine that you are a consultant and have been invited to design an intervention to address the issues raised in each case.

After reading Chapters 17–22, you might find it useful to review your approach to designing an intervention. You might also consider the nature of your change strategy in the light of the strategies considered in Chapter 15.

Case study 17.1   Designing an intervention to improve the effectiveness of primary healthcare centres in southwest India

A senior health official in an Indian State government has approached you for advice. The State has a rapidly growing population and a high demand for primary healthcare, but a tight budget which means that every effort has to be made to improve the effectiveness of the existing provision. There will only be limited resources to cope with the growing demand for primary healthcare services. The existing provision is good when benchmarked against World Health organisation (WHO) standards and exceptionally good when compared with countries at a similar stage of development and with most other States within India.

There are about 500 primary healthcare centres spread across the State, many in isolated rural areas. Their role is to offer medical care, mother and child welfare, family planning, improvements in environmental sanitation, control of communicable diseases, health education and school health. In addition they are required to collect statistics and provide a referral service. Each Centre is managed by a chief medical officer and has an establishment of approximately sixty staff. There is typically a main facility that has accommodation for clinics, operating theatres for minor surgery, three wards for short- stay patients and a pharmacy. In addition various outreach services maybe located at satellite sites in the community served by a Centre.

Up until now attempts to improve the effectiveness of primary healthcare provision have been limited to sending chief medical officers and other doctors who have been identified as candidates for promotion on a lengthy training programme at the State's Institute for Management in Government. The senior health official who has approached you for advice believes that there has been relatively little transfer of learning back into the primary healthcare centres and that the heavy investment in training has had little effect on performance.

Your task

1 Design an intervention that will improve the capability of the staff working in the health centres to improve the effectiveness of the services they provide.
2 Identify issues that might affect the success of your proposed intervention, and explain how you would address them.

Case study 17.2   Designing an intervention to increase the motivation and the flexibility of the work-force in a large dairy company

The new CEO and the director of HR of a large dairy company have sought your advice regarding the kind of intervention that might be effective in helping them involve employees in order to motivate them to work more flexibly and support the modernisation of the diaries.

The company is Danish-owned. It began production in the UK six years ago following the acquisition of a number of British dairies. It now employs 2,400 people at six dairies and one other plant that produces fruit drinks. The last few years have been a difficult time for the dairy industry in the UK and many companies have gone out of business. Supermarkets are selling milk at very competitive prices, presenting a fierce challenge to the doorstep-delivery business and the abolition of the Milk Marketing Board (MMB) has led to a sharp increase in the price of raw milk.

After the new CEO was appointed he initiated a restructuring of the UK business, creating strategic business units (SBUs) serving particular segments of the market and major customers such as the large supermarket chains. The company has also invested heavily in state-of-the-art processing and packaging equipment. But further action is still needed to ensure the company's success.

Labour requirements fluctuate considerably, as the demand for dairy products varies over the week and over the year. Operations managers cope with peak periods by making extensive use of overtime working. Many of the workers at the company's processing sites are low-paid and make a living wage by working overtime. It is not unusual for workers to work more than fifty hours over a six-day week and up to seventy hours at peak periods.* There is always plenty of overtime at peak times such as Christmas, but in order to ensure that overtime is available at other times employees operated machines inefficiently.

Managers experience great difficulty persuading employees to work flexibly or accept new practices. Over the years they have used supplementary payments as a way of getting things done. There are over ninety different rates of pay and no formal grading system to justify ninety differences.

The state of industrial relations varies across sites, ranging from good to difficult. Absenteeism is high, running at about 10 per cent.

The company needs a skilled and well-motivated workforce able and ready to react flexibly to customers' demands and willing to support the modernisation of the dairies.

Your task

1   Design an intervention that will involve the employees in order to motivate them to work more flexibly and support the modernisation of the diaries.
2   Identify issues that might affect the success of your proposed intervention and explain how you would address them.

Note: *This case describes a situation before the EU working time directive was introduced into the UK.

Case study 17.3   Designing an intervention to improve the treatment offered by the trauma orthopaedic care department in a large NHS hospital

The general manager responsible for orthopaedic services in a large acute NHS hospital has sought your advice regarding the kind of intervention that might be effective in helping to improve the treatment offered to patients who are admitted for trauma orthopaedic care.

Trauma orthopaedic care (which typically involve an emergency admission and immediate treatment for a condition such as a broken leg) and elective orthopaedic care (which involves non-emergency treatment such as a hip replacement operation) are provided by separate departments located in neighbouring hospitals within the same city. Because of a government initiative to reduce waiting times (that apply to elective treatments) extra resources have tended to be allocated to elective care rather than to trauma services. The situation confronting trauma orthopaedic care has worsened over the last three years because the department has had to cope with an 11 per cent increase in emergency admissions. This has undermined the department's ability to provide the quality of care that it, and other stakeholders, believe that patients should receive. While the hospital recognises that trauma services are under-resourced and has agreed to appoint more orthopaedic surgeons and increase their access to operating theatres, everybody recognises that these changes will not be in place for some time. As a result, staff morale is low.

Several surgeons and departmental managers are highly motivated to change what they refer to as a 'desperate situation' in trauma orthopaedic care. They are particularly concerned to improve patient care for one of the largest groups of patients – those admitted with a broken neck of the femur. There are approximately 800 such admissions each year and the average patient stay is twenty-four days.

The department has a traditional structure with four wards, each headed by a ward sister (a senior nurse who acts as ward manager). Occupational therapists and physiotherapists work with patients to facilitate their rehabilitation. Doctors, nurses, occupational therapists and physiotherapists maintain their own care notes and treatment plans. Many patients, especially the elderly, require support in the community post- discharge and social workers (who work for the Local Authority's social services department) assess this need and arrange social care packages.

Your task

1 Design an intervention that will improve the situation in trauma orthopaedic care. This could include delivering outcomes such as improved patient care and reduced length of stay in hospital.
2 Identify issues that might affect the success of your proposed intervention and explain how you would address them.

Case study 17.4   Designing an intervention to reduce absenteeism in the elderly care sector of Silkeborg Council, Denmark

An area manager responsible for the care of the elderly in Silkeborg has approached you for advice. (This case is based on a situation that existed in 2001.) Absenteeism is a problem for all departments of the Silkeborg Council. The average number of working days lost over the first six months of 2001 was 9.25 (an annual rate of just under twenty days per employee). One of the departments in which absenteeism is especially high is elderly care.

Over a period of several years the Council had taken several initiatives to reduce absenteeism. In the area of elderly care these have included:

● analysing the reasons for lost time
● introducing a 'stop-lift' policy to improve practices in moving and handling in order to reduce lost time caused by back injuries
● helping group leaders develop their supervisory skills
● educating the management team in the area of supervision and leadership
● helping the management team and care staff work together to develop an absenteeism policy.

An important element of the new absenteeism policy is that illness should be regarded as a common concern for both employer and employee rather than a private issue for the employee alone. If people are off sick frequently, or for a prolonged period of time, their managers should engage in a dialogue with them about work, health and satisfaction in order to explore ways of improving the situation for both the individual and the department.

These various initiatives have produced short-term improvements but little long- term change.

Your task

1 Design an intervention that will help the elderly care department provide a better service for patients and the wider community by ensuring that the 250 front-line staff are present more of the time and making a full contribution to the work of the department.
2 Identify issues that might affect the success of your proposed intervention and explain how you would address them.

Change efforts can be less successful than they might be because those responsible for managing the change are unaware of the full range of interventions that are available. Cummings and Worley (2001) define interventions as 'a set of sequenced planned actions or events intended to help an organisation increase its effectiveness'. They are deliberate acts that disturb the status quo. This chapter reviews some of the main types of intervention.

The first section of this chapter considers how the development of interventions over the twentieth century was influenced by theoretical perspectives. Burnes (2004) identifies the three main perspectives as the individual perspective, the group dynamics school and open systems thinking. These different perspectives focus attention on different aspects of organisational life and have implications for the focus of change efforts and how change is managed. Weisbord (1989) adopts a similar view and traces the development of interventions in terms of 'who should do what'. He identifies four main types of intervention:

- experts applying scientific principles to solve specific problems
- groups working collaboratively to solve their own problems
- experts working to solve system-wide problems
- everybody working to improve the capability of the whole system for future performance.

The second section introduces an alternative typology that classifies type of intervention in terms of the issues they address. Again, four main types of intervention are identified. They focus on:

- human process issues
- technology/structural issues
- strategic issues
- human resource issues.

A number of specific interventions are briefly considered under each of these headings and a selection of interventions is considered in more detail in Chapters 18–21.

A classification of interventions based on 'who does what'

Weisbord (1989) observes that there was a continuous development of new types of intervention over the twentieth century and suggests that this has been a response to environmental changes, particularly the trend towards greater turbulence and uncertainty.

Weisbord classifies the range of interventions available to change agents into four categories according to criteria relating to *who* does the intervening

Figure 17.1   Developments in the type of intervention over the twentieth century

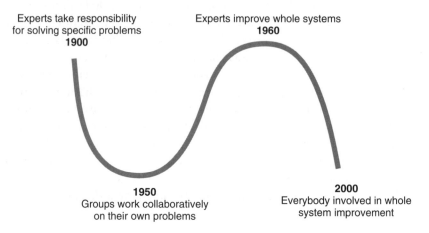

Source: Adapted from Weisbord (1989).

and *what* it is that they do to bring about improvement. In terms of who does the intervening, he notes that in the early 1900s the typical intervention relied on an expert to solve a problem, whereas today interventions often involve the whole system (including experts). In terms of what it is that the interventions focus on, Weisbord notes that there has been a shift from problem solving past mistakes in particular parts of the system to improving the capability of the whole system for future performance. This evolution in interventions is illustrated in Figure 17.1.

The use of technical experts to solve problems

Fredrick W. Taylor published his *Principles of Scientific Management* in 1911, in which he advocated a systematic experimental approach to problem solving. His principles involved a careful analysis of tasks and experimentation to determine, from the perspective of efficiency, how the task should be divided into segments and how the work in each segment should be done. One of the most frequently quoted examples of Taylor's work involves an assignment at the US Bethlehem steel plant designed to find the most efficient way of moving 100lb pigs (slabs) of iron from a loading dock into a railroad truck. He enlisted the help of a pig-iron handler called Schmidt and studied him while, on instruction, he moved the pigs in different ways. The outcome was an ideal approach to doing the job that also specified rest periods and included an incentive system that rewarded the jobholder for working efficiently. The new approach increased productivity by 280 per cent.

Taylor's approach led to the widespread use of experts to solve problems, such as methods engineers to identify the most efficient way of accomplishing a task and time and motion analysts to set standard times for the completion of each segment of the work.

Today many organisations still employ experts to solve specific problems – for example, to develop a new payments system or to design a new information management system. Experts are often used when a unit (or the organisation) has only occasional need for a specific kind of expertise, when the need is for 'cutting-edge' expertise which might be obtained only from specialist departments or external consultants, or when a solution has to be found urgently and the quickest approach is to buy-in external help. A potential problem associated with the use of experts is that members of the system may not share the expert's diagnosis of the problem and therefore may not be committed to implementing the prescribed solution. Members of the system may also not learn how to solve the problem for themselves, so should it reoccur they will continue to be dependent on the expert for the solution.

Interventions which involve groups working on their own problems

In the 1950s, the work of Kurt Lewin and his associates at the Research Centre for Group Dynamics began to produce evidence that supported the proposition that the behaviour, attitudes, beliefs and values of individuals are all based in the groups to which they belong. This led to the view that groups will exert a strong influence over whether individuals will accept or resist a change. A consequence was the development of new kinds of intervention that involved all members of a work group working together to solve problems. Interventions focused on changing the groups' norms, roles and values.

Cartwright (1951) summarised eight principles (that emerged from the early research on group dynamics) that influenced the design of interventions. The first five are concerned with the group as a medium of change and with how the group is able to exert influence over its members. The final three focus on the potential benefits of making the group the target of change, even when the prime aim is to change individual behaviour. Evidence suggests that by changing the standards, style of leadership and structure of a group it is possible to change the behaviour of individual group members. The eight principles are:

1 *If the group is to be used as a medium of change, those people who are to be changed and those who are to exert influence for change must have a strong sense of belonging to the same group*
   This implies that in situations where the change agents are regarded as part of the group, and when a strong 'we' as opposed to 'us and them' feeling exists, those trying to bring about change will have more influence over others. Cartwright cites research findings that show that there

is greater change in members' opinions when discussion groups operate with participatory rather than supervisory leadership.

2 *The more attractive a group is to its members the greater the influence it will exert over its members*
When individuals find a group attractive and want to be members of the group they are more ready to be influenced by other members of the group. Attractiveness promotes cohesiveness and a willingness, on the part of members, to conform with others when conformity is a relevant matter for the group.

A group is more attractive to members the more it satisfies their needs. Some of the ways that group attractiveness can be increased include:

(a) increasing the liking of members for each other
(b) increasing the perceived importance of the group goal
(c) increasing the prestige of the group in the eyes of others.

3 *A group has most influence over those matters that attract members to it*
Research evidence suggests that in attempts to change attitudes, values or behaviour, the more relevant they are to the basis of attraction to the group, the greater is the influence that the group is able to exert upon them. This helps to explain, for example, why a member of a local branch of a trades union might be willing to follow a union recommendation to engage in industrial action to influence the outcome of a pay negotiation but refuse to join a wider political protest targeted at government policies. While some members might be attracted by the union's political agenda others might not share the union's political affiliation. However, all may be attracted by the role the union can play in protecting their interests in the workplace.

4 *The greater the prestige of a member in the eyes of other group members, the greater the influence that member can exert*
The relevance of this principle, in the context of change management, is that the person who has greatest prestige and who exerts most influence may not be the manager or formal leader designated by the organisation. Also, in peer groups the most influential person may not be the person who behaves in ways that are valued by superiors. For example, in a classroom situation the 'teacher's pet' may have low prestige in the eyes of other members of the class and therefore will have low influence over them.

5 *Efforts to change individual members or sub-parts of a group which, if successful, would have the effect of making them deviate from the norms of the group, will encounter strong resistance*
In many groups the price of deviation is rejection. Consequently (especially where group membership is valued) there is pressure to conform to the norms of the group. This principle helps to explain why training interventions that involve taking individuals from different groups and

training (changing) them often have a poor record in terms of transfer of learning when compared with training interventions which are directed at all members of a natural work group. Where the focus is on changing an individual, that individual may be reluctant to continue to behave differently after training for fear of rejection. Where the intervention is targeted at the whole group, this problem is less likely to arise.

6   *It is possible to create strong pressures for change in a group by establishing a shared perception of the need for change, thus making the source of pressure for change lie within the group*
When groups are presented with 'facts' by an outsider (for example, by a manager, an internal or an external consultant) even where the facts 'prove' the case for change in the eyes of the outsider, the facts may not be accepted by the group. The group may reject the facts because it does not 'own' them.

   When groups collect and test their own facts they are more likely to accept the evidence. Cartwright notes that there appears to be all the difference in the world between those cases where external consultants are hired to do a study and present a report and those in which a technical expert collaborates with the group in doing its own study. Often external reports are not acted on, they are left to gather dust rather than stimulate lasting change.

7   *Information relating to the need for change and the consequences of change (or no change) must be shared by all relevant people in the group*
This principle is about getting people talking about the need for change. Changes can be blocked unless action is taken to improve communication. Evidence suggests that where the prospect of change creates feelings of threat, mistrust or hostility people avoid communicating openly and freely about the issues that concern them. Just at the point when the need for communication is at its highest, people act defensively and communicate less.

8   *Changes in one part of the group (or system) produce strain in other parts of the group (or system) that can be reduced only by eliminating the initial change or by bringing about readjustments in the related parts*
This principle is about alignment. For example, a training programme that has produced changes in one sub-group (nurses working on a hospital ward) will have implications for other sub-groups working above, below and around them as part of the total group of people dealing with patients on that ward.

The use of experts to solve systemic problems

Following the impact of Von Bertalanffy's (1950) seminal paper on 'the theory of open systems in physics and biology', social scientists began to pay more attention to *organisations* as systems of inter-related units that transact with a larger environment (some of the main implications of systems thinking for organisations are summarised in Chapter 3). This interest led to the development of a new class of intervention. Attention shifted from solving isolated problems to looking at more systemic issues. Organisations began to employ experts, such as operations researchers and systems analysts, to guide this approach to problem solving and in the UK social scientists at the Tavistock Institute of Human Relations in London began to develop interventions based on socio-technical theory. Much of their work was based on the principle that, in any situation, there is rarely only one single social system (work relationship structure) that can be used to accomplish a given task. Usually there are a number of such systems that can be used to operate the same technology and therefore there exists an element of choice in designing the work organisation (see Trist, 1969). This gives rise to the question of which social system will provide the optimum conditions and contribute most to the outcomes valued by various stakeholders.

These developments gave rise to a proliferation of other interventions that were directed towards systemic issues such as managing the organisation's relationship with its environment and helping to promote a better alignment of the elements within the organisation. While most early systemic interventions were led by experts, many of those that were developed later integrated representatives of the target system into the process of managing change. This development has been taken a stage further in whole systems interventions.

Whole system interventions to improve capability for future performance

The most recent development has been whole systems interventions in which *everybody* is involved in whole-system improvement. Many examples of this type of intervention, such as Weisbord's Strategic Search Conference, adopt a 'whole system in the room' or conference model format. The five principles that underpin the whole system approach are summarised below:

- *Parallel organisation versus whole system in the room approaches*   The effectiveness of attempts to introduce change, especially at the strategic level, is dependent on the actions and behaviours of *everybody* affected by the change. Therefore, wherever practicable, *everybody* should be involved in the change process.

  A typical intervention used, for example, to develop a shared vision and an agreed strategic plan is to set up a temporary parallel organisation involving representatives from different groups (and levels) across the regular organisation to work together in various committees and task forces to produce the desired output. It is assumed that this kind of approach creates a wide feeling of involvement and gains the commitment of all organisational members. Often, however, only the representatives and those close to them feel involved. While this minority may become excited and passionate about the changes, others may feel left out and unable to influence developments. This can undermine their commitment to the vision and strategic plan produced by this process.

An alternative approach, embedded in the 'whole system in the room' or conference model, involves a significant part of the whole system rather than a parallel organisation of representatives. This allows everybody to contribute. It is not uncommon to accommodate 500 or more members of the organisation in a single conference. In large organisations, several conferences may be required, with some mechanism for integrating the findings from the different meetings at key stages.

• *Problem solving versus preferred future approaches* Lippitt (1983) argues that trying to 'fix the past' by problem solving depletes energy whereas focusing attention on planning for a new future releases energy. Dannemiller and Jacobs (1992) report that when Lippitt compared a problem solving group and a group using a 'preferred futures' approach to planning the latter group envisioned the future they preferred and developed plans to achieve it whereas the former group restricted itself to problem identification and action planning. He also found that the 'preferred futures' approach was associated with higher levels of energy, greater 'ownership' of the situation and more innovative and future-oriented goals and plans. The focus of whole systems approaches tends to be on what the organisation might become, rather than the current problems that need to be solved.

• *Organisational biographies: understanding the past and the present as a basis for exploring a preferred future* All too often organisational members are unaware of the assumptions and consistent patterns that guide how they interpret and respond to situations, yet these assumptions and consistent patterns may blind them to threats and opportunities and may lead them to develop unrealistic strategic plans.

What an organisation is today has been influenced by the way organisational members have interpreted and responded to opportunities and threats in the past. But organisations are not victims of the past. It is possible to learn from past experience and to use this learning to challenge and modify assumptions, identify new possibilities and identify what needs to happen if these possibilities are to become reality. An element of many interventions, therefore, is the development of a better understanding of where the organisation has come from, where it is today, and how it moved from where it was to where it is.

• *Overcoming resistance to change* Change occurs when organisational members experience a tension that results from a discrepancy between their awareness of current reality and their desired future state (Fritz, 1984). They are motivated to reduce the tension by acting in ways that will help the organisation move towards the more desired future state. The conference method is designed to create this necessary tension across the whole organisation. Dannemiller and Jacobs (1992) advance this view and adapt Gleicher's change formula to argue that change will occur when the product of dissatisfaction with the present situation (*D*), a vision of what is possible (*V*) and practical first steps toward reaching the vision (*F*) are greater than the cost of change/resistance (*R*):

$$C = (D \ V \ F) > R$$

The conference method involves a process that openly explores organisational members' satisfaction with the status quo, develops a clear vision of the future possibilities and identifies practical first steps in order to motivate people to change.

- *Open systems planning*   Jayaram (1977) and others strongly advocate open systems planning. In the conference method external stakeholders, such as supplies and customers, are invited to contribute their views about the organisation's current performance and the opportunities and threats it will have to respond to in the future. This kind of input enriches the database available to organisational members.

The last 100 years has seen many developments in the types of intervention available to change agents, but all four types considered so far can be used to good effect in appropriate circumstances.

The next section of this chapter will review interventions from a different perspective.

A classification of interventions based on focal issues

Cummings and Worley (2001) offer an alternative typology for classifying interventions based on the kinds of issues that they are designed to resolve. Figure 17.2 shows the four main types of intervention. Systemic interdependencies are indicated by the double-headed arrows. Specific interventions within each of the four types can differ in terms of their intended target: individual, group, or whole organisation. For example, under the heading of Human Resource Management interventions, there might be some interventions, such as those concerned with reward systems, that could be targeted at all three levels, whereas other interventions, such as those concerned with performance appraisal, might be targeted only at the individual and group levels.

Human process interventions

These focus on people and the processes through which they accomplish organisational goals, such as communication, problem solving, decision making and leadership. Cummings and Worley (2001) provide a good overview of this type of intervention.

Figure 17.2   Cummings and Worley's typology of interventions based on focal issue

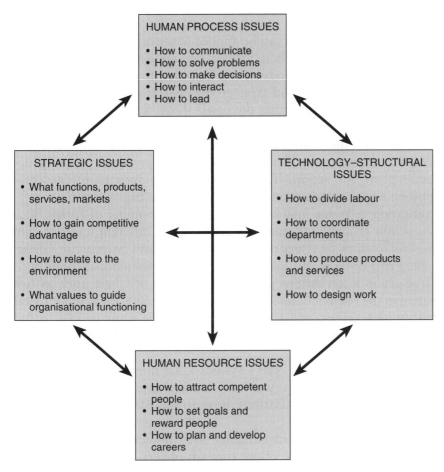

Source: From *Organization Development and Change*, 7th edition, by Cummings/Worley © 2001. Reprinted with permission of South-Western, a division of Thomson Learning: www.thomsonrights.com.

Interpersonal and group process approaches include interventions such as T-groups, process consultation, third-party interventions and-team building:

● T-groups, sometimes referred to as sensitivity training, involves trainees exploring group dynamics and providing each other with feedback about the impact of their behaviour on others

● Process consultation typically involves a consultant helping group members to diagnose what is going on in their group as they work on real issues, and helping them devise solutions to problems that undermine group effectiveness

● Third-party interventions involve an outsider helping organisational members resolve conflicts

- Team-building interventions are designed to improve team working, often by re-examining the group's task, members' roles and the strategies they use for completing the task.

Human process interventions can be applied at the organisational level to deal with more systemic issues. These include organisational confrontation meetings, inter-group relations interventions designed to help groups work with and through other groups and large-group interventions such as the 'whole system in the room' interventions discussed above, and Grid interventions:

- Confrontation meetings are interventions designed to mobilise organisation-wide resources to identify problems, set priorities and targets and devise plans for action. They are often employed to bridge the gap between senior management and the rest of the organisation.
- Inter-group relations interventions can take a number of forms, such as microcosm groups with members representing different interests coming together to work on issues relating to diversity, and interventions designed to help two or more groups work to resolve dysfunctional conflicts.
- Large-group interventions go under a number of labels, such as 'whole system in the room' conferences, search conferences, open space meetings and future searches, and are designed to involve many people, including external stakeholders, in the management of issues that affect the whole organisation.
- Grid interventions, and Likert's System 4, are normative in the sense that they specify a 'one best way' to manage organisations and involve processes that help organisations move to this ideal.

Action research and appreciative inquiry (see Chapters 18 and 19) are examples of human process interventions that adopt very different approaches to accomplishing organisational goals. Action research involves the application of scientific principles to problem solving whereas appreciative inquiry involves the identification and amplification of best practice.

Technostructural interventions

These are the second broad type of intervention referred to by Cummings and Worley (2001). They focus on structure, task methods and job design.

Interventions relating to the design of organisations include the grouping of activities, downsizing and re-engineering:

- Structural design encompasses interventions that aim to identify and move towards more effective ways of structuring activities. It often involves moving towards more process-based and network-based structures in order to provide the flexibility to cope with increasing turbulence and uncertainty.

- Interventions aimed at reducing the size of the organisation are referred to as 'downsizing'.
- Business process re-engineering (BPR) involves a fundamental re-think and radical redesign of business processes to achieve a step change in performance. It often involves the use of information technology (IT) systems to help organisational members control and coordinate work processed more effectively. This kind of intervention is considered in more detail in Chapter 21.

Interventions designed to increase employee involvement in order to enhance their commitment and performance often involve moving decision making downwards in the organisation, closer to where the work is actually done. To achieve this employees, at all levels, have to be provided with the power, information, knowledge and skills required to act effectively. Interventions of this type include:

- General interventions designed to improve the Quality-of-Work-Life such as job enrichment, self-managed teams and labour-management committees
- Interventions of various types that involve the creation of a parallel structure that operates in tandem with the formal organisation to provide alternative settings (such as away-days, project groups or quality circles (QCs)) in which organisational members can address problems and search for solutions
- Other broad-based interventions designed to increase employee involvement are high-involvement organisations which entail a joint manager–worker redesign of the organisation to promote high levels of involvement and performance (rather that the addition of parallel structures) and Total Quality Management (TQM) which is a long-term effort designed to focus all the organisation's activities around the concept of quality.

Work–job design interventions include engineering, motivational and socio-technical systems approaches to designing work for groups and individuals:

- Engineering approaches to work design focus on efficiency and job simplification
- Motivational approaches focus on enriching the work experience and are designed to motivate employees to work more effectively
- Socio-technical approaches to work design focus on integrating the technical and social aspects of work, they often involve the introduction of self-managed work groups.

Human resource management interventions

These are the third broad type of intervention referred to by Cummings and Worley (2001). They focus on personnel practices such as selection, training and development, goal setting, performance appraisal, incentives, internal promotion systems, career development and the like, and how they can be used to integrate people into the organisation.

Interventions designed to develop and assist organisational members can be grouped under three headings: career planning and development, managing work-force diversity and employee wellness:

- Interventions designed to promote career planning and development are often introduced to help employees manage their own careers and prepare themselves to respond to the uncertainties and lack of job security that are increasingly becoming a feature of organisational life.
- Work-force diversity interventions are designed to respond to the different needs, preferences and expectations of the various groups of employees who bring different resources and perspectives to the organisation. A key aim of these interventions is to help the organisation retain a diverse work-force and use it to gain competitive advantage.
- Employee wellness interventions are designed to promote the wellbeing of organisational members and to contribute to the development of a productive work-force. They include employee assistance and stress management programmes.

Performance management interventions focus on how goal setting, performance appraisal and reward systems can contribute to organisational effectiveness by aligning members' work behaviour with business strategy and workplace technology.

High-performance management is an HRM intervention that involves developing and implementing a 'bundle' of HR practices that are internally consistent and aligned with the organisation's strategy to achieve improvements in organisational effectiveness. This type of intervention is considered in Chapter 20.

Strategic interventions

These are the fourth broad type of intervention referred to by Cummings and Worley (2001). These are interventions that link the internal functioning of the organisation with the wider environment. They aim to align business strategy with organisational culture and the external environment.

Cummings and Worely highlight three interventions designed to improve the organisation–environment fit. They are open systems planning, integrated strategic change and trans-organisational development:

- Open systems planning is an intervention designed to help an organisation systematically assess its environment and develop strategic responses to it

- Integrated strategic change interventions are directed towards integrating strategic planning and operational and tactical actions
- Trans-organisational development is an intervention that focuses on the creation of beneficial partnerships with other organisations to perform tasks or solve problems that are beyond the capability of a single organisation.

Another sub-category of strategic interventions is that which focuses more directly on changing the organisation's culture and mental models. They involve diagnosing the existing culture and assessing the cultural risks associated with planned changes.

Exercise 17.1   Change programmes

Review some of the change programmes that have been pursued within your organisation and consider the types of intervention used. Do they all tend to fall within one or two of the categories reviewed in this chapter, or have a wide range of different types of intervention been employed?

Notes

Summary

This chapter has adopted two contrasting typologies to provide a brief overview of the wide range of interventions available to change agents.

References

Burnes, B. (2004) *Managing Change*, Harlow: Pearson Education.
Cartwright, D. (1951) 'Achieving Change in People: Some Applications of Group Dynamics Theory', *Human Relations*, 4 (2), pp. 381–392.

Cummings, T.G. and Worley, C.G. (2001) *Organisational Development and Change*, Cincinnati, OH: South-Western.

Dannemiller, K.D. and Jacobs, R.W. (1992) 'Changing the Way Organizations Change: A Revolution of Common Sense', *Journal of Applied Behavioural Science*, 28 (4), pp. 480–98.

Fritz, R. (1984) *The Path of Least Resistance*, Salem, MA: DMA, Inc.

Jacobs, R. (1994) *Real Time Strategic Change*, San Francisco: Berrett-Kochler.

Jayaram, (1977) 'Open Systems Planning', in T. Cummings and S. Srivastra (eds), *Management at Work: A Socio-technical Systems Approach*, San Diego: University Associates.

Lippitt, R. (1983) 'Future before you Plan', in R.A. Ritvo and A.G. Sargent (eds), *The NTL Managers' Handbook*, Arlington, VA: NTL Institute.

Taylor, F.W. (1911) *Principles of Scientific Management*, New York: Harper.

Trist, E.L. (1969) 'On Socio-Technical Systems', in W.G. Bennis, K.D. Benne and R. Chin (eds), *The Planning of Change*, New York: Holt, Rinehart & Winston, pp. 269–82.

Von Bertalanffy, L. (1950) 'General Systems Theory', in *General Systems, Yearbook of the Society for the Advancement of General Systems Theory*, 1, pp. 1–10.

Weisbord, M. (1987) *Productive Workplaces: Organising and Managing for Dignity, Meaning and Community*, San Francisco: Jossey-Bass.

Weisbord, M. (1989) *Building Productive Workplaces: Change Strategies for the 21st Century*, Lake Bluff, IL: Blue Sky Videos.

Action research

Action research is the basic model underpinning most organisational change interventions. It involves the application of scientific methods (fact-finding and experimentation) to organisational problems and underpins the generic process model of change presented in Chapter 5.

Kurt Lewin developed the action research model in the 1940s when he identified the need for social scientists to base their theory-building on research into practical problems. Early projects involved Coch and French (1948) working with employees at the Harewood Manufacturing Company to overcome resistance to change and Lewin working in the community to reduce violence between Catholic and Jewish teenage gangs (see Marrrow, 1969). These early projects involved social scientists collaborating with members of social systems to understand and take action to resolve problems. The action research methodology helped members apply scientific methods to guide their actions and helped social scientists develop knowledge about social processes that they could generalise to other situations.

Dickens and Watkins (1999) observe that Lewin originally conceived of action research as a process that involved cycling back and forth between an ever-deepening surveillance of the problem situation and a series of research-informed action experiments. These experiments formed an important part of the process. Action research is based on the traditional scientific paradigm that involves experimental manipulation and observation of the effects of the manipulation. However, as Dickens and Watkins note, there are important differences between action research and traditional science. Action research, unlike traditional science, does not attempt to set tight limits and controls on the experimental situation. Action research also uses information to guide behaviour in order to solve immediate problems, whereas traditional science involves studying information for the purpose of learning and typically ends at the point of discovery. Over time, this dual focus on problem solving and theory-building has changed as those concerned with facilitating change have focused more of their attention on improving organisational functioning within a particular context rather than helping social scientists contribute to the development of theoretical understanding. However, over the last few years there has been a growing body of social scientists using action research as the basis for developing theory. Brydon-Miller, Greenwood and Maguire (2001) refer to Lewin's assertion that there is nothing so practical as a good theory (Lewin, 1951: 169) as a major influence on their work. They argue that:

> action research goes beyond the notion that theory can inform practice, to a recognition that theory can and should be generated through practice, and . . . that theory is really only useful insofar as it is put in the service of a practice focused on achieving positive social change. (2001: 15)

Action research and organisational learning

Hendry (1996) reviews the role of learning in the management of change and refers to Lewin's three-stage process of change as a learning process. The motive force for learning and change is cognitive dissonance and the experience of disconfirmation. The initial questioning and unlearning associated with this 'unfreezing' experience provides the motivation for individuals and groups to engage in the information gathering, diagnosis and experimentation that leads to new learning.

Individuals, groups and whole systems are constantly faced with the need to learn and change in order to adapt to changing circumstances. Those that are best able to adapt are those who are able to learn from their experiences. Kolb (1984) elaborated Lewin's model and articulated a theory of experiential learning that conceptualizes learning as a four-stage cycle that translate experience into concepts which are used to guide the choice of new experiences (Figure 18.1).

Figure 18.1   The experiential learning model

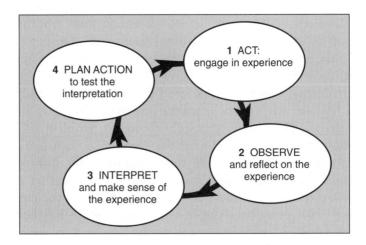

Stage 1 involves engaging in immediate concrete experience in order to provide the basis, at stage 2, for observation and reflection. At stage 3 these observations are interpreted and assimilated into a 'theory' from which new implications for action can be deduced. These implications (or hypothese) then serve as guides when planning, at stage 4, how to act to create new experiences. If individuals and groups are to be effective learners and action researchers they must be able to:

- involve themselves fully, openly and without bias in their experiences
- reflect on and observe these experiences from many perspectives
- create concepts that integrate their observations into logically sound theories
- use these theories to make decisions and solve problems.

Role of the facilitator

This process can be facilitated by a change agent. Nearly fifty years ago, Shepard (1960) was advocating a collaborative relationship between consultant and client. His view was that the role of the consultant is to *help* the client or client group design their fact-finding procedures and plan their actions in such a way that they can learn from them in order to serve the end of discovering better ways of organising.

The role of the change agent as facilitator rather then prescriber of solutions has received considerable attention. Action learning (Revans, 1980), for example, advocates an approach to learning that involves solving real problems. Mumford (1985) made the point more than twenty years ago that those who wish to assist learners should do so by helping them learn from the exposure to problems, and to each other. The role of the facilitator/trainer is to help learners formulate their own plans for action and to test them through implementation.

Since the 1950s action research has spawned many related action strategies that have been applied to individual learners, groups, organisations and even wider networks of institutions (see the special edition of *Management Learning* edited by Raelin, 1999, and the special issue of *Human Relations* edited by Eldon and Chisholm, 1993). In addition to the classical model of action research, Raelin (1999) refers to five other models: participatory research, action learning, action science, developmental action inquiry and cooperative inquiry. Appreciative inquiry is also regarded by many as a contemporary development of the classical action research model. This will receive separate and detailed attention in Chapter 19.

The participative nature of action research

All of these action strategies are inherently *participative*. Facilitators and members of the target system:

mutually open themselves up to an inquiry process that seeks to 'unfreeze' the assumptions underlying their actions. Their methodologies are experimental and predominantly conducted in group settings. (Raelin, 1999: 117)

Reason and Bradbury (2001) define action research as:

a participatory, democratic process concerned with developing practical knowing in the pursuit of worthwhile human purposes . . . It seeks to bring together action and reflection, theory and practice, in participation with others, in the pursuit of practical solutions to issues of pressing concern to people, and more generally the flourishing of individual persons and their communities. (2001: 1)

Most of those who advocate a collaborative approach to problem solving in organisations do so because they believe that much of the information relevant to resolving problems is widely disseminated throughout the organisation. Participation increases the likelihood that those who hold important information will share it with others. Collaborative approaches to problem solving also built commitment and facilitate the implementation of actions designed to resolve the problem.

Action research at the Harwood manufacturing company

Blake and Mouton (1983) report one of the early examples of action research to illustrate the importance of participation. It was undertaken at the Harewood Manufacturing Company at a time when the company was planning to recruit older workers to ease the labour shortage created by the Second World War. The proposal was fiercely resisted by supervisors, who feared that older workers would be inefficient and difficult to manage. The director of personnel responded by providing the supervisors with scientific 'proof' that older workers did possess the skills and aptitudes necessary to perform effectively. But the supervisors rejected the evidence and were not persuaded. However, rather than moving ahead and imposing the new hiring policy, the director of personnel decided to try to change attitudes by involving the supervisors in a research project designed to investigate the efficiency of the older workers. The study focused on older workers already employed in the plant. Some had been with the company for many years and others had been employed more recently for social reasons – for example, because they had been widowed. Members of staff were given full responsibility for designing the project and deciding how to collect the data. The findings of the study were a surprise to the supervisors. They found that it was not age, but a range of other factors, that were the main determinants of performance. Blake and Mouton report that while the supervisors had rejected 'expert' evidence, they were convinced by their own findings. Their involvement in the project helped them 'unlearn' some of the beliefs that they had been convinced were true and changed their attitudes towards the employment of older workers. Marrow, Bowers and Seashore (1967) cite Lewin on the importance of participation. This kind of result occurs 'because the facts become really their own facts (as against other people's facts). An individual will believe facts he himself has discovered in the same way that he believes in himself.'

The process of action research

The classical model of action research involves collecting and analysing data about the nature of a problem, taking action to bring about a change and observing the effects of the action in order to inform further actions to improve the situation. Sometimes the process starts following the identification of a problem by a senior member of the organisation who has the power and influence to make things happen. However this 'top-down' approach is not the only way of introducing action research methodologies into organisations. Sometimes group members are aware that a problem exists but, for a variety of reasons, find it difficult to manage the problem more effectively. This may motivate them to take the initiative and seek help from an external facilitator. Whatever the start point, Lewin (1946) argued that an essential prerequisite for action research is a 'felt-need', an inner realisation that change is necessary. Unless the group is willing to work on their problem, this kind of collaborative intervention is unlikely to succeed.

Following the identification of an issue that requires attention, action research involves successive cycles of *action* and *evaluation*. Each cycle comprises five steps. Succeeding cycles begin with the collection and analysis of data to evaluate the consequences of the action taken at the end of the preceding cycle. The five steps are:

1 *Data gathering for diagnosis*   This step involves collecting data about the problem. This can be done in a number of ways. Several methods of collecting data have been discussed in Chapter 8, such as interviews, questionnaires, observations and reference to performance data and other records that are collected as a normal part of day-to-day operations. The choice of method needs to be influenced by the nature of the problem and the people involved. For example the 'organisational mirror' (see Marguilies and Wallace, 1973) is a technique that might be appropriate when the problem involves the quality of relationships between a group and other organisational units or external parties, such as suppliers and customers. These other units reflect back to the focal group their perceptions and information about its performance. They act as a 'mirror' and provide the group with their view of the situation. Data can be collected by the whole focal group in a meeting with representatives of other units, or by a designated person interviewing others on behalf of the group.

2   *Data feedback to client group*   Often members of the focal (problem solving) group are delegated to investigate particular aspects of the problem or an external facilitator collects data on behalf of the group. Consequently, in order for the process to be truly collaborative, data needs to be fed back to all members of the group.

3   *Discussion of the data and diagnosis of the problem*   One of the defining features of action research is that system members collaborate with each other and with an external facilitator to review the data, clarify issues and formulate hypotheses about cause and effect.

4   *Action planning*   Following on from diagnosis, action planning involves identifying possible interventions to improve the situation and selecting a preferred way forward.

5   *Implementation of action plan*   The final step involves taking action to improve the situation (see Figure 18.2).

Following the first cycle of the process the original hypothesis about cause and effect and the action taken to improve the situation are evaluated through a further cycle of data gathering, feedback and analysis. This evaluation might suggest ways of refining the original hypothesis (or the

Figure 18.2   The action research process

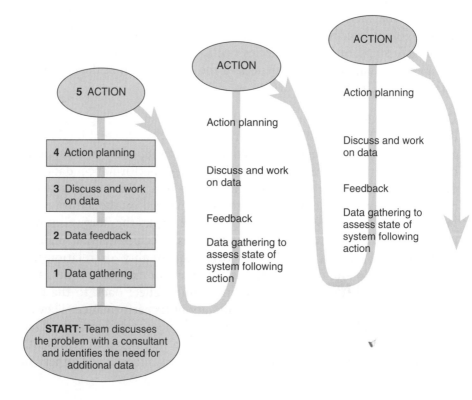

implementation of alternative actions), or it might prompt the formulation of a completely different hypothesis regarding the nature of the problem. And so the process continues.

Results from action research

Action research is widely acknowledged as an effective means of bringing about change. Reference has already been made to projects in the Harewood Manufacturing Company that illustrate how it can be used overcome resistance to changes proposed by senior management. Greenwood, Whyte and Harkavy (1993) report a successful action research project in the Xerox Corporation that involved employees (union members and managers at plant level) persuading senior management to radically change their proposal to outsource the manufacturing of selected components (Case study 18.1).

Case study 18.1   Action research in the Xerox Corporation

During the 1980s the Xerox Corporation introduced a series of major changes in response to a decline in market share and profits. One outcome of this process was the development of an employee involvement programme at the Webster plants, the company's major US manufacturing facility. Some time later this was integrated with a quality improvement programme and was jointly administered at plant level by local managers and members of the union. They received training in group problem solving so that they could be involved in the programme as internal consultants and facilitators. This high level of collaboration provided the context of a successful action research project.

As part of a competitive bench-marking program, Xerox decided to 'outsource' the production of parts that could be manufactured externally at lower cost. The first outsourcing decision targeted the production of wire harnesses. Bench-marking and cost comparison studies indicated that the company could save $3.2 million a year by outsourcing production and shutting down the wire harness department. It was anticipated that an immediate outcome of this outsourcing decision would be the loss of 180 jobs, but the union feared that this might be just the beginning of a major programme of redundancies as the competitive bench-marking exercise was rolled out to include a wider range of components, and local managers also recognized that their jobs were at risk.

Greenwood, Whyte and Harkavy report that after several weeks of discussions with high-level union and management officials it was decided to institute a cost study team, composed of six workers and two members of management. The team was established to determine whether Xerox could cut its manufacturing costs sufficiently to meet the outside bid and thus save the jobs. Inputs were sought from many sources including industrial engineers, cost accountants and a social psychologist. Greenwood, Whyte and Harkavy describe the outcome of this action research intervention as spectacular. The team was able to demonstrate cost savings sufficient to persuade senior management to retain wire harness production within the company. The exercise was successfully extended to include four other cases and led to 900 jobs being saved.

The team also reported other benefits. Management developed greater trust in workers' abilities and this led them to promote a variety of other initiatives involving workers in new plant design and the restructuring of the R&D programme for discovering new products and new manufacturing methods. Union leaders and workers experienced a raised level of confidence in their own ability to make an intellectual contribution to the solving of manufacturing problems. In terms of contributing to theory, the cost study teams learned how conventional forms of allocating indirect costs to industrial products could lead management to make decisions adverse to the economic interests of both company and workers. Greenwood, Whyte and Harkavy also assert that their analysis led to a theoretical reformulation of the relations between worker participation and productivity.

Hendry (1996) reports several examples of how Lewin's three-stage model of change and Kolb's experiential learning cycle provided the conceptual framework for action research in Courtaulds Aerospace Advanced Materials. In one case the action researchers described their main contribution in terms of developing focus in response to a situation where mangers were trying to do too much. The organisation was beset with 'initiative-itis', never sustaining attention long enough on one activity. In a related example the need was to develop an integrated management team in which people were willing to engage in strategic dialogue and listen and learn from each other. Another, very different example, involved a group of twelve middle–senior managers learning about themselves and their effects on people through a process that involved them making presentations which the others then critiqued. An HR manager observed that nothing these managers had ever done with their staff had ever given them this kind of feedback about themselves as to the way they were perceived by others.

Summary

Lewin led the development of action research by using communities and work organisations as laboratories for field experiments designed to help scientists develop theories about social processes that they could generalize to other situations while helping members of the focal community understand and manage their circumstances more effectively. During the 1960s OD practitioners began to use action research as a basis for intervening to promote change in organisations.

A wide range of change management interventions are rooted in action research methodologies in so far as they involve some form of fact finding and action taking designed to improve the way that problems are managed. Many also reflect the principles of interactive or participatory action research in so far as they involve organisational members in the problem solving process in order to promote the kind of learning that will support the ongoing development of their group or organisation.

Action research is traditionally an intervention that is targeted at groups or whole systems but, as with action learning, the group sometimes provides a context for individual learning and development. There is also a growing interest in 'first-person' action research which involves using inquiry practices to examine personal experience. White (2004) provides an excellent example of this development with her account of how she used her experience working as a practitioner with police and local communities in post-apartheid South Africa to develop a grounded theory of conflict resolution.

Action research, according to the typology presented in Chapter 17 (Figure 17.2, p. 279), is a human process intervention that addresses processes such as learning, problem solving communication and decision making.

References

Blake, R.R. and Mouton, J.S. (1983) *Consultation: A Handbook for Individual and Organization Development*, 2nd edn, Reading, MA: Addison-Wesley.

Brydon-Miller, M., Greenwood, D. and Maguire, P. (2001) 'Why Action Research?', *Action Research*, 1 (1), pp. 9–14

Coch, L. and French, J.R. (1948) 'Overcoming Resistance to Change', *Human Relations*, 1, pp. 512–32.

Dickens, L. and Watkins, K. (1999) 'Action Research: Rethinking Lewin', *Management Learning*, 30 (2), 127–40.

Eldon, M. and Chisholm, R.F. (1993) 'Emergent Varieties of Action Research: Introduction to the Special Issue', *Human Relations*, 46, pp. 121–42.

Greenwood, D. J., Whyte, W.F. and Harkavy, I. (1993) 'Participatory Action Research as a Process and as a Goal', *Human Relations*, 46, 2175–93.

Hendry, C. (1996) 'Understanding and Creating Whole Organizational Change Through Learning Theory', *Human Relations*, 49 (5), pp. 621–41.

Kolb, D.A. (1984) *Experiential Learning*, Englewood Cliffs, NJ: Prentice Hall.

Lewin, K. (1946) 'Action Research and Minority Problems', *Journal of Social Issues*, 2 (4), pp. 34–46.

Lewin, K. (1951) *Field Theory in Social Science*, New York: Harper.

Marguilies, N. and Wallace, J. (1973) *Organizational Change: Techniques and Applications*. Glenview, IL: Scott, Foresman.

Marrow, A.J. (1969) *The Practical Theorist: The Life and Work of Kurt Lewin*, New York: Teachers College Press.

Marrow, A.J., Bowers, D.G. and Seashore, S.E. (1967) *Management by Participation*, New York: Harper & Row.

Mumford, A. (1985) 'A Review of Action Learning', *Management Development*, 11 (2), pp. 3–18.

Raelin, J. (1999) 'Preface to Special Issue on Action Strategies', *Management Learning*, 30 (2), pp. 115–25.

Reason, P. and Bradbury, H. (eds) (2001) *Handbook of Action Research: Participative Inquiry and Practice*, London: Sage.

Revans, R.W. (1980) *Action Learning*, London: Blond & Briggs.

Shepard, H.A. (1960) *An Action Research Model in an Action Research Program for Organization Improvement*, Ann Arbour: University of Michigan, The Foundation for Research on Human Behaviour, pp. 33–4.

White, A.M. (2004) 'Lewin's Action Research Model as a Tool for Theory Building', *Action Research*, 2 (2), pp. 127–44.

Appreciative inquiry

Appreciative inquiry is a process that involves exploring the best of what is (or has been), and amplifying this best practice. It seeks to accentuate the positive rather than eliminate the negative; it focuses attention on what is good and working rather than on what is wrong and not working.

This chapter examines appreciate inquiry from three perspectives; a philosophy of knowledge, an intervention theory and a methodology for intervening in organisations to improve performance and the quality of life.

The social construction of reality through dialogue and negotiation

Social constructionist thinking challenges the view that there is an objective universe 'out there' that is in some sense enduring and physically observable. It posits that reality is a *social construction*. Elliot (1999) describes a simple exercise that illustrates how readily we make and defend our own versions of reality, even when the data we use are ambiguous. The exercise involves presenting a group with a set of squiggles on a flip chart and inviting each person to take a couple of minutes to decide what they represent. He reports that after a short while each person begins to see (or think they can see) some emergent shape. If they are then allocated to small groups of three or four and asked to come to a consensus about what the squiggles really mean, members usually start with different interpretations, imagine that their interpretations are correct and try to convince the others that this is the case.

Everything we encounter and experience is open to multiple interpretation. Social constructionists assert that our perceptions of reality are the product of *dialogue* and *negotiation*. Dixon (1997), for example, argues that organisational members construct a shared mental model of the organisation through a process of dialogue and interaction. She believes that, in the process of articulating one's own meanings and comprehending the meanings others have constructed, people alter the meanings they hold. There is no single objective reality.

The way we behave and the consequences of our behaviour are critically dependent on the way we construct reality, on the way we see the world, and the way we see the world is determined by what we believe. Srivastva and Cooperrider (1990) argue that our beliefs govern what we look for, what we see and how we interpret what we see: 'The reality perceived . . . is often a consequence of the reality believed, a situation that leads to self-fulfilling expectations within groups, organisations, or even whole societies.'

Cooperrider and Srivastva (1987) argue that to the extent that action is predicated on beliefs, ideas and meanings, people are free to seek a transformation in conventional conduct by modifying their beliefs and idea systems.

A widely held belief is that organisational life is problematic. This belief promotes a *deficiency perspective* that focuses attention on the dysfunctional aspects of organisations and has led to many interventions being designed on the assumption that organisations are 'problems to be solved'. Such interventions typically involve (a) identifying key problems, (b) analysing causes, (c) analysing solutions and (d) developing action plans to manage these problems more effectively. Cooperrider and Srivastva (1987) argue that this kind of OD intervention is conservative in so far as the formulation of a problem implies that somebody has knowledge of what 'should be' and therefore any remedial action is bounded by what is already known. Advocates of appreciative inquiry argue that this kind of approach typically leads to single-loop learning – continuous improvement within the existing paradigm – and is relatively ineffective when it comes to facilitating organisational transformation (see Chapter 4).

An alternative belief about organisations, and one that underpins appreciative inquiry, is that rather than 'problems to be solved', they are 'possibilities to be embraced'.

Advocates of appreciative inquiry argue that not only are organisations social constructions open to revision, but that this process of revision can be facilitated by a *collective inquiry*. They also argue that this collective inquiry should attend to the life-giving forces of the organisation rather than to a set of problems that have to be resolved. It involves appreciating the best of 'what is' and using this to ignite a vision of the possible. The process is generative; it takes nothing for granted and challenges the beliefs and assumptions that guide behaviour. The organisation is viewed as an unfathomable mystery, offering many as yet unknown possibilities. The advocates of appreciative inquiry argue that this social constructionist perspective is more likely to produce double-loop learning (that will lead to the organisation doing things differently or even doing different things) than is a perspective that is more narrowly focused on organisational dysfunction.

A theory of intervention

Cooperrider (1990) refers to the 'heliotropic hypothesis' as the core of a powerful theory of change. The essence of this theory is that social systems have images of themselves that underpin self-organising processes and that they have a natural tendency to evolve towards the most positive images held by their members. They are like plants: they evolve towards the 'light' that gives them life and energy. This leads to the proposition that interventions that promote a conscious evolution of positive imagery offer a viable option for changing social systems for the better.

It has already been noted that a widely held belief about organisations is that they are problematic. There is a tendency to focus on what is wrong rather than to celebrate what is working and going well. Elliot (1999) reports that when he asked a group of forty-five managers to write down twenty adjectives that accurately caught the flavour of their organisation, 72 per cent of the words they used were critical, negative or hostile (for example, 'chaotic', 'inefficient', 'inward-looking', 'lazy', 'poorly structured', 'over-bureaucratic', 'slow', 'careless', 'unaware'); 13 per cent were neutral (for example, 'mainstream', 'averaged', 'contended', 'unambitious'); and only 15 per cent were positive and approving (for example, 'creative', 'exciting', 'thrilling', cutting-edge', 'determined', 'satisfying', 'customer-oriented', 'high-tech', 'achievement-oriented').

Appreciative inquiry is based on the assumption that we are free to choose which aspects of our experience we pay attention to. Elliot suggests that one of the most important things that appreciative inquiry seeks to achieve is:

> the transformation of a culture from one that sees itself in largely negative terms – and therefore *is inclined to become locked into its own negative construction of itself* – to one that sees itself as having within it the capacity to enrich and enhance the quality of life for all the stakeholders – *and therefore move toward this appreciative construction of itself*. (1999: 12, emphasis in the original)

Elliot highlights the role of *memory* and *imagination*. Memory is important because every organisation has a history, but this history is not an indisputable fact, it is an artefact of those who do the remembering. Organisational memory is based on how those who do the remembering interpret what happened, and one of the factors that influence their interpretations is where they are now and how they construct the present. Elliot argues that it is this plasticity of memory and our freedom to remake the history of our organisations that is essential for the appreciative approach:

> For what is at stake is the capacity to construct a narrative of the organization that highlights the worthwhile and life-enriching themes without denying the darker or more sombre tones that are likely to be present. It is only when we can read the history from this perspective that we are likely to transcend the problematic present or the fearsome future. (1999: 37)

The way organisational members construct and reconstruct the present and the past is a prelude to the way they imagine the future. Appreciative inquiry does not promote the imagination of unachievable fantasies; it promotes the imagination of a future that is based on an extrapolation of the best of what is or has been.

Cooperrider (1990) maintains that one of the greatest obstacles to the wellbeing of an ailing group is the affirmative projection that currently guides it. He argues that to affirm means to 'hold firm' and it is the strength of affirmation, 'the degree of belief or faith invested, that allows the imagery to carry out its heliotropic task'. He goes on to argue that when a group finds that its attempts to fix problems create more problems, or that the same problems never go away, the group's current affirmative projection is inadequate. Like Elliot, Cooperrider contends that 'every new affirmative projection of the future is a consequence of an appreciative understanding of the past or present'. We do not have to appreciate the present in terms that accentuate the negative. We can appreciate the present and build affirmative images of the future in terms that accentuate the positive. The heliotropic hypothesis posits that the future we imagine is the future we create. Strong affirmative images create a powerful 'pull effect' that can help the organisation evolve towards this more positive future.

Advocates of appreciative inquiry point to studies of the Pygmalion and placebo effects as sources of evidence that support the validity of the heliotropic hypothesis. The 'Pygmalion effect' refers to the power of self-fulfilling prophesies. Many studies have shown that the performance of individuals and groups such as soldiers (Eden and Shani, 1982), trainee welders (King, 1970) and students (Rosenthal and Jacobson, 1968) is shaped by the expectations of others. Rosenthal and Jacobson, for example, argue that teachers convey messages of expected success and failure to their students and their students live up to these expectations. However, we not only behave in response to the mental attitudes of those around us, especially those in authority over us, but we also behave in response to our own mental attitudes and expectations of ourselves. In the field of medicine, studies of the 'placebo effect' have shown that those who expect an improvement in their condition are more likely to improve than those who expect no improvement. Similarly, those who remain hopeful and determined in extreme life-threatening circumstances are the ones who are most likely to survive. In other words, nothing succeeds like the expectation of success and nothing fails like the expectation of failure.

While this provides the basis for a very attractive theory of intervention, Golembiewski (1999) sounds two notes of caution. The first concerns the outcome of appreciative inquiries. As predicted by the heliotropic hypothesis, social forms gravitate towards an imagined future that amplifies 'peak experiences' because people are motivated to move in that direction. People are less likely to resist this kind of change because, as Golembiewski says: 'You can catch more flies with honey than with vinegar.' However, the search for social forms faces a far larger issue than whether or not people are motivated to change. Golembiewski raises the question: 'motivation for what purpose?', and notes that there are many examples where people have been motivated to *level down* human systems to the bestial (see, for example, Chang, 1997) as well as *level them up* to pursue some noble purpose. He advises that consultants should cultivate a sense of the difference: 'A powerful learning design may attract, but well-targeted ones make more progress, more safely, more of the time'. He acknowledges that appreciative inquiry can induce powerful forces, but he is concerned that those who adopt a social constructionist view may pay insufficient attention to the normative character of the social form that is the imagined future: '[appreciative inquiry] in its dominant form assumes the social constructionist view that there is nothing special about any social form or norm'. This said, the evidence seems to indicate that appreciative inquiry not only engages the attention of organisational members but facilitates a process of organisational learning that moves the organisation in a direction that yields benefits for all stakeholders.

His second note of caution relates to appreciative inquiry's apparent aversion to 'negative' stories. He suspects that this could encourage an incautious optimism about facts or beliefs. Elliot (1999), however, is less concerned. He argues that non-blaming, non-judgemental appreciative conversations enable people to acknowledge that the best is not the norm. For example, someone might describe an example of the best of what is and then go on to elaborate: 'But it isn't usually like this. Usually we spend too much time arguing or hating the other department, distrusting them, seeing what is bad about them.' While this kind of comment acknowledges deficiencies it can facilitate positive thinking. Elliot (1999: 76) suggests that a skilled interviewer might achieve this be asking questions along the lines: 'What is special about the good times? What do you think you and your colleagues need to do or to be in order to be able to maximise the chances that the good times will become the norm?'

A methodology for intervening in organisations

The essence of appreciative inquiry is the generation of a shared image of a better future through a collective process of inquiry into the best of what is. It is this imagined future that provides the powerful 'pull effect' that guides the development of the group or the organisation.

The critical part of the intervention is the *inquiry*. The mere act of asking questions begins the process of change. Based on the assumption that the things we choose to focus on and the questions we ask determine what we find, it follows that the more positive the questions the more positive the data, and the more positive the data the more positive are the beliefs that people are likely to develop about what contributes to peak experiences. The more positive are these beliefs, the more positive is the vision of the organisation at its best, and the more positive is this image, the more energy it generates for change.

Figure 19.1   The five steps of an appreciative inquiry

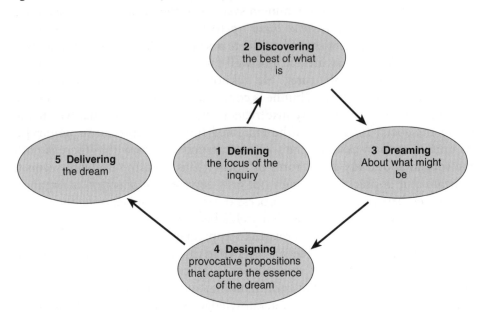

Bushe (1999) describes the process of appreciative inquiry as consisting of three parts:

- *Discovering the best of . . .* This involves discovering the best examples of organising and organisation within the experience of organisational members
- *Understanding what creates the best of . . .* This involves seeking insights into the forces that lead to superior performance and what it is about the people, the organisation and the context that creates peak experiences at work
- *Amplifying the people or processes that exemplify the best of . . .* This involves reinforcing and amplifying those elements of the situation that contribute to superior performance.

A widely accepted methodology for discovering, understanding and amplifying the best of what is involves five steps (see Figure 19.1).

Defining the focus of the inquiry

In the early 1990s appreciative inquiry was often viewed as a macro-organisational intervention that studied the organisation as a whole. More recently, however, the scope of appreciative inquiries has been extended to include more focused inquiries into issues such as retention, team-building, leadership, customer service, conflict management, cross-gender relationships and culture change.

Defining the precise field of inquiry is often undertaken by some kind of *steering group*, possibly one that represents the different categories of organisational member who might be involved in the inquiry. The inquiry needs to be defined in a way that focuses attention on the positive rather than negative aspects of people's experience. For example, if an organisation has an issue with high labour turnover, rather than focusing attention on why people leave the inquiry might focus attention on why people choose to stay. Similarly, if there is an issue related to sexual harassment, rather than focusing on the problems associated with cross-gender interactions the inquiry might focus on the conditions and factors that promote good cross-gender working relationships.

Discovering examples of excellence and achievement

Appreciative inquiry involves getting people to tell stories about the best of what is. It can involve pairs of people interviewing each other or a group of interviewers each having appreciative conversations with ten or twenty other people and then reporting their findings back to a core group. Whatever the format of the inquiry, interviewers need to be good listeners, able to attend to what others are saying and understand their thoughts and feelings from their perspective. They also need to be good at getting others to tell their stories of excellence and achievement. Key to this is the questions they ask. Whitney *et al.* (2002) have produced an *Encyclopedia of Positive Questions* that some practitioners may find helpful.

The questions the interviewer asks frame the way people look at an issue. Consider, for example, alternative ways of framing questions designed to discover the factors that contribute to good cross-gender working relationships. Even apparently neutral questions such as: 'Tell me about male–female relationships here' may elicit stories about problems rather than about the best of what is. An alternative approach is to frame questions along the following lines.

- 'You have been identified as someone who has a good cross-gender relationship. Can you tell me about it, starting with how it began?'

This kind of opening question might be followed with questions such as:

- Reflect on your experience of this relationship. What have been the high points when you felt that the relationship was working well and that you were making a real contribution to what the organisation is trying to achieve?
- Select an example of one of these high points and describe the circumstances: what were you doing, who was involved, what were they doing, what was the result, why did it feel good?
- Tell me about another example.

There is considerable evidence that people enjoy being interviewed appreciatively. It creates a 'feel-good' experience but, as Bushe (1999) observes, care must be exercised to ensure that talking about peak experiences does not degenerate into social banter. The successful appreciative interview is one that provides at least one insight into the root causes of success. The interview needs to go beyond identifying what it is that works well and explore *why* it works well and *how* this success can be reinforced, amplified and extended to other parts of the organisation.

A final step in this discovery phase involves sharing the stories that have been collected and identifying themes about the strengths of the organisation. This can be done in a number of ways. Interviewers can verbally report their stories in an open meeting to all who have been involved in the inquiry process, or they can share their stories with a core group that has been tasked to interpret the data and identify important themes. All those present can then be involved in a discussion of the stories to identify and reach a consensus about what the key themes are.

Bushe (1999) suggests that when there are lots of stories to review, organising the data according to an 'inquiry matrix' can help focus attention on themes relating to the purpose of the inquiry. He suggests that prior to data collection the steering group might highlight the elements of the organisation they want to attend to and amplify the best of (for example, these elements might be cross-gender working relationships, team work or customer service) and identify an organisational model that they feel captures the major categories of organising (for example, structure, technology, culture, leadership, job design, rewards and so on). This information can be used to construct a matrix that can be employed to *categorise emerging themes* from the stories. The matrix might be relatively simple and include, for example, cells for team work and structure, team-work and technology, and team-work and rewards, or it might be more complex and include a similar set of cells for other elements that may have been part of the inquiry, such as customer service.

An alternative but less structured approach, similar to one reported by Elliot (1999), involves each member of the core group of interviewers reviewing a sample of written reports of the appreciative conversations in their own time and then coming together to agree key themes. In the case reported by Elliot a core group of ten had conducted 100 interviews. In order to manage the workload, three members of the group read all 100 reports and everybody else read and analysed ten reports plus the ten reports of the interviews they had conducted. To aid their analysis the facilitator, who had been closely involved with every stage of the inquiry, distributed a list of issues that he though might emerge as key themes. This kind of list provides a *category set* that group members can use to help them identify key themes but it is important that they do not feel that they must restrict themselves to simply testing the validity of this suggested list. If the inquiry is to be an inclusive and collaborative process, everybody must feel free to identify other clusters of statements that might suggest alternative themes. Members bring their impressions of the content of the reports to a meeting and share and discuss their findings until they are able to agree a list of key themes that reflect the positive present and past.

Dreaming about what might be

Drawing on these themes to inspire a vision of a more positive future is the essence of the 'dreaming' phase. Organisational members are encouraged to envision what the future might be like if the best of what is or has been became the new norm. Elliot provides the following guidance to those who are involved with analysing the stories of excellence and achievement:

> You are looking for repeated themes which, together, point to a possibility that currently lies just outside the grasp of the company. You are *not* looking for a major-ity view nor a way-out odd-ball, but for a gathering set of ideas that, pulled together, given coherence and shape, will command an 'Ah, yes . . .' from a large majority of stakeholders who will recognise it as building on the best of the past but unlocking a new future. (1999: 137, emphasis in the original)

Elliot suggests that despite all the emphasis in the literature on visioning, relatively few organisational members believe that their imagination is a significant resource that they can bring to the workplace. Consequently many employees do not do much of it as part of their everyday work activ-ity. He goes on to argue that imagination is like many of our faculties, from memory to muscles; if they are not used, they wither. It is possible, therefore, that some organisational members may need to be helped and encouraged in order to use their imagination to envision a more positive future. Elliot suggests some 'warm-up' exercises that might help people gain the confidence to envision new possibilities. These include asking people if they have ever visited another organisation and seen things that they would like to introduce here, or asking them, if one of their grand-children were eventually to work here, what they would hope it might be like for them.

When organisational members have arrived at a consensus about their preferred future the process moves on to the design phase.

Designing provocative propositions that will achieve the dream

In order to facilitate the achievement of the vision it has to be translated into a set of *statements of intent*. These are 'provocative propositions' that will stretch organisational members and show them the way to an achievable preferred future.

Designing the provocative propositions typically generates considerable energy and involvement and it is through the dialogue associated with testing, redrafting and refining them that the possibilities for amplifying the best of the present and past are realised.

If the provocative propositions have been developed by a sub-group it is essential that they are presented to and validated by other organisational members, thus widening the net of those involved in the dialogue. Bushe (1999) suggests that when many people need to be involved it is possible to test the propositions using an *organisational survey*. Alongside each proposition there might be questions such as: 'To what extent do you believe this proposition is an important component of the topic under study?' and 'To what extent do you believe the organisation exemplifies the proposition?' He argues that simply filling out the questionnaire can generate energy and do a lot towards spreading the ideas across the organisation. People are encouraged to reflect on future possibilities and debate them with others. Communicating the results of the survey, informing everybody about the strength of feeling regarding each proposition, can also stimulate action, licensing organisational members to begin implementing the propositions in their everyday work.

These provocative propositions are design principles that can be used to identify the structures, processes and practices that will move the organisation towards the 'dream'. Finegold, Holland and Lingham (2002) describe them as *filters* that can be used to evaluate any proposed changes.

Delivering the dream

Guided by the design principles embedded in the provocative propositions the system (group or organisation) is propelled to fulfil its destiny. Sometimes those leading the inquiry help organisational members write implementation strategies and action plans and develop score cards or other procedures for monitoring progress. However, amplifying the best of what is and moving the organisation towards a more positive future does not necessarily require those leading the appreciative inquiry to get involved with the details of implementation. While there are some who see this as important, most practitioners restrict their involvement to the point where organisational members develop and validate their vision. If the vision and its associated provocative propositions are sufficiently compelling they not only generate the energy for change but also provide the guiding focus for individual and group initiatives and action taking across the organisation.

Joep de Jong, a Dutch consultant interviewed by Elliot (1999), offers a slightly different perspective. He observes that once organisational members move back into their normal day-to-day roles they may not find it easy to use the provocative propositions to steer their every action, but they may frequently use them as an encouragement to get back into the appreciative way of thinking. While it can be difficult to constantly pursue the realisation of the provocative propositions, the process of developing them changes their way of conceiving of themselves, their colleagues and their organisation. This, according to de Jong, changes their day-to-day work in a manner that makes it more probable that the essence of the provocative proposition will become reality.

Dick (2004) draws attention to a number of publications that practitioners might find useful when designing appreciative inquiries. Cooperrider, Whitney and Stavros (2003) have published an Appreciative Inquiry Handbook that provides a practical guide and a rich collection of resources, and Whitney and Trosten-Bloom (2003) have produced what Dick describes as a practical and informative introduction to appreciative inquiry 'suitable for novices'.

Applications

Appreciative inquiry has been used in a wide range of different situations. Sorensen, Yaeger and Bengtsson (2003), after reviewing 350 papers, report that there is considerable evidence pointing to its successful application in many settings. Projects vary in terms of scale, organisational context and focus. Elliot (1999) presents a detailed account of an appreciative inquiry with a private healthcare provider in the UK and several accounts of the use of appreciative inquiry to develop communities in Third World settings. The interventions Elliot describes extend over relatively long periods and involve a considerable investment of time on the part of members of the core work group. This contrasts with Jeop de Jong's much shorter (two-day) interventions with three secondary schools that had to merge and with two fast-growing computere dealers who were also involved in a merger (see Elliot, 1999). Zemke (1999) refers to a number of large-scale projects. An appreciative inquiry at Nutrimental Foods in Brazil involved 700 stakeholders interviewing each other over the course of half a day, after which, over a period of four days, 150 of them used the data generated from these interviews to develop a new corporate vision. He reports that this led to three new business initiatives and a massive increase in sales. In Chicago a project involved 4,000 school children conducting 1 million 'peak experience' interviews with older city residents to vision what the City could be like if the norm became Chicago at its best. Avon had a problem with male–female relationships and used appreciative inquiry to address the issue. Following a request on the company's email system for male–female pairs who believed they exemplified high-quality communication in the workplace, fifteen pairs were selected to interview 300 other exemplary pairs. Their stories were used to generate thirty principles for positive cross-gender working relationships. Finegold, Holland and Lingham (2002) describe an appreciative inquiry in a Midwestern university. It started with 400 members of the Administrative and Finance Division being asked, in pairs, to reflect on their whole span of employment at the university and tell each other a story about a peak experience, a time when they felt most energised, alive and valued.

They were then invited to tell each other what they valued about themselves, their work and the University and to think about the way they wanted the University to be. For many, it was the first time they had been invited to give voice to their hopes and visions. They were able to present propositions for staff training and development and for better communication between departments to senior management. The intervention was so successful that it became the methodology for annual strategic planning in the Division and eventually developed into a University wide process where the focus was: 'Discovering the power of partnership: Building a University-wide community to advance to the next tier of nationally recognised excellence.'

Bushe (1998) describes the use of appreciative inquiry in the context of team development. His basic approach involves asking team members to recall their best team experience. Each member, in turn, describes their best team experience and other members are encouraged to question the focal person about what it was about the person, the situation and the task that contributed to the peak experience. When everybody has told their stories, the group reviews the stories and tries to reach a consensus on the attributes of highly effective teams. Bushe's final step involves members mapping these attributes onto their experience with their current team, acknowledging anything they have seen in others that has helped the group to be like any of the listed attributes and identifying possibilities for amplifying these attributes. This approach can be applied to new teams as well as existing teams because even though members of a new team may not have much, if any, shared experience, everybody will be able to talk about some examples of best team experiences in other contexts. Bushe actually recommends that members of on-going teams do not use examples of best team experiences drawn from their experience with the current group because it is likely that members may recall the same experience and, after it has been talked about a few times, the process may lose steam.

It will be evident from the examples of applications presented above that appreciative inquiry can be adapted to provide a methodology for intervening in many different settings and for addressing a range of different issues.

Summary

Appreciative inquiry is a process that involves exploring the best of what is (or has been) and amplifying this best practice. Whereas action research promotes learning through attending to dysfunctional aspects of organisational functioning, appreciative inquiry seeks to accentuate the positive rather than eliminate the negative. It focuses attention on what is good and working rather than on what is wrong and not working. This chapter has examined appreciate inquiry from three perspectives; a philosophy of knowledge, an intervention theory, and a methodology for intervening in organisations to improve performance and the quality of life. It has also provided a number of examples of how appreciative inquiry had been used in a variety of settings.

References

Bushe, G.R. (1998) 'Appreciative Inquiry with Teams', *Organization Development Journal*, 16 (3), pp. 41–9.

Bushe, G.R. (1999) 'Advances in Appreciative Inquiry as an Organization Development Intervention', *Organization Development Journal*, 17 (2), pp. 61–8.

Chang, I. (1997) *The Rape of Nanking*, New York: Basic Books.

Cooperrider, D. (1990) 'Positive Image, Positive Action: The Affirmative Basis of Organizing', in S. Srivastva and D.L. Cooperrider (eds), *Appreciative Management and Leadership*, San Francisco: Jossey-Bass. pp. 91–125.

Cooperrider D. and Srivastva, S. (1987) 'Appreciative Inquiry in Organizational Life', *Research in Organizational Change and Development*, 1, pp. 129–69.

Cooperrider, D., Whitney, D. and Stavros, J. (2003) *Appreciative Inquiry Handbook*, San Francisco: Berrett-Koehler.

Dick, B. (2004) 'Action Research Literature: Trends and Themes', *Action Research*, 2 (4), pp. 425–44.

Dixon, N. (1997) 'The Hallways of Learning', *Organizational Dynamics*, Spring, pp. 23–34.

Eden, D. and Shani, A.B. (1982) 'Pygmalion Goes to Boot Camp: Expectancy, Leadership, and Trainee Performance', *Journal of Applied Psychology*, 67, pp. 194–9.

Elliot, C. (1999) *Locating the Energy for Change: An Introduction to Appreciative Inquiry*, Winnipeg: International Institute for Sustainable Development.

Finegold, M.A., Holland, B.M. and Lingham, T. (2002) 'Appreciative Inquiry and Public Dialogue: An Approach to Community Change', *Public Organization Review*, 2, pp. 235–52.

Golembiewski, R.T. (1999) 'Fine-Tuning Appreciative Inquiry: Two Ways of Circumscribing the Concept's Value-Added', *Organization Development Journal* 17 (3), pp. 21–6.

King, A.S. (1970) 'Managerial Relations with Disadvantaged Work Groups,: Supervisory Expectations of the Underprivileged Worker', PhD dissertation, Texas Tech University.

Rosenthal, R. and Jacobson, L. (1968) *Pygmalion Effect in the Classroom: Teachers' Expectations and Pupil Intellectual Development*, New York: Holt, Rinehart & Winston.

Sorensen, P.E., Yaeger, T.F. and Bengtsson, U. (2003) 'The Promise of Appreciative Inquiry: A 20-Year Review', *OD Practitioner*, 35 (4), pp. 15–21.

Srivastva, S. and Cooperrider, D. (1990) *Appreciative Management and Leadership: The Power of Positive Thought and Action in Organizations*, San Francisco: Jossey-Bass.

Whitney, D., Cooperrider, D., Trosten-Bloom, A. and Kaplan, B.S. (2002) *Encyclopedia of Positive Questions, Volume 1: Using Appreciative Inquiry to Bring Out the Best in your Organisation*, Euclid, OH: Lakeshore Communicatons.

Whitney, D. and Trosten-Bloom, A. (2003) *The Power of Appreciative Inquiry: A Practical Guide to Positive Change*, San Francisco: Berrett-Koehler.

Zemke, R. (1999) 'Don't Fix the Company', *Training*, 36 (6), pp. 26–34.

20 High-performance management

'High commitment', 'high involvement' and 'high performance' are terms that are often used interchangeably to refer to an approach to managing an organisation's human resource that involves employing HR practices to achieve sustainable improvements in productivity and financial performance.

Rather than focusing on separate HR practices, high-performance management involves developing and implementing a 'bundle' or system of HR practices that are internally consistent, aligned with other business processes and aligned with the organisation's business strategy. It is an approach to improving organisational performance that is consistent with open systems thinking and the concept of 'fit' discussed in Chapter 3.

Bailey (1993) contends that human resources are frequently under-utilised because employees perform below their maximum potential. High-performance management seeks to improve performance through HR practices that elicit discretionary efforts from employees.

MacDuffie (1995) argues that high-performance management systems can contribute to improved economic performance when employees possess knowledge and skill that managers lack; when employees are motivated to apply this skill and knowledge through discretionary effort; and when the organisation's business strategy can be achieved only when employees contribute such discretionary effort. He goes on to argue that skilled and knowledgeable workers who are not motivated are unlikely to contribute any discretionary effort, and motivated workers who lack knowledge and skill may contribute discretionary effort, but with little effect on performance.

'Soft' and 'hard' models of HRM

Walton (1985) identified two profoundly different approaches to HRM: one based on imposing *control* and the other based on eliciting *commitment*. This distinction is similar to that made by Truss *et al.* (1997) when they referred to 'hard' (control) and 'soft' (commitment) strategies when investigating HRM practice in eight UK organisations. Arthur (1992) found empirical support for Walton's control and commitment categorisation when he studied human resource policies and practices in thirty US steel minimills. He identified six clusters of practices which could be grouped under two broad headings – cost reduction and commitment maximisation. These approaches are based on fundamentally different views about human nature, and the most effective way of exercising control.

The cost reduction or control approach

This focuses on the use of controls to reduce direct labour costs and improve efficiency. This is achieved by enforcing compliance through the application of specific rules and procedures. It is an approach that shares many of the assumptions that underpin Beer's (2001) Economic change strategy which focuses on the drive for economic value through tough, 'top-down', results driven action. Truss *et al.* (1997) observe that this 'hard' approach is based on the 'economic model' of man and McGregor's (1960) Theory X proposition that people dislike work and must be controlled and directed to get them to put forth adequate effort toward the achievement of organisational goals. Walton (1985) refers to the kind of situation in which control strategies flourish. He describes a plant in which employees are responsible for fixed jobs and are required to perform up to a minimum standard, and where peer pressure keeps them from exceeding this standard and from taking initiatives to improve performance. In such circumstances, because motivation is low, management seeks to secure adequate work effort through close monitoring and supervision, and what MacDuffie (1995) refers to as 'efficiency wages'.

The commitment maximisation approach

This is based on the assumption that people work best and contribute most to organisational performance when they are fully committed to the organisation. It is an approach that shares many of the assumptions that underpin Beer's OD strategy for change in so far as it involves creating the capabilities required to sustain competitive advantage and high performance over the long term. Truss *et al.* (1997) argue that 'soft' HRM has its roots in the human relations movement, the utilisation of individual talents and McGregor's (1960) Theory Y that proposes that 'man will exercise self direction and self control in the service of objectives to which he is committed'. It focuses on developing committed employees who can be trusted to use their discretion to work in ways that are consistent with organisational goals. This approach assumes that commitment is generated when employees are trusted and allowed to work autonomously. It assumes that individuals can work hard and smart without being controlled through sanctions and other external pressures. The commitment maximisation approach is the approach that underpins high-performance management practices.

Theoretical foundations: how commitment strategies work

Huselid (1995), building on the work of Bailey (1993), argues that HRM practices can affect an individual's performance by (a) improving employees' knowledge and skills; (b) motivating them to engage in discretionary behaviours that draw on their knowledge and skill; and (c) modifying organisational structures in ways that enable employees to improve the way they perform their jobs. Some of the practices that contribute to these outcomes are listed below.

Improving employee knowledge and skills

There are a number of practices that can enhance employee knowledge and skill. These include:

- *Recruitment practices that provide a large pool of qualified applicants* It may be possible to improve recruitment practices by focusing attention on what the organisation does to attract appropriately qualified individuals and how this affects the kind of people who present themselves for selection.
- *Selection practices that identify those individuals who possess required competencies* It may be possible to improve selection practices by focusing attention on how the organisation goes about selecting new employees, and what steps it takes to identify and validate its selection criteria. Pfeffer (1998), for example, argues that emphasis should be placed on screening for 'cultural fit' and attitudes rather than skills. He makes a case for *selecting* on those attributes that are both important and difficult or impossible to change, and *training* people in those behaviours or skills that are more readily learned.
- *Induction practices that affect the way people are socialised into the organisation* It may be possible to improve induction practices by focusing attention on what happens to new employees after they join the organisation and how this affects the development of competencies. (Induction might also be considered as a practice that affects employees' motivation to engage in discretionary behaviours and influence their motivation to work harder and smarter).
- *Training practices that develop knowledge and skills required by organisational members* It may be possible to improve training practices by focusing attention on the kind of issues considered in Chapter 12 and questioning whether sufficient attention is being given to the development of those competencies that are critical to the achievement of the organisation's purpose. Pfeffer (1998) argues that training is an essential component of high-performance work systems because these systems rely

on front-line employees exercising their skill and initiative to identify and resolve problems, introduce changes in work methods and take responsibility for quality. However, some organisations fail to invest sufficiently in training and many more are too quick to cut training budgets when times are hard:

> because training budgets often fluctuate with company economic fortunes, a perverse, procyclical training schedule typically develops: training funds are most plentiful when the firm is doing well. But when the firm is doing well, its people are busiest and have the most to do, and consequently, can least afford to be away for training. By contrast, when the firm is less busy, individuals have more time to develop their skills and undertake training activities. But that is exactly the time when training is least likely to be made available. (Pfeffer, 1998: 89)

- *Other development activities*, such as coaching, mentoring, on-the-job learning, secondments, or job rotation that develop the *knowledge, skills and job behaviours required for effective performance* Consideration might be given to whether these practices are as effective as they might be, and whether there is an appropriate balance between these practices and more formal training activities. Performance appraisal is listed below as a practice that affects employees' motivation to engage in discretionary behaviours, but it can also provide a vehicle for developing competencies.
- *Retention practices that encourage valued employees to stay with the organisation* Do they motivate those most likely to be poached away by competitors to remain with the organisation?
- *Attendance practices* Do they encourage employees to attend regularly and work contacted hours?
- *Information-sharing practices* that provide employees with the knowledge about immediate *job-related issues and wider business matters that they require in order to perform effectively* Consideration might be given to how and when information is provided, and whether it is the right kind of information.

Motivating employees to engage in discretionary behaviours

Huselid (1995) argues that the effectiveness of even the most highly skilled employees will be limited if they are not motivated to perform. A number of HRM practices can encourage organisational members to (a) work harder and (b) work smarter. These include:

- *Employment security* Consideration might be given to whether employees are regarded as a variable cost or a valued asset, and how this affects their commitment to the organisation.
- *Redeployment and severance* When workers are no longer required in their current roles, how does the organisation manage this situation, and

how does this affect the motivation of both those who are to be redeployed and their colleagues?

- *Performance appraisal*   It may be possible to improve the benefits from appraising performance by considering questions such as: What are the objectives of the performance appraisal system? What does it measure? Are individuals or groups appraised? Who does the appraising? Is the process perceived to be fair?
- *Incentives*   A wide range of factors can affect the link between incentives and performance (see Chapter 13) but some of the questions that might be considered under this heading include: How are individuals compensated? Are rewards linked to the acquisition of skills or to the achievement of performance targets? If they are linked to performance, is compensation based on individual, group or organisational performance?
- *Internal promotion systems*   How are people identified and prepared for promotion?
- *Status distinctions*   These can affect motivation, so it might be useful to review the kind of status distinctions that exist and the effects they may have on performance.

Enabling motivated employees to engage in discretionary behaviours

Bailey (1993) notes that the contribution of highly skilled and motivated employees will be limited unless their jobs are structured in ways that allow them to apply their knowledge and skills in order to improve the way they perform their jobs. There are a number of interventions that enable employees to engage in such discretionary behaviours. These include:

- *Organisation structures*   How is the organisation structured, and how does this affect the ability of individuals to improve the way they do their jobs? (For example, does the organisation have a functional structure with people working in 'silos', or is it process-based?)
- *Parallel and temporary structures*   Does the organisation use structures such as quality circles and away-days to facilitate the sharing of ideas about performance improvement?
- *Job design*   Are people employed to perform narrowly defined tasks that require little skill, or does job design emphasise a whole task and combine doing and thinking? Do people work on their own, or in teams?
- *Locus of decision making*   Is decision making concentrated high up in the organisation or is it decentralised and delegated?
- *Employee voice*   Is employee input encouraged? Is it allowed on a narrow agenda or a wide range of issues? What methods are used to facilitate upward, lateral and downward communication?

Pfeffer (1998) advocates the adoption of self-managed teams and decentralised delegated decision making as the guiding principles for organisational design. He argues that teams offer several advantages. They can substitute peer-based for hierarchical control: peer-based control can be very powerful, for example, when a team member is absent all the difficulties of that absence fall on other team members, producing enormous peer pressure against absenteeism (Parker and Slaughter, 1988). Pfeffer also points to other advantages. Team working encourages people to pool ideas and come up with better ways of addressing problems and provides a framework within which workers can more readily help each other and share their production knowledge (Shaiken, Lopez and Mankita, 1997).

Other benefits from high-performance management practices

Pfeffer (1998) argues that high-commitment work practices can produce savings by reducing administrative overheads. Delegating more responsibility to people further down the organisation eliminates the need for many supervisory roles. High-commitment work practices can also reduce many of the costs associated with having an alienated work-force that is engaged in an adversarial relationship with management.

The alignment of HRM practices

Many attempts to improve performance through the introduction of new HRM practices fail because changes are introduced piecemeal and are focused on particular practices such as selection, performance appraisal, compensation or training. Investing more resources in just one practice, such as training, may have little effect if other practices remain unchanged. For example, the potential benefits of training may be wasted if jobs are not redesigned in ways that give workers the freedom to apply their new knowledge and skills. HRM practices need to be aligned with each other if employees and the organisation are to benefit from what MacDuffie (1995: 197) refers to as 'multiple, mutually reinforcing conditions'.

Some view alignment as the defining feature of high-performance management systems and they do not believe that it is necessary to prescribe the kind of practices that are aligned, so long as the practices are internally consistent. However, there is a strong body of opinion that the most effective way of securing high performance is through high commitment. Those who subscribe to this school of thought advocates a configuration of practices that support the commitment rather than the control approach to management (see Pfeffer, 1998: 56). The theoretical foundation of the three- pronged approach to improving performance outlined above is based on the assumption that HRM practices should be targeted at increasing commitment in order to elicit discretionary behaviour. Pfeffer's (1998) seven practices that characterise systems that produce profits through people (employment security; selective hiring; self-managed teams and decentralised decision making; high compensation contingent on performance; extensive training; reduced status distinctions; extensive sharing of information) are all high-commitment management practices.

Implementation is not always easy. Moving from a control- to a commitment-oriented set of management practices can be difficult, because many managers are wedded to a control philosophy. Pfeffer (1998: 29) refers to 'the one-eighth rule' which states that only about half of all senior managers believe that there is a possible connection between how organisations manage their people and the profits they earn. Of these, only about a half will do more than attempt to change a single people management practice, not realising that the effective management of people requires a more comprehensive and systematic approach. In those organisations where managers do make comprehensive changes, only about a half will persist with these changes long enough to derive any economic benefit.

The introduction of a commitment-based high-performance management system often requires a paradigm shift in the way some managers think. Pfeffer argues that if managers see their staff as costs to be reduced; as recalcitrant employees prone to opportunism, shirking and free-riding; as people who can't be trusted and who need to be closely controlled through monitoring, rewards and sanctions; then any attempt to introduce high-performance management practices is likely to fail. Successful implementation requires a mind-set which regards people as fundamentally trustworthy, intelligent and motivated.

Results from high-performance management systems

Pfeffer (1998) presents an impressive review of studies that provide evidence of substantial gains from implementing high-performance management systems. His review includes a study of five-year survival rates of initial public offerings (Welbourne and Andrews, 1996); studies of profitability and stock price in a large sample of companies from multiple industries (Huselid, 1995); and detailed research in the automobile industry (MacDuffie, 1995), apparel (Dunlop and Weil, 1996), semiconductors (Sohoni, 1994), steel (Arthur, 1995), oil refining (Ricketts, 1994) and service industries (Schneider, 1991; Johnson, Ryan and Schmit, 1994). These findings suggest that high-performance management can produce economic benefits in a wide range of settings, including low- and high-technology industries and in manufacturing and service settings.

Exercise 20.1   Diagnosing the alignment of HRM practices

One of the first things that need to be done when developing and implementing a high-performance management system is to diagnose the extent to which existing management practices are aligned with each other and with the organisation's business strategy. Pfeffer (1998) describes the essential steps of an 'alignment diagnosis' that provides the basis for the diagnostic exercise presented below. You may find it useful to complete this exercise for your organisation or some other organisation that you are familiar with.

The alignment diagnosis is in two parts. The first is concerned with *external* alignment and involves diagnosing the extent to which management practices are congruent with the organisation's business strategy. The second part is concerned with *internal* alignment and involves diagnosing the extent to which HRM practices are aligned with each other.

Diagnosing external alignment

This first part of the exercise involves four steps:

1 Reviewing the organisation's strategy.
2 Identifying the critical behaviours and related competencies that are required to achieve the strategy.
3 Identifying practices that the organisation uses to manage people.
4 Assessing the alignment of each people management/ HRM practice with the competencies and behaviours required to achieve the organisation's strategy (does each practice support the availability and application of critical competencies and behaviours?).

Each step will be considered in turn.

Specifying the organisation's strategy

Strategy is a statement of purpose that indicates how the organisation will match its resources with the opportunities, constraints and demands in the environment. Implicit in this statement are the *value* propositions the organisation offers to stakeholders.

Summarise your organisation's strategy in the space below.

Identifying the critical behaviours and related competencies that are required to achieve the strategy

If the organisation's strategy is premised on the provision of excellent customer service and if the majority of staff are customer-facing then the organisation needs people who have the competencies necessary to support this value proposition. If, on the other hand, the strategy is premised on being first to market with innovative products, then a different set of competencies will be required. Pfeffer recommends that attention is restricted to the six or so behaviours and related competencies that are the most important. These can be entered at the head of the columns of the external alignment matrix presented (Figure 20.1).

Figure 20.1   External alignment matrix

Practices that affect:	Critical behaviours competencies required to implement the organisation's strategy						
1 The development and availability of competencies							
Recruitment							
Selection							
Induction							
Training							
Other development							
Information-sharing							
Other							
2 Motivation							
Employment security							
Performance appraisal							
Incentives							
Internal promotion systems							
Status distinctions							
Other							
3 Ability to use competencies to improve performance							
Organisation structures							
Job design							
Locus of decision making							
Employee voice							
Other							

Identifying practices that the organisation uses to manage people

The external alignment matrix is divided into three parts in line with Bailey's (1993) model of how HR practices can affect performance. The first part relates to the policies and practices that affect the *availability and development of* the competencies necessary to deliver required behaviours. These practices include:

recruitment, selection, induction, training, other development activities, and information-sharing.

The second part relates to practices that affect employees' *motivation* to engage in discretionary behaviours that involve applying critical competencies in order to improve performance. These practices include employment security, redeployment and severance, performance appraisal, incentives, internal promotion systems and status distinctions.

The third part relates to practices that *enable* motivated employees to engage in discretionary behaviours that lead to performance improvements. These practices include organisation design, parallel and temporary structures, job design, locus of decision making and employee voice.

Review your organisation's HR practices and amend the list included in the external alignment matrix (Figure 20.1) to reflect your organisation's current approach to HR management. You may also amend this list to include additional practices that, if applied appropriately, could contribute to high performance.

Assessing the alignment of each HRM practice with the competencies and behaviours required to achieve the organisation's business strategy

This step involves assessing the extent to which each of the HRM practices listed in your external alignment matrix is likely to promote the competencies and behaviours that you identified as critical for the implementation of the strategy. Pfeffer suggests using a three-point scale where +1 indicated that the practice is aligned with the organisation's business strategy and will support the development of required competencies and behaviours, 0 where the practice has a neutral effect and –1 where it is mis-aligned. This procedure is a useful way of identifying where there is substantial mis-alignment and a clear need for action to develop and implement a revised HRM practice.

Alignment-related problems   Pfeffer (1998: 111) identifies some of the most common alignment-related problems. Two of these involve the link between training activities and competencies, and the link between compensation and the achievement of key performance targets:

- With regard to training and required competencies, in many organisations training activities are focused on generally useful topics (such as negotiating skills and time management) but neglect the crucial competencies that are tightly linked to the achievement of strategic objectives
- With regard to compensation and key performance targets, Pfeffer high-lights the problem with an example of a firm rewarding managers for 'making budget numbers' when the really important targets had to do with being innovative, fast and customer-focused.

Diagnosing internal alignment

The second part of the alignment diagnosis involves assessing the internal consistency of the HRM practices. One way of doing this is to list the management practices identified as part of the external alignment exercise across the top as well as down the left-hand side of a matrix and taking each practice in turn and reviewing it for alignment against each of the other practices. For example, in terms of job design, if work is allocated to self-managed teams are employees given training that supports this practice? Also, is performance appraisal focused on individuals or teams and is compensation based on individual or team performance? Again the three- point scale can be used to signal the degree of alignment and highlight potential problems (Figure 20.2).

This kind of alignment diagnosis can help change agents identify the system of HR practices that will assist the organisation to achieve its strategic objectives.

You may find it useful to reflect on your findings regarding the extent of external and internal alignment in your organisation and the areas where alignment problems might arise.

Figure 20.2   Internal alignment matrix

Practices that affect:	← Management practices →														
1 The development and availability of competencies	a	b	c	d	e	f	g	h	i	j	k	l	m	n	o
a Recruitment	–														
b Selection		–													
c Induction			–												
d Training				–											
e Other development					–										
f Information-sharing						–									
2 Motivation															
g Employment security							–								
h Performance appraisal								–							
i Incentives									–						
j Internal promotions										–					
k Status distinctions											–				
3 Use of competencies															
l Organisation structures												–			
m Job design													–		
n Locus of decision making														–	
o Employee voice															–

Summary

This chapter has considered how HRM practices can affect performance by (a) improving employees' knowledge and skills; (b) motivating them to engage in discretionary behaviours that draw on their knowledge and skill; and (c) modifying organisational structures in ways that enable employees to improve the way they perform their jobs.

Rather than focusing on separate HRM practices, high-performance management involves developing and implementing a 'bundle' or system of practices that is internally consistent, aligned with other business processes and aligned with the organisation's business strategy.

Alignment is the defining feature of high-performance management interventions. However, while some argue that any HRM practices can be effective so long as they are aligned, others (such as Pfeffer, 1998) advocate a configuration of practices that supports a commitment rather than a control approach to people management.

In terms of the typology presented in Figure 17.2 (p. 279), high-performance management is an HRM intervention.

References

Arthur, J.B. (1992) 'The Link between Business Strategy and Industrial Relations Systems in American Steel Minimills', *Industrial and Labor Relations Review*, 45, pp. 488–506.

Arthur, J.B (1995) 'Effects of Human Resource Systems on Manufacturing Performance and Turnover', *Academy of Management Journal*, 37 (3), pp. 670–87.

Bailey, T. (1993) 'Discretionary Effort and the Organisation of Work: Employee Participation and Work Reform since Hawthorne', Working Paper, Columbia University, New York.

Beer, M. (2001) 'How to Develop an Organization Capable of Sustained High Performance: Embrace the Drive for Results–Capability Development Paradox', *Organizational Dynamics*, 29 (4), pp. 233–47.

Dunlop, J.T. and Weil, D. (1996) 'Diffusion and Performance of Modular Production in the US Apparel Industry', *Industrial Relations*, 35, pp. 337–8.

Huselid, M.A. (1995) 'The Impact of Human Resource Management Practices on Turnover, Productivity, and Corporate Financial Performance', *Academy of Management Journal*, 38 (3), pp. 635–72.

Johnson, R.H., Ryan, A.M. and Schmit, M.J. (1994) 'Employee Attitudes and Branch Performance at Ford Motor Credit', Paper presented to the ninth annual conference of the Society of Industrial and Organisational Psychology, Nashville, TN, April.

MacDuffie, J.P. (1995) 'Human Resource Bundles and Manufacturing Performance: Organizational Logic and Flexible Production Systems in the World Auto Industry', *Industrial and Labor Relations Review*, 48 (2), 197–221.

McGregor, D. (1960) 'Theory X and Theory Y', in D.S. Pugh (ed.), *Organization Theory: Selected Readings*, London: Penguin.

Parker, M. and Slaughter, J. (1988) 'Management by Stress', *Technology Review*, 91, p. 43.

Pfeffer, J. (1998) *The Human Equation: Building Profits by Putting People First*, Boston, MA: Harvard Business School Press.

Ricketts, R. (1994) 'Survey Points to Practices that Reduce Refinery Maintenance Spending', *Oil and Gas Journal*, 4 July, 38.

Schneider, B. (1991) 'Service Quality and Profits: Can you have your Cake and Eat it, too?', *Human Resource Planning*, 14, p. 151.

Shaiken, H., Lopez, S. and Mankita, I. (1997) 'Two Routes to Team Production: Saturn and Chrysler Compared', *Industrial Relations*, 36, p. 31.

Sohoni, V. (1994) 'Workforce Involvement and Wafer Fabrication Efficiency', in C. Brown (ed.), *The Competitive Semiconductor Manufacturing Human Resources Project: First Interim Report*, Berkeley, CA: Institute of Industrial Relations.

Truss, C., Gratton, L., Hope-Hailey, V., McGovern, P. and Stiles, P. (1997) 'Soft and Hard Models of Human Resource Management: A Reappraisal', *Journal of Management Studies*, 34 (1), 53–73.

Walton, R. E. (1985) 'From Control to Commitment in the Workplace', *Harvard Business Review*, 63, pp. 77–84.

Welbourne, T. and Andrews, A. (1996) 'Predicting Performance of Initial Public Offering Firms: Should HRM be in the Equation?', *Academy of Management Journal*, 39, pp. 910–11.

Business process reengineering

Business process reengineering (BPR) is often presented as a 'top-down', organisation-wide approach to transforming organisations. The structure of most organisations has been influenced by the principle of the division of labour, first articulated by Adam Smith (1776) in *The Wealth of Nations*. Smith observed that it was much more efficient to break the process of pin making down into several steps that could be undertaken by specialist workers, rather than to delegate the whole process to one generalist worker. This principle manifests itself today in organisations that structure activities according to specialist functions rather than value-creating processes. Hammer and Champy (1993) argue that: 'Companies today consist of functional silos, or stovepipes, vertical structures built on narrow pieces of a process.'

They illustrate how this affects organisational functioning with reference to the order fulfilment process that starts when a customer places an order and ends when the goods are delivered:

> The person checking a customer's credit is part of the credit department, which is probably a part of the finance organisation. Inventory picking is performed by workers in the warehouse, who may report to the vice president of manufacturing. Shipping on the other hand, is part of logistics. People involved in a process look *inward* towards their department and *upwards* towards their boss, but no one looks *outwards* toward the customer. (Hammer and Champy, 1993: 28, emphases in the original)

BPR involves switching attention away from fragmented functional-based thinking towards *cross-functional processes* that create value for the organisation. Kaplan and Murdock (1991) argue that focusing attention on and redesigning core processes can make them faster and more flexible, and make organisations more responsive to changes in competitive conditions, consumer demands, product lifecycles and technologies.

The nature of BPR

Hammer and Champy (1993) define BPR as the fundamental rethinking and radical redesign of business processes to achieve dramatic improvements in performance. They argue that reengineering is 'fundamental' because it involves asking the most basic questions about how an organisation operates, questions that challenge many widely held assumptions. Rather than simply asking whether it is possible to improve the way something is done, reengineering involves questioning *why* the organisation does what it does. For example, those responsible for reengineering the order fulfilment process, referred to above, might question the need to perform credit checks rather than assuming that they are an essential part of the process. It is possible that checking a customer's credit fails to add any value because the cost of performing a check is greater than any losses that might be incurred from bad debts. Hammer and Champy state that new thinking should not be influenced by embedded assumptions or any existing processes, activities and systems. They advocate a 'clean-sheet' approach to process redesign.

Davenport and Stoddard (1994) challenge this view. Based on conversations with managers from more than 200 companies and rigorous research on thirty-five reengineering initiatives (Javenpaa and Stoddard, 1993), they assert that in practice a clean-sheet approach is rarely found. Those companies that do adopt this approach tend to make a clear distinction between clean-sheet *design* and clean-sheet *implementation*. They may adopt a clean-sheet approach to design because it can provide a vision of a 'best-of-all-processes' world towards which the organisation can focus its change efforts. However, they recognise that implementation, more often than not, needs to be piecemeal and incremental. They quote one manager who said: 'You can design assuming a clean slate, but you must implement assuming the existing state.' They also report that designers often start with a 'dirty slate', taking into account both the opportunities for enabling a new process and the constraints that disable it:

> With both design elements in mind, the design team [can] construct the best possible process given the enablers and the constraints. Whereas this is a less exciting and more difficult design method, 'designing with a dirty slate' will normally yield a more implementable process. (1994: 123)

Hammer and Champy also argue that process reengineering is 'radical and dramatic' because, to be successful, it must entail *rapid and wholesale transformation* rather than incremental and piecemeal change. Davenport and Stoddard (1994), however, do not see reengineering as incompatible with continuous improvement. While they agree with the proposition that reengineering is a process that can contribute to organisational transformation they do not agree that it is synonymous with it. They report observing numerous firms trying to change too many processes at once and failing in their ambition to achieve radical transformation. However, they also report observing several firms that were successfully creating hybrid configurations, adding a process dimension to their functional structures. McNulty and Ferlie (2002), in their in-depth study of business process reengineering within the Leicester Royal Infirmary, report findings which support Davenport and Stoddard's position. They found that while the intended strategy was radical and revolutionary the emergent strategy of reengineering proved to be evolutionary and convergent in both overall approach and impact:

> as the reengineering programme unfolded the initial radical ambition for organisational process redesign was tempered and reshaped in line with functional organisational principles that underpinned the existing pattern of specialties and clinical directorates. Reengineers learned quickly that they were dependent on the support of managers and clinicians . . . to effect change at specialty and clinical directorate levels. (2002: 116)

Those who argue that reengineering offers a system-wide and radical approach to change also tend to view it as an essentially 'top-down' process. Hammer and Champey, for example, believe that people near the front line lack the broad perspective that reengineering demands:

> They may see – probably better than anyone else – the narrow problems from which their departments suffer, but it is difficult for them to see a process as a whole and to recognise its poor overall design as the source of their problems. (1993: 208)

They also argue that middle managers lack the required authority to change processes that cross organisational boundaries. There are, however, those who believe that reengineering can be a more participative process. While Davenport and Stoddard (1994) accept that innovative designs for broad processes are unlikely to come from those whose heads are 'buried deep in the bowls of existing process', they see no reason why all members of design teams must be high in the organisational hierarchy. They argue that those who are at the front line may make a very valuable contribution to the design of detailed process activities. They also cite examples of organisational members who have failed to implement newly designed processes because they had had no hand in their creation.

Reengineering at Leicester Royal Infirmary started as a 'top-down' programme to identify, redesign and roll out core processes across the hospital. A central reengineering capability was created using an infrastructure of reengineering committees, reengineering laboratories (physical spaces in which teams or reengineers could work on the redesign of processes) and internal and external change agents. This initial strategy began to flounder and was eventually replaced by a decentralised approach which involved responsibility for reengineering shifting from a dedicated team of reengineers to managers located within clinical directorates. McNulty and Ferlie (2002) note that it was at this point that the energy and momentum for change increased because individuals felt more able to 'adopt, adapt and customise' reengineering ideas to suit local circumstances and purposes.

The application of BPR

BPR typically involves seven steps:

Process mapping

A process is a series of actions that lead to an *outcome*. Process maps show how work flows through an organisation. People tend to be more familiar with organisational units, such as the manufacturing, R&D or marketing, than with the processes to which these units contribute. Examples of processes in a business organisation are order fulfilment (order to payment – including intermediate steps such as manufacturing), product development (concept to prototype) and sales (prospect to order). Examples of processes in a healthcare organisation include patient test (referral to diagnosis) and patient stay (admission to discharge). In most organisations there are relatively few core processes, but each of these might involve a number of sub-processes. The start point for any process reengineering project is to map the processes that contribute to the organisation fulfilling its purpose.

Identifying processes for reengineering

Even when the ambition is to use process reengineering to radically transform the organisation in the shortest possible time it will normally prove impossible to reengineer all the organisation's processes simultaneously. Hammer and Champy suggest three criteria for choosing which processes to reengineer and the order in which this might be done. They are: *dysfunction* (which processes are in deepest trouble), *importance* (which processes have the greatest impact on the organisation's customers) and *feasibility* (which of the processes are most susceptible to successful redesign).

Understanding the selected process

The reengineering team needs to understand the process, what it does, how well it does it and any critical issues that govern its performance, but it does not, according to the classical school of process reengineering, need to undertake any detailed analysis. Hammer and Champy (1993) caution against too much analysis because it directs attention inside the process and directs attention away from challenging embedded assumptions. They argue that attention should be focused on seeking a high-level understanding, starting with what the process delivers and how well these outcomes match what customers really want. This high-level overview provides the basis for a 'clean-sheet' design activity.

There are those, however, who see value in starting with a 'dirty slate' and looking for opportunities for incremental process improvement. While improving the patient journey in a healthcare setting might involve starting

Figure 21.1   GP referral for a routine X-ray at a local hospital

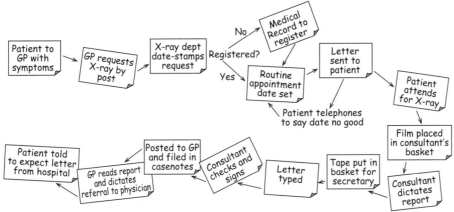

from a clean sheet and radically transforming a process, it might also involve working with an existing process and seeking out opportunities for incremental improvement. For example, the aim of a reengineering project might be to improve the service provided to patients who go to their local doctor (GP) with symptoms that require a diagnostic test involving an X-ray (Figure 21.1). The process might be defined as starting when the patient first goes to a doctor with symptoms, and ending when the doctor communicates the X-ray results to the patient.

There are several ways of *mapping this process*. One method is to gather all the stakeholders together for a mapping workshop. Another is for members of the reengineering team to physically walk through the process and record what happens at each stage. This mapping for understanding might involve identifying:

- The number of steps in the process for the patient
- The number of hand-offs (occasions when the patient or information related to the patient's diagnostic test is passed from one person to another)
- Task time (the time taken for each step)
- Wait time (the time between each step)
- 'Dead time' when nothing happens (a letter sits on a dictated tape for three days before being typed)
- Steps that fail to add any value (can they be eliminated?)
- Blockages (steps that slow the rest of the process down)

Mapping a targeted process is often done in two steps. The first involves producing a high-level process map that provides an overview of how inputs are transformed into outputs, focuses attention on the relative value of the outputs produced by the process (are they worth the effort required to produce them?, do they really satisfy customers' needs?) and the value added by particular steps in the process (can a step be eliminated, integrated with another step or replaced with an entirely different sub-process?). Experience suggests that analysing this kind of high-level map helps to expose embedded assumptions and identify those parts of the overall process that offer the greatest potential for improvement. The second step involves mapping these parts in more detail.

Defining key performance objectives

Key performance objectives are based on what the reengineering team and other stakeholders believe the customer requires from the process. They provide a basis for specifying measures that will indicate whether the changes have been successful. Sometimes bench-marking is used to help define performance objectives but reengineers need to be alert to the possibility that bench-marking may limit ambition to what is currently being achieved by 'the best of the rest' and inhibit 'out-of-the-box' thinking about what the process could deliver. Base-lining, collecting and recording data about existing (pre-reengineered) performance can also help with the definition of realistic performance targets and provide a basis for assessing the successes of the reengineering project.

Designing new processes

'Redesign is the most nakedly creative part of the entire reengineering process. More than any other, it demands imagination, inductive thinking, and a touch of craziness' (Hammer and Champy, 1993: 134). Hammer and Champy illustrate this with the example of an insurance company that believed it was costing more than it should to settle claims relating to motor accidents.

There is no set format for redesigning a process, but it often involves people sharing ideas about how the process might be changed and others 'piggybacking' on these ideas to suggest other possibilities. In Hammer and Champy's example of the claims settlement process, somebody noted that it cost the same per hour to work on a big claim as it did to work on a small claim. This led to two related suggestions: introduce a step early in the process that would separate out those claims that will cost a lot to settle (usually those involving a claim for personal injury) and those that will not, and redesigning the process for small claims that will cut the time required to settle them. One suggestion was to immediately settle any claim for less that a certain amount. Some members of the team felt that this could encourage fraud and escalate the cost of claims, but others felt that this danger could be managed by only offering immediate settlement to policy-holders who had a good no-claims record. A related idea was to let the agent handle claims below a specified amount. This led to somebody else suggesting that the garage be allowed to deal with the claim, thereby eliminating the need for many steps in the existing process. This proposal was initially dismissed because it was feared that garages might inflate the cost of repairs. However, somebody brought the team back to this idea and suggested that there would be many garages willing to work for modest margins if this enabled them to win more business from the insurance company. It was also recognised that not only could this reduce costs for the insurance company, but it would also lead to greater customer satisfaction. What customers wanted most was their car back on the road as quickly as possible.

This first meeting came up with some challenging new ideas, some of which merited further attention and testing. It also involved the application of a number of reengineering principles, such as organising work around outcomes – for example reduced cost and increased customer satisfaction – and involving as few people as possible in the process to reduce hand-offs and wait-time. In addition it involved destroying some embedded assumptions such as that garages could not be trusted.

Testing

An important part of process reengineering is the *testing* of ideas to see if they will work in practice. Langley *et al.* (1996) advocate a Plan, Do, Study, Act (PDSA) model for process improvement that involves *planning* a change that can be tested on a small scale or over a limited period (an hour, day, or week), *doing* or carrying out the test, *studying* base-line data and the effect of the test and looking for improvement, and *acting* to implement the tested change. This process has many similarities with action research (see Chapter 18) and can involve several iterations before final implementation.

Implementation

If the tests are successful the redesigned process can be implemented and rolled out, as appropriate, to other parts of the organisation. However, great care needs to be exercised if the redesigned process is to be rolled out to powerful individuals or groups who were not part of, and committed to, the reengineering process. Process reengineering can be highly politicised and often involves jurisdictional disputes when managers are required to 'let go' of activities and decisions they value.

Results from BPR

Research findings regarding the results of reengineering are mixed. Cummings and Worley (2001) cite a study of 497 companies in the US and

1,245 companies in Europe. While 60 per cent of US firms and 75 per cent of European firms had engaged in at least one reengineering project, only 15 per cent of them reported positive outcomes. This is quite different to the findings reported by Caron, Javenpaa and Stoddard (1994). They found that while only half of twenty reengineering projects undertaken by CIGNA, a leading provider of insurance and related financial services, were successful first time round, the impact of reengineering was very positive, and the company saved more than $100 million overall. They also reported that some of the most successful projects were those that were undertaken in self-contained areas.

McNulty and Ferlie (2002) report that attempts to radically transform a large hospital through process reengineering were highly contested and the outcome of the change was uneven across the organisation. *Contextual* factors had an important effect on outcomes, especially those relating to the extent to which doctors retained control over work practices. They also found that it was easier to secure change in those processes (or parts of processes) that did not cross boundaries between clinical directorates or between directorates and external agencies. This echoes one of the findings reported by Caron, Javenpaa and Stoddard (1994) that some of the most successful projects were those that were undertaken in self-contained areas. Despite the many difficulties encountered when trying to reengineer the hospital, McNulty and Ferlie observed that the reengineering methodology did make an important contribution to securing change. For example, in trauma orthopaedic care there was a number of positive outcomes. The base-lining activity produced 'facts' about patient activity on which the case for change could be built. Process mapping enabled the reengineers and other stakeholders, such as doctors, to analyse and understand the care process and develop a vision of change. Finally, piloting allowed some changes to be introduced, often without people realising that an important change had taken place.

Summary

This chapter has examined the nature of BPR. While it is often regarded as a fundamental rethinking and radical redesign of business processes to achieve a dramatic improvement in performance, the benefits of less ambitious approaches that adopt reengineering principles to achieve process improvement have also been considered.

The seven stages of BPR have been discussed and the results from applying process reengineering in different contexts reported.

In terms of the typology presented in Figure 17.2 (p. 279), BPR is a techno-structural intervention.

References

Caron, J.R., Javenpaa, D.L. and Stoddard, D. (1994) 'Business Reengineering at CIGNA Corporation: Experience and Lessons Learned from the Last Five Years', *MIS Quarterly*, September, pp. 233–50.

Cummings, T.G. and Worley, C.G. (2001) *Organization Development and Change*, 7th edn, Cincinnati, OH: South-Western College Publishing and Thomson Learning.

Davenport, T.H. and Stoddard, D.B. (1994) 'Reengineering Change in Mythic Proportions', *MIS Quarterly*, June, pp. 121–7.

Hammer, M. and Champy, J. (1993) *Reengineering the Corporation: A Manifesto for Business Revolution*, London: Nicholas Brealey.

Javenpaa, D.L. and Stoddard, D.B. (1993) 'Managing IT-Enabled Radical Change', Research Proposal, University of Texas/Harvard Business School.

Kaplan, R. and Murdock, L. (1991) 'Core Process Design', *McKinsey Quarterly*, 2, pp. 27–43.

Langley, G., Nolan, K., Norman, C. and Provast, L. (1996) *The Improvement Guide: A Practical Approach to Enhancing Organisational Performance*, San Francisco: Jossey Bass.

McNulty, T. and Ferlie, E. (2002) *Reengineering Health Care: The Complexities of Organisational Transformation*, Oxford: Oxford University Press.

Smith, A. (1776) *The Wealth of Nations*, Volume 1 (1950 edition), London: Methuen.

Selecting interventions

This chapter examines the factors that need to be considered when selecting which type of intervention to use. Consideration is also given to the factors that can affect decisions regarding the sequencing of interventions in those circumstances where it might be necessary to use more that one type of intervention. This is important because sometimes an inappropriate sequence can undermine the effectiveness of a change programme.

Beware fashions and fads

There is a real danger that change agents under-use many traditional well-tried interventions in favour of those that are new and 'fashionable'. Ettorre's (1997) lifecycle theory of management fads suggests that the adoption of an intervention follows five stages:

1   *Discovery* – intervention just begins to come to people's attention.
2   *Wild acceptance* – uncritical adoption.
3   *Digestion* – critics begin to suggest that it is not a panacea.
4   *Disillusionment* – recognition of problems associated with the intervention.
5   *Hard core* – only a minority continue with the intervention.

But the most fashionable interventions may not always be the most effective. After surveying the 100 largest *Fortune* 500 firms, Staw and Epstein (2000) found that while the use of popular interventions, such as TQM, empowerment and team working was positively associated with corporate reputation (organisations were admired, seen as more innovative and rated as having higher-quality management) and positively related to CEO pay, it was not associated with improvement in economic performance (assessed over a one–five-year period). It is important to select and apply those interventions that will be effective in a particular context. At times this might involve using interventions that have been around for some considerable period.

Factors indicating which interventions to use

Consideration is given first to those factors that need to be taken into account when deciding which interventions are likely to contribute most to achieving the goals of a change programme. Attention is given to three main factors: the *nature* of the problem or opportunity that the intervention has to address (diagnosed issue), the *level* of change target (individual, group, etc.) that is to be the focus for change and the *depth* of intervention required. Two additional factors are also considered. These are the *time available* for the change and the *efficacy* of different types of interventions.

Diagnosed issue

A key determinant of the appropriate intervention is the nature of the diagnosed problem or opportunity. This underpins the aim of the change programme and indicates the issues that have to be attended to in order to move an organisation or unit from the current position to a more desirable future state.

At a macro level the issue might be defined in terms of either *transformational* or *incremental* change.

Where the issue is defined in terms of a need for *transformational change*, Burke and Litwin (1992) suggest that the most effective interventions will be those that are targeted at changing system-wide elements such as mission and strategy, leadership and culture. Interventions that successfully change these elements will have knock-on effects that will affect just about every other element in the system.

On the other hand, where the issue is defined in terms of *incremental change* (or fine tuning) the most effective interventions may be those that address elements that, if changed, may have a more localised impact in terms of units or levels affected. These include interventions targeted at elements such as structure, systems, climate, tasks and roles. For example, the focal issue might be to improve task performance in a particular department. The intervention selected to address this issue might be work redesign. Redesigning the work to improve task performance may affect other elements of the departmental organisation (such as the competencies required of those who do the work, or departmental structure if redesigning the work involves reducing the number of levels in the hierarchy). However, this kind of intervention may have relatively little impact on how the entire organisation functions, even if it does have some implications for how the target unit performs and interacts with related units.

At a micro level, issues may simply be defined in terms of the organisational elements that are most closely associated with the diagnosed problem or opportunity. The twelve elements of the Burke–Litwin model (see Figure 7.6, Chapter 7) could provide a basis for classifying issues in this way. An alternative, used in the three-dimensional model presented in Figure 22.1 (p. 334), is the typology used by Cummings and Worley (2001) to classify interventions. It points to four broad types of diagnosed issue:

- *Human process issues* which include communicating, problem solving, decision making, interpersonal and inter-group interactions, and leadership
- *Technology and structural issues* which include horizontal and vertical differentiation, coordination, technology and production processes and work design
- *HR issues* which include attracting, selecting, developing, motivating and retaining competent people
- *Strategic issues* which include managing the interface between the organisation and its environment, and deciding which markets to engage in, what products and services to produce, how to gain competitive advantage and what values should guide the organisation's development.

Level of change target

Schmuck and Miles (1971), Blake and Mouton (1986), Pugh (1986) and others all include the individual, group, inter-group and organisation in their classifications of units that can be the target for change. Blake and Mouton also include the larger social system as the potential client or target for change and Schmuck and Miles include a group as small as a dyad as a separate unit.

In the three-dimensional model for selecting interventions presented in Figure 22.1 (p. 334) the four *levels* are individual, group, inter-group and organisation. A diagnostic analysis might indicate that the critical issue has to do with a mismatch between task demands and individual competencies, suggesting that the target for change is at the individual level. Alternatively, the diagnosis might point to poor working relationships within a group, indicating that the group should be the target for change. Another possibility is that the diagnosis focuses on poor relationships between groups, suggesting that inter-group relations should be the target. At the level of the organisation the diagnosis may suggest that organisational strategy is not matched to market conditions or is not properly appreciated by organisational members at all levels, indicating that the target for change is the whole organisation.

Depth of intervention required

Harrison (1970) argues that the depth of individual emotional involvement can be a key factor in determining whether an intervention will be effective. This factor is concerned with the extent to which core areas of personality or self are the focus of change events. He posits a dimension running from surface to deep. Interventions that focus on external aspects of an individual and deal with the more public and observable aspects of behaviour are located at the 'surface' end of the continuum. Interventions that touch on personal and private perceptions, attitudes or feelings, and attempt to affect them, are located at the 'deep' end.

Operations research (OR) is an example of an intervention that can be classified at the 'surface' end of the continuum because it is a process of rational analysis that deals with roles and functions without paying much attention to the individual characteristics of the persons occupying these roles. An example of a deeper intervention is management by objectives (MBO). This involves a boss and subordinate establishing mutually agreed goals for performance and monitoring performance against these goals. Typically the exchange of information is limited to that which is observable. Further along the continuum are interventions such as management counselling that, for example, involves a consultant working with managers to increase their awareness of how their personality, role relationships and previous experience affect their management style. 'Deeper' interventions might involve members of a group discussing with peers the interpersonal processes that affect their contribution to group performance. This kind of intervention can involve group members sharing very personal information about themselves, how they perceive their own behaviour and the behaviour of others and exploring with them how they and others might modify their attitudes, roles and behaviour to improve group performance.

Harrison (1970) argues that as the level of intervention becomes 'deeper' the information needed to intervene becomes less available. For example, the information needed by the OR change agent is easily obtained because it is often a matter of record. The information required by those engaged in MBO can often be observed. However, people may not be prepared to discuss freely their attitudes and feeling towards others or to be open to feedback from others about their own interpersonal style.

These considerations led Harrison to suggest that change agents should intervene at a level *no deeper than that required to produce an enduring solution to the problem at hand*. However, this criterion, while necessary, is not sufficient for determining the depth of intervention. While the change agent may have a view about the nature of the information required and the depth of intervention necessary to produce this information, the change target (individual, group or system) may not be comfortable working at this level. Harrison argues that any intervention, if it is to be successful, must be legitimised in the norms of the group or organisation and must be seen to relate to the felt needs of organisational members. This led him to suggest a second criterion. Intervene at a level *no deeper than that at which the energy and resources of the client can be committed to problem solving and change*.

Harrison suggests that in those circumstances where the change agents suspect that the required information is located at a depth greater than that at which the client is comfortable working, they should resolve the dilemma by selecting an intervention on the basis of the second criterion. Once the client has gained confidence they may be prepared to engage in an intervention that will involve the sharing of information such as attitudes and feelings that they would normally regard as private and confidential.

A three-dimensional model to aid choice

The factors considered so far can be combined to produce a three-dimensional model that can be used as a rough guide to the type of intervention that might be most effective in a given situation. This is presented in Figure 22.1.

Figures 22.2–22.5 provide examples of interventions for each of the four types of diagnosed issue.

Some cells in Figures 22.2–22.5 are blank because they represent situations that are unlikely to call for an intervention that complies with all three criteria. For example, there may not be many (any?) situations that call for a deep-level techno-structural intervention targeted at the individual.

Some interventions could appear in more than one cell. Team building, for example, is an example of a human process intervention that is targeted at the group. In terms of depth, however, some team building interventions are shallow and others rather deep. At the shallow end interventions might be concerned only with agreeing the purpose of the group, indicators of effective performance and performance strategies that could contribute to achieving this level of performance. On the other hand, at the deep end interventions could involve an exploration of inter-personal relationships and how these promote or undermine performance.

Figure 22.1   A three-dimensional model to aid choice of interventions

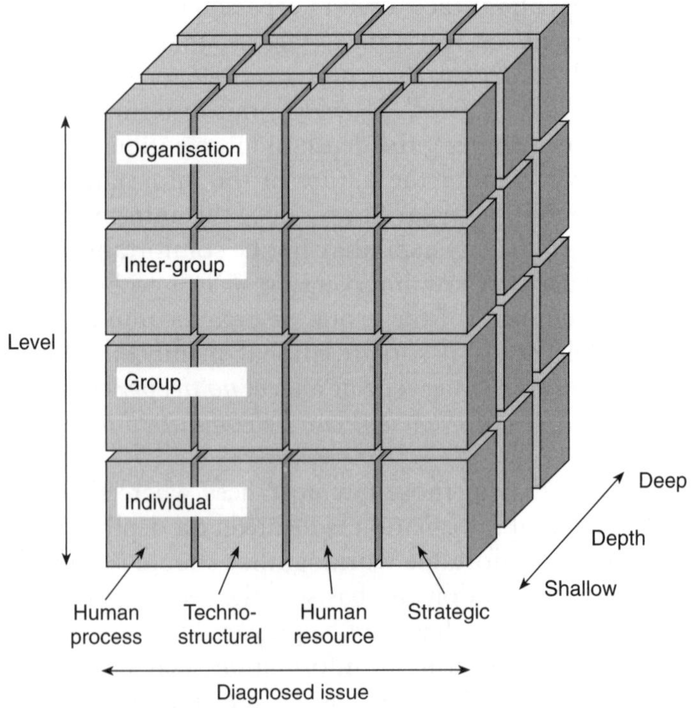

Figure 22.2   Examples of human process interventions

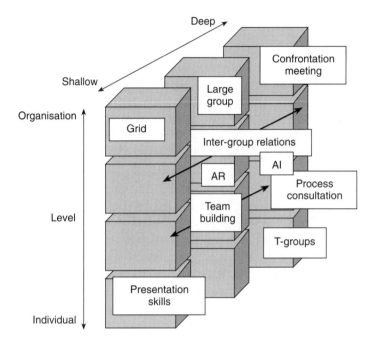

Figure 22.3   Examples of techno-structural interventions

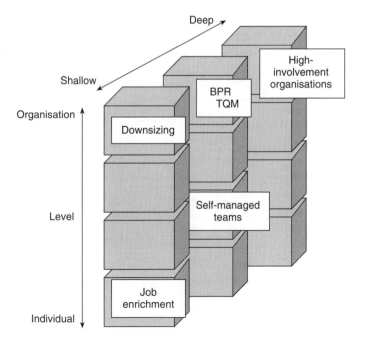

Figure 22.4   Examples of HR interventions

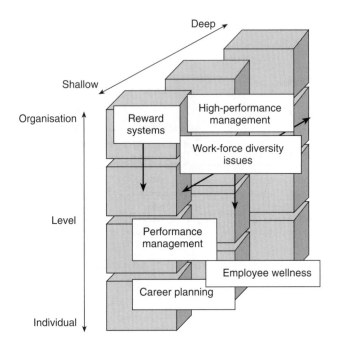

Figure 22.5   Examples of strategic interventions

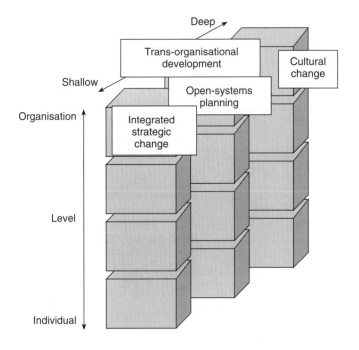

Figures 22.2–22.5 contain only a sample of the interventions that are available to change agents. The literature on the management of change is a rich source of other possibilities.

Two additional factors might also influence choice of intervention.

Time available to implement change

Where the need for change is urgent and the stakes are high there may be insufficient time to employ some of the more time-consuming interventions that offer organisational members the opportunity to be involved in deciding what needs to be changed or how the change will be achieved. It might be necessary to restrict choice to those interventions that can be implemented quickly and this might, for example, involve the use of experts who can rapidly prescribe solutions. Prescriptive/directive interventions can be effective, especially over the short term and where organisational members recognise the need for this kind of action. However, there is always the possibility that organisational members may resent the way the change was managed, experience little sense of ownership of the process or the outcome and therefore may go along with the change only so long as their behaviour is being closely supervised and there is a perceived threat of sanctions for non-compliance.

Where the need for change is less pressing, the change agent may be able to consider a much wider range of interventions.

Efficacy of interventions

A basic question that needs to be addressed when considering whether or not to choose a particular intervention is 'will it produce the intended result?' Some very popular interventions are not always as effective as many would like to believe. There are frequent reports in academic journals and the business press indicating disappointment with the outcome of major change programmes that have involved interventions such as BPR, TQM, job design or interpersonal skills training.

Sometimes the problem is that the change agents select an *ineffective intervention*. This kind of problem can be avoided by seeking evidence about the efficacy of interventions from reports, colleagues and elsewhere. Often, however, the problem is not that the intervention is ineffective, but that its success is dependent on a number of contingent factors. In these circumstances it is important to take account of these factors when selecting interventions.

There are many examples of interventions that are affected by contingent variables.

T-group training

This is a form of social skills training which provides participants with an opportunity to increase their awareness about themselves and their impact on others in order to learn how to function more effectively in groups. Some of the early evidence on the effectiveness of T-groups indicated that they can be very effective. Cooper and Mangham (1971), for example, report that they can improve skills in diagnosing individual and group behaviour, lead to clearer communication, greater tolerance and consideration and greater action skill and flexibility. However, other reports suggest that, while there is evidence of learning and behaviour change, this may not always be transferred to the work situation. Transfer is dependent on a number of factors, one of which is the 'match' between the structures and norms that characterise the work and training situations; the closer the match, the greater the transfer and vice versa.

Job design

This is another example. It is often presented as the universal answer to low commitment and poor performance in situations where people are required to perform repetitive, sort-cycle, simple tasks. Motivation theory suggests that people will be more committed and will perform best when they are engaged in varied and challenging work that (a) provides feedback about how well they are doing, (b) allows them to feel personally responsible for outcomes and (c) offers them the possibility of producing outcomes that are perceived to be worthwhile and meaningful. In practice, job design has been found to be very effective in some circumstances and not in others. One of the most important contingent variables related to the success of this intervention is the level of *need* that employees are seeking to satisfy at work. Job design appears to be most effective where employees are seeking to satisfy what Maslow (1943) referred to as the higher-order needs for personal growth and development.

TQM

This is an organisation-wide, long-term change effort designed to orient all of an organisation's activities around the concept of quality. Cummings and Worley (2001) report that in the US a survey of *Fortune* 1000 companies showed that about 75 per cent of them had implemented some form of TQM. They also report that the overwhelming majority (83 per cent) rate their experience with TQM as either positive or very positive. However, other reports of the success of TQM initiatives are less optimistic. Crosby (1979), for example, asserts that over 90 per cent of TQM interventions by US companies fail and Burnes (1996) lists a number of studies that suggest that European companies have experienced a similar rate of failure. It is not immediately obvious why TQM interventions are very successful in some settings and less so in others, but one possibility relates to the attitude of top management. In those settings where TQM is viewed in instrumental terms – for example, as a way of gaining a kite mark such as ISO 9000 that will provide competitive advantage – it may be less successful than where there is a genuine commitment to routinely meeting or exceeding customer expectations. Where the aim is merely to gain a kite mark organisational members may experience the intervention as a requirement to comply with a new set of rules. This may have little long-term affect on their values and attitudes towards customers. Also, once the kite mark has been secured top management may shift attention elsewhere, and any movement towards a more customer-focused culture may be short lived.

Where there is a need to use more than one type of intervention

Because of the nature of the problem or opportunity, systemic interdependencies and the need to maintain alignment it may often not be possible to think in terms of selecting a single intervention to respond to an isolated issue. For example, the recognition of a new opportunity and the decision, by senior management, to intervene in order to develop a strategy to exploit it might require a range of further interventions. The organisation may have to introduce a new technology, adapt its structures and systems, introduce new management practices, redesign tasks, reallocate employees to new roles and provide training to equip people to perform as required. The change agent has to decide whether to pursue all of these simultaneously or to *sequence* them in some way.

Sequencing interventions

The organisation's capacity to cope with change is often limited. Consequently decisions have to be made about *priorities* and the sequencing of interventions. Several factors can influence these decisions. These include the overall purpose or intention of the change, organisational politics, the need for an early success, the stakes involved and causal links in the change process.

Intent

Where the intention is to transform the organisation, interventions that address the *transformational variables*, such as mission and strategy, leadership, and culture, need to be given priority (see p. 331 above and Chapter 7 on diagnostic models). Where, on the other hand, the intention is to seek an incremental change, the focus of attention might be on the *transactional variables* identified by Burke and Litwin, such as structure, management practices, systems, work climate, etc. (see Chapter 7).

Politics

The change agent needs to be aware of how political factors can affect who is prepared to support different kinds of intervention. Some of the issues that relate to this have been considered elsewhere (for example, Chapter 9 on power, politics and stakeholder management, Chapter 13 on motivating others to change, and earlier in this chapter when the factors influencing the depth of intervention were considered). Other issues include:

1 *Professional orientation* Many managers have been socialised, over the course of their training and work experience, to focus attention on certain variables rather than others. For example many managers are more comfortable with interventions that focus on changing structures, technology and manufacturing and information systems rather than with interventions that focus on 'softer' people issues.

2 *Fashion and fad* can influence choice of intervention. In the 1990s many managers were keen to adopt certain interventions, such as performance- related pay, in order to be seen as progressive and attuned to the latest developments. Change agents who propose favoured interventions might receive more encouragement than those who propose an intervention that has 'gone out of fashion', even if is the most appropriate intervention to deal with the issue at hand.

3 *Past experience with certain interventions* Change agents who have a track record of success with certain interventions may be more inclined to recommend their use than interventions they are less familiar with. While it may be wise to take account of a change agent's skills and experience, other factors also need to be considered. Just because a change agent is skilled at hammering does not mean that nails are the only means of 'fixing things'. There may well be occasions when 'screws or glue' may be much more effective.

Need for an early success

It has already been noted in Chapter 9 (on power, politics and stakeholder management) that long-term change efforts can slow down if people lose their initial sense of urgency. One way of countering this is to select problems and interventions that offer the promise of some early successes.

Stakes involved

Priority needs to be given to those interventions that can resolve issues that threaten the survival of the organisation. Where survival is not an issue, priority might still be given to issues where the potential gains and losses are relatively high.

Dynamics of change

In some circumstances the dynamics of change may suggest that the best way to proceed is to adopt an indirect approach rather than addressing the prime issue or change target first:

1 *Causal links*   Consideration needs to be given to causal links and the relative strength of the inter-relationships between the elements of the organisational system. The Burke–Litwin model points to the relative strength of high-level elements such as strategy, leadership and culture over lower-level elements such as structure, systems and management practices. While culture and systems can affect one another, culture is seen to have a stronger influence over systems than vice versa. This kind of consideration can influence which elements are selected as the initial targets for change, thereby influencing the sequencing of interventions.

2 *The effect of groups on individuals*   A related dynamic relationship that can affect the sequencing of interventions is the effect that the group can exert over individual behaviour. This was discussed in Chapter 17 (on types of intervention). Research evidence suggests that there may be occasions where the most effective way of changing individual behaviour is to intervene at the level of the group. Group-level interventions, such as team building activities designed to produce a more cohesive group that has high prestige in the eyes of other organisational members, might *motivate* individuals to change their behaviour to support group goals. A follow-up intervention might involve training selected individuals to provide them with the *competencies* they might need to make a more effective contribution to group performance. If individual training had been the first intervention, it might only have had limited success because of low member motivation. After a group-level intervention, individual members might be much more highly motivated to acquire the competencies that would enable them to play a full and active part in the work of the group.

3 *The effect of attitudes on behaviour and vice versa.* There have been many debates about whether the most effective route to lasting change is to target attitudes and values first, or behaviour first. While there is support for the view that strongly held values and attitudes influence behaviour, the evidence that interventions targeted at values and atti-tudes can change behaviour is more equivocal. An alternative view is that the most effective route to lasting change is to intervene to create condi-tions that require people to behave differently because over the longer term attitudes and values will be re-aligned with the new behaviour.

Porter, Lawler and Hackman (1975) offer a third way. They suggest that an effective route to change is to intervene in ways that simultane-ously modify structures (in order to create the conditions that will elicit new and desired behaviours) *and* modify interpersonal processes (to address issues of managerial style, attitudes and the social climate of the organisation). This approach employs structural interventions to support intrapersonal and interpersonal learning.

They suggest that structural interventions might include:

(a) modifying *work* structures in order to change how individual employees actually spend most of their time
(b) modifying *control* structures in order to determine what individuals attend to
(c) modifying *reward* structures in order to influence what individuals will do when they have choice.

While there are no hard and fast rules about whether interventions should address interpersonal processes or structures first, there is a growing body of opinion that intervening to change one without the other is less effective than intervening to change both.

There is no easy formula that can be used to identify the most effective intervention for all types of situation. However, there are some useful principles that can be applied to aid the selection of appropriate interventions and assist with decisions about how they should be sequenced.

Summary

This chapter has reviewed some of the factors that need to be considered when selecting interventions. The main factors (diagnosed problem, level of change target and depth of intervention) have been integrated into a three-dimensional model to aid choice.

Attention has also been given to the factors that can affect the sequencing of interventions. These include intent or purpose of the change, organisational politics and how they affect the support for different interventions, the need for an early success to maintain motivation, the stakes involved and causal links that affect the dynamics of change.

Exercise 22.1   Choice of interventions

Review some of the change programmes that have been pursued within your organisation and, with reference to the content of this chapter, critically assess the choice of interventions.

Are you able to identify occasions when inappropriate interventions have been used?

Give reasons and suggest interventions than might have been more effective.

Notes

Exercise 22.2   Case studies

Reflect on the content of chapters 17–22 and review your approach to designing an intervention for each of the four case studies presented at the beginning
of Chapter 17. You might also consider the nature of your change strategy in the
light of the strategies considered in Chapter 15.

In the light of what you have read, would you now revise the design of any
of your proposed interventions? Why would you do this?

Learning points

References

Blake, R.R. and Mouton, J.S. (1986) *Consultation: A Handbook for Individual and
    Organization Development*, 2nd edn, Reading, MA: Addison-Wesley.
Burke, W.W. and Litwin, G.H. (1992) 'A Causal Model of Organizational Performance and
    Change', *Journal of Management*, 18 (3), pp. 523–45.
Burnes, B. (2006) *Managing Change: A Strategic Approach to Organisational Dynamics*,
    Harlow: Pearson.

Cooper, C. and Mangham, I. (1971) *T-groups: A Survey of Research*, London: Wiley.

Crosby P.B. (1979) *Quality is Free*, New York: McGraw-Hill.

Cummings, T.G. and Worley, C.G. (2001) *Organisational Development and Change*, 7th edn, Cincinnati, OH: South-Western.

Ettorre, B. (1997) 'What's the Next Management Buzzword?', *Management Review*, September, pp. 33–5.

Harrison, R. (1970) 'Choosing the Depth of Organizational Interventions', *Journal of Applied Behvioral Science*, 6 (2), pp. 182–202.

Maslow, A.H. (1943) 'A Theory of Human Motivation', *Psychology Review*, 50, pp. 370–96.

Porter, L.W., Lawler, E.E. and Hackman, J.R. (1975) *Behavior in Organizations*, London: McGraw-Hill.

Pugh, D. (1986) *Planning and Managing Change*, Milton Keynes: The Open University Press.

Schmuck, R.A. and Miles, M.B. (1971) *Organization Development in Schools*, Palo Alto, CA: National Press Books.

Staw, B. and Epstein, L.D. (2000) 'What Bandwagons Bring: Effects of Popular Management Techniques on Corporate Performance and Reputation', *Administrative Science Quarterly*, 45 (3), pp. 523–60.

Keeping the change on track

Managing change involves implementing and, where necessary, modifying plans to move the organisation towards a more desirable state. Issues associated with maintaining control during the implementation phase have already been highlighted in Chapter 16, and other issues that need to be addressed if change plans are to be successfully implemented have been considered in Chapters 9–22.

Chapter 23 addresses issues associated with managing, reviewing and sustaining change. Special attention is focused on how the process of reviewing progress can provide change managers with feedback that they can use to assess whether interventions are being implemented as intended, whether the chosen interventions are having the desired effect and whether the change plan continues to be valid.

The utility of the Balanced Scorecard as a template for designing a system for managing change is also discussed.

Keeping the change on track

Reviewing and sustaining change

This chapter focuses special attention on how the process of reviewing progress can provide change managers with feedback that they can use to assess whether interventions are being implemented as intended, whether the chosen interventions are having the desired effect and whether the change plan continues to be valid.

The utility of the Balanced Scorecard as a template for designing a system for managing change is also discussed.

Managing the implementation stage of the change process

It was noted in Chapter 5 (on process models of change) that there are two main approaches to implementation.

Implementing blueprint change

In the case of blueprint change the desired end state is known in advance and change managers are in a position to formulate a clear plan of action to achieve this vision. Implementation involves rolling out this plan, monitoring the effect of interventions and taking corrective action as and when required in order to ensure that the desired end state is achieved. Change managers do not typically think in terms of re-examining the validity of the blueprint or the assumptions that underpin the change plan designed to achieve the desired end state.

The learning associated with this kind of change tends to be restricted to single-loop learning. Assumptions about what needs to be changed and assumptions about how the change will be achieved tend to go unchallenged unless the feedback from implementation is so unexpected that it shocks the change managers into making a radical re-assessment.

Implementing evolutionary change

In the case of evolutionary change it may be difficult or impossible to specify an end point in advance. Change managers have to develop an implementation plan on the basis of broadly defined goals and a general direction for change. Sometimes, because of a high rate of change in the operating environment, ideas about the desired future state have to be constantly revised, even in those cases where the original vision has been defined in only the broadest of terms.

In such circumstances, change managers have to adopt a very open-ended approach to planning and implementation. Managing evolutionary change involves taking tentative incremental steps and, after each step, reviewing the intervention(s) that constituted that step (did it/they work as planned?) and the general direction of change (does it still hold good or does it need to be revised?). This questioning of the validity of the desired future state and the plan for achieving it calls for double-loop learning.

Monitoring the implementation of the change plan

A plan for change reflects a set of hypotheses about cause and effect. Kaplan and Norton (1996) view the measurement and review process as a means of making these hypothesised relationships explicit. They argue that once they are clearly articulated and widely understood the change process can be more easily managed. The process of managing change involves validating or, where necessary, revising the assumptions and hypotheses that underpin the change plan. The desired future state (vision) is reflected in the outcome measures embedded in the change plan. *Performance drivers* are the variables that determine whether the desired outcome will be achieved. Specifying these in the change plan signals to organisational members what they need to do in order to contribute to the achievement of the desired future state.

Some of the questions that need to be addressed when managing change and validating the hypothesised cause and effect relationships that underpin the change plan are considered below.

Are interventions being implemented as intended?

Sometimes it is more difficult than anticipated to roll out a plan for change. The change manager may respond by reviewing the situation and identifying those factors that have hindered implementation first time round. These might include a lack of commitment and motivation on the part of those immediately affected by a proposed intervention, a lack of political support from those in a position to champion or sabotage the change, or insufficient resources to ensure that the change initiative gets the attention it requires. The content of previous chapters points to ways of addressing these kinds of problem.

Are interventions producing the desired effect?

Change managers need to be alert to the possibility that while the intervention might have been implemented as intended, it might not be producing the effect that was anticipated. An example will illustrate this possibility and indicate ways in which the change manager might address the situation:

1   A company might be losing market share because it is lagging behind competitors in the time it takes to bring new products to market.
2   A factor contributing to this predicament might be diagnosed as the high level of conflict between members of the product engineering department (responsible for developing new products) and members of the production engineering department (responsible for developing the manufacturing system required to produce a new product).
3   Informed by this diagnosis, the change manager might send members of both departments on a variety of external courses to learn about inter-group dynamics and the management of conflict.
4   After monitoring the effect of this intervention, the change manager might discover that while members of both departments are much more aware of constructive ways of behaving in conflict situations, this awareness has had little effect on the level of manifest conflict between the two departments.

An initial response might be to explore ways of modifying the original intervention in order to make it more effective – for example, by seeking out opportunities to improve the transfer of learning from the training activity to the work situation:

•   Rather than sending individuals on external courses the change manager might decide to facilitate an in-house workshop that involves members of both departments working together to identify ways of managing their differences in a more constructive way.

If modifying the original intervention in this way still fails to produce the desired effect on the targeted performance driver (the quality of inter-departmental relationships) the change manager might begin to question the assumed cause and effect relationship between poor conflict management skills and high levels of inter-departmental conflict. This questioning might point to other possible causes of the immediate problem (high levels of inter-departmental conflict) and lead the change manager to consider ways of modifying the change plan to include interventions that target them:

•   It might be found that the original diagnosis was valid in so far as it identified the level of inter-departmental conflict as a major cause of delay in getting new products to market (and, therefore, of loss of market share). However, it may have been flawed when it focused on poor conflict management skills as the root cause of this damaging behaviour.

- A re-examination of the situation might suggest that the main source of conflict is rooted in the way the company is structured. This broad heading could include a number of possible causal factors. One might be the siting of work-groups in locations that make it difficult for members of one department to communicate on a face-to-face basis with members of the other. Another might be mis-aligned performance criteria that results in competing sets of priorities in the two departments.

This questioning of the taken-for-granted cause-and-effect assumptions involves a process of double-loop learning.

Is the change plan still valid?

There may be occasions where the interventions have been implemented as intended and where the interventions have produced the desired effect. However, this chain of events may have had little or no impact on overall organisational performance. This kind of outcome poses another challenge to the validity of the change plan and the hypothesised cause-and-effect relationships on which it is based. Faced with this kind of outcome, the change manager may decide to embark on a further re-examination of the original diagnosis and the causal models that were used to inform the design of the change plan:

- This further re-examination might reveal that, despite what many managers in the company accept as given wisdom, improvements in the time it takes to get new products to market may have had little effect on the gradual decline in market share. Further investigations might suggest that customers are more concerned about other value propositions such as product reliability, price and so on and might feel that competitors are better able to satisfy their needs in these areas.
- On the other hand, it may be that the further investigations reveal that the original diagnosis was correct at the time, but has been overtaken by new developments (for example, changes in customer requirements) that challenge its validity, with obvious implications for the change plan.

There may also be (hopefully, many) occasions when the interventions have been implemented as intended, where they have produced the desired effect and where this has had a positive impact on organisational performance. This kind of positive outcome signals a need to consolidate this achievement and use it, as appropriate, as a basis for achieving further improvements in performance.

The role of performance measures in the management of change

Some of the issues that encourage or inhibit learning are considered in Chapter 4 (on organisational learning and organisational effectiveness). This chapter focuses attention on how the cycle of monitoring, reviewing, planning, acting and further reviewing can facilitate double-loop learning during the process of managing change. Central to this process is the collecting and feeding back of information about how interventions affect performance.

Attention has already been given to some of the different ways in which performance can be measured (see Chapter 2 on organisation effectiveness and the role of change management). It is essential that performance measures should be related to the outcomes that are important to key stakeholders and to the hypotheses about cause-and-effect relationships that are embedded in the change plan. Without the feedback that such measures can provide, change managers will be unable to monitor what is going on and determine what further action may be required to successfully implement the change plan.

Approaches to measuring performance

It was noted in Chapter 16 (on maintaining control during the change) that many control systems are designed to reward current practice and offer little incentive for people to invest effort in changing the organisation to promote long-term effectiveness. Even in those organisations where change is given a high priority, the monitoring and feedback process may focus attention on only a limited set of performance measures. Many organisations direct most of their attention to financial measures. Often too little attention is given to other performance indicators that relate to important outcomes and key cause-and-effect relationships that are central to the change plan.

One of the early attempts to widen the base of performance monitoring on an organisation-wide and systematic basis was the development, by Analog Devices, of a 'Corporate Scorecard'. This included, alongside a number of traditional financial measures, measures of customer delivery time, quality and cycle times of manufacturing processes and effectiveness of new product development.

Kaplan and Norton (2004) report that they became interested in new ways of monitoring performance when they recognised the importance of knowledge-based assets, such as employees and information technology, as determinants of competitive success. They believe that managers and others pay attention to what is measured and that they are not good at managing that which is not measured. If they are to manage, develop and mobilise the organisation's intangible assets, managers need a performance management system that measures how these assets are used. This led them to develop what is now referred to as the 'Balanced Scorecard'.

The Balanced Scorecard

The Balance Scorecard (Kaplan and Norton, 1996) integrates financial measures of past performance with measures of the 'drivers' of future performance. It provides a template that can be adapted to provide the information that change managers need to monitor and review the effects of their interventions and to plan what they might do next to move the organisation towards a more desirable future state. The Scorecard includes four categories of measure: financial, customer, internal business process and innovation and learning:

- *Financial measures,* such as return on investment, economic value added, sales growth and generation of cash flow, summarise the economic consequences of past actions. This financial perspective considers how the organisation needs to appear to its shareholders if it is to achieve its vision.
- *Customer-related measures* include indicators of business performance that relate to the customer and market segments that are important to the organisation. Examples include measures of satisfaction, retention, new customer acquisition, customer profitability, account share and market share. They might also include measures of those performance drivers that affect the value propositions that influence customer loyalty, such as on-time delivery and product innovation. This customer perspective considers how the organisation needs to appear to its customers if it is to achieve its vision.
- *Internal business processes measures* such as quality, response time and cost relate to the internal business processes that make a critical contribution to the organisation's current and future performance. They might measure the performance of the processes that enable the organisation to deliver value propositions that attract and retain important customers, that satisfy shareholders by contributing to the delivery of excellent financial returns or that deliver other outcomes that are important to key stakeholders.
- *Measures of the infrastructure that facilitates long-term growth and improvement* Kaplan and Norton (1996) argue that organisational learning and growth comes from three principle sources: people, systems and organisational procedures. They suggest that the financial, customer and internal business process objectives of the Balanced Scorecard typically reveal large gaps between the existing capabilities of people, systems and procedures and the capability that is required to achieve a performance breakthrough. In order to transform an organisation (or even to

achieve a more modest level of change) these gaps have to be addressed. This can involve intervening in the normal process of organisational functioning to enhance this infrastructure and improve the organisation's capacity for innovation and learning.

Developing tools to help with implementation

The Balanced Scorecard approach can be adapted to focus on those performance drivers and measures that are identified as important in specific situations and used as a change management tool to clarify and gain consensus about the change strategy.

This kind of tool can help managers articulate and communicate their strategy for change. It might, for example, be based on a hypothesised relationship between employee satisfaction, customer satisfaction, financial performance and sustained growth. Translating the vision and strategy into operational goals can stimulate the kind of debate that will help ensure that the change strategy is shared, tested and understood. Specifying operational goals can help everybody concerned think about the plan for change in systematic terms and can facilitate the development of a shared view of how and why the various change goals are related in terms of cause-and-effect (Figure 23.1).

The feedback that this kind of tool can provide on how the organisation (or unit of an organisation) is performing will enable change managers to test the validity of the cause-and-effect relationships embedded in the change plan.

The employee satisfaction-profit cause-and-effect chain is only one of many possible change hypotheses but it has been found to be related to organisational performance in a number of studies. Heskett, Jones and Loveman (1994) argue that customer satisfaction is a critical intervening

Figure 23.1 Translating the change strategy into a set of operational goals

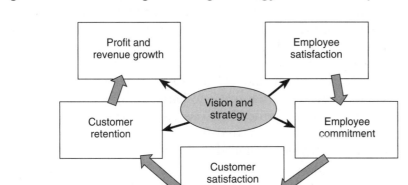

Figure 23.2   The service–profit chain

variable in the employee attitude-profit relationship. Their work has stimu-lated a lot of interest in the service-profit chain (Figure 23.2).

The basic premise is that employee satisfaction is positively related to employee commitment and that increased commitment promotes customer satisfaction and motivates customers to stay with the company longer and recommend the company's products and services to others. This, in turn, stimulates revenue growth and profitability.

Kaplan and Norton cite the example of Echo Engineering where change managers were able to test and validate their assumption that employee morale was a key performance driver. They found that employee morale correlated with a number of important performance indicators. For exam-ple, they found that the most satisfied customers were those who were served by the employees with highest morale. They also found that the most satisfied customers were the ones who settled their accounts in the shortest period.

Several studies report findings that suggest that favourable employee perceptions are related to superior business performance. Koys (2001) found that level of employee satisfaction and commitment in a chain of restaurants was positively related to profitability. Gelade and Young (2005) cite a meta-analysis by Harter, Schmidt and Hayes (2002) of 7,939 work units in thirty-six companies that found small but significant correlations between business unit productivity and profitability, and a composite of items they labelled 'employee engagement'. They also cite a study by Patterson, Warr and West (2004) that reports significant associations between company climate and productivity in a sample of forty-two manufacturing companies.

Management tools such as the Balanced Scorecard not only facilitate the development of a shared view of how and why the various change goals are related in terms of cause-and-effect, but can also help change managers communicate their plan for change throughout the organisation and provide a framework for consultation and debate about what a more desirable future state will look like and what needs to happen if it is to be achieved.

This kind of management tool can also help to ensure that the range of change initiatives that might be started in different units and at different levels in the organisation will be aligned to contribute to the strategic goals of the change programme.

This approach, based on the concept of the Balanced Scorecard, is presented here as one example of a tool that can help change managers manage the change process. In any change programme plans have to be operationalised and communicated widely. Furthermore targets for change have to be specified as clearly as possible if progress is to be monitored and if the change plan is to be kept under review and adjusted as circumstances require.

Sustaining the change

Managing change rarely involves moving from one steady state to another and Lewin's goal of 're-freezing' seldom, if ever, involves achieving a new state that will last indefinitely. However, the goal of change normally involves more than just reaching a desired future state. If change managers fail to give sufficient attention to sustaining the change, at least until they are ready to lead the organisation into a phase of further adjustment or transformation, the new situation may be short-lived and may drift back towards its previous condition. Buchanan *et al.* (2005) observe that for many organisations it is a strategic imperative to embed change in order to achieve a new level of organisational effectiveness, but that in many situations this goal is frustrated by 'initiative decay' or what the NHS Modernisation Agency (2002) refer to as the 'improvement evaporation effect'. They go on to argue that sustainability may be defined in different ways, ranging from relatively static to more dynamic conceptualisations. For example it 'may concern the stability of work methods, or the consistent achievement of performance goals independent of the methods deployed, or the development of a consistent trajectory of changes generating performance improvement beyond initial expectations'. But all of these definitions embrace some notion of 'stickability' and the avoidance of initiative decay.

On the basis of a thorough review of the literature, Buchanan *et al.* (2005) identify ten categories of factors that interact in different ways to affect sustainability, such as the scale and type of change; individual commitment and competencies, managerial style; the quality of leadership; organisational culture; political processes and the like. The relative importance of these factors is determined by context. For example, a management style that elicits enthusiastic commitment in one setting may trigger cynicism, resentment and a lack of support for change in another. Consequently Buchanan *et al.* (2005) are unable to offer change managers any simple prescription for sustaining change. However, they do point to three issues that seem to affect the extent of initiative decay. The first relates to how the change is perceived. Is it peripheral or central to organisational performance, and is it perceived as acceptable or threatening by key stakeholders? Often change managers can influence the way a change is perceived and this will have consequences for sustainability. The second relates to how the change is implemented. As noted above, there is no one implantation process that will be effective in all settings but doing everything possible to identify and adopt an appropriate process can affect whether or not the change will be sustained. The third issue is the timing, sequencing and pacing of the change process. For example, while a relaxed timetable might help people digest the need for change, delays can undermine commitment and divert attention to other pressing issues. On the other hand when a change is rushed people may not feel involved and a succession of change initiatives may lead to 'initiative fatigue'.

Several writers (Beckhard and Harris, 1987; Nadler, 1993) argue that tailored feedback mechanisms can not only facilitate monitoring and control during the transition phase of a change, but can also be effective in helping to sustain change. Change managers can work with operational managers (who will have ongoing responsibility for day-to-day management) to design and introduce feedback mechanisms that they can use for themselves to monitor and manage the situation over the longer term.

Summary

This chapter has considered how monitoring and reviewing the implementation of the change plan can help managers adjust and adapt the plan for change to help ensure that the organisation moves towards a more desirable future state.

Attention has been given to the kind of information change managers need in order to, at one level, determine whether interventions are being implemented as intended and assess whether they are having the anticipated effect and, at a higher level, to assess whether the change plan continues to be valid. Assessing the continued validity of the change plan, and updating it as required, is especially important when managing evolutionary type change.

It has been argued that change managers need to identify measures of organisation effectiveness that relate to those outcomes that are important to the organisation's long-term survival and growth: this might involve attending to more than just the short term interests of shareholders.

It has also been argued that, when monitoring the effectiveness of interventions, attention needs to be paid to the hypotheses of cause and effect that have influenced the design of the change plan. Where feedback raises questions about the validity of these hypothesised relationships the change manager needs to review the change plan and consider whether alternative ways of intervening to move the organisation towards a more desirable future state might be more effective.

The Balanced Scorecard has been considered as an example of a management tool that can help the manager attend to these points when managing change.

References

Beckhard, R. and Harris, R.T. (1987) *Organizational Transitions: Managing Complex Change*, Reading, MA: Addison-Wesley.

Buchanan, D., Ketley, D., Gollop, R., Jones, J.L., Lamont, S.S., Neath, A. and Whitby, E. (2005) 'No Going Back: A Review of the Literature on Sustaining Organizational Change', *International Journal of Management Reviews*, 7 (3), pp. 189–205.

Gelade, G.A. and Young, S. (2005) 'Test of a Service Profit Chain Model in the Retail Banking Sector', *Journal of Occupational and Organizational Psychology*, 78 (1), pp. 1–22.

Harter, J. K., Schmidt, F. L. and Hayes, T. L. (2002) 'Business-Unit-Level Relationship between Employee Satisfaction, Employee Engagement, and Business Outcomes: A Meta-Analysis', *Journal of Applied Psychology*, 87, pp. 268–79.

Heskett, J.L., Jones, T.O. and Loveman, G.W. (1994) 'Putting the Service-Profit Chain to Work', *Harvard Business Review*, 74 (2), pp. 164–70.

Kaplan, P. and Norton, D.P. (1996) *The Balanced Scorecard*, Boston, MA: Harvard Business School Press.

Kaplan, P. and Norton, D.P. (2004) *Strategy Maps: Converting Intangible Assets into Tangible Outcomes,* Boston, MA: Harvard Business School Press.

Koys, D.J. (2001) 'The Effects of Employee Satisfaction, Organizational Citizenship Behaviour and Turnover on Organizational Effectiveness: A Unit-Level, Longitudinal Study', *Personnel Psychology*, 54, pp. 101–14.

Nadler, D.A. (1993) 'Concepts for the Management of Organisational Change', in C. Mabey and B. Mayon-White (eds), *Managing Change*, London: Paul Chapman, in association with the Open University.

NHS Modernisation Agency (2002) *Improving Leaders' Guide to Sustainability and Spread*, Ipswich: Ancient House Printing Group.

Patterson, M., Warr, R. and West, M.A. (2004) 'Organizational Climate and Company Productivity: The Role of Employee Affect and Employee Level', *Journal of Occupational and Organizational Psychology*, 77, pp. 193–216.

Developing and maintaining helping relationships

Lippitt, Watson and Westley (1958) observed that most change agents are oriented to two objectives. The first is to select and/or design interventions which will help client systems solve problems and deliver desirable change. This objective is addressed throughout the book but especially in Part V which considers a wide range of interventions such as process reengineering, action research and high-performance management. The change agents' second objective is to develop and maintain an appropriate relationship between themselves and their client system so that the client will willingly acknowledge and use the resources they offer. This final part of the book addresses the issue of developing and maintaining an appropriate helping relationship.

Chapter 24 explores the helping skills required by effective change agents. Attention is focused on intervention styles – high-level approaches to facilitating change. Reference is made to other levels of behaviour but these are considered in much more detail elsewhere (see Hayes, 2002). The intervention Style Indicator provides you with the opportunity to assess your own style of intervening.

Chapter 25 presents a six-stage model of helping and facilitating that is designed to provide you with a cognitive map that will help you understand your relationship with clients, and give you a sense of direction when thinking about ways of facilitating change.

References

Hayes, J. (2002) *Interpersonal Skills at Work*, 2nd edn, Hove: Routledge.
Lippitt, R., Watson, J. and Westley, B. (1958) *The Dynamics of Planned Change*, New York: Harcourt, Brace & World.

Modes of intervening

There are many ways in which change agents can intervene to facilitate change. Blake and Mouton (1986) argue that even where the change agents have correctly diagnosed the issue or problem that is of concern to the client, their efforts may not be successful if they adopt an *inappropriate* mode of intervening.

When people think about change agents, they often only think about external consultants, but within organisations there are many people who occupy roles that are almost exclusively concerned with facilitating change. Examples include systems analysts, business development advisors, OR people, management development specialists, trainers, project managers and the transition managers referred to in Chapter 16. Often the role of transition manager is a temporary role, but there are many managers who, as part of their normal day-to-day responsibilities, intervene to facilitate change. They intervene to facilitate the introduction of new working practices, to find ways of reducing costs, to help staff develop better relationships with customers, to help others identify and exploit opportunities offered by changing circumstances, or to help colleagues who are experiencing problems that are affecting their performance or general wellbeing. Throughout this chapter all those who facilitate change will be referred to as 'change agents' or 'helpers' and those who are being helped (be they colleagues, subordinates, or clients in the more conventional sense) will be referred to as 'clients'.

Paraphrasing Mangham (1986), the successful change agents are those who can conduct themselves in the complexity of the organisation as subtle, insightful, incisive performers. They require a highly developed ability to read the actual and potential behaviour of others around them and to construct their own conduct in accordance with this reading. This is an ability we all have to a greater or lesser extent but, according to Mangham, 'the most successful among us appear to do social life with a higher degree of skill than the rest of us manage'.

Much has been written about the skills required by change agents. Greiner and Metzger (1983) refer to a wide range of skills, but argue that consulting is essentially a human enterprise and, irrespective of whether the problem being addressed concerns a new accounting system or the need for better strategic planning, the success of the project will be largely determined by the quality of the change agents' interaction with the client or client group. Margerison

(2000) echoes this view and highlights the importance of personal and interpersonal skills.

The hierarchical nature of interpersonal skills

Social skill, according to Argyle (1994) and others, has a *hierarchical structure* in which the larger, higher-level units consist of integrated sequences and groupings of lower-level units. Wright and Taylor (1994) identify three levels in this hierarchy: primary components, structure and style.

1 *Primary components*   These are at the lowest level of the hierarchy and are what we actually say and do; our verbal and non-verbal behaviours. Skilled change agents are those who, at this level, have a wide range of verbal components (for example, questions and statement types) at their disposal and are able to select the one most appropriate to the situation and purpose at hand. They are also able to perform it well with the appropriate non-verbal cues.
2 *Structure*   This is the next level up, and refers to the way we sequence the primary components of behaviour. At this level, interpersonally skilled change agents are those who can organise and integrate the primary components into purposeful sequences which steer the interaction towards their objective. For example, in a problem solving interview this might involve adopting a 'funnel sequence' of questions which begins with very open questions and then progresses towards more closed ones.
3 *Style*   This is the highest level in the hierarchy. The primary components change agents use in an interaction and the way in which these are structured will depend, at least in part, on the type of interaction they intend to have with clients. Skilled change agents are those who are able to develop an approach to the interaction that is congruent with both their objectives and with the probable reactions of the others involved. For example, managers who want to help members of their team become more effective may decide to adopt a helping style that involves helping them to help themselves. They might place a high priority on empowering them to experiment and learn from their own mistakes and they might deliberately resist the temptation to 'take them by the hand' and tell them precisely what they need to do to improve their performance. Some change agents may choose to behave this way because they believe that a more prescriptive approach to helping would encourage others to become too dependent on their guidance and advice and that this would inhibit their learning.

This hierarchical model highlights the possibility of adopting a range of different styles and component behaviours, and focuses attention on the value of identifying ways of relating, in particular situations, which will contribute to the achievement of desired outcomes. Being supportive and avoiding confrontation or consulting and collaborating might be effective in some circumstances, but not in others. For example, in those situations where people do not share a common goal or, because of a crisis, where there is insufficient time for consultation, the most effective helping style might be directive and involve telling other people what to do.

This chapter focuses attention on intervention styles – high-level approaches to facilitating change. Reference is made to other levels of behaviour but these are considered in much more detail elsewhere (see Hayes, 2002).

Intervention styles

Change agents can intervene to help in many different ways. The Intervention Style Indicator in Exercise 24.1 has been designed to help you identify your preferred approach to facilitating change. You might find it useful to complete it now and refer back to your intervention style profile as you read on. It will provide you with a point of reference when thinking about how you might improve the effectiveness of your helping interventions.

Exercise 24.1   The Intervention Style Indicator

Five cases (problem situations) are presented and, for each case, there are five examples of how a change agent/helper could respond. For *each* of the five responses to each case, circle the number on the scale that most closely reflects the probability that you would use that response. For example:

NEVER USE → | 1 | ② | 3 | 4 | 5 | ← DEFINITELY USE

There are no 'right' or 'wrong' answers.

Case A

A newly appointed supervisor has complained to you that her subordinates are hostile, moody, only hear what they choose to hear and often fail to obey instructions. She likened their behaviour to rebellious school children who are determined to 'break' the new teacher. Her account placed all the blame for the rapidly deteriorating situation on to her subordinates. You had not expected this kind of conversation because she had joined the company with glowing references and a ten-year record of successful people management. In addition, her work group has never created problems before. All of them have been with the company for at least ten months, most are very well qualified and two have recently been through the company's assessment centre and identified as having potential for promotion.

How likely is it that you would use each of the following responses?
(Circle one number on each of the five scales)

1 Introduce the supervisor to a theory that might help her better understand the situation. For example, you might explain the basics of transactional analysis and ask her to (a) apply it to her problem and consider whether her subordinates see her as a controlling parent dealing with a group of inexperienced children rather than an adult interacting with other competent adults, and (b) speculate how she might apply the theory to improve the situation.

A1 NEVER USE →

1	2	3	4	5

← DEFINITELY USE

2 Tell her that she has failed to recognise the quality of her subordinates, that she is under-valuing the contribution they can make and that she needs to delegate more and give them greater responsibility.

A2 NEVER USE →

1	2	3	4	5

← DEFINITELY USE

3 Listen carefully and attempt to see the problem through her eyes, in the hope that by being supportive you can encourage her to open up and tell her story, which in turn may help her to develop a better understanding of the problem and what needs to be done about it.

A3 NEVER USE →

1	2	3	4	5

← DEFINITELY USE

4 Suggest to her that it may not only be her subordinates who hear what they choose to hear and ask her if she has really paid attention to all the messages she has been sent by the members of her work group.

A4 NEVER USE →

1	2	3	4	5

← DEFINITELY USE

5 Help her to get to the bottom of the problem by assisting her to gather more information which she can use to develop a better understanding of what is going on and what can be done to improve matters.

A5 NEVER USE →

1	2	3	4	5

← DEFINITELY USE

Case B

You have been approached by the head of a strategic business unit (SBO) in your organisation with a request for help. She has been in post for six months and has come to the view that the way her top team is working together is adversely affecting performance.

How likely is it that you would use each of the following responses?
(Circle one number on each of the five scales)

1 Offer to collect information from people who are affected by how well the team is performing and feed this back to her and her senior colleagues to

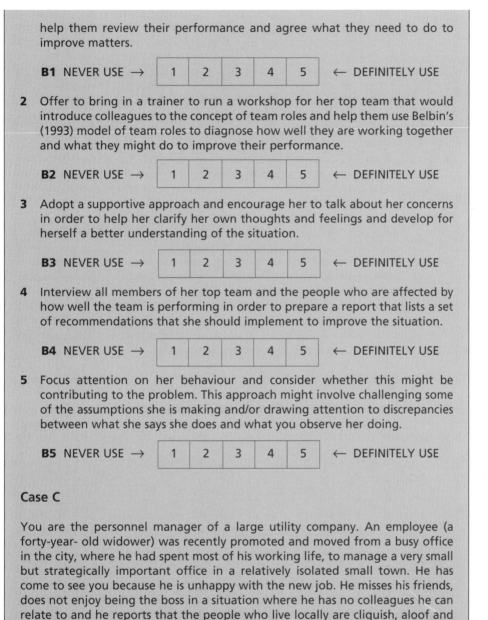

help them review their performance and agree what they need to do to improve matters.

B1 NEVER USE → | 1 | 2 | 3 | 4 | 5 | ← DEFINITELY USE

2 Offer to bring in a trainer to run a workshop for her top team that would introduce colleagues to the concept of team roles and help them use Belbin's (1993) model of team roles to diagnose how well they are working together and what they might do to improve their performance.

B2 NEVER USE → | 1 | 2 | 3 | 4 | 5 | ← DEFINITELY USE

3 Adopt a supportive approach and encourage her to talk about her concerns in order to help her clarify her own thoughts and feelings and develop for herself a better understanding of the situation.

B3 NEVER USE → | 1 | 2 | 3 | 4 | 5 | ← DEFINITELY USE

4 Interview all members of her top team and the people who are affected by how well the team is performing in order to prepare a report that lists a set of recommendations that she should implement to improve the situation.

B4 NEVER USE → | 1 | 2 | 3 | 4 | 5 | ← DEFINITELY USE

5 Focus attention on her behaviour and consider whether this might be contributing to the problem. This approach might involve challenging some of the assumptions she is making and/or drawing attention to discrepancies between what she says she does and what you observe her doing.

B5 NEVER USE → | 1 | 2 | 3 | 4 | 5 | ← DEFINITELY USE

Case C

You are the personnel manager of a large utility company. An employee (a forty-year- old widower) was recently promoted and moved from a busy office in the city, where he had spent most of his working life, to manage a very small but strategically important office in a relatively isolated small town. He has come to see you because he is unhappy with the new job. He misses his friends, does not enjoy being the boss in a situation where he has no colleagues he can relate to and he reports that the people who live locally are cliquish, aloof and unfriendly.

How likely is it that you would use each of the following responses?
(Circle one number on each of the five scales)

1 Tell him that there is a vacancy at his old grade in the department he used to work in and indicate that you think that the best solution would be for him to move back.

C1 NEVER USE → | 1 | 2 | 3 | 4 | 5 | ← DEFINITELY USE

2 Explore how he feels about the situation without passing judgement or jumping to conclusions. Make sure that you really understand why he is unhappy and do every thing you can to help him clarify his own feelings about what the problem might be. You might listen hard to what he has to say and then reflect back to him the essence of what you think you heard. For example, 'What you seem to be saying is . . . Have I got it right?'

C2 NEVER USE → | 1 | 2 | 3 | 4 | 5 | ← DEFINITELY USE

3 Help him adopt a balanced problem solving approach and encourage him to thoroughly explore every aspect of the problem and, where necessary, gather information that might help him identify and evaluate possible solutions. (For example by helping him identify opportunities to meet new people.)

C3 NEVER USE → | 1 | 2 | 3 | 4 | 5 | ← DEFINITELY USE

4 Give him the kind of feedback that might push him into taking a new initiative, for example by telling him that you have listened to what he has said and not once heard him mention anything that he has actually done to try to make new friends. (All he seems to do is moan about others and complain that they do nothing to make him welcome.) You might try to encourage him into action by asking him if he has thought about what he might do that would make others want to get to know him better.

C4 NEVER USE → | 1 | 2 | 3 | 4 | 5 | ← DEFINITELY USE

5 Lend him a copy of Dale Carnigie's (1936) book *How to Win Friends and Influence People* and suggest that if he could master some of the techniques and skills it contains then making friends might be something which he could do more easily.

C5 NEVER USE → | 1 | 2 | 3 | 4 | 5 | ← DEFINITELY USE

Case D

The CEO of a fast-growing software company has approached you for help following the second time within twelve months that a project team has failed to deliver a major project within budget and on time. She told you that on both occasions similar problems appeared to have been associated with the failures. She also told you that relationships between members of the project team have deteriorated and they all appear to be blaming each other for the failures.

How likely is it that you would use each of the following responses?
(Circle one number on each of the five scales)

1 Interview the CEO and the manager in charge of the project team to ensure that you have a good understanding of what happened before advising the CEO what she should do to ensure that in future projects will be managed more efficiently and effectively.

D1 NEVER USE → | 1 | 2 | 3 | 4 | 5 | ← DEFINITELY USE

2   Run a workshop on new approaches to managing projects and use the models presented to help team members review the way they managed the last two projects and identify lessons that they might use to inform the way they will manage the next project.

D2 NEVER USE → | 1 | 2 | 3 | 4 | 5 | ← DEFINITELY USE

3   Talk to each member of the team individually in order to help them express any frustrations, anxieties or other feelings that might be inhibiting their ability to make an objective assessment of the situation.

D3 NEVER USE → | 1 | 2 | 3 | 4 | 5 | ← DEFINITELY USE

4   Interview all members of the project team and other stakeholders in order to identify key issues related to the failures and then convene a workshop where you can feed this information back and use it to stimulate a discussion of the problem and help them explore ways of improving their performance.

D4 NEVER USE → | 1 | 2 | 3 | 4 | 5 | ← DEFINITELY USE

5   Work with the CEO to help her clarify the issues she wants to raise with the project team, and then facilitate a meeting where she can confront members with her concerns.

D5 NEVER USE → | 1 | 2 | 3 | 4 | 5 | ← DEFINITELY USE

Case E

A colleague has come to you for help. He does not want to be an autocratic boss and believes that people work best when they are given the freedom to get on with their job. However his department is beginning to get itself a reputation for not getting it right. He has explained that while he always tries to pursue an 'open-door' policy there are some people who never cross his threshold. Consequently he is badly informed and avoidable mistakes have been made. He is obviously upset and you suspect that his boss has just had him in and torn a strip off him.

How likely is it that you would use each of the following responses?
(Circle one number on each of the five scales)

1   Share with him a similar problem you once had and tell him what you did about it. Also, suggest that there can come a time when democracy has to go out of the window and you have to read the riot act. And that is what he should do now.

E1 NEVER USE → | 1 | 2 | 3 | 4 | 5 | ← DEFINITELY USE

2 Tell him about a theory you are familiar with that argues that the best style of leadership might vary from one situation to another, and suggest that one way forward might be for him to consider whether his current style appears to be a 'best fit' or whether the theory would suggest an alternative leadership style.

E2 NEVER USE → | 1 | 2 | 3 | 4 | 5 | ← DEFINITELY USE

3 On the basis of what you have observed, challenge his view that he always operates an 'open-door' policy. You might, for example, tell him that you have heard that he is never around when he is needed. Also that while he might believe he is approachable others see him as aloof and distant. You might follow this up by asking him to consider how true this is.

E3 NEVER USE → | 1 | 2 | 3 | 4 | 5 | ← DEFINITELY USE

4 You can see that he is upset so decide that the best thing you can do is to sit him down with a cup of coffee and let him get it off his chest.

E4 NEVER USE → | 1 | 2 | 3 | 4 | 5 | ← DEFINITELY USE

5 Help him identify some specific circumstances where things have gone wrong and then question him about a number of these problems to sort out precisely what happened and whether there are any patterns that he could do something about.

E5 NEVER USE → | 1 | 2 | 3 | 4 | 5 | ← DEFINITELY USE

Scoring

In the grid below all of the available responses to each case have been arranged into columns that reflect five different styles of helping.

- Taking each case in turn, enter the *number you circled* for each response alongside the appropriate response code in the grid. For example, for case A, you may have circled 2 for response A1, so enter '2' in the square for A1; and you may have circled 5 for response A2, so enter '5' in the square for A2, and so on.

Note that for cases B–E the response codes are presented in different sequences and are not arranged in order from 1 to 5.

- Calculate the total score for each column and enter this in the box provided.

The total score for each column indicates your relative preference for the different helping styles.

Response grid

	THEORISING	ADVISING	SUPPORTING	CHALLENGING	INFORMATION GATHERING
Case A	A1 ☐	A2 ☐	A3 ☐	A4 ☐	A5 ☐

(Note that from B to E the response codes are not arranged in order from 1 to 5)

Case B	B2 ☐	B4 ☐	B3 ☐	B5 ☐	B1 ☐
Case C	C5 ☐	C1 ☐	C2 ☐	C4 ☐	C3 ☐
Case D	D2 ☐	D1 ☐	D3 ☐	D5 ☐	D4 ☐
Case E	E2 ☐	E1 ☐	E4 ☐	E3 ☐	E5 ☐
TOTAL	☐	☐	☐	☐	☐

You should now have a score for all five modes of intervening. Note whether your scores are equally spread across all five intervention styles or whether your response pattern indicates that you prefer to use one or two approaches much more than the other modes of intervening.

The goal of intervening

Egan (1988) argues that the management of change is not about planning or action but about *achieving results* – system-enhancing outcomes such as innovations realised, problems managed more effectively, opportunities developed or new organisation-enhancing behaviours in place.

Change agents intervene to facilitate change. Blake and Mouton (1986) describe their interventions as a cycle-breaking endeavour. They argue that behaviour tends to be cyclical in character – that is, sequences of behaviour are repeated within specific time periods or within particular contexts or settings. Some of these patterns of behaviour are advantageous to the client or client group but some do little to promote their interests and may even be harmful. They go on to argue that individuals, groups or larger client systems (such as entire organisations) may engage in behaviour cycles by force of habit: they may not be conscious of the possibility of harmful or self-defeating consequences. They may be aware that things are not going well, but they may not understand why or what they could do to improve matters. The change agent's function is to help clients identify and break out of these damaging kinds of cycles.

This cycle-breaking endeavour can take many forms. It can be prescriptive or collaborative. Egan (2004) argues that problem management and opportunity development is not something that helpers do to clients. He advocates a collaborative approach that involves clients achieving their goals through the facilitation of the helper (change agent). However, much of the help offered by external consultants and internal change agents is not collaborative in nature.

Prescriptive modes of intervening

The mode of intervening referred to as 'advising' on the Intervention Style Indicator is prescriptive. Many change agents intervene by giving advice and telling their clients what to do in order to rectify problems or develop opportunities. Change agents who adopt this mode of intervening assume that they have a greater level of relevant expertise than their clients and can discern their real needs. They also appear to assume that clients lack the necessary competence either to make a sound diagnosis or to plan corrective actions for themselves.

In many circumstances consultants or senior managers can see a solution because they are more experienced than their clients/subordinates, but if they intervene by offering advice and telling people what to do they deprive them of the opportunity to learn how to solve the problem for themselves. Clients can become dependent on the change agent and the next time they experience a difficulty they again have to seek help.

Often clients actively seek advice, especially when they are under great pressure to find a solution and/or when they are at their wits' end. Steele (1969) argues that the needs of both the client and the change agent may propel the change agent towards exclusive occupancy of the role of expert in their relationship and that in those circumstances where the client accepts the change agent as expert there may be some benefits. However, he also identifies some costs. One is the increased dependency, which has already been mentioned, and the other has to do with the change agent's neglect of the clients' knowledge about their own problem. Even where clients do not attempt to withhold this knowledge the helper may choose to ignore it:

> The client often has great wisdom (intuitive if not systematic) about many aspects of his own situation, and an overweighing of the consultant's knowledge value may indeed cause poorer choices to be made than if there were a more balanced view of that which each can contribute to the situation. (1969: 193)

Although clients often seek advice, there are circumstances when they may reject any advice that they are offered. For example, they are likely to reject advice when they lack confidence in the expertise of the change agent. They may also reject advice when it is offered by a change agent who appears to be insensitive to their needs.

Collaborative approaches to helping

The remaining four modes of intervening featured in the Intervention Style Indicator (supporting, information gathering, challenging and theorising,) are non-prescriptive. Change agents adopting these approaches work with clients to help them develop opportunities or manage their own problems, rather than intervene by telling them what they should do.

A number of factors can contribute to clients being ineffective opportunity developers or problem managers. Emotional states such as anger or insecurity may undermine their ability to function normally, they may lack the information they need to understand the problem or develop a plan for change, they may be locked into an ideology or set of beliefs that inhibits their ability to respond effectively, or they may not have access to concepts and models that will help them identify the cause-and-effect relationships that maintain the status quo or offer opportunities for change. There is also the possibility that they have already tried to introduce changes and their efforts have failed to deliver desired outcomes. All of these conditions can contribute to clients lacking confidence in their own ability to develop opportunities or manage problems.

Seligman's (1975) theory of 'learned helplessness', mentioned in Chapter 2, states that when individuals are subjected to events which are uncontrollable (that is, when the probability of an outcome is the same irrespective of how they respond) they will develop *expectations* of non-contingency between response and outcome. The theory suggests that the incentive for clients to initiate activity directed towards resolving a problem depends upon their expectation that responding will produce some improvement to the problematic situation. If clients have no confidence in their own ability to achieve any improvement, they will not try. Hiroto (1974) illustrated this effect with an experiment that exposed groups of college students to either loud controllable noises that they could terminate by pressing a button four times or uncontrollable noises which were terminated independently of what they did. Another group included in the experiment was not exposed to any noise. All subjects were then tested in a situation in which it was possible for them to exercise control over noise termination. Hiroto found that the groups which had either been subjected to controllable noise or no noise learned to terminate the noise in the later test situation, whereas subjects who had previously been subjected to uncontrollable noise failed to terminate the noise during later tests.

Abramson, Seligman and Teesdale (1978) distinguish between 'universal helplessness' (where the client believes that the problem is unsolvable by anyone) and 'personal helplessness' (where the client believes that the problem is solvable, for example, by the helper but not by self). The danger with the prescriptive/advising approach to helping outlined above is that it can promote a sense of *personal helplessness* in the client and the client may become dependent on the help of others.

Egan (2004) discusses the notion of *empowerment* in the helping relationship. He notes that some clients learn, sometimes from a very early age, that there is nothing they can do about certain life situations. They engage in 'disabling self-talk' (see Ellis, 1977) and tell themselves that they cannot manage certain situations and that they cannot cope. Egan's position is that whether clients are victims of their own doing or the doings of others they can and must take an active part in managing their own problems, including the search for solutions and efforts towards achieving those solutions. He also argues that helpers can do a great deal to help people develop a sense of agency or self-efficacy. Change agents can help clients challenge self-defeating beliefs and attitudes about themselves and the situation. They can help clients develop the knowledge, skills and resources they need to succeed and they can encourage them to take reasonable risks and support them when they do. The function of the change agent, according to Egan, is to encourage clients to apply a problem solving approach to their current problem situation and to learn from this experience so that, over the longer term, they will apply a problem solving approach to future problem situations. In other words, Egan's approach is one that is directed towards eliminating feelings of personal helplessness and empowering clients to act.

Facilitating change by supporting the client

The supportive mode of intervening is very different to the other four featured in the Intervention Style Inventory. It involves the change agent working with clients to help them clarify their views and express feelings and emotions that impede objective thinking about a problem or opportunity.

Margerison (2000) refers to change agents helping clients 'give themselves permission'. In the first instance, this involves giving themselves permission to talk about difficult issues, which leads on to giving themselves permission to act rather than to worry. He reports that in his consulting experience an effective intervention has sometimes been to just listen and help managers open up difficult areas and talk about matters that they have so far avoided. He observes that clients appear to experience this kind of intervention as a great relief, it is as though a load has been taken off their mind.

Change agents adopting a supportive mode of intervening listen empathetically, withhold any judgement and help clients develop for themselves a more objective view of the situation. It is assumed that this new level of awareness will often be sufficient to help them go on and solve their problem for themselves.

Supportive interventions have many similarities with the way client-centred counsellors work with their clients (Rogers, 1958). They listen, reflect and sometimes interpret what clients have to say about themselves and their relationship with others and the situation, but they do not intervene or develop any active strategies for dealing with clients' problems. It is a *person-centred*, as opposed to a *problem-centred* approach to helping.

An example will help to clarify how this approach can be effective. Blake and Mouton (1986) describe a case in which a consultant, who was working in the Hawthorn Plant of Western Electric, used a supporting approach to help a shop floor worker. The consultant overheard the worker complaining, in very emotional tones, about his supervisor and decided to intervene. He asked what had been going on and was told, in the same emotional tones, that: 'The bosses were not worth a damn because when you have a rise coming to you they will not give it.' The worker went on to tell the consultant that he thought the place stank and that he wanted to get out. The consultant's response was to avoid siding with either the worker or the supervisor, but to invite the worker into his office to 'talk it over'. As the interaction progressed, the worker unloaded his feelings about his supervisor. As he went on, he began to ramble from one complaint to another. He had been refused a rise, and because he was at the top of his grade he could not advance any higher. He then complained about the machine setters who did everything they could to protect their own position and stop others learning anything that would help them to improve the work they do. All the way through this interaction the consultant maintained his neutral stance and refrained from making any evaluation of the worker's complaints. He assumed the role of active listener and did little more than reflect his sympathetic understanding by repeating what he had been told. For example, in response to the complaint about the machine setters he said: 'I see, they seem to be pretty selfish about their knowledge of screw machines.'

In this case the consultant's strategy was to allow the worker to vent his anger because he believed that until he had done this he would be too wound up to think straight. It appeared to work. Slowly, as the tension eased, the conversation moved away from gripes towards problem solving. The consultant confined his interventions to supportive listening and clarifying but eventually the worker (client) began to work through his problems for himself.

Supportive modes of intervening can be very effective, but there are situations where this approach to helping clients develop a better understanding of their situation may not be sufficient to produce change. In these circumstances, other modes of intervening might be required, but supporting can still have an important role to play in the early stages of helping.

Using theory to help clients move to a preferred state

The theorising approach involves change agents identifying theories and conceptual models that are pertinent to the clients' problem situation, presenting these to clients and helping them learn to use them to facilitate a better understanding of their situation in an analytical cause-and-effect fashion. The change agents then build on this understanding and use it to help clients identify what they can do to move towards a more desirable state of affairs.

This mode of intervening might be adopted when change agents feel that some kind of theoretical framework could help clients organise their thoughts and provide the basis for a fresh appraisal of their predicament. For example the stakeholder grid discussed in Chapter 9 might be used to help a management team identify important stakeholders and develop strategies for winning their support, or the Burke–Litwin causal model of organisational performance might be used to focus attention on important cause- and-effect relationships that affect performance. Change agents can also use theories to facilitate the discussion of potentially delicate or sensitive issues. For example, a discussion of Belbin's (1993) team roles might provide a relatively safe and non-threatening way of exploring how members of a management team work together. This theory-based approach can also provide a way of exploring and testing implicit assumptions and values in a way that avoids direct confrontation, and it can provide a basis for increasing the client's capacity for independent action.

Blake and Mouton (1986) argue that theories can help clients free themselves from blind reliance on intuition, hunch, common sense and conventional wisdom and enable them to see situations more objectively. Theories can be applied to all classes of problem in a wide range of situations, so long as the theory is valid and the clients are willing and able to internalise the theory and make it a personally useful source of guidance. Theory-based interventions might be less effective than other approaches if the change agent introduces clients to a theory they perceive to be invalid, irrelevant or too complicated, or if the client is unreceptive to the possibility of using theory as a basis for managing problems. Even valid, user-friendly theories may be rejected, for example, when clients are emotionally charged. In such circumstances a supportive mode of intervening might be used before adopting a theory-based approach to helping.

Challenging

One mode of intervening that has great potential for facilitating change is 'challenging'. It is an approach that involves the change agent confronting the foundations of the client's thinking in an attempt to identify beliefs, values and assumptions that may be distorting the way situations are viewed. Blake and Mouton observe that:

> Values underlie how people think and feel and what they regard as important and what is trivial. Sometimes guidance from a particular set of values is sound – things go smoothly, results are good. Sometimes values cause problems – they are inappropriate, invalid, or unjustified under the circumstances. Often people who must work in concert hold different values; failure to achieve agreement in such situations results in antagonisms, disorder or outright chaos. (1986: 210)

An assumption underlying this challenging mode of intervening is that effective action can be undermined by the clients' inability or unwillingness to face up to reality. They may not be aware of some aspects of their behaviour or its consequences, or they rationalise or justify their behaviour and in so doing create or perpetuate an unsatisfactory situation. Challenging interventions are designed to call attention to contradictions in action and attitude or challenge precedents or practices that seem inappropriate. The aim of this approach is to identify alternative values and assumptions that might facilitate the development of opportunities or lead to the development of more effective solutions to problems.

Hayes (2002) illustrates this approach. He refers to a head teacher of a small school who had worked tremendously hard to improve the school's external reputation and had invested a great deal of effort in building a good team spirit among his staff. When one of them applied for a job elsewhere the head teacher interpreted this as a sign of disloyalty. He communicated his reaction to the individual concerned and made his disapproval public by excluding him from management team meetings. The deputy head intervened. He confronted the head with his own early career progress and pointed out how this was little different from the progress that the teacher who had applied for the job elsewhere was seeking. The deputy pointed out that the head had rarely stayed in one job for more than three years whereas this individual had already been in post and had performed very satisfactorily for almost four years. He also asked the head how he thought others would interpret his action and what effect it was likely to have on the team spirit he prized so highly. Eventually the head accepted that the teacher's application was a timely and appropriate step to take. He also accepted that he had not only overlooked the career development needs of this individual but had given insufficient attention to the career development of all of his staff. He also accepted that his response had been inconsistent with the management culture he was trying to create.

Great care needs to be exercised when change agents adopt a challenging style. Egan (2004) argues that confrontation can be strong medicine and, in the hands of the inept, can be destructive. Effective challenges are those which are received by clients as helpful invitations to explore aspects of a problem from a new perspective. Change agents adopting this approach ask questions or provide feedback that draws the client's attention to inappropriate attitudes, values, discrepancies and distortions, but they avoid telling the client how they should think or act. Challenges that clients perceive as 'punitive accusations or the shameful unmasking of inadequacies' (Egan, 2004) are likely to be met with some form of strong defensive reaction and are rarely effective, especially over the longer term. Consequently, even in circumstances where a challenging style of intervention promises to be effective, this promise may not be realised if change agents are inept at challenging and confronting.

Information gathering

This approach to helping involves change agents assisting clients collect data that they can use to evaluate and reinterpret a problem situation. Hayes (2002) illustrates this with the example of a trainer in the sales department of a machine tool company faced with a very demotivated young representative who had recently lost three important accounts. The trainer suggested that he get in touch with the buyers he used to deal with and ask them why they had changed suppliers. The trainer suspected that it was because the representative had not been attentive enough but he felt that it would be more effective if the representative discovered this and decided what he needed to do about it for himself.

The assumption underlying this approach is that *deficiencies of information* are an important cause of malfunctioning. The helpers' objectives are to help clients arrive at a better level of awareness of the underlying causes of a problem and to help them identify what action is required to resolve it. Many change agents adopting this approach assume that any information they might present will be less acceptable and less likely to be understood than information that individuals (or groups) generate for themselves. Another assumption often made by change agents adopting this approach is that clients will be less resistant to proposals and action plans that they generate for themselves. Pascale and Sterin (2005) point to 'positive deviance' as an example of an intervention that relies on helping others gather and use information for themselves. It involves helping clients identify and investigate examples of innovation and superior performance in order to share their findings and use them as a basis for exploring ways of spreading this best practice. Pascale and Sterin argue that because the process of information gathering is undertaken by members of the client system ownership is high, and because the innovators who are responsible for superior performance are members of the same system ('just like us') disbelief and resistance are easier to overcome.

Sometimes change agents might be more directly involved in the collection of data (see, for example, the accounts of action research offered in Chapter 18) but when this happens they are often working on behalf of their clients and they feed the information back to them for them to use to develop a better understanding of their problem and explore ways of improving the situation.

Prescriptive versus collaborative modes of intervening

It has been argued that the most effective way of helping others is to help them to help themselves, and that this will normally involve adopting a collaborative mode of intervening. There may, however, be occasions when a more prescriptive style might be appropriate. Clients may be faced with a critical problem that, if not resolved quickly, could have disastrous consequences. If the change agent has the expertise to help them avoid this disastrous outcome it might be appropriate to adopt a prescriptive mode to provide the required help quickly. While this kind of intervention is likely to provide only a 'short-term fix' it might be effective if it can buy time to help clients develop the competencies they require to manage any similar situations they may encounter in the future.

Helping skills

The focus of attention in this chapter has been on high-level intervention styles and how they can be applied to facilitate change over the course of the helping relationship. Passing reference has also been made to some of the specific helping skills that change agents need to use to intervene effectively. These 'helping skills' are not a special set of skills reserved exclusively for the helping relationship (Hopson, 1984). Helping involves the appropriate use of a wide range of 'everyday and commonly used' interpersonal skills. Some of these are:

- self-awareness
- establishing rapport and building relationships
- empathy
- listening to facts and feelings
- probing for information
- identifying themes and seeing the bigger picture
- giving feedback
- challenging assumptions.

These and many other relevant interpersonal behaviours are considered in detail in Hayes (2002).

Identifying effective helping behaviours

Exercise 24.2 is designed to help you reflect on the discussion so far, and on your experience of being a client.

Exercise 24.2   Identifying effective helping behaviours

The aim of this exercise is to use your own experience to identify effective helping behaviours.
   Think of a number of occasions when others have tried to help you.

1   Identify people whose behaviour towards you was very helpful:

● What did they do that you found helpful?
● How did you respond to this behaviour? (Why was it helpful?)

Record your observations below.

✎ List the helpful behaviours	Explain why the behaviours were helpful

2   Identify people who, while trying to help, behaved towards you in ways that you found *un*helpful:

● What did they do that you found unhelpful?
● How did you respond to this behaviour? (Why was it unhelpful?)

✎ List the *unhelpful* behaviours	Explain why the behaviours were *unhelpful*

Reflect on your findings and consider how they relate to the modes of intervention referred to in this chapter. Does you experience highlight any skills not discussed but which appear to have an important bearing on the outcome of the helping relationship?

Summary

This chapter has considered five modes of intervening to facilitate change: advising, supporting, theorising, challenging and information gathering. Some of the factors that can affect the efficacy of different approaches have been considered. While acknowledging that advising may be an appropriate mode of intervention in some circumstances, this chapter has highlighted the benefits of those modes of intervening that help clients help themselves.

References

Abramson, L.Y., Seligman, M.E.P. and Teesdale, J D. (1978) 'Learned Helplessness in Humans: Critique and Formulations', *Journal of Abnormal Psychology*, 87 (1), pp. 49–74.

Argyle, M. (1994) *The Psychology of Interpersonal Behaviour*, 5th edn, London: Penguin.

Belbin, R.M. (1993) *Teach Roles at Work*, London: Heinemann.

Blake, R.R. and Mouton, J.S. (1986) *Consultation: A Handbook for Individual and Organization Development*, Reading, MA: Addison-Wesley.

Carnegie, D. (1936) *How to Win Friends and Influence People*, New York: Pocket Books, Simon & Schuster.

Egan, G. (1988) *Change Agent Skills B: Managing Innovation and Change*, San Diego, CA: University Associates.

Egan, G. (2004) *The Skilled Helper: A Problem Management and Opportunity Development Approach to Helping*, Pacific Grove, CA: Brooks/Cole.

Ellis, A. (1977) 'The Basic Clinical Theory of Rational-Emotive Therapy', in A. Ellis and G. Grieger (eds), *Handbook of Rational-Emotive Therapy*, Monterey, CA: Brooks/Cole.

Greiner, L.E. and Metzger, R.O. (1983) *Consulting to Management*, Englewood Cliffs, NJ: Prentice Hall.

Hayes, J. (2002) *Interpersonal Skills at Work*, Hove: Routledge.

Hiroto, D.S. (1974) 'Locus of Control and Learned Helplessness', *Journal of Experimental Psychology*, 102, pp. 187–93.

Hopson, B. (1984) 'Counselling and Helping', in C. Cooper and P. Makin (eds), *Psychology for Managers*, Leicester: British Psychological Society.

Mangham, I.L. (1986) *Power and Performance in Organisations: An Exploration of Executive Process*, Oxford: Blackwell.

Margerison, C.J. (2000) *Managerial Consulting Skills*, Aldershot: Gower.

Pascale, R.T. and Sterin, J. (2005) 'Your Company's Secret Change Agents', *Harvard Business Review*, 83 (5), pp. 72–81.

Rogers, C.R. (1958) 'The Characteristics of a Helping Relationship', *Personnel and Guidance Journal*, 37, pp. 6–16.

Seligman, M.E.P. (1975) *Helplessness*, San Francisco: W.H. Freeman.

Steele, F.I. (1969) 'Consultants and Detectives', *Journal of Applied Behavioural Science*, 5 (2), pp. 193–4.

Wright, P.L. and Taylor, D.S. (1994) *Improving Leadership Performance: Interpersonal Skills For Effective Leaders*, Hemel Hempstead: Prentice Hall.

Chapter

25

Effective helping and the stages of the helping relationship

This chapter discusses helping in terms of six stages. The first stage involves early encounters and the beginnings of a helping relationship. Stages 2–4 involve the change agent helping clients assess the problems or opportunities that are of concern, explore a range of preferred futures and establish an agenda for change, and develop and implement plans for moving towards their preferred future. Stage 5 involves working with clients to help them develop ways of consolidating those changes that have been achieved. Finally the change agent withdraws from the helping relationship and leaves the clients to get on with the ongoing process of developing opportunities and managing problems.

Nearly fifty years ago Lippett, Watson and Westley (1958) noted that the helping relationship rarely progresses in an orderly and sequenced way through a series of stages. Like Burke (2002) they see change and the helping relationship as a kind of *cyclical process* which starts over and over again as one set of problems are resolved and new ones are encountered, and as new actors are drawn into the situation. Consequently, at any point in time the change agent might be involved in activities associated with more than one aspect of the helping process. Even in situations that are less complex and more ordered than this, the helping process may still not unfold as a linear sequence of distinct stages. For example, as noted in Chapter 5, reviewing the present state and identifying a preferred future are not separate and distinct activities. In practice, they are often integrated and these two steps frequently go through several iterations, progressing from broad concepts toward something that is sufficiently concrete and detailed to be implemented. Notwithstanding this inevitable 'messiness' of the helping relationship, it will be considered here as if it does progress through six distinct stages, and the role of the change agent as helper and facilitator will be examined at each stage.

Mode of intervening and the stage of the helping relationship

Chapter 24 considered *modes of intervening*. The most effective mode of intervening might vary over the course of a helping relationship. The supportive mode that involves the use of empathetic listening to help clients develop a new level of understanding might be especially effective at the beginning of the helping process. As well as helping clients clarify their thinking about an opportunity or problem, it can contribute to the development of trust and a supportive relationship between change agent and client. However, as the helping relationship develops, it might be necessary for change agents to modify their initial approach and begin to adopt a more challenging, information gathering or theorising style of facilitation. They may need to confront clients about discrepancies between what they say and what they do, provide them with feedback or help them gather for themselves new information that will help them view their problem from a different perspective. It might also be beneficial to introduce clients to theories and conceptual frameworks that will facilitate their diagnosis and action planning. In other words, any one approach, used in isolation, might not always lead to an adequate level of understanding about a problem, or to the development and implementation of plans to move toward a preferred future. It might be necessary to draw upon a number of different modes of intervening as the clients' needs change. Egan (2004) argues that helpers should be competent in all aspects of the helping process because they are all interdependent. For example, helpers who specialise in challenging may be poor confronters if their challenges are not based on an empathic understanding of the client or if they confront clients too early in the helping relationship.

Stages in the helping process

This section elaborates a six-stage model of helping and facilitating that is designed to provide you with a cognitive map that will help you understand your relationship with clients and give you a sense of direction when thinking about the way forward. While it is a stage model, as noted above, it does not assume that helping and facilitating will necessarily involve a sequential progression through each of the six stages. It might be necessary to move backwards as well as forwards throughout the model because, for example, while planning for action the client may raise new concerns that have to be clarified and understood before the problem can be resolved.

The model draws on the broad framework offered by Lippett, Watson and Westley (1958), but many of the details of stages three–five are grounded in Egan's (2004) three-stage model of helping.

Stage 1: developing the helping relationship

Relationship-building plays an important part in the early stages of the helping process. The change agent has to gain the confidence of the client because, while some find it easy to seek or accept help and to share their thoughts and feelings, many are reluctant to talk about their problems with anyone. There is also the possibility that a client may not believe that the change agent has the ability to provide the help they require or they may not be confident that they can trust the change agent's intentions. Margerison (2000) likens the change agent's early encounters with the client to 'knocking at doors which are half open and seeing them either close it in your face, or open fully'.

Lines *et al.* (2005) argue that trust and trustworthiness have a direct bearing on the change agent's access to knowledge and cooperation. When clients feel that they can trust the change agent they are more likely to be open, share information with those involved in managing the change and avoid defensive behaviours. Change agents who are new to the situation have a special problem because it can be hard for clients to trust people who are relative strangers. Normally it takes time to build trust, it is an incremental process. Lines *et al.* define 'trust' as a state that depicts how individuals and groups view other individuals and social units. They argue that it is based on the processing of numerous experiences, normally over a long period of time. But individuals and groups who feel vulnerable (and many do in times of change) will actively process any information that they feel has a bearing on the extent to which they can trust the change agent. Morgan and Zeffane (2003) view organisational change as a critical event that can either create trust or destroy a long-standing trusting relationship in an instant.

First impressions can have an important impact on any relationship, and studies have shown that clients actively form early impressions of change agents, especially in terms of their competence, ability to offer help, friendliness and inferred motives. This latter point is considered in Chapter 11 on communicating.

Egan (2004) and Reddy (1987) point to respect and genuineness as core values that affect the way change agents behave and the kind of relationship they are able to build with clients. According to them, respect involves:

1 *Being 'for' the client*   This entails helpers behaving in a manner that indicates that they are 'with' or 'for' the client in a non-sentimental caring way. If clients feel that the change agent might be against them, they are unlikely to trust them sufficiently to reveal anxieties, weaknesses or specific information that they fear could be used against them.
2 *Signalling that the other's viewpoint is worth listening to*   This reflects the change agents' willingness to commit to working with their clients. It also suggests a minimum level of openness to the clients' point of view.

Without this openness, empathic listening is impossible. Too often, even when change agents go though the motions of asking clients for their views they are not really committed to listening. The effective helper needs to respect the clients' point of view and needs to clearly signal this respect if they are to be encouraged to work with the change agent.

3   *Suspending critical judgement*   Change agents need to keep an open mind and avoid reaching premature conclusions. Egan (2004) and Reddy (1987) assert that this does not mean that they should signal approval of everything they hear or observe. It involves communicating that the clients' point of view has been heard and understood, but it does not involve making judgements because this could push clients into a position that they may resist. The act of suspending judgement (and trying to understand the other's viewpoint) can encourage them to explore their position and it can give them the freedom to change their view. According to Reddy, suspending judgement and keeping an open mind does not come naturally. He argues that we have been conditioned to persuade others to our point of view. At school, there is nearly always a debating society but rarely a listening club. It may be that we often fail to keep an open mind because if we listen we may end up agreeing, and if we agree we may appear to have lost. However, the aim of the helping relationship is not to win. Suspending judgement encourages clients to believe that the change agents are 'for' them and have their interests at heart.

4   *Working with clients as unique individuals or groups*   This involves being willing to support clients in their uniqueness and not relating with them as just another 'case'. It requires change agents to personalise their interventions and tailor them to the needs, capabilities and resources of their clients.

5   *Assuming that clients are committed to the goal of developing opportunities or managing problems more effectively*   Some clients may not have referred themselves for help and therefore may be reluctant to engaged in a relationship with the change agent. However, their initial reluctance to work with the helper does not necessarily imply that they are not committed to finding ways of managing their problems more effectively. Egan (2004) suggests that respectful change agents will assume the clients' goodwill and will continue to work with them until this assumption has been clearly demonstrated to be false. Clients who recognise that change agents respect them and are oriented to their needs are more likely to engage positively in the change process than clients who observe little evidence of any respect.

Genuineness

This is also an important ingredient in the helping relationship. Many change agents are good at controlling what they say, but most of us are less good at managing our non-verbal behaviours, the signals that we 'give off'.

If our respect for the client is not genuine, and if we try to fake attitudes of openness and interest in the client, than there is a high probability that this will be detected and that it will seriously damage or even destroy, the helping relationship. Being genuine involves being honest, sincere and without facade. Egan defines it as a value that can be expressed as a set of behaviours that include being oneself, being open, spontaneous, assertive and consistent.

Exercise 25.3   Monitoring core values

Next time you are involved in a helping relationship, observe yourself. Open up a 'second channel' and monitor what you are *thinking* when you are relating with a client. Consider what this tells you about your values:

● Are you able to suspend critical judgement?
● Do you believe that the client's point of view is worth listening to?

Stage 2: helping clients understanding the problem situation

This stage is important because problem situations cannot be managed or unused opportunities developed until clients are able to identify and understand them. Egan originally (see the first edition of *The Skilled Helper,* 1976) presented the process of identification and clarification as one which involves two steps: the inward journey and the outward journey:

The inward journey

This is concerned with helping clients tell their stories and develop a subjective understanding of the opportunities or problems that they are aware of. It focuses on how the client sees things. No attempt is made, at this stage, to persuade clients to consider alternative ways of thinking about their problems or opportunities. Change agents help by assisting clients to clarify their situations *from within their own frames of reference.* They can do this by attending and responding in ways that help clients explore their own feelings, attitudes and behaviours. They can help them consider what it is that they do (or fail to do) that has a bearing on their problems. It is important that helpers empathise with clients, that they show that they understand what the clients are saying and how they are feeling from within their own frames of reference. They may also have to nudge clients into dealing with concrete and specific issues and feelings if they are to clarify and better understand their problem situations. Vague generalities provide a poor foundation for the generation of strategies to develop unused opportunities or manage problem situations.

Relationship-building is not a discrete phase at the beginning of the help-ing process. It is integral to the whole process and it plays a central role in this diagnostic phase. Strong (1968) defines helping in terms of a *social influence process*. He goes on to suggest that helpers need to establish a power base that they can use to influence clients. This is clearly what happens in prescriptive helping relationships where clients define helpers as experts and bow to their expertise. However, in the more collaborative help-ing relationships advocated here, change agents must be careful to avoid using their ability to influence in ways which will increase the clients' feel-ings of powerlessness. Nonetheless, where clients trust the change agents and believe that they are 'on their side' and are working 'for' them they will be more likely to share sensitive information. It will also help to ensure (in the next phase of this diagnostic stage – the outward journey) that clients will be receptive to suggestions from change agents that point to alternative ways of looking at the problem.

The outward journey

This is concerned with helping clients identify 'blind spots' and develop new perspectives. While the inward journey focuses on helping them clarify prob-lems from within their own frames of reference, the outward journey focuses on the development of a more objective assessment. Old and comfortable frames of reference may keep clients locked into self-defeating patterns of thinking and behaving, and the change agents may need to help them iden-tify blind spots and develop alternative frames of reference.

There are a number of ways that change agents can persuade clients to consider their problem situations from alternative perspectives. As clients tell their stories, they may draw attention to recurring themes and to what appears to be the 'bigger picture'. To do this, the change agent or facilitator needs to be able to communicate what Egan refers to as 'advanced empathy' – to communicate to clients an understanding not only of what they say but also of what they imply, what they hint at and what they convey non-verbally. In this phase, the change agent might also begin to constructively challenge clients in those situations where their old frames of reference appear to be preventing them from identifying opportunities or better ways of managing their problems.

There is also a need to motivate clients to recognise the need for action. While helping them develop a better understanding of the problems can contribute to this goal there is also the possibility that this diagnostic process might produce the opposite effect. A problem which at first seemed rela-tively straight forward may begin to appear much more complicated as clients begins to broaden and deepen their understanding of the issues. Lippitt, Watson and Westley (1958) note that sometimes clients can begin to feel that the redefined problem is too pervasive and too fundamental to be remedied and therefore may be tempted to give up trying, or may continue working to resolve the problem but in a way that is less receptive to any new information that might further complicate the diagnosis. Often this kind of difficulty can be resolved by helping the client recognise that it may not be possible to deal with all aspects of the problem at once, and that it might be necessary to establish priorities and work on those issues that will make an important difference. Egan identifies 'focusing' as a vital part of helping clients clarify problem situations. If the diagnostic process reveals several problems or a very complex problem situation, it will be necessary to establish some criteria that they can use to help decide which aspects of the problem to focus on. Egan offers some useful guidelines – for example: begin with issues that clients see as important and that they are willing to work on, if the problem situation is complex begin with a manageable sub-problem that shows some promise of being successfully handled by the clients, and focus on problems where the benefit is likely to outweigh the cost.

Stage 3: helping clients identify a preferred scenario and establish change goals

Insight is seldom sufficient, however interesting it may be. Egan (2004) asserts that the helping relationship should promote problem managing *action*. He argues that assessment for the sake of assessment, exploration for the sake of exploration, or insight for the sake of insight is close to useless. This third stage of the helping process – identifying and clarifying problem situations and unused opportunities – can be judged to be effective only to the extent that it helps clients construct more desirable scenarios in terms of realistic and achievable goals that provide a basis for action.

Developing a range of possible scenarios

All too often clients tend to lock on to the first scenario they generate, and in so doing lock out the possibility of considering alternatives. Change agents need to help clients think about alternative scenarios before choosing which to pursue. The importance of identifying the right goals is illustrated by Covey (1989), who argues that it is incredibly easy to get caught up in an activity trap, in the 'busy-ness' of life, and to work harder and harder at climbing the ladder of success only to discover that it's leaning against the wrong wall. It is possible to be busy, very busy, without being very effective. Effective problem management requires the direction of effort towards the achievement of appropriate goals. All too often people faced with problems fail to think of alternative courses of action. Many, as soon as they become aware of a problem, are so eager to resolve it that they fail to clarify the problem before dashing off in search of a solution. Heirs (1986) argues that managers 'should be thinkers first, doers second – and *equally* competent at both' (emphasis in the original). This third stage of the helping process is concerned with helping clients to be *thinkers*.

Choosing which goal to pursue

Once a client or client group has generated a range of possible future scenarios, choosing which to pursue is the critical next step. Clients have to be motivated to achieve their goals because the course of action necessary to achieve them might require 'letting go' of a number of things that they value, such as certainty, power and many other outcomes that have been a source of satisfaction. The loss of these sources of satisfaction may threaten their commitment to change and therefore they need to be confident that the benefit will be worth the sacrifice. Helping clients develop their own criteria for selecting a goal and using these to reach a decision can create a sense of 'ownership' which can be a powerful source of motivation.

Locke and Latham (1984) believe that goals can help clients in a number of ways: they provide a vision and a focus for their attention and action; they mobilise energy and effort, people are motivated to achieve goals to which they are committed; goal setting increases persistence, people try harder and are less willing to give up when goals are both clear and realistic; finally, goals provide clients with the motivation to search for strategies that will help them achieve their objective.

Stage 4: helping clients plan and take action

An important measure of the success or failure of the helping relationship is the extent to which clients are able *to take action* to bring about a more desirable state of affairs. While stage three of the helping model is concerned with goals (*ends*) stage four is concerned with the *means* of achieving these goals. It involves identifying different strategies for action and selecting and implementing the strategy which offers the greatest promise of success.

An important aspect of the helper's role is to guide clients away from *convergent thinking* (which leads them to think in terms of only one cause of the problem situation, only one solution to improve matters and only one strategy for achieving that solution) to *divergent thinking*, in which alternative causes, solutions and action plans are explored. Whereas in stage three change agents might feel the need to intervene to encourage clients to generate more than one goal, in stage four they might intervene to help them think about alternative strategies for achieving their chosen goal. Techniques such as brainstorming can provide a useful aid for helping clients identify different ways of achieving goals, and the chosen route may well end up comprising a combination of the best ideas derived from a number of different action plans.

Throughout the helping process change agents need to both encourage divergent thinking to ensure that a range of possibilities are considered and focus on specifics rather than vague generalities. At an early stage, they might need to encourage clients to think in terms of specific issues and factors that contribute to their predicament. At a later stage, attention may shift to thinking in terms of specific goals and targets for change rather than vague and non-specific aims. In this stage of the helping process change agents might need to encourage clients to think in terms of specific actions that need to be taken if these goals are to be achieved.

Force-field analysis offers an approach to systematically searching out viable courses of action. It is a method, based on the work of Lewin (1951) for identifying the psychological and social forces which affect behaviour, for identifying how the forces opposing change can be diminished and how the forces pushing for change can be strengthened, and for thinking about the development of an action plan that takes account of the secondary effects associated with manipulating both kinds of force (Case study 25.1).

Case study 25.1   Using force-field analysis to develop action plans

Bill had been recruited by a large multinational auto components manufacturer to transform the organisation's manufacturing capability so that the company could regain its previous world-class status and ensure its survival in an increasingly competitive environment. Some time after his appointment he began to worry about his lack of progress. The senior managers of the operating divisions located in several countries around the world were resisting his efforts to introduce change. The author met Bill when he was working on another project in the company. They talked about the problem for about twenty minutes and Bill suggested a further conversation. This happened the following week.

The story Bill told revealed a complex set of related problems, but eventually he focused on an immediate goal that was to engage more effectively with senior mangers and persuade them to provide him with detailed information about the current situation in the manufacturing units they were responsible for. Initially, Bill focused on why managers should provide him with this information. He needed it to be able to assess how well the group was doing in relation to leading competitors and to assess the company's strengths and weaknesses in terms of its current manufacturing technology. He also wanted to be in a position to identify opportunities for rationalisation and to identify areas where efforts to introduce new technologies might be productive. He expressed a genuine desire to help divisions raise their performance and felt that the information he was seeking would help him make this contribution. He also felt that the information would be of value to managers for their own use within their own divisions. Given all these powerful reasons why the provision of this information was in the company's interest he failed to understand why divisional managers insisted on keeping him at arm's length and were resistant to his requests for information. In terms of Lewin's force-field, Bill had focused his attention on the driving forces. His initial plan for achieving his goal was to further increase these driving forces by enlisting the support of the CEO and asking him to instruct the divisional managers to comply with his requests for detailed information.

The author suggested that before pursuing this course of action Bill might consider some of the restraining forces. Why were the divisional managers resisting his requests and was there anything Bill could do to lower this resistance? (In Chapter 5 it was noted that Lewin favoured action to reduce restraining forces.) The author suggested that Bill might find it helpful to view the situation through the eyes of the divisional mangers. As he did this, he began to speculate about whether they truly understood his role and what he was trying to achieve. He also recognised the possibility that they feared that the detailed reporting that he was requesting could threaten their autonomy, that unfavourable comparisons might be made between the divisions, and that the information – in its raw form – might be misinterpreted by others at corporate headquarters who might access it when making decisions about resources, promotions and bonuses. He also recognised that he had not involved any of the divisional managers in specifying the information requirements, nor had he given them the opportunity to discuss the information that would be of help to them in their own businesses. There was also a possible problem relating to the cost of collecting this new set of information. Who was to pay for it? This analysis helped Bill develop a better understanding of the situation and provided a good basis for planning action to achieve his goal. Bill decided that his first initiative would not be to appeal to the CEO to increase pressure on the divisional managers to comply with his requests. He didn't rule this out, but decided that actions directed towards reducing the restraining forces might be more productive, especially bearing in mind that achieving this particular goal was only one part of his overall plan for change.

The author continued to work with Bill to help him prioritise the forces he wanted to work on and to identify specific actions he could take to achieve his aim. In this case it transpired that all of Bill's priorities for action involved reducing the power of selected restraining forces. It is not essential that plans should be be based only on reducing the power of restraining forces, but plans that only involve actions to increase the power of driving forces might deserve another look!

In a few cases, the need for detailed planning can be minimal. Where the problem is relatively straightforward it is possible that the analysis that enabled clients to identify specific goals might point to an obvious course of action. However, in other cases it may not be enough for clients to have generated a range of possible strategies and selected the one which offered the greatest promise of success. It might also be necessary to help them develop a step-by-step programme for action which includes milestones and measures of success which they can use to assess whether each step has been achieved. Sometimes, however, it may not be possible to develop a very detailed plan because there may be too many uncertainties in the situation. This was the position with Bill. In such circumstances, the client has to adopt an *incremental approach* (see the discussion of logical incrementalism in Chapter 4) that will accommodate new factors and issues as they emerge. However, it may be possible to anticipate what some of these issues might be and to explore ways in which they might be addressed. This need for contingency planning is especially important when the facilitator cannot always be present to 'coach' the clients while they are implementing their action plan.

Stage 5: consolidating the change

As noted in Chapter 23, the benefits of change can quickly evaporate unless attention is given to consolidating the change. One of the things change agents can do to help clients maintain the changes they have secured is to work with them identify possible sources of feedback that already exist and/or encourage them to develop new sources of feedback, such as setting up review meetings with significant others, developing new statistical indicators, or implementing a regular survey of customer or employee attitudes that will help them assess the effect of their actions.

Stage 6: withdrawing from the helping relationship

The position adopted in this chapter is that the role of the change agent is to help clients help themselves. Consequently there will come a point in every helping relationship where the change agent needs to withdraw. Identifying this point is not always easy because some clients need more help than others. For example, one group of clients may experience problems understanding their predicament, but once they have been helped to diagnose the situation they may be perfectly capable of solving the problem for themselves, and the facilitator may be able to terminate the helping relationship at that point. In another situation, a client group may be experiencing difficulties diagnosing the situation but while help in developing a better understanding of the problem might be necessary it may not be sufficient to enable them to act independently to manage their own problem more effectively. In addition, to help with their diagnosis they may also require help in identifying achievable goals. A third client group may have a good understanding of the situation and may have identified a clear and appropriate goal they want to achieve, but they may lack the ability to transform this intention into action. In this case, the facilitator may not have to help the client group with its diagnosis or goal setting and may be able to confine any intervention to helping them plan and take action to improve the situation.

In other words, some clients may require help with every stage of opportunity development or problem management (understanding the situation, goal setting, planning and taking action and consolidation) whereas others may require help only with particular stages. The six-stage helping model presented here provides a map that can be used to assess where the clients are, and what help they require. Armed with this kind of conceptual map the change agent is in a better position to identify when to intervene, the kind of intervention that will be most effective and when it will be appropriate to withdraw from the role of helper and leave the clients to get on with managing the situation for themselves.

Summary

An important factor that can affect the outcome of attempts to manage change is the quality of the relationship between the change agent and the client system. This chapter has outlined a six-stage model of the helping relationship in order to explore some of the ways the change agent can relate with clients in order to facilitate change.

References

Burke, W.W. (2002) *Organization Change: Theory and Practice*, Thousand Oaks, CA: Sage.

Covey, S.R. (1989) *The Seven Habits of Highly Effective People*, London: Simon & Schuster.

Egan, G. (2004) *The Skilled Helper: A Problem Management and Opportunity Development Approach to Helping*, Pacific Grove, PA: Brooks/Cole.

Hayes, J. (2002) *Interpersonal Skills at Work*, Hove: Routledge.

Heirs, B. (1986) *The Professional Decision Thinker*, London: Sidgwick & Jackson.

Lewin, K. (1951) *Field Theory in Social Sciences*, New York: Harper & Row.

Lines, R., Selart, M., Espedal, B. and Johansen, S.T. (2005) 'The Production of Trust during Organizational Change', *Journal of Change Management*, 5 (2), pp. 221–45.

Lippett, R., Watson, J. and Westley, B. (1958) *The Dynamics of Planned Change*, New York: Harcourt Brace Jovanovich.

Locke, E.A. and Latham, G.P. (1984) *Goal Setting: A Motivational Technique that Works*, Englewood Cliffs, NJ: Prentice Hall.

Margerison, C.J. (2000) *Managerial Consulting Skills*, Aldershot: Gower.

Morgan, D.E. and Zeffane, R. (2003) 'Employee Involvement, Change and Trust in Management', *International Journal of Human Resource Management*, 14, pp. 55–75.

Reddy, M. (1987) *The Manager's Guide to Counselling at Work*, London: British Psychological Society/Methuen.

Strong, S.R. (1968) 'Counselling: An Interpersonal Influence Process', *Journal of Counselling Psychology*, 15, pp. 215–24.

Author index

Subject index